Critical Issues in Air Transport Economics and Business

T0300304

In many ways, the airline sector is like a laboratory where new developments and trends serve as an indicator of what it about to happen in the rest of the economy. This book takes a look at the critical issues facing the airline industry. Which existing airline activities will expand and which will disappear? Where will new opportunities arise? What factors drive change? In a series of chapters, a number of key elements for success and failure in the airline industry are discussed in detail, whereby attention is devoted to all the major players in the air transport industry.

As such this book offers material for strategic thinking featuring contributions from key figures in Europe, the US and Asia. The focus of the book expands from economic to legal issues, bankruptcy and safety and security. The carefully selected papers offer a thorough and structured analysis of major current developments in the air transport industry. Fully up to date, topics covered include competitive strength, capacity utilisation and risk.

The most likely future scenarios are more or less known. Only the timeframe remains uncertain. The speed at which the various market players in the air transport chain will implement their strategies remains the key question. This depends on a whole range of exogenous and endogenous variables, as this book aspires to demonstrate. As both an overview of the current issues affecting the industry and as a cohesive set of strategic documents, therefore, this collection will prove invaluable for policy makers and researchers alike.

Rosário Macário is Assistant Professor in Transportation at Lisbon Technical University. **Eddy Van de Voorde** is Full Professor at the University of Antwerp, Faculty of Applied Economics

Routledge studies in the modern world economy

Critical Issues in Air Transport Economics and Business

Edited by Rosário Macário and
Eddy Van de Voorde

Routledge
Taylor & Francis Group

LONDON AND NEW YORK

First published 2011
by Routledge
2 Park Square, Milton Park, Abingdon, Oxfordshire OX14 4RN

Simultaneously published in the USA and Canada
by Routledge
711 Third Avenue, New York, NY 10017

First issued in paperback 2014

Routledge is an imprint of the Taylor & Francis Group, an informa business

Typeset in Times by Wearset Ltd, Boldon, Tyne and Wear

British Library Cataloguing in Publication Data
A catalogue record for this book is available from the British Library

Library of Congress Cataloging in Publication Data
Critical issues in air transport economics and business/edited by Rosário
Macário and Eddy Van de Voorde.
p. cm.
1. Aeronautics, Commercial–Finance. 2. Airlines–Cost of operation. 3.
Aeronautics and state. I. Macário, Rosário. II. Voorde, E. van de (Eddy)
HE9782.C75 2010
387.7′1–dc22

2010006943

ISBN 13: 978-1-138-88078-8 (pbk)
ISBN 13: 978-0-415-57055-8 (hbk)

Contents

1 Introduction

Rosário Macário and Eddy Van de Voorde

The air transport industry, by its very nature, is highly sensitive to cyclical economic movements. Periods of boom and strong economic growth coincide with the entry of new carriers, expanding business, and considerable profit-making. By the same token, downturns impact heavily on the sector and nearly always prompt thorough rationalisation, characterised by waves of mergers and take-overs, as well as bankruptcies and market exits. Moreover, developments in the air transport sector often foreshadow events to unfold in the rest of the economy over the next few months. Hence, the airline sector is like an economic laboratory where new evolutions and trends tend to come to light.

As in the maritime sector, thought and action in the airline business have evolved rapidly in recent years. Increasingly, players are approaching the industry from the perspective of air transport chains. Prospective customers are no longer selecting airports and airlines on the basis of their individual merits, but because they belong to an air transport chain that meets their preferences maximally and corresponds to their willingness to pay, despite having their loyalty challenged by low-fare airlines. Hence, the success of those airports and airlines depends crucially on whether or not they belong to a successful air logistics chain.

This new approach has gone hand in hand with a degree of specialisation, low-cost passenger transport and air freight being two typical examples. Take the case of air freight. Whereas freight used to be regarded as a 'side product' of passenger transport, there are now a number of carriers focusing exclusively on this market and in some cases it is freight that allows the cross-financing of the lower passenger fares, enabling traditional companies to compete in the low-fare market. Likewise, there are now airports (albeit smaller ones) that consider freight transport as their core business. This growing significance of full-freighter services has been occasioned by a combination of factors, including insufficient freight capacity and stricter safety regulations on passenger planes, a trend towards scale increases, and substantial imbalances between incoming and outgoing flows.

So what does the future hold? Which existing air transport activities will expand and which will disappear? Where will new opportunities arise? Which factors drive change? The answers to these questions have implications that go far beyond air transport as such. Each decision has direct and indirect consequences for – among other things – employment, investments, achievable value added and funding requirements. No wonder, then, that the airline industry is attracting growing interest from scholars and policymakers alike!

Clearly it is important that any new developments in the air transport sector should be acknowledged as soon as possible, so that the actors involved can take suitable action. This book intends to contribute to this process of insight. In a series of papers, a number of key factors for success and failure are discussed in detail, whereby attention is devoted to all the major players in the air transport industry. In other words, here is a collection of papers that offer ample food for strategic thought.

1   A highly competitive playing field

A number of recent developments demonstrate that the air transport sector is evolving rapidly towards a new market form. Therefore, it is crucially important that we should have adequate insight into how the major players – from airlines to airport authorities – determine their strategies. Each move by an individual carrier has immediate and substantive consequences for the rest of the air logistics chain and thus impacts on airport transport competition.

We may summarise some of the most important recent developments in the global airline industry as follows:

- The derived nature of transport demand is in clear evidence, in the sense that the air transport industry is driven by the global economy. This world economy is prone to rapid change, witness the swift growth in international trade, the international redistribution of labour and capital, and the far-reaching integration and globalisation of markets.
- Airlines are obviously major, strategically important, customers of airports. Among these carriers, we have in recent times observed significant scale increases, primarily through horizontal cooperation (cf. the three large alliances) and/or mergers and takeovers. For the time being, this trend has not really expanded towards service providers and hinterland transport. However, such an evolution cannot be ruled out in the future, given the growing tendency to view transport services in terms of complex logistics chains, whereby each link is expected to contribute to the constant optimisation of the chain as a whole. Any such development would inevitably affect the competitive balance, with carriers acquiring much greater market power.
- The airport industry has also undergone momentous change. Traditional ground handling companies have evolved towards more complex 'handling holdings' – more often than not as a consequence of capital needs – in a process likewise involving mergers and takeovers, as well as externally funded expansion projects. Airport authorities and public regulators have thus far observed these evolutions rather passively.

Now the question arises of which scenarios may unfold in the future. Will long-term economic growth persist or will short-term crises occasion structural shifts? And if economic growth does persist, will it continue to translate automatically into growing demand for air transport services? Or does demand depend on growth in services rather than in industrial output? Will the trend towards scale increases, through horizontal and vertical forms of integration, continue? What will the market impact be of the expected deployment of ever-larger aircraft (e.g. the A380)? Which timeframe are carriers looking at in their search for new collaborative structures? What are the likely response strategies of the other market players, i.e. non-carriers? Will some carriers become so powerful that they are able to impose their will upon the other players, including airport authorities and ground handling agents? Will air transport intensify partnerships with other modes or choose ring fencing strategies?

Each of these crucial issues is surrounded by uncertainty. Moreover, the airline market is a highly dynamic environment, so that one may reasonably assume the various players anticipating one another's moves and devising proactive strategies. In other words: here we have competition at its purest!

Like costing and pricing, the matter of air transport competition – both horizontally between carriers and vertically between other players in the logistics chain – invariably comes down to a related key concept, i.e. available capacity. Capacity is therefore a critical factor in airport selection and it comes into play at various levels of competition.

Let us take the example of competition between airports. Carriers' primary consideration in airport choice is the potential market: the volume of traffic on a specific route must be adequate to guarantee a viable capacity utilisation rate. Furthermore, available capacity is not only a factor in attracting new flows; it is equally instrumental in retaining flows. Carriers tend to pick airports that are free of congestion and bottlenecks, both in the air and on the ground. After all, congestion wastes time and money, and it can thus compromise the competitive strength of carriers and their air logistics chains.

The most likely future scenarios, which consequently merit close scientific study, are more or less known. Only the timeframe remains uncertain. The speed at which the various market players in the air transport chain will implement their strategies will depend on a whole range of exogenous and endogenous variables, as this book hopes to demonstrate.

2 Overview of contributions

The carefully selected papers included in this book offer a thorough and structured analysis of the main current developments in the air transport industry. The various contributions are also complementary, in the sense that they all focus on air transport competition and highly relevant subtopics such as competitive strength, capacity utilisation and risk.[1]

Figure 1.1 provides a schematic overview of the content of this book. In Chapter 2, a number of hypotheses are formulated with regard to possible future evolutions in the air transport industry. Subsequently, the focus shifts to the industry's two principal players, namely the airlines (Chapters 3–5) and the airports (Chapters 8–9). In view of its specific nature, a separate section is devoted to air freight (Chapters 6–7). Then, in Chapters 10–21, some characteristic and crucial topics in air transport competition are discussed. The concluding chapter is a synthesis in the context of major challenges for the future air transport sector.

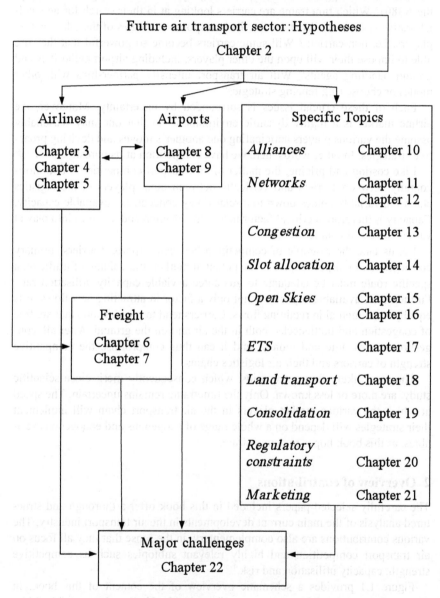

Figure 1.1 Overview of contributions.

The dynamic nature of the airline sector to some extent explains the growing interest it is attracting from policymakers, researchers and leading figures in the world of business. In their contribution, *Hilde Meersman, Eddy Van de Voorde* and *Thierry Vanelslander* attempt to outline some of the likely developments in the air transport industry beyond 2010. If the trends that have unfolded in recent decades persist in the coming years, that alone will inevitably result in an altered market and ownership structure. The authors first present an analysis of the present situation in the air transport business against the backdrop of developments over the past decade. Subsequently, they describe potential scenarios and strategies, as well as business models that are able to cope with the dynamic nature of the sector.

The survival of an airline depends crucially on its operational and financial performance. Hence, airlines' short-term liquidity, return on assets and long-term solvency are based on current ratio, productivity of assets and debt ratio, as in any other business. With such fierce competition in the air transport market, airlines cannot pursue any other primary strategy than to strive for cost leadership. In their contribution, *Juan Carlos Martín* and *Concepción Román* analyse airlines and their focus on cost control and productivity.

Rosário Macário and *Vasco Reis* discuss the impact of and reaction patterns to the emergence and growth of low-cost airlines. The focus is on a set of domains that arguably have been most affected by the phenomenon of LCAs: full service airlines; travel distribution agencies and distribution agents; other modes of transport; airports; and regions. The authors provide a general overview, which is in contrast with literature that typically explores a single aspect of the issue at hand.

Over the last decade the airline industry has experienced extreme financial adversity. Whereas external low-probability, but high-impact factors have been partially to blame, some airlines have performed noticeably worse than others. Predicting differences in airlines' financial performance is of interest to various stakeholders. While much performance prediction research has focused on corporate distress and bankruptcy, little attention has been paid to firms' operating profits or losses. Therefore, in his contribution, *Sveinn Vidar Gudmundsson* constructs a neural network performance prediction model, i.e. a multi-country single industry model, and compares a multi-year and single year model. The industry is the international airline business, the data are non-financial, and the input parameters are selected on the basis of significant differences between the means of performance states.

Air cargo transport has developed very rapidly in recent years. Until not so long ago, air freight was essentially considered to be a by-product of passenger transport. Today, however, it is fully recognised that air cargo can codetermine airline companies' success, and there are now airlines that specialise in this particular submarket. *Franziska Kupfer, Hilde Meersman, Evy Onghena* and *Eddy Van de Voorde* set out to explain the economic rationale behind the air cargo market with a view to creating a better understanding of how the sector works. A regression analysis is carried out to identify factors affecting the development of the air cargo market.

Since integrators are able to control the total supply chain (cf. 'one-stop shopping'), their strategic and operational significance to the commercial and production processes of shippers is great. In her contribution, *Evy Onghena* deals with the integrator market, focusing on its structure and supply side. More specifically, her contribution situates the integrators in the global air cargo business and offers insight into their cost structure. In addition, some challenges and opportunities specific to the integrator market are examined.

Traditionally, airports regard airlines as their primary customers, as they are bound by legally enforceable agreements and because airlines pay various charges, including landing and parking fees, as well as charges per passenger or tonne of freight handled. Today, in a more commercial and privately operated environment where there is growing awareness of the value of business models to airports, these complex infrastructures are becoming more and more dependent on non-aeronautical revenues and thus passengers are now increasingly perceived as a primary customer section. Within this context, the chapter written by *Rosário Macário* deals with airports of the future, and considers some essentials for a renewed business model.

The airport city concept has been embraced in different ways by airports of varying sizes around the world. Airports everywhere have diversified their landside revenue sources through non-aviation-based commercial and industrial development, with a view to boosting income and spreading risk in the notoriously volatile aviation market. The contribution by *Douglas Baker* and *Robert Freestone* provides an overview of the issues that have arisen as a result of the changing role of airports in the development of land for non-aeronautical uses. The analysis focuses on two mid-sized airports, Athens and Brisbane, with specific reference to issues relating to land-use planning, infrastructure and governance. The authors provide a descriptive review of the two cases and offer insight into how these airports have embraced the airport city concept to develop land within their perimeter.

Airline alliances are hot. The first global alliances typically included one US airline and one European airline operating a number of code-share flights in the USA and Europe. However, as the alliances have expanded, they have incorporated additional US and European carriers, as well as carriers from other parts of the world. By the early 2000s, many of the global airlines had entered into one of four global alliances, each headed by at least one US carrier and one European carrier. In his contribution, *Martin Dresner* offers a comprehensive exploration of the economic impacts of airline alliances, with emphasis on the role that code-sharing agreements play in determining costs and benefits to carriers and passengers.

In the chapter entitled 'The transmogrification of hub-and-spoke airline networks', *Kenneth Button* looks at the factors that initially stimulated the growth of airline hub-and-spoke networks, and the forces that have subsequently led to their being modified, and the forms that they now take. The examination not only looks at the underlying economic forces involved, but also at the political economy of such things as the emergence of mega-trade blocks, attitudes towards anti-trust and merger activities, and increasing amounts of environmental regulation. Markets for air services, and with them the relevance of hubs, are not independent of the institutional structures in which they function, and changes in these institutions, along with new technologies and innovations in management, inevitably affect the types of service networks airlines offer.

Jan Veldhuis addresses the impact of network changes for the users (passengers) of the airports of Amsterdam Schiphol and Paris Charles de Gaulle. The author first deals with the possible effects of the partnership between the two airports and then provides a brief theoretical introduction on a methodology for assessing consumer benefit variations. He demonstrates the effects of network integration for the route between Amsterdam and Dallas. Additionally, he shows similar effects to exist on other routes and finds indications of possible other impacts.

The contribution of *Paul Roosens* deals with the significant challenges posed by congestion in air transport. Transport congestion in general occurs when demand for infrastructure exceeds capacity, causing delays in travel time as one of the main symptoms. Most of the congestion issues in air transport discussed here are based on the European and US experiences. Many of the available European and US solutions have either already been adopted or are in the process of being adopted elsewhere in the world. The author deals exclusively with airport- and airspace-related or en-route congestion issues and delays. The immediate challenge is to decrease congestion while maintaining safety levels as traffic intensity increases.

In view of the current situation in the airline industry, the problem of airport congestion in Europe may have been postponed for a while, but irrespective of the temporary reduction in aircraft movements, substantial shortages of airport capacity are foreseen in the long run. Over the next two decades, the European air transport industry will experience a growing need for more efficient allocation methods with regard to increasingly scarce airport capacity. *Jaap de Wit* and *Guillaume Burghouwt* consider market-based options that may satisfy that need. After discussing the current slot allocation system in Europe and its inefficiencies, various market-based options are compared and contrasted with the US experience. Subsequently, the focus of attention shifts to whether secondary slot trading as a market-based option at European hubs such as Amsterdam airport will result in more concentrated downstream air transport markets at these hubs.

The chapter by *David Pitfield* deals with the impact assessment of Open Skies agreements. He proposes a methodology for dealing with the issue of the counterfactual in passenger numbers in the assessment of the EU–US Agreement. If the first application of the model can produce good fit for the period before any interventions, then the significance of those interventions when added to the model will demonstrate their contribution. It is suggested that this methodology could address the significance of the change in passenger numbers attributable to the EU–US Open Skies Agreement.

The North Atlantic is the busiest inter-regional route in the world, accounting for around a quarter of all inter-regional traffic. *Anne Graham* assesses the impact on airports of recent aviation developments on the North Atlantic. The focus is exclusively on passenger services. Conclusions are drawn with consideration of prospects for the future, both with regard to the major short-term problems associated with the effects of the credit crunch and the severe economic recession which the industry now faces, as well as in relation to the longer term.

The contribution by *Yulai Wan* and *Anming Zhang* deals with the effects of emission trading schemes. Climate change has aroused much public concern around the world in recent years. The rapid growth in air traffic over the last few decades has led to a significant increase in greenhouse gas (GHG) emissions from the aviation sector, and these emissions are expected to continue to grow rapidly in the future. Significant public pressure has been mounted on both the aviation industry and its regulators to better control GHG emissions. Therefore it is important to get to grip on the direct and indirect impacts of climate change.

Werner Rothengatter discusses competition between airlines and high-speed rail services. The development of transport demand after the opening of high-speed railway lines (HSR) between large agglomerations shows that fierce competition between air transport and HSR may occur on distances up to 1000 km. The author considers developments in air and high-speed rail traffic on major relationships in Europe, and discusses empirical findings regarding competition between short-distance air transport services – particularly those operated by low-cost carriers (LCC) – and HSR services. In some cases, the competitive performance of HSR services has been encouraging, but in others the huge investment has proven not to be financially viable

Competition is crucial to any liberalisation process, where regulatory authorities should retreat and economic agents take over. Only free and open markets, in fact, force companies to compete on their merits. *Marco Benacchio* explores the role and the tools of competition policy in the evaluation of the consolidation phase that is re-shaping the air transport industry, after the implementation of the EU deregulation packages. In this contest, the role for anti-trust enforcers should not be to influence the market outcomes, but – as a referee – to preserve the contestability of the air transport markets in the light of the current regulation.

Air transport is arguably the most regulated industry in our society, even after deregulation. One could ask: why? What makes air transport different from maritime or road transport, and how can we legitimise government intervention in all of its aspects? Most chapters of this book deal with economic and business topics. At first glance, the contribution by lawyer *Mia Wouters* would appear not to fit the bill. However, in today's air transport industry, there is only a thin line separating law from economics, and, with the advent of deregulation, the two areas are bound to interact more than ever before. The combination of law and economics inevitably brings us to the issue of 'policy'. But what exactly is air transport policy? And what precisely is the role of government as a policymaker?

Joel Zhengyi Shon deals with essential airline marketing strategies. The concept of marketing can be quite confusing to those who are unfamiliar with business, management and economics. To put it in the simplest terms: marketing is an intermediary, helping supply to meet demand on the market. Without marketing processes and activities, transaction costs may become too high, leaving all parties involved in the transaction process without ever reaching an agreement.

In the final chapter, *Rosário Macário* and *Eddy Van de Voorde* present a synthesis of the main conclusions. These serve as a basis for a tentative research and policy agenda for the coming period. Because of its dynamic nature, the airline sector is after all like a laboratory for scientific research and, by extension, also for business and policy processes. Hence, a research agenda would certainly seem a worthwhile tool.

Note

1 We thank the editorial board and publisher of the *European Journal of Transport and Infrastructure Research* for granting us the right to revise and update six papers that appeared earlier in their journal, and to incorporate them in this book.

2 The future air transport sector
A modified market and ownership structure

*Hilde Meersman, Eddy Van de Voorde and
Thierry Vanelslander*

1 Introduction

The airline business is almost like the laboratory of transport economics. It is an environment where technological and organisational developments unfold in rapid succession. Among the world's air transport companies, one observes all kinds of industrial and economic evolutions, with frequent new entries, mergers, takeovers and bankruptcies. Airports are increasingly confronted with ecological and capacity issues. Regions are constantly competing with one another to attract players in the airline business. New and innovative products, including low-cost airlines and full-freighter cargo services, are claiming an ever greater proportion of available capacity.

The dynamic nature of the airline sector explains to some extent the growing interest from policy makers and researchers, as well as leading persons in the world of business. Here, two issues come to the fore time and again: the economic significance of the air transport industry and the future that lies in store for that industry.

This chapter attempts to outline some of the likely developments in the air transport industry beyond 2010. If the trends that have unfolded in recent decades persist in the coming years, that alone will inevitably result in an altered market and ownership structure. This chapter consists of four parts: the analysis of the present situation in the air transport business taking into account the development process of the last decade, the description of potential scenarios and strategies, the business models to cope with the dynamic nature of the sector, and finally some concluding remarks.

2 Trends from the past

The best starting point to gain an understanding of sectoral developments is by analysing figures and trends from the past, over a sufficiently long period of time. In the case of the international air transport business, indicators of demand, supply and market structure can give a good insight in the past and present situation of the sector.

In the early 1990s, the air transport industry went through a deep, structural crisis, occasioned by, among other things, a combination of relatively weak economic activity and rising oil prices. In addition, there was the direct impact of the 1991 Gulf War and the Asian economic slump from 1992. Furthermore, there was the structural problem caused by the liberalisation of the air transport market, with initial overcapacity putting downward pressure on yields and profits and resulting in an entirely new market environment.[1]

Prior to the deregulation process, only national authorities, through their flag carriers, were able to organise scheduled services on the major routes. There was no question of competition, and operational efficiency was regarded as inessential. With the movement towards deregulation, however, the quasi-monopoly power of those flag carriers was seriously eroded, not least because it had become relatively simple for new companies to enter the marketplace. New and successful products were developed, as was apparent in the rise of so-called low-cost carriers. Innovative pricing strategies allowed companies to benefit maximally from a different willingness to pay in different market segments. The continuous search for opportunities for cooperation in relation to reservation systems, frequency of service and slot allocation resulted in the emergence of a limited number of strategic alliances.

This movement towards a profound liberalisation, coupled with the cyclical impact of economic activity, translates into the evolution outlined in Figures 2.1 and 2.2.

In the period under consideration, there is clear evidence of substantial growth in the industry, as is aptly summarised in Table 2.1.

There are, however, notable differences in respect of where the growth was achieved, which in turn impacts on the structure of the air transport sector:

•   In the period under consideration, there was very strong growth in terms of passengers carried.

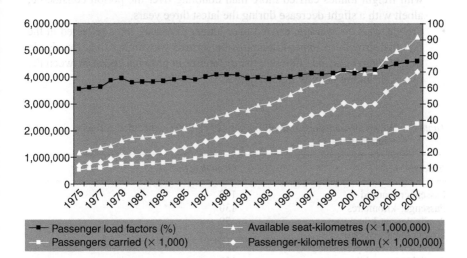

Figure 2.1 World air transport scheduled services (domestic + international) – passengers (source: IATA).

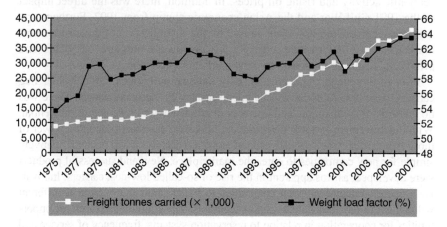

Figure 2.2 World air transport scheduled services (domestic + international) – freight (source: IATA).

- The even greater growth recorded in passenger-kilometres performed indicates that the average air passenger travelled greater distances; the passenger-kilometres flown increased quite strongly during the most recent years.
- While still strong, growth in the number of available seat-kilometres was slower than that in passenger-kilometres performed, resulting in a marked improvement in the seat-occupancy rate.
- The growth figures recorded in freight transport are even more impressive, with freight tonnes carried more than doubling over the period considered, albeit with a slight decrease during the latest three years.
- Freight was, on average, carried over longer distances, as is reflected in the fact that growth in tonne-kilometres performed was higher than the rise in freight tonnes carried, although the difference in growing speed between the two is shrinking heavily in later years.

Table 2.1 World air transport: growth figures (1991–2007, scheduled services, domestic + international)

Indicator	Growth rate (%)
Passengers carried	102
Passenger-kilometres	130
Available seat-kilometres	99
Freight tonnes carried	138
Tonne-kilometres performed	140
Available tonne-kilometres	122

Source: IATA (1991–2008).

• As in passenger transport, freight transport saw a substantial improvement in capacity utilisation, as growth in available capacity was lower than growth in tonne-kilometres performed; here again, the growth difference is shrinking.

While the above graphs and table undeniably provide an overview of the most significant developments in the air transport business, they do also 'mask' a number of evolutions. First and foremost, there are the short-term effects and potential regional differences. The air transport sector faces potential great risks on the demand side, including volatile oil prices, the impact of Influenza A (H1N1) and terrorist threats. Cash flow is affected by weak demand, leading to capacity adjustments, and worsened by fare discounting upon several years of continued cost reduction, making it difficult to cut costs any further. Table 2.2 shows evidence of how the economic context is affecting the sector in the different geographical markets.

The developments described above have altered the air transport landscape profoundly. Particularly in respect of the actual carriers, the industry has evolved towards a typology consisting of at least four categories: network airlines, regional and smaller network airlines, charter companies, and low-cost airlines. Starting from this typology, one can discern quite divergent evolutions:

• The picture in Europe is mixed. The three largest carriers (British Airways, Lufthansa and Air France) have performed well. However, there have also been a number of bankruptcies (e.g. Sabena and Swissair), while other companies have had to contend or continue to contend with looming crisis (e.g. Alitalia). In the charter market, there were some successful start-ups (e.g. TCAB), followed by a concentration movement resulting in a limited

Table 2.2 IATA recorded load factors(*) – 2009 vs 2008

YTD 2009 vs YTD 2008	RPK growth (%)	ASK growth (%)	PLF	FTK growth (%)	AFTK growth (%)
Africa	–9.2	–5.6	69.0	–22.5	–19.8
Asia/Pacific	–12.0	–7.7	70.6	–22.3	–16.4
Europe	–7.6	–4.8	73.5	–21.6	–9.4
Latin America	–3.2	1.0	70.4	–19.6	–8.6
Middle East	7.1	12.5	71.1	–5.5	11.5
North America	–8.9	–5.3	76.6	–22.2	–9.9
Industry	**–7.6**	**–3.9**	**72.6**	**–20.6**	**–10.4**

Source: IATA.

Notes
(*) RPK: Revenue Passenger Kilometres measures actual passenger traffic.
ASK: Available Seat Kilometres measures available passenger capacity.
PLF: Passenger Load Factor is % of ASKs used. In comparison of 2009 to 2008, PLF indicates point differential between the periods compared.
FTK: Freight Tonne Kilometres measures actual freight traffic.
AFTK: Available Freight Tonne Kilometres measures available total freight capacity.

number of large groups (e.g. Thomas Cook and TUI). Another notable trend has been the rise and growth of some important low-cost airlines (Ryanair, easyJet, Air Berlin,...).

- In the United States, recent years have brought a thorough reorganisation in the air transport market. With the exception of American Airlines, all major companies (United Airlines, US Airways, Delta, Continental Airlines,...) have gone through Chapter 11, resulting in reorganisation and a healthier cost structure.
- The impressive economic growth rate in Asia has also had a positive impact on the Asian carriers. Importantly, though, Asian growth is generating scarcity, including of pilots.
- In the Arab world some carriers faced a strong growth (including Qatar, Etihad, Emirates,...); the strategy pursued by these carriers is clearly linked with the striving for diversification among the region's political leaders.

The question that now confronts the airline industry and its business environment is how matters will evolve further. Will this long-term growth persist in the coming decade? What will be the long-term effect of the economic crisis that started in the second half of 2008? Does it justify investments in additional capacity, in terms of both aircraft and airports? Does it make sense in the short run for political attention to focus on possible bottlenecks, including in respect of air space and slot allocation?

3 Towards a new business model?

Too often, the air transport sector has been considered as a homogeneous sector. This is not correct. The air transport business involves a highly heterogeneous array of actors. Some remain subject to a form of state control, others are fully privatised, and yet others operate under a mixed regime. As far as the privately controlled players are concerned, the corporate objective is obviously profit maximisation. The non-privately controlled players, on the other hand, usually pursue other goals, such as maximisation of employment and/or value added, or, more generally, the maximisation of socioeconomic surplus.

A thorough analysis of the strategic behaviour of a number of carriers shows that, while each airline tends to position its own product in a specific way, the available tools are invariably the same. The approach taken always combines control over the unit cost and optimisation of the seat occupancy or load factor with a striving to maximise the yield.

In the future, ever greater emphasis will be placed on achieving a sufficiently high yield, with carriers also generating income from non-flying activities through every passenger. Ryanair is a case in point. Not only does the company apply many surcharges, including a luggage check-in fee and a fee for payment by credit card, but significantly, in recent financial years, Ryanair generated more than half of its operational result (earnings before interest and tax) through activities that had little or nothing to do with flying. Typical examples are such diversification activities as car rentals and hotel room reservations, for which Ryanair earns a commission.

There are clearly links between the various actors, both within a particular subsector (e.g. the airline industry) and beyond (e.g. between airlines and ground-handling companies). Table 2.3 provides an overview of the different kinds of links encountered.

Each company operating in the air transport business may have committed to different types of agreement with different players. French carrier Air France, for example, has effectively taken over Dutch airline KLM in a merger/acquisition, while at the same time entering into code-share agreements with numerous other carriers. Moreover, the company is part of the SkyTeam airline alliance. German carrier Lufthansa, for example, has effectively taken over control of a number of airlines like Brussels Airlines, Austrian and bmi, while at the same time entering into code-share agreements with numerous other carriers and also promoting the entry into the air transport network of the German rail network, causing a very significant improvement of accessibility to and from German territories. Moreover, the company is a core partner of the Star airline alliance. Each merger or acquisition can have consequences for the relationships with other actors, e.g. at ground-handling level. Hence, for each enterprise, a specific cell can distinctly be completed in Table 2.3, as every market player has a specific structure and corporate history.

It is equally interesting to highlight and subsequently quantify the existing links between partners at airport level. In this context of company strategies and linkages, the major questions are who provides which services to whom, and to what extent are actors dependent upon specific suppliers and clients. Consider the example of easyJet, which in 2007 launched flights from Brussels to Nice and Geneva. This new entry was, first and foremost, in direct competition with Brussels Airlines and Swiss, both of which companies were already operating flights on these routes. Second, there were derived effects for service suppliers, including ground-handling companies.

Figure 2.3 provides insight into the structure of relationships between actors in the air cargo business. The arrows indicate existing relationships and their direction. These relationships may, in a subsequent phase, be quantified. A similar methodology was already applied to port and maritime relations within the port of Antwerp in Coppens *et al.* (2007).

The above overview shows quite clearly how the airline industry is subject to constant change and how it is evolving towards new business models. Hence the importance of being able to understand the potential impact of that evolution on the future airline market.

4 An outline of the future market

Predicting a future market is inevitably fraught with uncertainty. So too in the air transport sector. Uncertainty can never be eliminated entirely. At best, it can be channelled to some extent.

Table 2.3 Control and cooperation between subsectors in the air transport industry

Market actors	Airlines	Handling companies	Airport operators	Authorities
Airlines	*Mergers and acquisitions* (e.g. Air France and KLM) *Alliances* (e.g. Star, SkyTeam, Oneworld, WOW) *Code-share agreements* *Joint ventures* (e.g. Lufthansa Cargo and DHL Express) *Financial participations*			
Handling companies	Previously mostly integrated in airline, nowadays often *outsourced* to third party handling companies *Specific contracts* (e.g. in 2007 Martinair with Aviapartner, for nine German airports, for three years)	*Concentration* by take-overs (e.g. Menzies, Globeground, Aviapartner,…)		
Airport operators	*Financial participation* (e.g. Lufthansa in Munich) *Co-operation* between airports and airlines (e.g. Charleroi and Ryanair)	*Concessions and licences* *Integration*	*Mergers and acquisitions* (e.g. Brussels Airport by Macquarie Airports)	
Authorities	*Participation* of governments in Flag carriers (e.g. TAP)		Monopoly by airport authority or its sole concessionaire *Participation* of government in airports, including (partial) privatisation	*Participation* of two governments in an airline

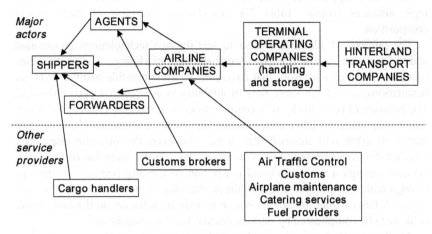

Figure 2.3 Air transport actors (cargo business case).

The starting point for the outline of possible future developments is invariably a combination of the present situation, recent trends and a set of endogenous and exogenous variables. Among the exogenous variables under consideration are such factors as economic activity and fuel prices. Endogenous variables are the yields, the cost structure (cf. hedging agreement or not), financial indicators, capacity utilisation, mergers and acquisitions.

The future developments which could impact and shape the sector are:

- a total split between global network carriers and niche players;
- more privatisation;
- alliances influenced by cross-border mergers and acquisitions;
- survival of the Southwest model?
- more bankruptcies;
- increasing aggressiveness;
- decreasing influence of government;
- extreme volatility of the air freight market;
- increasing international capital flows.

4.1 A total split between global network carriers and niche players

In the most recent past, a clear market split has come about between global network carriers on the one hand and niche players on the other. The global network carriers have consolidated through so-called strategic alliances into a limited number of fiercely competing networks, both in passenger and in freight transport. Niche players have been able to exploit market opportunities that presented themselves because of geographic characteristics, for instance by operating strongly from small regional airports, or through specific services, such as low-cost activities and express freight transport.

After the disappearance of the Qualiflyer Group in 2001, three important strategic alliances remain. Table 2.4 provides an overview of their present composition.

The purpose of alliances is clear to see: through technological cooperation and the tool sharing that it implies (code sharing, interlining,...), potential customers are offered a network that covers the greatest possible number of major destinations, and at the same time profitability is assured and even enhanced. The pressure of profitability will continue to exist in the near future, so that one may assume that a further concentration movement will ensue. The crisis that started in 2008 will intensify this trend. However, the question does arise whether this concentration will be achieved through the inclusion of new partners, or through a more profound integration of existing partners, or perhaps through both. The positive effect on the profitability of the alliance must be clear to see. A far-reaching integration within an existing alliance, on the other hand, is likely to be complicated by intercontinental legal discrepancies.[2]

Another question arises, namely whether more concentration can result in market dominance by a limited number of carriers, with the risk of abuse of market power. Within the Star Alliance for instance, Lufthansa has increasing market power, as in its capital control of Austrian, bmi and Brussels Airlines. The move towards market dominance has been accelerated by the lack of capital of smaller companies.

The niche market is in trouble. In 2005, a totally new product was launched that is known as 'business-only transatlantic travel'. Aircraft are converted into a configuration to suit the business traveller, with personal space and a check-in procedure that is faster and less stressful than in services offered by traditional carriers. Promoted as a low-fare, all-business-class service, the aim is to persuade economy-class customers to pay slightly more in return for a more personalised service. In the London to US market, three airlines were operating such a service in 2007: EOS Airlines, Maxjet Airways and Silverjet. All of them

Table 2.4 Composition of strategic alliances (December 2009)

Alliance	Air companies
Star Alliance	Air Canada, Air China, Air New Zealand, ANA, Asiana Airlines, Austrian, bmi, Brussels Airlines, Egyptair, LOT Polish Airlines, Lufthansa, Scandinavian Airlines, Shangai Airlines, Singapore Airlines, South-African Airways, Spanair, Swiss, TAP Portugal, Thai Airways International, United, US Airways Regional members: Adria, Blue1, Croatia Airlines
SkyTeam	Aeroflot, Aeromexico, Air France, KLM, Alitalia, China Southern, Continental Airlines, Czech Airlines, Delta Air Lines, Korean Air Associates, Air Europa, Copa Airlines, Kenya Airways
Oneworld	American Airlines, British Airways, Cathay Pacific, Finnair, Iberia, Japan Airlines, LAN, Malev, Quantas, Royal Jordanian

Sources: Star Alliance (2009), SkyTeam (2009) and Oneworld (2009).

disappeared before June 2008. Lufthansa, KLM and Swiss International Airlines launched their own all-business transatlantic flights from continental Europe. To this end, they cooperate with the Swiss operator PrivatAir.[3]

4.2 More privatisation

The former air transport market, dominated by flag carriers that were completely or largely controlled by national authorities, has disappeared. Former flag carriers have been or are in the process of being wholly or partially privatised. New entries are almost always financed with private capital. The cases of British Airways, Air France, Alitalia and others show very clearly how public stakes in carriers are becoming smaller or, in some cases, have disappeared altogether. Equally interesting is the fact that some airlines are now participating in the capital of other carriers. This trend has been intensified by the need for re-capitalisation of some airlines.

However, privatisation does not necessarily mean that the prevailing competition rules are being respected. In February 2006, for example, the European Commission and the US Department of Justice announced an investigation into alleged collusion in the air cargo market. This was followed by an investigation in the long-haul passenger market, focusing on possible price collusion and, in particular, on fuel surcharges on top of normal fares, including in deals negotiated with large enterprises and holding companies.

Privatisation movements also generate competitive strategies. In 2006, Ryanair acquired a blocking minority in Aer Lingus, facilitating its own bid for the former flag carrier and enabling it to prevent others from bidding. The Irish state retained a 25.4 per cent stake. This battle for control over Aer Lingus illustrates how the public authorities can become involved in a tug of war over a largely privatised carrier.

The privatisation wave is also noticeable in the airport sector. Carriers will in the future be increasingly confronted with privatised airports. Unlike when these airports were publicly operated, the main goal is now profit maximisation. The result is bilateral negotiations between two profit maximisers that (must) take into account the portfolio of alternative solutions available to their adversary.

4.3 Alliances influenced by cross-border mergers and acquisitions

The purpose of alliances, mergers and takeovers are similar: to enhance operational and marketing efficiency, to achieve better financial results, and to realise industrial–economic improvements through scale effects and by lowering barriers to entry.

Mergers and takeovers also have a clear impact on the composition of alliances, and thus on their economic performances. Here, there is much to be learnt from past experiences in maritime transport. The example of P&O Nedlloyd is quite illustrative in this respect. In 1998, this shipping company helped establish the Grand Alliance. However, after the takeover by Maersk in 2005, it pulled out. To compensate for this loss, the Grand Alliance concluded deals with the New World Alliance on a number of routes. Clearly, then, alliances as such are not stable, but subject to continuous movements and the associated entry and exit of partners.

A similar situation is threatening to unfold in the air transport business. The takeover of Alitalia by Air France/KLM did not result in a reshuffle of alliances, as both companies belonged to the SkyTeam group, but matters would have been quite different had US Airways' 2006 bid for Delta Air Lines succeeded. The new merger would have created the world's largest carrier. The effect on existing alliances would have been twofold. The alliance to which the merged company belonged would have become the dominant player, and within that alliance, the merged company would have become the dominant partner over the other participating carriers. The other alliance would have lost an important American partner and would thus have been weakened substantially.

It has also become apparent that a consolidation wave is inevitable. In the United States, five of the six international carriers were involved in merger talks in 2007.[4] Especially a merger/takeover involving both Continental and United Airlines would generate substantial benefits given the limited overlap between their respective networks. However, the two carriers belong to different alliances. Moreover, there are industrial–economic barriers to take into account in these kinds of mergers.[5]

In Europe, too, a consolidation movement is gaining momentum, with possible consequences for the existing alliances. Since 1999, the Spanish company Iberia has been operating in an alliance with British Airways, in which the latter carrier, for that matter, has a financial stake in the listed company Iberia. At the beginning of 2007, the Iberia management was not excluding the possibility of an alliance with Air France/KLM or Lufthansa. In September 2009, Iberia asked for an immediate merger with British Airways.[6] This movement illustrates what typically lies in store: a consolidation movement towards three large European groups, gravitating around the three largest carriers, namely Lufthansa, British Airways and Air France/KLM. The current crisis will probably accelerate this evolution.

4.4 Survival of the Southwest model?

The Southwest model has proven to be successful, and hence has been copied in the rest of the world. The model was based on strict adherence to a number of principles: short-haul, point-to-point, dense routes only, maximisation of flying hours, use of secondary airports, high frequency of service, no delays. It strove to combine low costs, low fares and high demand and capacity utilisation.

The European low-cost market is heavily influenced by the economic recession. But at the same time, Ryanair announced for the period 1 April–30 June 2009 a profit increase of 21 per cent, compared to the same period last year. Low-cost companies are increasing their market share vis-à-vis the traditional carriers and charter companies. The important question arises whether the growth rate of the past can be maintained in the future.

In an analysis by Deutsche Bank from May 2007, it was calculated that the low-cost market will continue to experience a volume growth of roughly 15 per cent, as a consequence of a combination of shifts from other air transport segments, GDP growth, and a very modestly rising propensity to travel. All major low-cost companies are expected to achieve annual growth rates of less than 15 per cent, while Ryanair is expected to grow by 20 per cent annually (Deutsche Bank, 2007, p. 5). This outlook is enhanced if one considers the investment strategy of carriers such as Air Berlin, Ryanair and easyJet. Table 2.5 provides an overview of aircraft orders and deliveries.

It is clear that current economic activity is continuing to stimulate the growth of the low-cost airlines. At the same time, it is more likely that certain inputs will become more expensive, resulting in a slowdown in growth. Moreover, there are signs that the market is reaching a degree of maturity (Mintel, 2006). This is undoubtedly why initiatives have been announced or indeed are already being launched in relation to long-haul low-cost routes.[7] Here, the question arises of what the price difference with the traditional carriers will be and, more importantly still perhaps, how customers will respond to this product.

4.5 More bankruptcies

Bankruptcies and takeovers used to be rare in the air transport sector during the era of the so-called flag carriers. More recently, however, such events have become more common and have had a significant impact on the market functioning and competition. By way of illustration, Table 2.6 provides an overview of recent bankruptcies, mergers and takeovers in the European airlines sector. Strikingly, the companies in question are often medium-sized international airlines.

Table 2.5 Estimated number of aircraft and passengers carried by European LCAs until 2012

	2005	2006	2007 F	2008 E	2009 E	2010 E	2011 E	2012 E
Number of aircraft								
easyJet	108	120	143	160	177	194	211	228
Ryanair	87	113	132	152	172	192	212	225
Others	152	181	221	260	302	347	395	458
Total	347	414	495	572	651	733	818	910
Passengers (millions)								
easyJet	28	34	38	42	46	51	55	60
Ryanair	31	41	48	55	62	69	76	81
Others	45	56	67	79	92	106	122	141
Total	105	130	152	176	201	227	253	262

Sources: Lopes (2005), airlines websites, authors' calculations. Cols 2007F and 2012E.

Notes
F – forecast; E – estimate.

Doganis (2001) asserts that these airlines are 'too small to be global players, too big to be a niche player'. Their mission is unclear, they usually find it hard to take optimal strategic decisions and, in most cases, they are undercapitalised.

In the United States the situation is different. First and foremost, the recent past has seen many companies file for Chapter-11 protection against creditors. At the same time, reorganisation measures have been pushed through and new, cheaper deals have been negotiated with partners.[8] The consequence is twofold: the majors generally get out of Chapter-11 with a lower cost structure and hence greater competitive strength, but their regional partners come under greater pressure and must adapt their strategies. This can influence the competitive position of European carriers, not having a kind of Chapter-11 protection scheme, e.g. to lower their costs.

It would appear that the trend of recent years will persist in the future, resulting in consolidation into a limited number of large network carriers as well as a limited number of large low-cost carriers. This evolution will undoubtedly impact on the market structure and on market behaviour, and possibly holds the risk of abuse of market power. Carriers that do not belong to strategic alliances will then become likely victims of bankruptcy and prime targets for takeovers and mergers.

4.6 Increasing aggressiveness

The air transport sector provides a good example of the potential response to new market entries in an industrial economy. Consider the hypothetical example

Table 2.6 Bankruptcies, mergers and takeovers in the European airlines sector (data of 2009, until 10 September)

Date	Airline	Country	Ops started	Event
17–Jan–09	FlyLAL	Lithuania	1938	Bankruptcy
19–Jan–09	Apatas Air	Lithuania	1994	Bankruptcy
24–Jan–09	Nordic Airways	Sweden	2006	Bankruptcy
16–Mar–09	EuroAir	Greece	1995	AOC withdrawn
31–Mar–09	Blue Wings	Germany	2003	
27–Apr–09	Air Sylhet	United Kingdom	2007	Bankruptcy
01–May–09	LTU International Airways	Germany	1955	Merged into Air Berlin
01–May–09	ThomsonFly	United Kingdom	2004	Became Thomson Airways
01–May–09	First Choice Airways	United Kingdom	1987	Became Thomson Airways
06–May–09	Open Skies	United Kingdom	2007	Transferred to Elysair
01–Jul–09	Cargo B	Belgium	2007	Bankruptcy
09–Jul–09	Clickair	Spain	2006	Merged into Vueling
24–Jul–09	MyAir	Italy	2004	Bankruptcy
01–Sep–09	SkyEurope	Slovakia	2002	Bankruptcy

Source: www.airlineupdate.com/airlines/airline_extra/defunctairlines/defunctairlines_index.htm.

of a new entrant in the marketplace launching a service on a particular route. The carriers already operating on that route will almost always respond with sharp price cuts, combined with increased capacity. As soon as the new carrier retreats, capacity is decreased again and prices are increased. Alternatively in such a situation, flag carriers might purchase or launch an in-house low-cost carrier.

While, initially, the low-cost airlines tended to exhibit aggressive behaviour vis-à-vis the flag carriers, now the opposite is happening. The large flag carriers are challenging the low-cost carriers on their short-haul destinations, and feeding these passengers to their more profitable full-service long-haul routes.[9] Flag carriers such as British Airways, Lufthansa and Air France/KLM have all changed the product of 'short-distance flights' quite drastically: more straightforward economy classes, the introduction of on-line reservation, the elimination of travel agents' commissions, no or exclusively paid-for catering.

This increasingly aggressive behaviour will persist in the future, as one can already infer from the sometimes strange developments at the takeover front. An example that comes to mind is Air Berlin, a low-cost carrier operating in the European market which in 2007 acquired LTU, an airline focusing on the long-haul holiday market. Also in 2007 there was the hostile bid from Ryanair, Europe's largest budget carrier, for the other Irish airline, Aer Lingus. It is a bid, for that matter, which stands very little chance of succeeding, if only because of the fact that the European Commission will not accept the dominant position that Ryanair would thus acquire at Dublin airport.

4.7 Decreasing influence of government

While for decades the air transport business was directed and controlled by public authorities, this government influence is now far less apparent. The traditional flag carriers are disappearing, not least because the public authorities are partially or wholly selling their share in the capital of these companies. Deregulation is gaining momentum, and the influence of the national authorities is now restricted mainly to two areas.[10] First and foremost, the public sector will most likely continue to provide the basic airport infrastructure. Second, they are still generally expected to act against any abuse of monopoly status in relation to pricing, landing slot allocation or access to terminals.

The (supra)national authorities for their part may be expected to assume a more prominent role in the environmental field. The European Commission, for example, is committed to a reduction in CO_2 emissions. The airline industry has been included in an EU emissions trading scheme (European directive 2008/101/EC).

The airline industry is already responding to this trend. In 2007, easyJet introduced its own so-called 'eco-friendly aircraft design', which uses existing technologies that could halve carbon dioxide emissions and produce 75 per cent less NO_x by 2015.[11] IATA, meanwhile, has launched a zero emission goal for the airline industry. The environmental issue, then, is likely to become one of the most significant points of debate within the airline sector. Here, government clearly has an important regulatory and supervisory role to play.

4.8 Air freight: from by-product to success factor

Till 2008, air freight was a growth market. Traditionally regarded as a by-product of passenger transport, there are now a number of companies focusing exclusively on this segment (Herman and Van de Voorde, 2006).[12] Air freight indeed became a heterogeneous product, from belly space operations till express operations and integrators (see Figure 2.4).

The relatively growing importance of full-freighter transport is occasioned by a combination of factors. For one thing, the available freight capacity in passenger aircraft is insufficient to satisfy growing demand. Second, on certain air freight routes, there is a strong imbalance between incoming and outgoing freight, so that a different network structure imposes itself. In addition, there is an ongoing consolidation trend whereby freight is combined at hubs, and these larger volumes are resulting in more competitive full-freighter operations.

Air freight was expected to continue to expand more rapidly than passenger transport. However, in 2009 some airports reported extreme decreases in throughput, some of them of up to −50 per cent. This is the result of a combination of several effects: carriers moving to other airports (e.g. Ethiopian from Brussels to Liège), lower frequency, merged routes, and bankruptcies. However, as long as air freight can contribute to profit maximisation and market share, carriers will want to operate in this market, be it as a by-product of air passenger flows or in a full-freighter configuration.

4.9 Increased foreign capital

The dilution of the flag carrier concept, which is characterised by a declining involvement of public funds and the entry of more private capital, has resulted in an important evolution in terms of industrial and capital structure. In the case of some airlines, and indeed airports, there was a three-step movement. First, there was the disintegration phase, with companies refocusing on the core business. In the second step, such non-core activities as catering, handling and maintenance

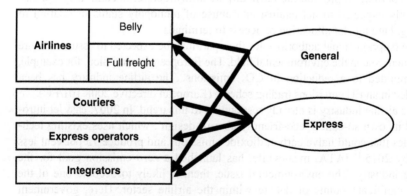

Figure 2.4 Airfreight, a heterogeneous product.

Table 2.7 Private equity in the Belgian airline industry

Date	Target	Purchaser	Million €
November 2004	BIAC (70%)	Macquarie Bank	735
July 2005	Aviapartner	3i	165

Source: own composition.

were sold off. Finally, in the third phase, this evolution was commonly combined with the entry of external capital.[13]

Increasingly, it appears to be private equity that enters the sector. Table 2.7 provides an overview of a number of significant capital movements involving private equity in the Belgian airline market.

The question that arises is whether the entry of private equity capital in the airline industry is not at odds with companies' long-term interests. Private equity groups tend to sell relatively quickly, i.e. within a period of three to five years. It remains to be seen, though, to what extent the strong cyclical movements in the airline industry may pose a problem in this respect. And to what extent may possible 'exits' from the capital of airlines and airports by private equity groups result in new consolidation movements?[14] Due to the economic crisis that started in 2008, the behaviour of some venture capitalists became quite nervous. They tried to sell (part of) their participation because of their need for cash. However, at such a moment, the number of potential buyers is limited and prices are low.

5 Conclusion

Being a capital-intensive business that is undergoing very rapid technological and organisational change, the air transport industry is in constant need of insight into future market evolutions. Hence, the purpose of this chapter has been to provide an understanding of likely developments in the sector after 2010.

There is no such thing as a single homogeneous air transport market. It is rather a configuration of various submarkets that are interconnected and therefore interact. The general feeling is that growth will persist beyond 2010. And, if one looks at the market from an international and aggregated perspective, this will indeed most likely be the case, if only because of the expected further expansion of the Asian growth market. However, aggregated data often mask underlying, sometimes opposite evolutions.

In summary, the air transport market after 2010 will be characterised by:

- further specialisation, from global network carriers over full air freight carriers to niche players, including the low-cost or low-fare market;
- the establishment of new alliances, and the international transfer of capital that this entails;
- relatively easy market access, resulting in frequent entries and exits, which in itself will lead to more aggressive behaviour in the market;

- less public intervention and more private investment, with the role of the public authorities restricted to core tasks, such as basic infrastructure provision and safety and security.

It is within this broad future framework, marked by a considerable degree of uncertainty, that the market players will position themselves.

Notes

1 In the United States, the Airline Deregulation Act was introduced in 1978. The liberalisation of the European market was implemented much later. Europe's deregulation programme was based on three packages of measures (1988, 1990, 1993), with each phase impacting on four areas: pricing, market access, competition and licensing (Button *et al.* 1998, pp. 30–44). Cabotage has been permitted within Europe since 1 April 1997.

2 A typical example is the US prohibition on foreign companies acquiring a stake of over 25 per cent in an American carrier.

3 The system works as follows: PrivatAir leases the aircraft and draws up a wet-lease contract. A wet lease is a leasing arrangement whereby one airline (lessor) provides an aircraft, complete crew, maintenance and insurance to another airline (lessee), which pays by hours operated, with the airline in question. PrivatAir provides the crew, catering and in-flight entertainment, it takes care of maintenance and bears all operational risks. The partner airline markets the service and sells the tickets.

4 Delta Air Lines is, for example, talking to Northwest Airlines, while United Airlines is engaged in separate negotiations with Continental and Northwest Airlines.

5 In 2001, Northwest Airlines and Continental struck a deal whereby they could sell tickets on each other's flights. Also, Northwest acquired the right, under certain conditions, to block any merger between Continental and another company.

6 The merger negotiations between British Airways and Iberia have been going on for a long period. This is the consequence of a dramatic decrease in the share price of British Airways. The latter heavily depends on transatlantic flights and revenues, and as such the company is much more sensitive to the economic recession than Iberia. That weakened the negotiating power of British Airways and that is the reason why they are trying to slow down merger talks.

7 Examples include Oasis Hong Kong Airlines (flights between Hong Kong and London), Air Asia, Virgin Blue, Zoom, etc.

8 In this context, David Field writes: 'Wielding the power of bankruptcy, US majors have forced their regional partners to fly for less, but given them more leeway to fly for other airlines.' And he adds: 'Through their powers in bankruptcy, both Delta and Northwest put almost all regional flying out for competitive re-bidding, and the downward pressure on margins spread through the industry' (*Flight International*, 22–28 May 2007, p. 32).

9 Flag carriers such as British Airways, Lufthansa and Air France/KLM generate around two-thirds of their revenues through long-distance flights, where they face no competition from low-cost/low-fare airlines. A carrier such as Alitalia achieves just a third of its revenues from long-distance flights, and is therefore much more sensitive to aggressive behaviour on the part of low-cost carriers.

10 In addition, the public authorities will continue to be involved in the funding of aircraft construction, especially in the fields of research, design and the launch of new aircraft types.

11 *Flight International*, 19–25 June 2007, p. 14.

12 The genuine full-freighter companies often operate in the 'ad hoc', irregular air freight market. Moreover, it often concerns small, unquoted companies so that there are

virtually no official data on their operational and financial performance (Herman and Van de Voorde, 2006).

13 There is much to be learnt from individual cases. An interesting example is the battle for the acquisition of the American company Midwest Airlines. In 2005, AirTran Airways, a low-cost carrier based in Florida, approached the management of Midwest Airlines, with headquarters at Milwaukee, Wisconsin. The purpose was to merge the two regional networks into a national network. In 2007, the bid was eventually rejected. The management of Midwest Airlines was, however, prepared to accept another bid, led by TPG Capital, a private-equity firm, in partnership with Northwest. It was Northwest's purpose to prevent AirTran from establishing a low-cost hub in Milwaukee, in the proximity of its own hubs at Minneapolis and Detroit.

14 In the airport sector, we are already seeing a strong concentration into a number of large groups: BAA (United Kingdom), Aena (Spain), Fraport (Germany), Aéroport de Paris (France), Macquarie Airports (Australia), Schiphol (Netherlands), Ferrovial (Spain). We have a similar trend in the third party handling sector, with companies like Ferrovial, Aviapartner (or 3i as the holding company), Menzies and Globeground.

References

Barret, S. (2004) 'How do the demands for airport services differ between full-service carriers and low-cost carriers?', *Journal of Air Transport Management*, 10 (1), 33–39.

Bazargan, M. (2004) *Airline Operations and Scheduling*, Aldershot: Ashgate.

Ben-Yosef, E. (2005) *The Evolution of the US Airline Industry: theory, strategy and policy*, Dordrecht: Springer.

Bieger, T. and Agosti, S. (2005) 'Business models in the airline sector: evolution and perspectives', in Delfmann, W., Baum, H., Auerbach, S. and Albers, S. (eds) *Strategic Management in the Aviation Industry*, Aldershot: Ashgate.

Burghouwt, G. (2007) *Airline Network Development in Europe and Its Implications for Airport Planning*, Aldershot: Ashgate.

Button, K., Haynes, K.E. and Stough, R. (1998) *Flying into the Future: air transport policy in the European Union*, Cheltenham: Edward Elgar.

Coppens, F., Lagneaux, F., Meersman, H., Sellekaerts, N., Van de Voorde, E., Van Gastel, G., Van Elslander, T. and Verhetsel, A. (2007) *Economic Impact of Port Activity: a disaggregate analysis – the case of Antwerp*, Working paper document no. 110, National Bank of Belgium, Brussels.

Deutsche Bank (2007) *Aviation Deviation: EU Parliament Sends Bullish Signal for Phase 3*, Frankfurt.

Doganis, R. (2001) *The Airline Business in the Twenty-first Century*, London: Routledge.

Doganis, R. (2006) *The Airline Business*, London: Routledge.

Francis, G., Fidato, A. and Humphreys, I. (2003) 'Airport–airline interaction: the impact of low-cost carriers on two European airports', *Journal of Air Transport Management*, 9 (4), 267–273.

Graham, B. and Vowles, T. (2006) 'Carriers within carriers: a strategic response to low-cost airline competition', *Transport Reviews*, 26 (1), 105–126.

Herman, F. and Van de Voorde, E. (2006) 'Bijdrage tot de economische analyse van het full-freighter luchtvrachtvervoer', *Tijdschrift vervoerswetenschap*, 42 (4), 16–23.

IATA (1970–2008) *World Air Transport Statistics*, Montreal.

Jarach, D. (2001) 'The evolution of airport management practices: towards a multi-point, multi-service, marketing-driven firm', *Journal of Air Transport Management*, 7 (2), 119–125.

Lopes, T. (2005) *Evaluating easyJet's Low Cost Model*, Toulouse: Toulouse Business School.
Macário, R., Mackenzie-Williams, P., Meersman, H., Monteiro, F., Reis, V., Schmidt, H., Van de Voorde, E. and Vanelslander, T. (2008) *The Consequences of the Growing European Low-cost Airline Sector*, Brussels: European Parliament.
Macário, R. and Van de Voorde, E. (2009) *The Impact of the Economic Crisis on the EU Air Transport Sector*, Brussels: European Parliament.
Mintel (2006) *Low-cost Airlines: International*, Mintel International Group.
Morrison, S. and Winston, C. (1995) *The Evolution of the Airline Industry*, Washington, DC: The Brookings Institution.
Oneworld (2009) www.oneworld.com.
Oum, T. H. and Yu, C. (2004) 'Measuring airports' operating efficiency: a summary of the 2003 ATRS global airport benchmarking report', *Transportation Research Part E*, 40, 515–532.
SkyTeam (2009) www.skyteam.com.
Star Alliance (2009) www.staralliance.com.
Taneja, N.K. (2004) *Airline Survival Kit*, Aldershot: Ashgate.

3 Airlines and their focus on cost control and productivity

Juan Carlos Martín and Concepción Román

1 Introduction

The deregulation of air transportation in the US in 1978 had a demonstrative effect for other regions of the world, and since then, the air transportation market has become more competitive and airlines are subject to important challenges with respect to their operational performance. Since the air transport deregulation of the US, many domestic markets have been totally deregulated or substantially liberalized. Another paradigmatic example of air transport deregulation was the gradual approach of the EU, in which the final phase of 1 April 1997 proposed a single internal market within the 15 European Member States, Finland and Norway. Following this process, in Europe, the former flag carriers have seen the total number of competitors increase during the last decade. For example, the total number of domestic airlines and routes has grown considerably in this period, after the completion of the European Air Transport Deregulation. Some of the former legacy carriers or full service carriers (FSCs) have faced financial problems and were forced to disappear or merged as a result. With such fierce competition in the air transportation market, airlines cannot have any other primary strategy than being cost leaders in the industry. The survival of an airline is directly influenced by its operational and financial performance. Thus, airlines' short-term liquidity, return on assets and long-term solvency are based on current ratio, productivity of assets and debt ratio as in any other business.

Airlines' operational performance is based on a set of indicators which can be characterized by three different aspects of their operations, namely: resource input (labour; capital; fuel; materials), service output (aircraft-hours; aircraft-km; seat-km), and service consumption (passengers emplanements; cargo; passenger-km; operating revenue), which constitute the three corners of an operational triangle. These three sides represent different efficiency concepts: resource-efficiency (measuring service output against resource input), resource-effectiveness (measuring service consumed against resource input), and service-effectiveness (measuring service consumed against service output), respectively.

As Oum and Yu pointed out, an airline is cost competitive

> if its unit costs are consistently lower than those of competitors. An airline may have lower unit costs than its competitors because it is more efficient, pays less

for inputs or both. That is, airline cost differentials are determined by differences in input prices and productivity efficiency. Knowledge about existing levels and sources of cost differentials are essential for analyzing public policies and strategies designed to enhance airline competitive positions.

(Oum and Yu, 1998: 1)

Increasing competition and other important drawbacks, such as the terrorist attacks of 11 September 2001, the severe acute respiratory syndrome (SARS) and the global economic downturn, have led airlines to face unprecedented and severe financial turbulence. It is usually argued that the bottom line of this crisis is larger than the impact of 9/11 since so many airline managers have been forced to undertake cost reduction programmes which allow airlines to survive in this global industry.

The rest of the chapter is structured as follows. A review of the European air transport deregulation is presented in Section 2; Section 3 reviews the different business models of the airlines. In particular, we will focus our attention on the development of low-cost carriers' (LCCs) competition. The different legacy carriers' strategies with respect to the new threats introduced by the competition of low-cost carriers will be analysed in Section 4; in Section 5, we will study the role of other sectors such as airports, air traffic control and regulators, and how these sectors affect the competitive result of air transport markets. Section 6 concludes.

2 The European air transport deregulation

Until the US air transport deregulation, market forces did not play any role in the provision of air services. Air transport was closely regulated according to the principles of the International Air Transport Association (IATA) which recognized that "every state has complete sovereignty over the airspace above its territory." Some over-fly and technical stops were recorded in the case of international services but the commercial rights were left to bilateral agreements to be negotiated between the countries involved. The International Civil Aviation Organization (ICAO) is an inter-governmental agency which provides a forum for discussion of key aviation issues and the basis for world-wide coordination of technical and operational standards and practices.[1]

In recent years and in most parts of the world air transport has become liberalized as institutional setting of fares, market entry, and capacity agreements have been abolished allowing market forces to operate instead. The 1978 US Airline Deregulation Act began the process and the positive results and the favourable opinion of the media provoked subsequent developments such as the liberalization of the internal European market and the spread of Open Skies bilateral air service agreements between different areas and countries.

The changes in the EU followed a more gradual approach in comparison with the air transport deregulation process where a "Big Bang" approach was favoured. Here, we do not further discuss why this process was slower, but it is clear that the demonstrable effects of the US regulation helped European regulators to promote a similar one in Europe. In Europe, the different institutional structures and the number of agents involved provoked this slow and gradual approach because of a lack of unique governance. Changes in regulatory regimes are also not costless, and especially given prevailing knowledge about the details of the ultimate losers, many countries which were involved in the provision of air services needed a temporary phase in order to accommodate the significant effects in these public airlines. In summary, they needed time to make a profound industrial reconversion regarding the internal air transport before being prepared to compete in the new situation.

The first aviation package, adopted by the European Community in 1987 (Vincent and Stasinopoulos, 1990), introduced a degree of flexibility in the air transport industry and set up a mechanism for a gradual liberalization. The second package, adopted in June 1990, went a stage further and made it possible for the EC Transport Ministers to commit themselves to full liberalization after December 1991.

When the European Community Transport Ministers adopted the second package of measures in June 1990, they again took a cautious step towards the definitive EU air transport liberalization. The governments compromised to loosen the rigid schemes of the past regarding the fixing of tariffs and the rights of airlines to determine what services and routes to offer in the territories of other Member States.

Without any doubt, the most important premise of this package was the promise to fully liberalize air transport by 1 January 1993, with measures to ensure:

- freedom for airlines to fix their own fares;
- new opportunities to operate in and between other EC countries under common rules for the certification of air carriers;
- the ending of capacity-sharing arrangements between governments, which hitherto had guaranteed to each country a given share of traffic on a particular route.

Stasinopolous (1992) explained how the main motivation for these two packages was the belief that a flexible and liberal framework for air transport would benefit passengers, because the airlines would be obliged to increase their efficiency and performance in order to survive in the market. However, these benefits could be hindered by two interrelated factors, namely, the corporate restructuring of the airline industry (which could be based on collusive agreements) and the shortage of adequate capacity at congested airports. In fact, as Keeler (1989) argued, the reasons for concentration of the industry in the US experience are not easy to identify. Nevertheless, the undesirable results of reduced competition can be mitigated by regulatory action. Solving problems caused by inadequate capacity is more difficult; rationing or better pricing policies only resolve partially the problem under a short-term perspective, but important scarcity costs can still be present.

Finally, on 22 and 23 June 1991, the Council adopted the third package of air transport liberalization consisting of regulations on:

- the licensing of air carriers;
- access for air carriers to intra-Community air routes;
- air fares and rates for air services.

The intention of the package was to open up the twelve national markets creating a unique interior market in which airlines could compete freely.

Stasinopoulos (1993) remarked that if the Community sought to maximize social welfare from the introduction of the third package, it would be necessary to introduce additional measures beyond the opening-up of market access and the freeing-up of price setting. In fact, he established different measures (p. 326):

- Short term

  - monitoring anti-competitive practices;
  - spreading the demand and reducing the incentive for carriers to resort to hubbing;
  - improving administrative procedures of the slot allocation systems;
  - looking at the feasibility of using under-utilised military airfields to relieve peak-time saturation.

- Long term

  - creating a central authority for flight planning in Europe;
  - expanding investment in airport infrastructure.

He also argued that because the air transport industry is global it is necessary to go beyond the traditional framework of bilateral agreements and to orient the industry towards a system of multilateral agreements. With this perspective, the role of the Community becomes a necessity to prevent a third country from exploiting the fragmentation of the bilateral system to its advantage, obtaining better conditions in Europe than can be enjoyed by the EC carriers under provisions of reciprocity. Therefore EC initiatives are a *sine qua non* condition for the success of the internal aviation market.

Stasinopoulos was completely right and he was anticipating some problems that we are actually seeing with the signature of Open Skies agreement between the US and the EU and the so-called restructuring of the EU airline industry. In fact, as many international routes are still based on bilateral agreements between different countries, there is a magical threshold foreign ownership value which cannot be exceeded in order to maintain these privileges. To be designated by a signatory government under the bilateral agreement to serve the international route, a carrier must be at least 50 per cent owned by nationals of the designator state. Therefore, if control of the carrier lost the national status, it would lose the right to service routes under all the bilateral agreements for which it is designated, so the EU internal market is affected by all the overlapping routes between the EU and other countries not included in the area, such as the US, Canada, South America, Africa, Asia and Australia. This has been and is a difficult obstacle for some airlines to take over other domestic airlines. This is also a barrier to real competition in the European arena, because for carriers serving EU destinations only (e.g. some European LCCs like Ryanair or Air Berlin), national ownership need only be at least 50 per cent by EU nationals rather than Irish or German nationals. However, Ryanair or Air Berlin could not start to serve Madrid–Buenos Aires, without changing their ownership to Argentina or Spain (a highly unlikely scenario). So, the international airline industry creates important peculiarities which affect the internal competition in the area.

The European Commission (EC) was given a mandate to negotiate a transatlantic deal with the United States (US), and a final agreement was signed in May 2007. It is likely to take a long time for the EC and the US to discuss the issues of foreign ownership restrictions and cabotage. Notwithstanding these difficulties, the agreement has achieved something that was demanded from the EU side: as provided in Article 22 of this new agreement, all the bilateral agreements between the US and Member States have been be suspended or superseded by this new agreement. After multiple formal rounds of talks and countless informal exchanges, the two sides finally signed a preliminary agreement. However, the largest and most important specific objective of the EU–US talks, the European Commission's need to eliminate the nationality clauses from the framework for air services agreements and cabotage in the US domestic market, has not been totally achieved and must jeopardize the success of the agreement.[2]

3 Airlines' business models

Porter (1985) suggests there are three strategies a company or organization can adopt to achieve competitive advantage: through cost leadership, differentiation or focus.

A firm sets out to become the low-cost producer in the industry when it follows a cost leadership strategy. To do so it must find and exploit all sources at cost advantage. Low-cost producers typically sell a standard, or no-frills, product and place considerable emphasis on reaping scale or absolute cost advantages from all sources. This strategy has been used by LCCs.

A company seeks to be unique in its industry along some dimensions that are extremely valued by passengers. It is usually rewarded for its uniqueness with a premium price. A firm that can achieve and sustain differentiation will be an above-average performer in its industry if its price premium exceeds the extra costs incurred in being unique. The logic of the differentiation strategy requires that a firm chooses attributes in which to differentiate itself that are different from its rival. This is the logic of the overall strategy of legacy carriers.

Focus involves adding value to the product or service and targeting it carefully at a niche segment of the market. Such a strategy does not apply to legacy and LCCs' current strategy, but corporate jet service providers could fall into this category.

34   *J.C. Martín and C. Román*

The terminology used to describe 'traditional, full-service or legacy' carriers is not unique or exact. In general, they operate extensive networks which inherit in part from the previous routes operated under strict regulatory provisions, thus the expression 'legacy carrier' has gained more adepts in academia. The definition of what we understand by an LCC is not unambiguous;[3] as we will see below there are numerous strategies to differentiate the product within the low-cost sector. However, all the airlines commit to a common premise: the 'cult of cost reduction' (Lawton, 2002). The low-cost model was pioneered by Southwest Airlines in the US and has been widely emulated by other North American carriers such as AirTran, JetBlue and WestJet and in Europe by Ryanair, easyJet and Air Berlin. The air transport deregulation in many areas of the world, principally the US and the EU, has allowed the entrance of new carriers in some markets which were previously protected and under the control of former legacy carriers. Table 3.1 shows the basic characteristics of the LCC business model.

The LCC business model is based on simplicity. This helped carriers to be cost leaders in the industry.[4] They also present higher load factors and labour productivity, thus they have been competing in fares (with important price reductions with respect to the fares charged by legacy carriers), promoting air traffic growth and creating new air transport markets. The growth of LCCs has produced more multi-contact markets with the networks of legacy carriers, and this trend has not ended. After ten years of the European air transport deregulation, many of the former legacy carriers have began to feel the level of competition of the LCCs, and it is not clear that the industry is now in equilibrium. Given the large number of aircraft that easyJet and Ryanair have on order, and

Table 3.1 Original low-cost carrier business model

Item	Attribute	Characteristics
Product	Fare	Low, simple and unrestricted
	Frequency	High
	Network	Point to point
	Connections	No
	Distribution	Call centres, internet, ticketless
	Class	Single class
	Seat comfort	High-density seating
	Food	No meals or free alcoholic drinks. Snacks and soda can be purchased
	Seat assignment	No
Operations	Aircraft fleet	Single type
	Aircraft use	High capital productivity >12 hours
	Airports	Secondary and uncongested
	Airports turnaround	20–30 minutes
	Sector length	Short 400 miles
	Staff	High labour productivity. Competitive salaries

Source: Adapted from Alamdari and Fagan (2005).

the latest news about the re-structuring of legacy carriers,[5] it is not difficult to affirm that carriers will definitely have more battles to fight.

European LCCs are growing and increasing their share of the market, especially in recent years. Figure 3.1 shows the evolution of the number of routes of LCC network in Germany for the period 2002–2005. It can be seen, looking at the numbers, that the growth is really spectacular. In a single decade, LCCs have transformed the European air transport scene beyond recognition. Europeans' leisure and travel habits have changed dramatically because new direct services between EU city pairs that were not serviced through the legacy carriers are now available. New regional airports have become popular, and some cities have benefited from the routes opened up by LCCs. Perhaps though, the most significant achievement for the LCCs, especially in the EU, is that they have allowed access to air transport to all the segments of society. Who could have predicted, ten years ago, that Ryanair would carry more passengers in Europe per month than British Airways? (OAG, 2006). This trend is predicted to continue in the next years, so legacy carriers need to react in order to survive.

Competition between LCCs and FSCs has been analysed by different authors who looked for factors influencing business travellers' behaviour in selecting flights between different carriers (Mason, 1999, 2000, 2001; Franke, 2004). Mason (1999) shows, in a previous research, that the decision-making behaviour of business travellers is influenced by the company they work for. Mason (2000) indicates that low-cost airlines are more likely to be successful in attracting business travellers from small and medium-sized companies. Mason (2001) shows that business passengers using LCCs do not form a separate market segment from those using FSCs. In fact, short-haul business passengers are, en masse, becoming increasingly price elastic, and corporate influence in purchase decision making is more evident in passengers choosing FSCs; this is partly a function of the size of the company, with larger companies favouring such carriers. Franke (2004) found that on continental travel routes, LCCs are able to deliver 80 per cent of the service quality at less than 50 per cent of the cost of network carriers.

Barbot (2005) studies how LCCs and FSCs compete in two markets (London–Berlin and London–Amsterdam), using daily collected web-based prices to estimate the reaction function on these two established low-cost carrier routes. In the first market, Air Berlin, Ryanair and easyJet compete with British Airways, and regarding the second market, easyJet and Transavia compete with British Airways and KLM. It was found that there is a separation of markets with the low-cost carriers competing with each other and the legacy carriers competing with each other.

4 Legacy carriers' strategies in competitive markets

The short-haul domestic operations of former legacy carriers such as British Airways, Air France, Iberia, Alitalia and Lufthansa have come under increasing pressure from the growth of low-cost carriers. In this section, we examine how these carriers have reacted to these new entrants. We eventually show that

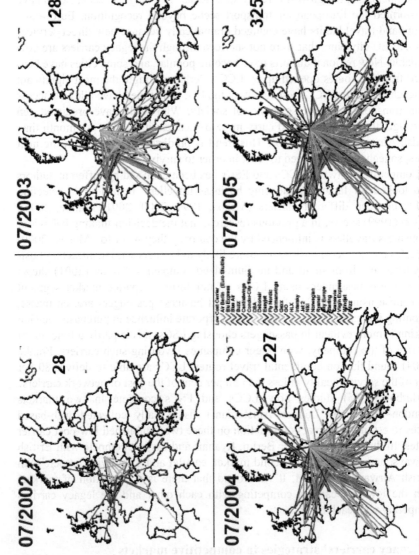

Figure 3.1 Development of LCC network in Germany for the period 2002–2005.

reductions in labour costs, greater use of regional aircraft and network reconfiguration, and more flexibility on minimum stay requirements on cheap fares have been introduced in many markets. Other important strategies with respect to the on-board service and direct distribution channels shrink the gap between former legacy and low-cost carrier products.

4.1 Focusing on costs and productivity

The strategies to reduce labour costs or increase labour productivity are the two faces of the same coin. Doganis (2001) argued that as a consequence of air transport deregulation and the entrance of new LCCs, a profound change in the nature of the airline industry since about 1990 has come to the operational arena because cost reduction is no longer a short-term response to declining yields or falling load factors, but a continued and permanent strategy when carriers want to survive in this competitive environment.

When airlines face strong opposition from well-organized labour unions, airline managers always have the option of transferring services to regional partners, franchises or alliances or even setting up a low-cost carrier subsidiary. These subsidiary carriers were created to compete fiercely with the new low-cost carriers and followed a similar business model.[6] However, this last strategy has been unsuccessful in many cases[7] (Morrell, 2005; Graham and Vowles, 2006).

BA set up GO to fly from some secondary airports located in the UK. This initiative failed and GO was eventually sold off to a consortium involving the management; and it was subsequently taken over by easyJet. Buzz was a subsidiary created in 1999 by KLM Royal Dutch Airlines from the remnants of KLM UK, an early casualty of the expansion of LCCs at London Stansted. This company was always condemned to be a failure by its lack of vision: high-cost airports mixed with low-density routes. Its years of existence were certainly tormented until 2003 when it was bought out by Ryanair. Lindstadt and Fauser (2004) analysed the case of Lufthansa, which owns a minority stake in Eurowings, a regional carrier serving low-density destinations in Europe. In addition, Germanwings, which is a subsidiary of Eurowings, is a typical low-cost carrier founded in 2002. This example shows how legacy carriers can own equity stakes in LCCs which operate with separate brands, staff, fleets and management. This has also been observed in other industries in which the cross ownership is always an object of debate. SAS set up Snowflake to take over low-yield/leisure type routes, but this was again the story of a failure. In fact, Snowflake is an example of an unsustainable strategy of high costs/low yields, with aircraft and crews mimicking the costs from the parent company. The company did not achieve much cost saving but yields were low because feeder traffic to the SAS network disappeared and large numbers of seats were simply transferred from the parent company by increasing the point-to-point markets. This was a clear example of cannibalism, and was a painful lesson that legacy carriers had to learn in order to succeed. The cost leadership is well established in the LCCs and the most viable strategy for a separate production platform is a ring-fenced leisure airline flying point-to-point routes without any substantive high-yield component and with substantially lower labour costs than the mainline operation (Graham and Vowles, 2006). This strategy has been followed by BA with its subsidiary GB Airways which operates mostly between Gatwick and holiday destinations in southern Europe. GB has lower cost levels than its parent and can operate viably on lower yields and compete more closely on price with the low-cost carriers. GB uses A320 and A321 aircraft which are used in destinations that were not in the BA network at all in recent times.

Distribution channels have also come under a more serious cost scrutiny, and many operations have been brought closer to the low-cost carrier model by reducing or overriding commission payments to travel agents. Many legacy carriers have revised their fare structures to become more aggressive and compete with the low-cost carriers. They have increased the fare differentiation, being more flexible with respect to minimum stays on the cheaper tickets for most European sectors. Legacy carriers have also started a downward trend regarding catering in economy class, and nowadays it is generally normal for passengers to pay for refreshments and food. The separation between different business models – charter, low-cost and legacy carriers – is more blurred than ever. In many domestic European routes there is a strong competition between these three apparently different carriers, and some web portals offer different fares from all the carriers that serve the market independently of their business model.

One area where the low-cost airlines outperform the legacy carriers is in terms of labour costs and productivity.[8] In the new competitive environment, the former legacy carriers need to revise their labour costs downwards through various measures which include increasing productivity, freezing or reducing nominal wages,[9] hiring new labour with lower wages and outsourcing more non-core activities, such as catering, ground handling and aircraft cleaning and maintenance. In some cases, airlines have sold or transferred to third parties some subsidiary firms which were in charge of those types of activities.

4.2 Network reconfiguration

Low-cost carriers have eroded many of the former well-protected legacy carriers' markets.[10] In these circumstances, legacy carriers need to revise their strategy in some of these markets. In some cases, they can simply transfer many short-haul routes to regional partner airlines. This strategy has been followed by Iberia for some short-haul domestic routes which are operated by Air Nostrum and Binter Canarias using regional propeller planes.[11] Thus, Iberia could maintain its frequency,[12] its network associated with the value of a frequent flier programme at a lower cost, without reducing the willingness to pay of passengers. Dennis (2007, p. 3) argued that "in Europe, there has been much less shift to regional jets due to capacity constraints at the major hub airports. The opportunity cost of using a precious slot for a 50 seats aircraft is enough to tip the balance in favour of the larger jets." However, this is the inherent cause of the search for secondary airports made by low-cost carriers. As Graham (2001) recognizes, regarding the relationships between LCCs and airports, the pressures are getting tougher and tougher, especially at secondary and smaller airports,[13] where aeronautically related revenues represent typically more than 64 per cent of total revenues. But as traffic grows, commercial revenue from the expansion of retail, catering and car-parking facilities builds up, forming an increasing share of total revenues. In other cases, legacy carriers have reduced their capacity by abandoning some routes to the low-cost carriers.

In the EU, one of the most noticeable impacts of the increased competition faced by the "legacy" carriers has been the network reconfiguration. The major European airlines have fortressed their main hub airports, where an increase in operations is more profitable,[14] and they have reduced or abandoned secondary hubs and point-to-point services. This process was the consequence of the era before the deregulation in which hub domination made it difficult to compete with carriers flying from a hub at the other end of the route.[15] As hub domination has been artificially created by the previous European regulation, the low-cost carriers needed to seek economic rents by identifying market point-to-point niches in which entry could be more beneficial. Thus, some secondary hubs such as Munich, Dusseldorf, Hamburg, Berlin and Stuttgart (Lufthansa); Barcelona (Iberia); Glasgow, London Gatwick, Manchester (BA); Amsterdam (KLM); Milan, Venice (Alitalia); and even other primary hubs like Copenhagen (SAS) have been more exposed. However, other airlines like Air France have not faced fierce competition on its secondary airports.

4.3 Yield management

The techniques that allow airlines to maximize revenues are known as "yield management" (YM), and were pioneered by American Airlines in the 1980s. The classical definition of YM, according to Smith *et al.* (1992), is the control and management of reservations inventory in a way that maximizes company profitability given the flight schedule and fare structure. It is based on market segmentation and real-time demand forecasting, with the final intention of establishing the best pricing policy for optimizing profits generated by the sale of a single seat for a certain flight. The application of this technique makes some additional requirements which fit perfectly well within the air transport industry, such as:

1   a perishable product (seat loses its value after departure);
2   a constrained capacity to satisfy a demand which is highly volatile;
3   the existence of reservation systems which permit the passengers to buy their tickets before departures;
4   multiple pricing structures (according to each segment);
5   and very low variable unit costs (airlines produce with high fixed costs due to the nature of the capital use).

Legacy carriers needed to redevelop new sophisticated systems of yield management that aimed to capture most of the consumer surplus using market segmentation according to different passengers' willingness to pay. Tretheway (2004) argued that carriers have been capable of offering a wide range of different fares for essentially the same product. The market segments were obtained according to different conditions. One of the best known so far has been the requirement to spend a Saturday night away to obtain a coach fare. The cheaper fares were normally sold only on a round-trip basis. This technique allows carriers to segment the market on the assumption that anyone returning before the weekend must be a business passenger who usually shows very low price elasticity because their firms pay for their flights. Coach fares were hence reserved for leisure passengers who present higher elasticity to price. Flexibility was also a requirement to segment both markets being only available in business class, again making coach fares unattractive to this segment in which travel plans may change frequently.

The low-cost airlines model is based on one-way fares, and their segmentation is done according to other factors such as the time of travel and the anticipation of the purchase of the ticket with respect to the departure date. Initially, the legacy carriers did not pay attention to the potential competition of low-cost carriers. They thought that business passengers would continue to buy expensive full-fare tickets to benefit from their differentiated product whose origin is a high-frequency service from primary hub airports, frequent flyer programmes based on international alliances and premium quality services (food, in-flight entertainment, beverages and VIP lounges at airports).

However, this idea was more an illusion than a fact, and all the legacy carriers have noticed the low-cost carriers' competition on most of their short-haul network, and this could not be ignored any longer. Legacy carriers have been forced to recognize that, nowadays, passengers have changed their expectations and become more elastic to prices than to service especially in the short-haul routes. For this reason, airlines have simplified their fare structures, reduced ticket prices, increased the number of cheap fares available and removed restrictions on lower fares. Recently, many legacy carriers have abandoned the minimum stay requirement for coach-class fares on short-haul European routes, and it is even possible to find cheaper one-way fares directly on the internet web sites of the carriers or other distribution channels like www.expedia.com or www.edreams.com.

In summary, all the legacy carriers have now adopted pricing strategies closer to those of the low-cost carrier counterparts, in this way increasing the revenues from the leisure segment. Of course, pricing strategies depend more on the market conditions of each individual route, in particular if there is direct competition from low-cost or legacy carriers, or even inter-modal competition from high-speed train (HST) services.[16]

4.4 No-frills service

In the old days, European passengers travelling within Europe have traditionally enjoyed a hot or cold meal, and business passengers received upgraded hot catering with a written menu, alcoholic beverages and fine cutlery. All legacy carriers provided a similar standard of catering, so for competitive reasons every carrier was forced to satisfy the European passengers' expectations.

However, in recent years, the fierce competition exerted by the growth of the low-cost carriers which offered no-frills service, has forced legacy carriers to make a serious assessment of the short-haul product regarding food and beverages. Román *et al.* (2007) analyse this topic in the routes connecting Madeira and Azores with Portugal mainland, and Canarias with Spain mainland. They find that the willingness to pay is different for each of the markets, because in the Portuguese markets, passengers see no price incentive for foregoing the food and drink. The authors conclude that the Portuguese value is higher than the Spanish counterpart because in the first case it can be seen as a willingness to accept instead of willingness to pay, because Portuguese travellers would forego food and drinks in the route reducing the flight to a no-frills service, and in the Spanish market fares are lower and no-frills services are the norm of Iberia, Spanair and Air Europa. In this case, the carriers started a gradual drift to reducing provision in coach class. The argument is that no one buys an air ticket because of the food, and therefore if the ticket price can be cut by x euros through cutting out the food (the cost of the service) and this frill is valued by less than x euros, then the strategy of not providing free catering will be profitable.

The danger for the legacy carriers, however, is that they can never match the cost levels of the low-cost carriers, so if inclusive economy class catering is eliminated, passengers may then see a more homogeneous product and find no reason for using these expensive carriers. In Europe, some legacy carriers provide non-inclusive catering tickets and sell food and beverages at reasonable prices. However, other legacy carriers still find it more efficient to provide some small snacks such as biscuits, cold sandwiches or a chocolate bar to all the coach passengers because the loss of image or reputation is not outweighed by the saving in costs.

5 The role of other sectors

The current situation of air transport can be explained by different issues, such as the potential unstable nature of providing pre-committed services in quasi-contestable markets to micro-studies of the management shortcomings of individual actors. However, as Button *et al.* (2007, p. 15) point out, "the fact that other players in the air transportation supply chain – airports, global distribution systems, airframe manufacturers, air traffic services, etc. – have often been earning higher and positive returns has also been noted." In fact, some of the sectors of the supply chain obtain important positive margins which are related to the degree of institutional and natural monopoly power that these elements enjoy.

5.1 Airports

So far, we have analysed how airlines have reacted to a new era in which market forces prevail in the air transport industry as a consequence of the introduction of new economic and regulatory conditions. Carney and Mew (2003) discussed how these conditions have changed for airports as well, and airport companies have been confronted with profound governance changes over the last decade. So, in this section we discuss different issues regarding the role of the airports with respect to the equilibrium of the air transport sector.

Origin and destination airports may have some impact on the market differentiation of the routes. This is especially true when several airports serve a city or an area like in London, Paris and Barcelona, where heterogeneous products are to some extent being provided by LCCs and FSCs. In the case of Paris, for example, airlines can fly to Charles de Gaulle and/or Orly.[17] In the case of London, airlines can fly to Heathrow, Stansted, Luton, London City and Gatwick. For example, it can be seen that the route Porto–London is served by three carriers using different London terminals: British Airways and TAP to Gatwick, and Ryanair to Stansted.[18] In the case of Barcelona, Ryanair and other LCCs sell tickets to Girona and Reus, two secondary Spanish airports located in the area of Barcelona, as if their flights were landing at Barcelona.

Some analysts have commented on how most of the busiest airports in Europe are congested and the considerable constraints on airport expansion have been cited as one of the most important obstacles impeding consumers from fully benefiting from European air transport deregulation. In particular, the issues of allocation of scarce capacity and the pricing policies of the airports are areas subject to an important debate in order to promote a more efficient equilibrium point.

It is possible to use prices to ration scarce airport capacity. Thus far, this has rarely been done, except occasionally to handle peaks.[19] Higher prices would ration demand to be closer to capacity, though the effects on actual demand would be less certain than slot limits.

However, the real difficulty with prices is that rationing prices would drive prices up, and airport profits would be correspondingly high (Forsyth, 2007). Most airports are required by government owners or regulators to keep revenues close to costs. A slot system enables capacity to be rationed tolerably efficiently, while at the same time keeping prices down. If there is to be regulation which seeks to keep prices close to costs, there also has to be slot rationing, or delays.

The primary criticism of slots is that there is no guarantee that they will be allocated efficiently, to the airlines with the greatest willingness to pay for them (Starkie, 1998; Lu and Pagliari, 2004). It is difficult for new airlines to obtain slots at busy airports even if they are prepared to pay for them. The slot-controlled airports have become an important weapon and anti-competitive barrier used by the legacy carriers. In fact, LCCs have difficulties in accessing the primary busiest airports of Europe, even when they would be willing to pay the price. Legacy carriers usually favour the slot system, since they possess most of the slots at busy airports. Thus, they can prevent the new entry of LCCs to the airports, and second, gain assets of considerable value. The access to slots is an important competitive advantage they have over LCCs, and they can charge a premium for using these preferred airports.

5.2 Aircraft manufacturers

There are only two major manufacturers of aircraft for large planes (Boeing and Airbus) and only three manufacturers of large jet engines. The number of regional jet manufacturers is only slightly larger. The main manufacturers of airframes have the advantage of being (or becoming) involved in military supply. This offers them a significant buffer to the adverse effects of downturns in the business cycle suggesting that their returns may need to be lower than normal market rates to attract necessary capital.

Vertical integration has taken a variety of forms in the air transport industry and we remark here that, in the early days of aviation, airlines were often vertically integrated with aircraft manufacturers (Boeing and United Airlines being an example).

Aircraft characteristics have an important role in airport planning and airlines competition. Regarding airport planning, both the airport airside and landside planning are based on operating characteristics of the aircraft. On the airside, the runway length and width, the minimum separation between runways and taxiways, the geometric projection of taxiways, and the pavement strength determine which type of aircraft can be served. Additionally, environmental issues such as noise and air pollution are also based on the aircraft that will make use of the airport. On the terminal area, aircraft characteristics will influence the number and size of gates, and consequently the terminal configuration. Finally, the aircraft passenger capacity will influence the size of facilities within the terminal – such as passenger lounges and passenger processing systems – and the size and type of the baggage handling system.

On the other hand, modern aircraft are also projected taking into account the constraints of actual airports. The costs of adapting an airport to changes in aircraft characteristics – for example, runway stretching to accommodate a larger aircraft – have become so high in the last decades that manufacturers now take into consideration fitting new development to existing airports. For instance, the new strategies of Boeing and Airbus to develop a new large aircraft with 500 to 800 seats and a new-generation supersonic aircraft are being carried out such that the runway requirements of these new products should not be excessive and preferably inferior to 3,500 metres (David, 1995; Boeing, 1994, 1996).

5.3 Air Traffic Control and National Airspace System

Airport capacity not only depends on the number of runways and the size of passenger terminals, but on the capacity of the Air Traffic Management (ATM) system which is usually divided into two different subsystems: Air Traffic Control (ATC) and National Airspace System (NAS). This is part of the air transport supply chain which needs to be analysed in order to understand and quantify the benefits of public and private investments in the system. Normally, the performance of the system is based on the quantification and monetization benefits and costs to the maximum extent possible taking into consideration a multiple stakeholder perspective.

While the need for studies on performance analysis of these systems is growing, industry stakeholders are also recognizing that their performance is multi-dimensional, and therefore not adequately captured by traditional delay-based metrics. For example, items such as predictability, flexibility and access can also be important for some level of service measured by the total delayed time. These items can be elements of value to the scheduled airline business passengers. Hansen *et al.* (2001) developed a cost model incorporating multiple dimensions of NAS performance.[20] They included in the model of costs some measures of NAS performance which are derived from the operational experience of carriers using the NAS, as captured by such metrics as average delay, variability of delay, and flight cancellation rates. As noted by the authors, these measures not only reflect the quality of service provided by the public aviation infrastructure, but also the carriers' ability to plan and manage their operations. They showed that poor NAS performance is, as expected, associated with increased airline operating cost. More surprisingly, one specific dimension of performance "disruption" emerges as the key cost driver. This challenges the traditional view that delay is the critical economic factor. So, the results may indicate that operational strategies that emphasize maintaining flights even when there are high delays are more efficient than cancelling flights to avoid such delays.

Many governments around the world have started a new era regarding ATM, leading to deregulation of some of these activities looking at other industrial sectors like telecommunications, passenger air transport and other transport activities which started this path previously. In this sense, the Single European Sky initiative was launched in 2004 by the European Commission aiming to set out regulatory principles with a view to restructure the airspace according to traffic flows rather than national boundaries, create additional capacity and improve the overall efficiency of the system.

Some steps have been taken but there is still too much to do. The United States has less than half the number of air traffic control centres and a standardized mainframe computer. Airspace in Europe has remained a national responsibility. It is controlled by different national centres, with different equipment, different operating standards and different management regimes. A pilot is transferred between fifty control centres, each with its unique computer system and equipment. Until the Europeans are able to impose solutions on the different national authorities that Eurocontrol attempts to coordinate, the system of "corridors" grouped into national route-maps will continue to be less than optimal.

At the end of 2008, Eurocontrol and the European Commission signed a Memorandum of Cooperation to enhance their synergy in five areas of cooperation: implementation of the Single European Sky; research and development; global navigation satellite systems, including Galileo; data collection and analysis in the areas of air traffic and environmental issues; and international cooperation in the field of aviation.

6 Conclusions

The entry of LCCs in the EU has dramatically changed the aviation market in recent years. The development of LCCs in Europe was different from what occurred in the US, as the informal sector of charter carriers, integrated vertically in the tourist industry, was a reality before the liberalization of air transport in the EU. So, the LCC business model in the EU made a slow and late appearance on the air transport scene, but since then its importance is increasing day by day. The competition exerted by the entry of LCCs has provoked the former legacy carriers to readapt their business model to the new situation. But not only airlines have adapted their behaviour: airport managers are also thinking about developing new terminals dedicated to the LCCs; passengers of different economic status can think about flying; other third parties, such as information technology providers, are developing new software programs to make consumers buy their flight tickets on the internet.

The implementation of the three packages of the EU air transport deregulation produced different effects on the European countries and their airlines. As a result of deregulation, some airlines like Sabena and Swissair disappeared in 2001, although both airlines have resurrected under different names. We have seen how FSCs have reacted to the new era of competition, adapting their pricing policies and route structure. The route structures have put more emphasis on the operations through hubs, rather than along linear routes, as occurred before deregulation. It is difficult to evaluate whether such "hubbing" has enhanced or not passenger convenience. We have seen how difficult it is to extract a definitive conclusion on whether nowadays the business models are more close or not, because FSCs have followed some patterns of LCCs, but they still differentiate their product in the long-haul segments which are not open to competition.

We have also dedicated a section to treating the problems associated with other sectors which affect the final equilibrium point of the industry. In particular, we have provided a thoughtful discussion of some important issues, including airport provision, aircraft manufacturers and Eurocontrol.

In summary, we can say that airline deregulation has been only a partial success, and that the benefits of air deregulation to passengers will continue to grow as LCCs could expand and as the rest of the sectors adjust to the new environment. In particular, regulators need to concentrate their efforts in enlarging more common aviation markets without considering the issues of foreign ownership and cabotage restrictions.

Acknowledgements

We acknowledge support from the Researchers Mobility Program of the Secretary of Education (Regional Government of the Canary Islands). We also want to express our gratitude to our colleagues H. Meersman, T. Vanelslander and E. Van de Voorde for helpful comments on an earlier draft, as well as the participants of the colloquium "The sky is not the limit. Trends in the air transport business", held in the University of Antwerp. This paper was written while we were visiting the Institute of Transportation Studies at the University of California at Berkeley. We also wish to thank to Samer Madanat and Mark Hansen for being considerate hosts during our stay. The usual disclaimer applies.

Notes

1 In the period 1950–1980, in general, air transport was highly dependent on the involvement of the state. It was a national interest sector, and for this reason it was highly regulated and in most cases, airlines, airports, air traffic control and air navigation systems were directly provided by public companies. Since the deregulation of the US in 1978, air transport has gradually changed its status as an industry requiring special treatment. Governments began to stand apart from direct provision of air services and liberalization was promoted as the best way to protect society's general interest.

2 According to Chang and Williams (2001), nationality clauses lie at the heart of bilateral Air Services Agreements. Without them, the value of such agreements is questionable. A key reason why foreign ownership rules remain in place is that they protect national airlines, and the US is reluctant to relax the ownership rules in a short time. Another obstacle to going beyond this is the treatment (in form of aid) that governments give to airlines in special circumstances such as terrorist attacks or bankruptcy clauses.

3 Alamdari and Fagan (2005) showed how the LCC business model is nowadays more differentiated and it is no longer based on the cost leadership factor as it used to be in the original model. They concluded that in pursuit of their differentiation strategy, the LCC deviated slightly more from the product features of the original model (40%) than from the operational features (36%). The evidence also suggests that European carriers tend to adhere to the original model more than their counterparts in the US. However, this could be the consequence of the number of years in which the air industry has been operating deregulated, and this change in the future may be less pronounced.

4 Doganis (2001) showed how the costs of these carriers are 40–50 per cent lower than those of the legacy carriers.

5 There are some indicia which suggest that airlines like Iberia, Alitalia and Olympic will be taken over by BA or Lufthansa.

6 In the US, Continental Airlines became the first US carrier to create a low-cost subsidiary with Continental Lite. This subsidiary carrier eliminated meals and first-class service, increased departure frequency, lowered fares and shortened turnaround time at the gate (Lawton, 2002).

7 Morrell (2005) discussed, looking at the US legacy carriers, the reasons behind this failure. The significant cost differences between legacy and LCCs are identified, and it is shown that full service carriers have made some sacrifices but are still far from closing the cost differentials. Some other reasons for the failure are suggested by examining operating differences: mixed fleets, keeping interlining and two-class cabins and the lack of progress on reducing labour costs. Labour union restrictions and the lack of separation from the main airline were also crucial.

8 easyJet and Ryanair, two of the most representative low-cost carriers, show leadership in low unit operating costs and high labour productivity. They base their flights on local home bases for the crews and reduce the turnover traffic time to a minimum in each of the airports. Thus they can use their capital assets (planes) more efficiently and save many overnight costs incurred by other legacy carriers, where some domestic sectors are based on crews who need to spend at least one night outside their home.

9 Dennis (2007) argued that employment with the major legacy carriers was historically a comfortable existence. However, once low-cost carriers like easyJet, Ryanair and Air Berlin showed there were employees willing to work in the airline industry with fewer privileges, it became difficult for the trade unions to justify maintaining these generous conditions.

10 Ryanair wants to be the biggest airline in Spain within five years. According to O'Leary, Ryanair will carry over 20 million people to and from Spain in five years' time. At the moment Iberia is the biggest airline in Spain but O'Leary expects that his airline will overtake Iberia in the future. Nowadays, Ryanair serves a variety of Spanish airports such as Barcelona–Gerona, Barcelona–Reus, Madrid, Valencia and Malaga.

11 On short-haul markets, up to about 300 miles, turbo-prop aircraft remain an altern-ative option for providing the optimal frequency and aircraft size, as they retain lower fuel and capital costs than the regional jets and their disadvantages of low speed and high internal noise levels are less apparent. Significant numbers of new turbo-props are still being ordered (Aviation Strategy, 2000).

12 Wei and Hansen (2005), using a nested logit model to study the roles of different vari-ables in airlines' market share and total air travel demand in competitive non-stop duopoly markets, found that airlines can obtain higher returns in market share from increasing service frequency than from increasing aircraft size. Therefore, they con-clude that airlines have an economic incentive to use aircraft smaller than the least-cost aircraft, since for the same capacity provided in the market an increase in frequency can attract more passengers.

13 Francis *et al.* (2003) argued that LCCs offer the potential of commercial viability to some smaller airports because they frequently seek locations away from major, con-gested hubs, stimulating rapid growth at such airports, for example, Ryanair at Stan-sted, Prestwick and Charleroi, easyJet at Liverpool and Luton, and bmibaby at East Midlands.

14 These practices have been criticized as they suppose an entry barrier which affects competition and an important driver to mark-up prices for hub passengers (Boren-stein, 1989, 1991).

15 This is the case of Madrid Barajas airport for Iberia. The airline enjoys a privileged position which comes before the air transport deregulation in Europe. In fact, the company, not only clearly enjoys a dominant position in the airport, but also can extract some monopolistic rents because some air transport markets, which are con-trolled by bilateral agreements (especially in routes to/from South America), are not subject to market forces.

16 Pels and Rietveld (2004) analysed the route Amsterdam–London, where low-cost car-riers and conventional carriers are active and addressed whether carriers react to each other's price adjustment. They found that easyJet closely follows the fares of British Midland and FSCs do not follow the price movements of the LCCs. Instead, some carriers seem to lower their fares when potential competitors raise their fares and all carriers increase their fares as the departure date gets closer.

17 Button *et al.* (2007) found that analysing the route Porto–Paris the fare pattern that emerges is one of comparable fares for the FSCs until quite close to departure, but more volatility for Air Luxor that serves a different airport (Orly). In the Lisbon–Paris case, where the same three carriers compete, the pattern is in some ways similar, with the legacy carriers, although not keeping constant fares, largely mirroring the fares they offer with Air Luxor standing-off somewhat.

18 Although Ryanair generally offers lower fares during the early phase of sales, there is still some degree of jockeying even before the immediate period before take-off when a more traditional pattern of yield management associated with the techniques of legacy US airlines emerges. Certainly, Ryanair does not stick to the textbook, low-cost model of continually raising fares until departure. Indeed, sometimes there

seems to be somewhat perverse behaviour with Ryanair lowering fares at times when both TAP and British Airways raise theirs. The legacy carriers would seem to be engaging in a more traditional yield management dance over time (Button *et al.*, 2007, p. 221).

19 Martín and Betancor (2006) analysed empirically this problem in the case of Madrid–Barajas airport, showing that social welfare from aeronautical services will increase by 6 per cent if a first-best pricing scheme (rather than the present pricing policy) is applied, where aeronautical demand usually exceeds capacity for the greater part of the day during all the weekdays. They also showed that a policy pursuing a higher level of capacity use does not provide higher social welfare and for this reason such a policy must not be encouraged.

20 The authors argued that, even when industry stakeholders recognize that NAS performance has many aspects, only delay is routinely monetized, and even in this case there is ample room for scepticism about the procedures. They commented that "virtually all delay cost calculations involve nothing more than the application of a cost factor based on reported values for the average direct aircraft operating cost per block hour to quantities of delay measured in time units. For air transport aircraft, the cost factor is in the range \$20–25 per min" (p. 3).

References

Alamdari, F. and Fagan, S. (2005). Impact of the adherence to the original low-cost model on the profitability of low-cost airlines. *Transport Reviews*, vol. 25, no. 3, pp. 377–392.

Aviation Strategy (2000). Turboprop manufacturing: reports of death exaggerated. 5–7 March 2000.

Barbot, C. (2005). How low-cost carriers compete amongst themselves and with full cost carriers. Paper presented at the 9th Air Transport Research Society Conference, Rio de Janeiro, Brazil, 3–7 July 2005.

Boeing Commercial Airplane Group (1994). *Large Airplane Development and Airports*. Seattle, WA.

Boeing Commercial Airplane Group (1996). *High Speed Civil Transport*. Program Review. Seattle, WA.

Borenstein, S. (1989). Hubs and high fares: dominance and market power in the US airline industry. *Rand Journal of Economics*, vol. 20, no. 3, pp. 344–365.

Borenstein, S. (1991). The dominant firm advantage in multi-product industries: evidence from the US airlines. *Quarterly Journal of Economics*, vol. 106, pp. 1237–1266.

Button, K., Costa, A. and Cruz, C. (2007). Ability to recover full costs through price discrimination in deregulated scheduled air transport markets. *Transport Reviews*, vol. 27, no. 2, pp. 213–230.

Carney, M. and Mew, K. (2003). Airport governance reform: a strategic management perspective. *Journal of Air Transport Management*, vol. 9, pp. 221–232.

Chang, Y.C. and Williams, G. (2001). Changing the rules: amending the nationality clauses in air services agreements. *Journal of Air Transport Management*, vol. 7, no. 4, pp. 207–216.

David, C. (1995). The impact of new aircraft developments on the design and construction of civil airports. *Proceedings of the Institution of Civil Engineers – Transportation*, vol. 111, pp. 59–69.

Dennis, N. (2007). End of the free lunch? The responses of traditional European airlines to the low-cost carrier threat. *Journal of Air Transport Management*, in press.

Doganis, R. (2001). *The Airline Business in the 21st Century*. London: Routledge.

Forsyth, P. (2007). The impacts of emerging aviation trends on airport infrastructure. *Journal of Air Transport Management*, vol. 13, pp. 45–52.

Francis, G., Fidato, A. and Humphreys, I. (2003). Airport–airline interaction: the impact of low-cost carriers on two European airports. *Journal of Air Transport Management*, vol. 9, pp. 267–273.

Franke M. (2004). Competition between network carriers and low-cost carriers: retreat battle or breakthrough to a new level of efficiency? *Journal of Air Transport Management*, vol. 10, pp. 15–21.

Graham, A. (2001). *Managing Airports: An International Perspective*. Oxford: Butterworth-Heinemann.

Graham, B. and Vowles, T.M. (2006). Carriers within carriers: a strategic response to low-cost airline competition. *Transport Reviews*, vol. 26, no. 1, pp. 105–126.

Hansen, M., Gillen, D. and Djafarian-Tehrani, R. (2001). Aviation infrastructure performance and airline cost: a statistical cost estimation approach. *Transportation Research Part E*, vol. 37, pp. 1–23.

Keeler, T.E. (1989). *Airline Deregulation and Market Performance: The Economic Basis for Regulatory Reform and Lessons from the U.S. Experience*. Economics Working Papers nos 89–123, University of California at Berkeley.

Lawton, T. (2002). *Cleared for Take-Off: Structure and Strategy in the Low Fare Airline Business*. Aldershot: Ashgate.

Lindstadt, H. and Fauser, B. (2004). Separation or integration? Can network carriers create distinct business streams on one integrated production platform? *Journal of Air Transport Management*, vol. 10, pp. 23–31.

Lu, C.C. and Pagliari, R.I. (2004). Evaluating the potential impact of alternative airport pricing approaches on social welfare. *Transportation Research Part E*, vol. 40, no. 1, pp. 1–17.

Martín, J.C. and Betancor, O. (2006). Evaluating different pricing policies on social welfare: an application to Madrid Barajas. *European Transport*, vol. 32, pp. 114–135.

Mason, K. (1999). The effects of corporate involvement in the short haul business travel market. *Journal of Air Transportation Worldwide*, vol. 4, no. 2, pp. 66–83.

Mason, K. (2000). The propensity of business travellers to use low-cost airlines. *Journal of Transport Geography*, vol. 8, no. 2, pp. 107–119.

Mason K. (2001). Marketing low-cost airline services to business travellers. *Journal of Air Transport Management*, vol. 7, pp. 103–109.

Morrell, P. (2005). Airlines within airlines: an analysis of US network airline responses to low cost carriers. *Journal of Air Transport Management*, vol. 11, pp. 303–312.

OAG (2006). *European Low-Cost Carriers White Paper. A Detailed Report Reflecting on the Impact Low-cost Carriers Have Had on the European Aviation Market*. London: OAG Worldwide Limited.

Oum, T. and Yu, C. (1998). *Winning Airlines. Productivity and Cost Competitiveness of the World's Major Airlines*. Boston: Kluwer Academic Publishers.

Pels, E. and Rietveld, P. (2004). Airline pricing behaviour in the London–Paris market. *Journal of Air Transport Management*, vol. 10, pp. 279–283.

Porter, T. (1985). *Competitive Advantage*. New York: Free Press.

Román, C., Espino, R., Martín, J.C., Betancor, O. and Nombela, G. (2008). Analyzing mobility in peripheral regions of the European Union: the case of Canarias–Madeira–Azores. *Networks and Spatial Economics* (NETS) (in press).

Smith, B., Leimkuhler, F. and Darrow, R. (1992). Yield management at American Airlines. *Interfaces*, vol. 22, no. 1, pp. 8–31.

Starkie, D. (1998). Allocation airport slots: a role for the market? *Journal of Air Transport Management*, vol. 4, no. 2, pp. 111–116.

Stasinopoulos, D. (1992). The second aviation package of the European Community. *Journal of Transport Economics and Policy*, vol. 26, pp. 83–87.

Stasinopoulos, D. (1993). The third phase of liberalization in community aviation and the need for supplementary measures. *Journal of Transport Economics and Policy*, vol. 27, pp. 323–328.

Tretheway, M.W. (2004). Distortions of airline revenues: why the network airline business model is broken. *Journal of Air Transport Management*, vol. 10, pp. 3–14.

Vincent, D. and Stasinopoulos, D. (1990). The aviation policy of the European Community. *Journal of Transport Economics and Policy*, vol. 24, pp. 95–100.

Wei, W. and Hansen, M. (2005). Impact of aircraft size and seat availability on airlines' demand and market share in duopoly markets. *Transportation Research Part E*, vol. 41, pp. 315–327.

4 Low-cost airlines
Strategies and reaction patterns

Rosário Macário and Vasco Reis

1 Introduction

The Low-Cost Airline (LCA) concept is arguably the most notable consequence of the deregulation wave that is sweeping the air transport sector worldwide, since the late 1970s. Over a period of three decades, the low-cost segment has continuously grown, bringing significant changes to the air transport sector's status quo and impacting societies and economies (for example, through tourism and regional development or enhancement of populations' accessibility). Such changes and impacts have already been largely identified and documented. The amount of literature dedicated to this subject is not therefore surprising, for example: Dobruszkes (2009, 2006), Graham and Shaw (2008), Dennis (2007), Gross and Schröder (2007), Francis *et al.* (2006) and Doganis (2005) analyse the LCA phenomenon; Mason (2001) discusses LCA marketing-related topics; Francis *et al.* (2007) analyse the possibility of transferring the LCA concept into long-haul flights; Davison and Ryley (2009) report the impacts of LCA in the promotion of tourism; O'Connell and Williams (2005) study the concept and passengers' perception of the level of service; or Francis *et al.* (2004, 2003), Warnock-Smith and Potter (2005), Dresner *et al.* (1996) research on the interaction and impact in airport operations; or Graham and Vowles (2006), Morrell (2005), Franke (2004), Gillen and Lall (2004), Windle and Dresner (1999) study the interactions between the LCA and the incumbents Full Service Airlines (FSA).

This chapter is built upon the literature[1] to discuss the impact and respective reactions of the growth of LCA along a set of domains. This set embraces, from the authors' point of view, the most impacted domains due to the emergence of LCAs. The domains are: full service airlines; travel distribution agencies and distribution agents; other modes of transport; airports; and regions. The chapter provides a general overview about these fives domains, which is in contrast with literature that typically adopts the research of a single topic. It is structured into four parts. The next part presents the LCA concept and philosophy. Part 3 is the core section and describes the main impacts and reaction along the abovementioned dimensions. The final part is the conclusion that gathers the main ideas of the chapter and highlights some of the areas for further research.

2 Concept and philosophy

Low-cost airlines, low-fare airlines, no-frills airlines, discount airlines or budget airlines are just some of the terms commonly used to designate the new breed of air transport companies that emerged in the late 1970s, in the United States, after the air transport market's deregulation. The fundamental reason for such an assortment of terms lies in their very origin. These terms were coined within the airline industry, referring to the newcomers with either low operating costs, or lower costs than incumbents. Soon after, this segment caught the attention of the media which generalized the terms to include any airline selling low-price tickets and offering limited services regardless of their operating costs (Humphreys *et al.*, 2006).

Nowadays, there is still no consensus around the definition of LCA (Mason and Morrison, 2008, Calder, 2008, Lawton, 2002). Nevertheless, it is generally accepted that an LCA is an air transport company that offers low fares and eliminates most traditional additional passenger services, the so-called frills. Their business design is mainly characterized by one or more of the following key elements: simple product, low operational cost combined with high productivity or specific market positioning (Bieger and Agosti, 2005, ELFAA, 2004, Doganis, 2005, Klaas and Klein, 2005, Taneja, 2004). Worthy of notice is that each LCA adopts a specific set of features, which is a function of their market positioning. For example, Air Berlin, in 2005, commenced UK domestic services as feeders to its German services out of Stansted, exploring the network effect, which is a rather uncommon feature in LCA business. Another relevant distinguishing feature amongst LCAs is how competition is perceived. Ryanair, for instance, prefers avoiding direct competition with any air transport company. Typically, it concentrates on smaller markets and regional airports and, thus, it generates its own market. Conversely, easyJet focuses on bigger markets and primary airports. Such markets are already served by other LCAs and FSAs, which denotes that easyJet does not avoid competition. So far, European LCAs have tried to avoid mutual competition.

An important question is whether this behaviour or that potential overcapacity might result in a price war and/or a consolidation wave. Experience in the air transport business (mainly in the FSA segment) points towards consolidation and the possible emergence of alliances (Meersman *et al.*, 2008), although this is an element so far not evident in the LCA market.

Diverse business models have already been documented (Dresner *et al.*, 1996, Doganis, 2005, Calder, 2008, Lawton, 2002, Francis *et al.*, 2004), which has already led some authors to put forth the designation 'low-cost model' for all the air transport companies that are pursuing different strategies aiming at the same outcome: low operating costs (Francis *et al.*, 2006). Indeed, these authors based on this assumption have proposed the following typology for the 'low-cost model' (Francis *et al.*, 2006, p. 84): southwest copy-cats, subsidiaries, cost cutters, diversified charter carriers, state-subsidized companies competing on price.

LCAs' core competitive advantage stems from having a lower cost structure than the FSAs. The lower cost structure allows them to offer fares below market average and still reap profits. Doganis (2005) computed at 49 per cent the average seat costs of a typical LCA in relation to a typical FSA. Cost advantage items included: higher seating density, higher aircraft utilization, use of cheaper secondary airports, no in-flight services or avoidance of travel agencies of Global Distribution System (GDS).

Cost reduction is indeed the main driver behind the operational and marketing properties of the LCA. Yet, there are limits to cost reduction and LCAs have been increasingly turning their attention to the other side of the equation: revenues. Typical examples for LCAs to optimize their revenues are commissions from hotels and car rental companies, credit card fees, (excess) luggage charges, in-flight food and beverages, advertising space. Additional growth could come from other in-flight services (e.g. telephone operations or gambling on board: Balcombe *et al.*, 2009). For FSAs the cost cuts privilege the production factors and the creation of segregated no-frills service. Although further evidence may be required, we may be on the brink of a turning point where the Low-Cost concept (and associated market) is evolving from pure cut cost into a Low-Fare concept irrespective of the source of revenues supporting the operation and sometimes also irrespective of the level of costs. In fact this should be the correct designation for this market – low-fare airlines (LFA). As an example, MINTeL (2006) states that Ryanair's revenue from sources other than ticket sales contributed €259 million to its 2005–6 net profit of €302 million. Those revenues already represent 16 per cent of the carrier's total revenue. For easyJet, that kind of income represented only 6.5 per cent of the airline's total revenue which increased by 41.3 per cent from 2004.

3 Evolution and forecast

The concept of LCA originated in the United States with Southwest Airlines. This airline was launched in the early 1970s, but it was not until the Deregulation Act of 1978 that it could grow and spread across the United States. The success of Southwest Airlines paved the way and, shortly after, many other LCAs have emerged in the United States. Meanwhile, the LCA concept has spread and emerged in many regions worldwide (see Table 4.1).

Liberalization of the air transport market is consensually considered to be an indispensable factor for the emergence of the LCA segment in every geographical context. Table 4.1 provides evidence of the close link between the emergence of LCAs and liberalization: invariably, LCAs have entered the market just after the liberalization process had taken place (or at least just a few years later). However, other factors are likewise considered catalysts for its development, namely: degree of entrepreneurship, density and level of income of populations, attitude towards travelling, supply of airports, or level of adherence to Internet and web-based communications (Macário *et al.*, 2007).

Table 4.1 Spread of LCA concept around the world

Region (country)	Year low-cost operations began	Year(s) in which market deregulation took place	Share of overall market (%)
North America			
USA	1978	1978	24–25
Canada	1996	1996	30
Europe			
UK/Ireland	1995	1993	40
EU	1999	1995	20
EU expansion	2002	2004	<1
Australia/NZ			
Australia	1990	1990	30+
New Zealand	1996	1984	–
Asia			
Malaysia	2001	2001	2
Singapore	2001	2001	<1
Japan	1998	1994	1
China	–	Ongoing	–
Thailand	2004	2003	<1
India		2003	<1
Rest of the world			
Brazil	2001	1998	3
South Africa	2001	1999	<1
Gulf States	2004	2003	1

Source: Francis *et al.*, 2006.

Differences in these factors may justify the differences in the evolution of the life cycle of the market development of LCAs worldwide (Table 4.2). The United States is the most developed market exhibiting properties of a mature market. The rest of the world lags considerably behind. Canada and the United Kingdom are undergoing the first wave of consolidation, whereas the other regions are still in the phase of either growth or entry of new LCAs. In the face of this evolution, Macário (2008) claims the existence of a 'liberalization wave' sweeping eastwards across the globe. Assuming the existence of such a wave, the current LCA market development worldwide evidences the key influence of liberalization, since the stage of development fairly coincides with the time of liberalization (Macário, 2008).

Looking into Europe, the LCA phenomenon has spread unevenly. European LCAs have benefited from a very liberal legal frame and a number of geopolitical factors such as the ones below (MINTeL, 2006):

- the Single European Aviation Act, which guarantees Seventh[2] and Eighth[3] Freedom traffic rights to airlines;
- underdeveloped air capacities in so-called 'secondary cities', such as Liverpool and 'secondary countries', such as Portugal, Ireland, etc.;

Table 4.2 Life cycle for market development of LCAs in different world regions

Life cycle stages	USA	Canada	Europe			Asia	Australia	New Zealand	Rest of the world
			UK	Mainland	East Europe				
Innovation	■								
Proliferation	■	■	■	■		■	■	■	■
Consolidation	■	■	■	■	■	■	■	■	■
Second phase of entrants	■	■	■						
Consolidation	■								
Market maturity	■								

Source: Francis *et al.* (2006) in Macário *et al.* (2007).

- the enlargement of the European Union;
- open-skies agreements with neighbouring non-EU countries, such as Morocco.

The LCA segment has proved to be a robust service concept from the financial and operational point of view. Since its inception this segment has consistently grown year after year, in every region. In 2005, the International Aviation Transport Association reported a market share of 45 per cent for the LCAs in the United States, and the European Association of Low Fare Companies (EALFC) claimed, in 2006, a market share of 30 per cent for the intra-European market (in terms of RPK). Figure 4.1 presents the evolution of the share of airport movements within Europe, measured by Eurocontrol. The market share is somewhat below the figures put forth by EALFC. Yet, considering that the average load factor of a LCA is normally higher than other carriers, a higher market share in terms of RPK is expected. In any case, Figure 4.1 evidences the major growth of LCAs over the past fifteen years.

Despite the robustness and continuous growth of LCAs, the segment has been revealed as highly volatile with many companies entering the market and many others exiting (either through bankruptcies or mergers). The following table (Table 4.3) provides an overview of the main bankruptcies and mergers in Europe in the past years.

This denotes that despite the overall success of the concept, individual survivability is rather difficult, which in turn provides some evidence about the nature of this market:

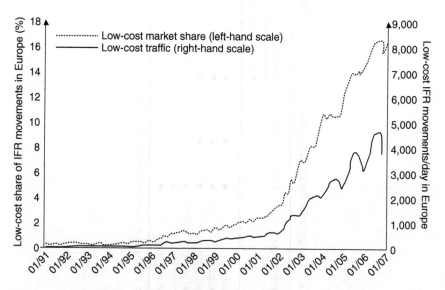

Figure 4.1 Evolution of market share of LCAs in terms of IFR movements in Europe (source: Macário *et al.* (2007)).

- The LCA market segment is harsh and very demanding, and only a few companies can actually achieve the necessary cost threshold to continue in the market.
- There is a misperception by entrepreneurs about an eventual simplicity of the LCA concept (after all, LCA is more than just cutting the frills or in-flight services).
- The LCA concept is only viable above a certain dimension, which may explain the success of the largest European LCAs. Smaller ones are condemned to failure.
- There is the advantage that the firstcomer and subsequent companies will have much more difficulty imposing its brand in the market.

Table 4.3 LCA bankruptcies or mergers in Europe

Year	Airline	Country	Event
1999	AB Airlines	UK	Bankruptcy
	Color Air	Norway	Bankruptcy
	Debonair	UK	Bankruptcy
2002	GO	UK	Bankruptcy
2003	Air Lib	France	Bankruptcy
	Buzz	UK	Merger with Ryanair
	Goodjet	Sweden	Bankruptcy
2004	Air Polinia	Poland	Bankruptcy
	Basic Air	Netherlands	Merger with Transavia
	Duo Airways	UK	Bankruptcy
	Flying Finn	Finland	Bankruptcy
	Germania Express	Germany	Merged with dba
	GetJet	Poland	Bankruptcy
	Jetgreen	Ireland	Bankruptcy
	Skynet Airlines	UK	Bankruptcy
	V-Bird	Netherlands	Bankruptcy
	VolareWeb	Italy	Bankruptcy
2005	Air Andalucia	Spain	Bankruptcy
	Eujet	Ireland	Bankruptcy
	Intersky	Austria	Bankruptcy
	Maersk Air	Denmark	Merged with Sterling
2006	Air Tourquoise	France	Bankruptcy
	Air Wales	UK	Bankruptcy
	Budget Air	Ireland	Bankruptcy
	dba	Germany	Merged with Air Berlin
	Flywest	France	Bankruptcy
	HiFly/Air Luxor	Portugal	Bankruptcy
	My Travelite	UK	Reintegrated into MyTravel Airways
	Snalskjusten	Sweden	Bankruptcy
2007	LTU	Germany	Merged with Air Berlin

Source: MINTeL, 2006 in Macário *et al.*, 2007.

The continuous economic depression, increasingly competitive environment and rise in fuel price provide no good signs for an eventual change in the level of volatility; on the contrary, further bankruptcies may occur. However, in an analysis by Deutsche Bank from May 2007, it was calculated that the LCA market will continue to experience a volume growth of roughly 15 per cent, as a consequence of a combination of shifts from other air transport segments, GDP growth, and a very modestly rising propensity to travel (Macário and Van de Voorde, 2009), meaning this market will continue to be a rather dynamic intertwining between cases of success and failure.

4 Impacts of the growth of the LCA segment

The notable growth of the LCA segment has greatly impacted the air transport markets and the regions. Yet, interestingly, the extent and nature of their effect has thus far had a clear regional scope. Two main reasons can be pointed out. First, because the liberalization processes have concerned (certain) air traffic within a bounded geographical region (e.g. United States or European Union), whereas traffic to and from elsewhere has remained regulated. Second, because LCAs operate on short to medium routes (continental routes). Thus, the impacts derived from LCAs' activities are restricted to a region, with few possibilities of spilling over into adjacent regions.

The authors have pinpointed five dimensions for conducting a deeper analysis of the nature of impacts and typical reactions. The dimensions have already been presented in the introduction, i.e. full service airlines; travel agencies and global distribution systems; other modes of transport; airports; regions.

4.1 Full service airlines

As mentioned above, there are essentially two strategies for choosing routes: entry on non-served routes (typically Ryanair's strategy) and creation of the air transport market; entry on served routes (typically easyJet's strategy) and competing against incumbents (either FSAs or other LCAs). In both strategies, however, there is competition with incumbents: in the latter strategy, there is direct competition on a route basis, while in the former strategy, there is indirect competition at city (or region) pair level. The entry of a new competitor always triggers some sort of reaction from the incumbents. The strategy depends upon a large variety of factors, such as: level of threat of the newcomer to incumbents' business, incumbents' business models or market's properties. The following reactions have been identified in the literature: no reaction; price reduction with eventual increase in capacity; withdraw from the route; establish an LCA subsidiary; or conversion into an LCA.

The first reaction is the simplest one and consists in having no reaction at all. The incumbent recognizes its lack of capacity to compete in terms of price and prefers losing market share to entering into a price war that it is obvious from the outset can never be won. In this reaction, the incumbent continues to do business as usual. The most visible consequence of this reaction is a significant loss of market share for the FSA, starting in particular with the leisure passengers.

The main reason for maintaining the route in service is to use it as a feeder for the long-distance network. Most FSAs have long-distance networks based on a hub and spoke structure. Yet, the region around a hub airport is commonly insufficient to generate enough traffic for the long-distance network, leaving the FSA to rely on a feeding network (the medium- to short-haul network). Since virtually no passenger is willing to buy two independent tickets (one for the short haul and another for the long haul), in real terms there is no direct competition in the long-haul market between the LCA and incumbents. An additional reason for an incumbent to keep the route is related to the existence of the highly profitable business passengers who remain loyal (because the incumbent has either better suitable schedules or higher frequency).

The second reaction refers to the immediate response of either reducing prices to match the LCAs, or increasing capacity, by either adding additional flights or increasing the aircrafts' size (Ito and Lee, 2003). Table 4.4 presents the evolution of fares (price in Euros) on the city pair London–Toulouse, after the entry of Ryanair and easyJet. The most striking fact is the incumbents' very high prices of tickets in 2002. Immediately after the entry of Ryanair, both Air France and British Airways drastically reduced prices and they continued to do so for around three years. The entry of easyJet with fares below market price represented the final blow in incumbents' intentions of competing in the market. Air France has eventually withdrawn. This example gives the evidence that this reaction, albeit possible in the short run, is not sustainable in the long run, simply because the

Table 4.4 Impact on fares from LCA market entry (€)

Airline	Route/special conditions	1 Out Mon. 15, Back Wed. 17, April 2002	2 Out Mon. 14, Back Wed. 16, April 2003	3 Out Tue. 2, Back Tue. 4, Dec. 2003	4 Out Mon. 4, Back Wed. 6, April 2005
Ryanair	Stansted–Carcassone	187	180	109	112
British Airways	Gatwick–Toulouse	910	273	183	193
Air France	Heathrow–Toulouse	910	606	185	discontinued
British Airways	if staying Saturday night	246	198	239	211
Air France	if staying Saturday night	234	193	185	discontinued
easyJet	Gatwick–Toulouse				91

Source: Doganis 2005.

higher cost structure of the FSAs is not compatible with the low prices. As a consequence, the route becomes a loss maker and the only way to keep it running is by cross-subsidizing from other routes, which, in the face of the adverse environment of the air transport business (Doganis, 2005), is scarcely possible to maintain for a long period of time.

A third reaction is to simply abandon the route, owing to, first, an expected reduction in demand and, second, an incapacity in competing head to head with LCA. This may occur either at the first signs of market contraction or, as in the above example, after the full assumption of the lack of capacity to compete. Albeit route withdrawal may prevent losses in the short term, it is not a sustainable strategy in the long term since it may lead to an excessive reduction of the FSA's network.

Fourth, the FSA may opt for establishing its own LCA subsidiary. The reaction of operating several business models within the same mother company is not unique to air transport. In sectors such as retailing, car rental, railroads, banking, insurance, news, power supply, tour operators or consulting, the establishment of (low-cost) subsidiaries is a common practice leading to success (Gillen and Gados, 2008). This may be done by either acquiring an existent LCA or charter company, or launching a new air transport company (Graf, 2005). Like the previous reaction, this one normally occurs when the FSA recognizes its inability to reduce its cost structure to profitably compete with the newcomers. Yet instead of simply withdrawing from the route, it opts for competing. This reaction has been followed by diverse companies as shown in Table 4.5 (Gillen and Gados, 2008).

Normally the new subsidiary embraces the most common features of an LCA, aiming to reduce the costs. The major sources of cost reduction include (Gillen and Gados, 2008): reduction of in-flight catering, single aircraft utilization, higher aircraft utilization and other asset utilization, improved crew utilization and reduced distribution costs. However, the large majority of the new subsidiaries failed. Examples include: Ted, Continental Lite, Delta Express or MetroJet (ibid.). Several reasons contribute to such an outcome. First, the subsidiary is for all legal purposes part of the incumbent, thus, the same rules of the incumbents apply to the LCA; this includes for example salaries or crews' block times. Consequently, the scope for reducing costs and increasing productivity is rather limited. Second, while an LCA normally uses brand-new fleets with very low maintenance costs, the FSA's LCA subsidiaries tend to use mother company's aircraft which normally are older. Third, brand confusion tends to occur between the LCA and the mother company. Customers may expect the same service quality in the LCA as in the FSA. An inferior service quality of the LFA may give a negative image of the FSA (Morrell, 2005).

In any case, there are examples of successful LCA subsidiaries. These include Jetstar from Singapore Airlines, Germanwings from Lufthansa or AirAsia from Malaysian Airlines. Gillan and Gados (2008) point out the following success factors: dominance of domestic market by the mother company, complete separation of the operations, no integration between both companies, non-overlapped networks (avoidance of cannibalization between companies).

Table 4.5 Closed down, active and planned low-cost units of incumbent airlines

Closed down		Active		Planned	
Low-cost unit	*Airline grouping*	*Low-cost unit*	*Airline grouping*	*Low-cost unit*	*Airline grouping*
Buzz	KLM	Song	Delta Air Lines	SAS Braathens	SAS
Go	British Airways	Zip, 'Tango'	Air Canada	Smart Wings	CSA
Lufthansa Express	Lufthansa	Ted	United Airlines	Nice Jet	Air France
Shuttle by United	United Airlines	Germanwings	Lufthansa/Eurowings	Iberia Express	Iberia
Delta Express	Delta Air Lines	Snowflake	SAS	Air India Express	Air India
MetroJet	US Airways	Bmibaby	British Midland	Virgin Express	SN Brussels Airl.
Continental Lite	Continental Airl.	Transavia (Basiq Air)	KLM	Indian Airlines	Alliance Air
People Express	Frontier Airlines	flynordic	Finnair/Nordic Airlink		
'Austrian Bratislava'	Austrian Airlines	Centralwings	LOT		
		'Swiss in Europe'	Swiss Intl. Air Lines		
		'Fare 4U'	Air Malta		
		'red ticket'	Austrian Airlines		
		Hapag-Lloyd-Express	TUI/Hapag-Lloyd		
		'SAS Economy'	SAS		
		Thomson Fly	TUI/Britannia		
		Freedom Air	Air NewZealand		
		'Express Class'	Air NewZealand		
		Australian Airlines	Qantas Airways		
		Jetstar	Qantas Airways		
		Jetstar Asia	Qantas Airways		
		JAL Express	Japan Airlines		
		Nok Air	Thai Airways		
		Tiger Airways	Singapore Airlines		

Source: Graf, 2005.

The final observed reaction consists in evolving towards an LCA configuration. The incumbent opts for embracing the philosophy inherent to an LCA. The most paradigmatic case has been the Irish national company Aer Lingus that due to the lack of capacity to compete with the LCA Ryanair has decided to convert herself into an LCA. This reaction is the most radical and demands a clear strategic vision, since it entails a complete change in the structure and mission of the company.

4.2 Travel Distribution Agents and Global Distribution Systems

When the LCAs entered the markets, the tickets' advertising and selling market was in the hands of third-party agents, namely: the Travel Distribution Agent (TDA) and the Global Distribution System (GDS). The FSAs had evolved towards an inferior market positioning. Figure 4.2 depicts the traditional organization of the ticket sales structure.

The TDA encompasses both travel agencies and tour operators. The GDSs emerged with the development of Information and Communication Technologies (ICT) in the mid-1970s and have consolidated the TDA's positioning within the market. Owing to the significant economies of size, the TDA segment is highly concentrated. Nowadays, the major GDSs are Travelport, Sabre and Worldpan. The large majority of the FSAs' tickets are sold through a TDA. Therefore, and in practical terms, the TDA has greater market power, since they are the ones who first control the selling channels, and second, control the relationship with the clients. Although we may argue that the GDSs also have a great amount of market power by determining the positioning of the air transport companies' flights on the display screens, the fact is that it is the TDA who actually chooses and sells the tickets. Furthermore, the various regulatory bodies have been implementing measures to reduce bias in the visualization of flights through the GDSs. The status quo was therefore very favourable for the TDA. They applied a fee over every fare, and in addition earned extra revenues from other services, such as hotels, car rental, airport transfers, etc. On the other hand, the risk was relatively low, since they did not need to invest any capital and, in case of an air transport company's bankruptcy, they only needed to shift to any other company in the market to avoid being exposed to that impact.

It is thus evident that LCAs have brought a major transformation to the relationship between the air transport companies and the TDA as highlighted in Figure 4.2. In their pursuit of cost reductions, one of the items to cut was the commissions to the travel agencies. Consequently, they have decided to directly sell the tickets to the passengers and, thus, avoid the TDA's commission fees, and regaining the direct contact with the passengers.

When the first LCA appeared in the United States, in the late 1970s the ICT was only taking its first steps and the only viable technological solution for massively advertising and selling fares was the telephone. This was the method followed by many LCA starters, such as Southwest. The advent of new ICT, in the

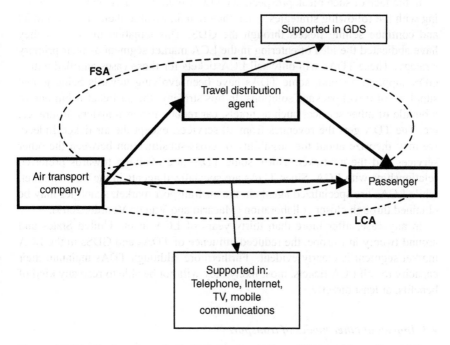

Figure 4.2 Distribution channels for Full Service Airlines (FSA) and Low Cost Airlines (LCA).

1990s, such as the internet, digital television or mobile communications, created new opportunities for the deployment of new distribution channels. This represented the final blow in the TDAs' and DGSs' hopes to have an active participation in the LCAs' distribution channels.

Recent moves are interestingly providing more clear evidence that GDSs and, inherently, TDAs, may after all have a place in the LCAs' distribution channels. In November 2007, easyJet was the first European LCA to sign an agreement with the GDS Travelport. Yet, the contract foresees an extra fee for booking through the GDS (BTOnline, 2007), which will render the ticket more expensive through the GDS than through easyJet's website. easyJet's official announcement states that the agreement was targeting the business travellers (easyJet, 2007), since many of these passengers have maintained loyalty to TDA and are more willing to pay premium prices. It is very likely that easyJet, well known for targeting the business passenger, is using this agreement to enter the business market segment.

More recently, in November 2009, the LCA Wind Jet announced a similar agreement with the same GDS provider (Travelport, 2009). Wind Jet was the fourth European LCA signing this agreement in 2009, which indicates the progressive entry of GDS in the LCA. However, despite the entry of some LCAs into GDS, the vast majority of them still avoid use of third-party agents.

In the face of such bleak prospects with LCA markets, TDAs have been react-ing with the following strategies. First, they remain loyal to their business model and continue selling tickets through the GDS. This situation means that they have abdicated the idea of entering in the LCA market segment as their primary strategy. These TDAs will only sell LCA tickets for those cases enrolled with a GDS supplier. Second, some TDAs have been evolving towards being global suppliers of travel package solutions. In this strategy, the air ticket is but one of a bundle of other services such as hotels, car rental, airport transfers, insurance, etc. The TDA gets the revenues from all services, except the air ticket. Indeed, we may theorize about the possibility of cross-subsidization between the other services and the air ticket. Third, some TDAs are evolving towards preferred relationships with LCA. Since TDAs are specialized agents in the travel market, while LCAs are specialized agents in the air transport market, synergies may be obtained through closer collaboration (Macário and Van de Voorde, 2009).

In any case, after more than thirty years of LCA in the United States and around twenty in Europe, the reduced influence of TDAs and GDSs in the LCA market segment is clearly evident.. Furthermore, although TDAs maintain their capacity to sell LCA tickets, most likely they will not be able to reap any kind of benefits, at least directly.

4.3 Impact in other modes of transport

Competition between modes of transport was for a long time, and continues to be in many regions of the globe, disallowed by governments. The transport sector is seen as a vital piece in countries' economic and social development, which should be protected from any disruptive force of competition. Con-sequently, for a long period of time there was no actual competition between the various modes of transport. This situation started to change with the progressive deregulation of the transport market in general and the air transport in particular. Although many governments still keep their transport sector under heavy regula-tion, in those countries that were deregulated modal competition has become a reality (Rothengatter, 1997).

In what concerns competition with air transport, Sinha (2001) found a sub-stantial increase in competition between air transport services and road and rail services, after the US liberalization. The two main US road companies were compelled to cut prices in order to reduce the shift of passengers to the LCAs. The rail company – Amtrak – had also to cut prices and introduced special deals for passengers. The same effects have been found in Australia.

Competition between road-based (car and bus) or conventional train and air transport may occur for short distances. Yet, for such distances, only in the case of network (road or railway) disruption or crossing of unsafe regions does it make sense to use air transport. For greater distances, due to differences in speed, road-based transport becomes non-competitive. Using cars may be prefer-able again in special situations, such as people carrying substantial amounts of luggage, or the access to remote locations not (or ill-) covered by air transport.

In the former situation, the private car may be preferred since it provides greater flexibility and privacy (Fröid, 2008). In the latter situation, the private car (or buses) may be the only or most suitable solution.

However, it is with the high-speed train[4] (HST) that the competition issues are more intense, because it is the only land transport solution that can directly compete in terms of travel times. Past experience shows that for distances up to 500 km, HST may be more competitive than air transport, mainly because it commonly offers city centre to city centre transport services, while many airports are in the outskirts, which implies extra transport time from/to the city centres. This competitive advantage is then progressively eroded until a threshold around 1,000 km, above which air transport has no direct competitors (Givoni, 2006). In terms of time, evidence shows that HST may compete for journeys up to three and half hours (Esplugas *et al.*, 2005). The following figure (Figure 4.3) compares, for the Swedish transport market, the travelling time of various land-based transport modes: private car, bus, conventional train, high-speed train on conventional tracks and high-speed train, including the connecting journeys. Reinforcing this evidence, a study by Dobruszkes (2006) computed the mean route distance of European LCAs as 634 kilometres, a value within the above mentioned values for competition with HST.

It seems to be consensual that the emergence of the LCA marked a watershed in inter-modal competition. Traditionally, air transport was essentially a luxury service, affordable to only wealthy or business travellers. Lower-income populations were thus forced to use the other cheaper modes of transport, namely bus and rail (Allaz, 2004). The LCA introduced a new concept of transport: low fares, similar to the other modes of transport, plus the speed and comfort of air

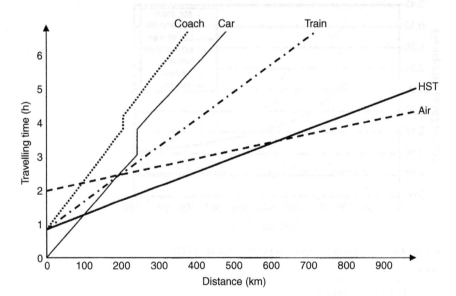

Figure 4.3 Modal comparison.

travel. Figure 4.4 compares the costs per revenue passenger-kilometre (RPK) for an LCA (in this case Ryanair average values, with an average load factor of 84 per cent), an HST and an FSA (in this case the SAS Airlines, average load factor of 64 per cent).

The results clearly demonstrate that operating costs of LCAs are competitive with HST and considerably lower than traditional carriers, which denotes that these modes of transport may compete directly on a fare basis. A 2003 survey by ELFAA concludes that around 8 and 4 per cent of LCA travellers were respectively former car and rail users that have meanwhile shifted towards air transport (ELFAA, 2004).

Similarly to the analysis of travel time, when considering the costs of transport, we should also consider the total generalized travel costs which, besides the fare, include other costs such as quality of the service, quality of the transfer service, comfort and adequacy of terminals or airports, or the total travel time (TTT). For price-sensitive passengers, direct cost is the most important factor, while for business passengers, TTT gains a primordial importance. Therefore the analysis of the competition between LCAs and the other modes of transport should include all these factors. In any case, there is strong evidence of competition since air transport is the fastest mode and LCAs have enough room to profitably offer low fares (in line with the other modes of transport). The main drawback of some LCAs is the choice of secondary airports, which tend to be far away from urban centres (which are already served by a main airport), and thus with lower accessibility, increasing the TTT and reducing the attractiveness to business travellers.

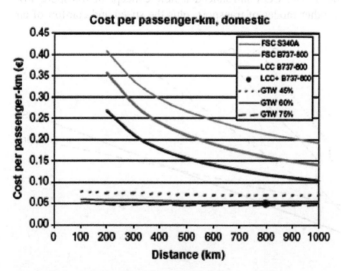

Figure 4.4 Costs per passenger-km (source: Fröid (2008)).

Notes
LCA = Low Cost Airlines.
FSC = Full Service Company.
GTW = High Speed Rail.

The interaction between LCAs and the other modes of transport is not, however, one of pure competition. Conversely, cooperation between air transport and other modes is required to produce door-to-door transport services. Normally, this cooperation occurs in the connection between the inter-urban modes (such as air transport or HST) and regional or urban modes (such as conventional rail, metropolitans or buses). So far, LCAs do not engage in any sort of cooperation with other modes, since that would represent costs or division of revenues. Instead, cooperation is normally promoted and supported by the airports or local authorities that extend the public transport network to the airport. There is, however, reason to believe that the evolutionary cycle of LCAs will in future lead these companies to engage in this type of partnership.

4.4 Airports

Airports have significant levels of fixed costs (e.g. maintaining runway and terminal, or security and handling equipment) and in the smaller ones the revenues (from aeronautical charges, retail or other sources) are not enough to cover these costs. Consequently, most of the smaller airports record financial losses and are publicly owned, being maintained through state or regional subsidies (Caves and Gosling, 1999). Fewings (1999) identified around 431 airports in Western Europe, the vast majority being underutilized since air traffic was essentially concentrated in the main airports, and around 200 had an annual throughput below one million passengers (Caves and Gosling, 1999). LCAs' main airport demands are: low charges, fast turnaround times and simply constructed terminals. Table 4.6 lists the main airport requirements sought by an LCA (Barret, 2004).

Moreover, passengers' comfort or the quality of the airport-related services are not a main concern, the priority is cost minimization. Typically, they contract the minimum level of services, and negotiate prices down to the minimum possible level. Commonly, they do not require business lounges, air bridges or baggage transfer services. They tend to use the aircraft parking stands adjacent to the terminal, so that passengers can walk directly to the aircraft.

Table 4.6 Airport requirements of low-cost airlines

Requirements
1 Low airport charges
2 Quick 25-minute turnaround time
3 Single-storey airport terminals
4 Quick check in
5 Good catering and shopping at airport
6 Good facilities for ground transport
7 No executive business class lounges

Source: Barret, 2004.

All these demands are reflected in the airports' design and services. In order to offer low prices, low-cost airports or terminals tend to have simple designs or be open spaces. The space per passenger tends to be smaller than in an airport or terminal meant for a traditional airline, in order to reduce the costs. In terms of retail services, the LCAs' demands result in a reduced amount of retail activity, simply because building and operating commercial space in airports can be particularly expensive (de Neufville, 2006, Francis, 2003).

LCAs are known for being very aggressive negotiators, typically demanding reduction of fees or financial support on the development of specific routes (on grounds of promotion of region, publicity, etc.). Their bargaining power is likewise very high, since secondary airports are eager to attract any kind of traffic and, therefore, more willing to accept their conditions.

Although the majority of LCAs avoid congested airports and expensive capital charges, there are those that operate on dense routes and serve bigger airports. In these situations, their bargaining power is limited. Commonly, they tend to use the airport in the periods of the day with lower activity (middle morning and afternoon), when slots are less scarce and, thus, less expensive. Additionally, they avoid using the larger terminals; instead they opt for the smaller ones, often located in remote places. Indeed, some main airports have been building new terminals or adapting older ones to the demands of LCAs, recognizing the relevance of having these airlines using the same airport as FSAs. Berlin/Schönefeld or Warsaw have dedicated a terminal to the use of easyJet; Geneva, Kuala Lumpur/Subang or Singapore/Changi have built a new LFA terminal; Paris/de Gaulle has converted Terminal 9 into a LCA terminal (de Neufville, 2006). The continuous growth of LCAs in some airports or the willingness to attract new companies is leading airports to develop tailored terminals, although maintaining the possibility for passengers to connect with the FSA.

4.5 Regions

There are few studies reporting the impacts of LCA activity in regions. In overall terms, the impacts of LCAs can be considered identical to the impacts on regional economies derived from air transport activity in general, which can be broken down into three main classes:

- Direct effects, which correspond to the increase in employment in activities directly related to air transport, such as airlines; handling, maintenance and catering companies; airports; shopping within airports; or parking facilities. It is estimated that 1,000 jobs are created for every million passengers through an airport (York Aviation, 2004).
- Indirect effects, which correspond to the increase in employment and economic activity in the region as a result of the increase in flows of people, for tourism and business purposes.
- Catalytic effects, which correspond to the attraction and retention of incoming investment and the stimulation of tourism. The increase in commercial

activity enhances a region's competitiveness by attracting leisure and business passengers, which ultimately leads to a sustainable growth in incomes and employment.

The LCA activity produces similarly positive effects in the regions where they operate. As they have a significant share of passenger travel for leisure purposes, the main economic sector to benefit is tourism. LCAs' business model leads these companies to choose regional airports, which are, in many cases, located in depressed and underdeveloped economic regions. Moreover, often regions are relatively unknown, and the LCA serves as an important vector for advertisement and publicity, improving regions' visibility. Thus, the benefits introduced by LCA activity are even more evident than the traditional air transport companies as they tend to fly to the well-developed economic regions.

In addition, by offering low fares, LCAs encourage air travel and, consequently, the number of people passing through the region, with inherent positive effects. Even in well-developed regions when competing with the established companies, LCAs lead to an overall reduction in fare prices, which further induces air travel to the region.

The benefits brought by LCA activity have been studied for several European regions. Table 4.7 summarizes the main findings. Another interesting example of market generation by the LCA is given by the route Frankfurt (Germany)–Dublin (Ireland). For a long time, the annual traffic volume was around two million passengers. After the entry of the LCA Ryanair on that route (Kerry (Ireland) to

Table 4.7 Benefits for regional economies from the LCA activities

Airport, region	Main findings
Carcassonne, France	Passengers generated (2003): 253,000 Direct income: €8.4 million Indirect income: €135 million Induced income: €272.4 million
Cologne/ Bonn, Germany	Taxes paid €91 million Cost and productivity advantages for companies in region: €147.6 million Average spent per incoming passenger: €285.42
Pisa, Italy	Passengers generated (2003): 316,000 Average spent per business incoming passenger: €431.40 Average spent per tourism incoming passenger: €496.52 Total economic impact of foreign passengers: €149.2 million

Sources: Ract Madoux Groupe Second Axe (2003) Rapport d'etude: impact socio-economique de la compagnie aerienne Ryanair dans la region et alentours de Carcassonne.

Institut fur Verkehrswissenschaft und der Universitat zu Koln (2004) die regionalwirtschaftlichen Auswirkungen des Low cost-Markets im Raum Koln/Bonn.

S. Anna University of Pisa (2003).

Frankfurt Hahn (Germany)), the annual traffic jumped to seven million passengers per year. The passengers included a significant share of business travellers, as the region around Kerry concentrates strong German investment in services and industrial activity (Barret, 2004).

We may conclude that between LCAs and regional authorities a symbiotic relationship is established. The former seeks for low-cost and high productive airports, whereas the latter seeks for higher accessibility, attracting visitors, business activity and employment. Typically, in Europe, secondary airports are publicly owned by the regional authorities, which may provide interesting fees and other compensations. The LCA makes accessible the region to outer regions, generating the market and providing regions with a continuous stream of foreign people. Although it could be argued that LCAs may get excessive advantages from airports, the regions are also liquid beneficiaries, since air travel is an important spur for economic development.

5 Conclusions

This chapter analysed the impacts and reaction owing to the arrival of a new philosophy of air transport providers: the low-cost segment. The emergence of low-cost airlines was arguably the most significant outcome of the liberalization processes occurring worldwide. The low-cost segment is overall very successful, exhibiting continuous growth in every market where it has emerged. However, it is also highly volatile, which denotes likewise difficult survivability. The two effects together result in a very dynamic sector and, inevitably, a risky one, as made evident by the number of bankruptcies in recent years (Macário and Van de Voorde, 2009).

The low-cost philosophy is based on cost minimization, which has produced a significant disruption with the status quo and the usual FSAs business. Due to the significant cost structure, FSAs cannot compete on prices against LCAs and still obtain profits. Several reactions have then been analysed including: do nothing, enter into a price war, establish a subsidiary or move towards the low-cost concept. Regardless of the reaction the outcome is inevitably a loss in revenues and eventually prices.

LCAs generalized air transport by making it affordable to most people. Consequently, LCAs entered into direct competition with the modes of transport that previously provided that kind of service. Yet, since air transport is the fastest mode of transport, in practical terms only the high-speed train can effectively compete against LCAs (and only up to a limit around the 800–1,000 km). Nonetheless it should not be forgotten that air transport only provides airport-to-airport transport service. Therefore, cooperation with other modes of transport is required, and we would say even inevitable, in order to achieve door-to-door transport service, which is what passengers demand. So far, LCAs have shown reduced interest in entering into any sort of modal cooperation, usually leaving this to the airport or local authorities.

An important innovation brought by LCAs was bypassing the TDA and inherently the GDS and selling tickets directly to passengers. In this way, they have eliminated the middle man, cut the fees and got direct access to passengers. The main drawback of this strategy is that a share of the market is out of bounds, since many passengers, essentially businesses, have remained faithful to the TDS. If for some of the LCAs this is not relevant since their main target is the leisure passengers, for those targeting the business passenger such facts represent a handicap. For this reason over the last few years several LCAs have signed contracts with GDS.

LCAs have also brought innovations in the relationship with airports. The choice of an airport is based on two basic promises: avoidance of congestion and minimization of capital costs (de Neufville, 2006). As a consequence, LCAs commonly chose secondary airports where rotation times can be as low as 25 minutes and with landing fees considerably lower than major airports. The secondary airports, mostly loss makers, willingly accept the LCAs' demands, and strength of negotiation, aiming to generate traffic. The main airports are also changing their attitudes towards the LCAs and have started adapting their infrastructure to accommodate LCAs' demands. Therefore, there is a visible trend towards a closer relationship between LCAs and airports.

Finally, in what concerns the impacts on regions, the low-cost segment was essentially positive or, at least, perceived as such. LCAs bring passengers to regions that otherwise had none or reduced traffic, and increase regions' accessibility to elsewhere.

For these reasons, public authorities are commonly willing to support the establishment of LCAs in the local airports (which are commonly public).

LCAs have been responsible for a major revolution in the production and perception of air transport services. Currently, in Europe and Asia the low-cost segment still shows signs of great vitality. Whereas in the United States this segment has already reached the maturity level, in other regions it is still in the growing stage, which evidences that further impacts are still to be expected.

Notes

1 Including the work undertaken by the authors and others to the European Parliament; for further details see Macário *et al.*, 2007.
2 The Seventh Freedom is the right of an airline to carry traffic between two countries outside its home country (e.g. Alitalia operating between Paris and London, without serving Italy).
3 The Eighth Freedom is also called 'cabotage' and is the right of an airline to carry domestic traffic in a foreign country as part of a service from/to its home country (e.g. Austrian conveying people from Barcelona to Madrid, on a flight originated in Vienna).
4 There are diverse types of HST, such as for example: the Shinkansen in Japan, the TGV in France, the AVE in Spain, the ICE in Germany, the X-2000 in Sweden, the Pendolino in Italy, KTX in Korea and the MAGLEV. There are significant differences between them, in terms of technology, types of railways or maximum speed, but all of them are able to reach the speed thresholds to be considered HST.

References

Allaz, C. (2004) *The History of Air Cargo and Airmail from the 18th Century*, London: Christopher Foyle Publishing.

Balcombe, K., Fraser, I. and Harris, L. (2009) 'Consumer willingness to pay for in-flight service and comfort levels: A choice experiment', *Journal of Air Transport Management*, Volume 15, Issue 5, pp. 221–226.

Barret, S. (2004) 'The sustainability of the Ryanair model', *International Journal of Transport Management*, Volume 2, pp. 89–98.

Bieger, T. and Agosti, S. (2005) 'Business models in the airline sector: Evolution and perspectives', in: Delfmann, W., Baum, H., Auerbach, S. and Albers, S. (eds) *Strategic Management in the Aviation Industry*, Aldershot: Ashgate, pp. 41–64.

BTOnline (2007) 'easyJet to charge steep fee for Amadeus, Galileo bookings', online: www.btnonline.com/businesstravelnews/headlines/article_display.jsp?vnu_content_id=1003668029 (accessed 20 November 2009).

Calder, S. (2008) *No Frills: The Truth Behind the Low-Cost Revolution in the Skies*, London: Virgin Books.

Caves, R. and Gosling, G. (1999) *Strategic Airport Planning*, Oxford: Pergamon.

Davison, L. and Ryley, T. (2009) 'Tourism destination preferences of low-cost airline users in the East Midlands', *Journal of Transport Geography*, in press.

de Neufville, R. (2006) 'Accommodating low cost airlines at main airports', Working Paper, Massachusetts Institute of Technology.

Dennis, N. (2007) 'End of the free lunch? The responses of traditional European airlines to the low-cost carrier threat', *Journal of Air Transport Management*, Volume 13, Issue 5, pp. 311–321.

Dennis, N. (2007) 'Stimulation or saturation? Perspectives on European low-cost airline market and prospects for growth', *Journal of Air Transport Management*, Volume 13, Issue 5, pp. 311.

Dobruszkes, F. (2006) 'An analysis of European low-cost airlines and their networks', *Journal of Transport Geography*, Volume 14, Issue 4, pp. 249–264.

Dobruszkes, F. (2009) 'New Europe, new low-cost air services', *Journal of Transport Geography*, Volume 17, Issue 6, pp. 423–432.

Doganis, R. (2005) *The Airline Business*, Oxford: Routledge.

Dresner, M., Lin, J. and Windle, R. (1996) 'The impact of low-cost carriers on airport and route competition', *Journal of Transport Economics and Policy*, Volume 30, Issue 3, pp. 309.

easyJet (2007) 'easyJet signs break-through distribution deals with Amadeus and Galileo for the corporate travel market', online: www.easyjet.com/EN/news/amadeus_and_galileo_for_the_corporate_travel_marke.html (accessed 20 November 2009).

ELFAA (2004) *Liberalization of European Air Transport: The Benefits of Low Fares Airlines to Consumers, Airports, Regions and the Environment*, Brussels: European Low Fares Airlines Association.

ELFAA (2005) 'Challenges facing low fares airlines: The European perspective', Asia Pacific Low-cost Airline Symposium – Singapore, 26 January 2005.

Esplugas, C., Teixeira, P., Lopez-Pita, A. and Saña, A. (2005) 'Threats and opportunities for high speed rail transport in competition with the low-cost air operators', Thredbo 9, 5–9 September, Lisbon.

Fewings, R. (1999) 'Provision of European airport infrastructure', *Avmark Aviation Economist*, Volume 7, pp. 18–20.

Francis, G., Dennis, N., Ison, S. and Humphreys, I. (2007) 'The transferability of the low-cost model to long-haul airline operations', *Tourism Management*, Volume 28, Issue 2, pp. 391–398.

Francis, G., Fidato, A. and Humphreys, I. (2003) 'Airport–airline interaction: The impact of low-cost carriers on two European airports', *Journal of Air Transport Management*, Volume 9, Issue 4, pp. 267–273.

Francis, G., Humphreys, I. and Ison, S. (2004) 'Airports' perspectives on the growth of low-cost airlines and the remodeling of the airport–airline relationship', *Tourism Management*, Volume 25, Issue 4, pp. 507–514.

Francis, G., Humphreys, I., Ison, S. and Aicken, M. (2006) 'Where next for low cost airlines? A spatial and temporal comparative study', *Journal of Transport Geography*, Volume 14, Issue 2, pp. 83–94.

Franke, M. (2004) 'Competition between network carriers and low-cost carriers: Retreat battle or breakthrough to a new level of efficiency?', *Journal of Air Transport Management*, Volume 10, Issue 1, pp. 15–21.

Fröid, O. (2008) 'Perspectives for a future high-speed train in the Swedish domestic travel market', *Journal of Transport Geography*, Volume 16, Issue 4, pp. 268–277.

Gillen, D. and Gados, A. (2008) 'Airlines within airlines: Assessing the vulnerabilities of mixing business models', *Research in Transportation Economics*, Volume 24, pp. 25–35.

Gillen, D. and Lall, A. (2004) 'Competitive advantage of low-cost carriers: Some implications for airports', *Journal of Air Transport Management*, Volume 10, Issue 1, pp. 41–50.

Givoni, M. (2006) 'Development and impact of the modern high-speed train: A review', *Transport Reviews*, Volume 26, Issue 5, pp. 593–611.

Graf, L. (2005) 'Incompatibilities of the low-cost and network carrier business models within the same airline grouping', *Journal of Air Transport Management*, Volume 11, pp. 313–327.

Graham, B. and Shaw, J. (2008) 'Low-cost airlines in Europe: Reconciling liberalization and sustainability', *GEOFORUM*, Volume 39, Issue 3, pp. 1439–1451.

Graham, B. and Vowles, T. (2006) 'Carriers within carriers: A strategic response to low-cost airline competition', *Transport Reviews*, Volume 26, Issue 1, pp. 105–126.

Gross, S. and Schröder, A. (2007) *Handbook of Low Cost Airlines: Strategies, Business, and Market Environment*, Berlin: Erich Schmidt Verlag.

Humphreys, I., Ison, S. and Francis, G. (2006) 'A review of the airport–low cost airline relationship', *Review of Network Economics*, Volume 5, Issue 4, pp. 413–420.

Ito, H. and Lee, D. (2003) 'Incumbent responses to lower cost entry: Evidence from the U.S. airline industry', Working Paper, Providence, RI: Brown University.

Klaas, T. and Klein, J. (2005) 'Strategic airline positioning in the German low-cost carrier', in: Delfmann, W., Baum, H., Auerbach, S. and Albers, S. (eds) *Strategic Management in the Aviation Industry*, Aldershot: Ashgate, pp. 199–142.

Lawton, T. (2002) *Cleared to Take Off*, Aldershot: Ashgate.

Macário, R. (2008) 'Airports of the future: Essentials for a renewed business model', *European Journal of Transport and Infrastructure Research*, Volume 8, Issue 2, pp. 165–182.

Macário, R. and Van de Voorde, E. (2009) 'The impact of the economic crisis on the EU air transport sector', Directorate General for Internal Policies Policy Department B: Structural and Cohesion Policies, Transport and Tourism IP/B/TRAN/IC/2009_055, PE 431.570, October 2009, European Parliament, October 2009.

Macário, R., Reis, V., Viegas, J., Meersman, H., Montiero, F., Van de Voorde, E., Vanelslander, T., Mackenzie-Williams, P. and Schmidt, H. (2007) 'The consequences of the growing European low-cost airline sector', Policy Department Structural and Cohesion Policies, European Parliament, Study: IP/B/TRAN/IC/2006-185.

Mason, K. (2001) 'Marketing low-cost airline services to business travellers', *Journal of Air Transport Management*, Volume 7, Issue 2, pp. 103–109.

Mason, K. and Morrison, W. (2008) 'Towards a means of consistently comparing airline business models with an application to the "low cost" airline sector', *Research in Transportation Economics*, Volume 24, pp. 75–84.

Meersman, H., Van de Voorde, E. and Vanelslander, T. (2008) 'The air transport sector after 2010: A modified market and ownership structure', *European Journal of Transport and Infrastructure Research*, Volume 8, Issue 2, pp. 71–90.

MINTeL (2006) 'Low-cost airlines', Mintel International Group.

Morrell, P. (2005) 'Airlines within airlines: An analysis of US network airline responses to low cost carriers', *Journal of Air Transport Management*, Volume 11, Issue 5, pp. 303–312.

O'Connell, J. and Williams, G. (2005) 'Passengers' perceptions of low cost airlines and full service carriers: A case study involving Ryanair, Aer Lingus, Air Asia and Malaysia airlines', *Journal of Air Transport Management*, Volume 11, Issue 4, pp. 259–272.

Rothengatter, W. (1997) 'Liberalisation and structural reform in the freight transport sector in Europe', OECD Joint Session of Trade and Environment Experts, Paris.

Sinha, D. (2001) *Deregulation and Liberalisation of the Airline Industry: Asia, Europe, North America and Oceania*, Aldershot: Ashgate.

Taneja, N. (2004) *Airline Survival Kit*, Aldershot: Ashgate.

Travelport (2009) 'Italian low cost carrier signs up for GDS participation', online: http://travelport.mediaroom.com/index.php?s=43&item=451 (accessed 20 November 2009).

Warnock-Smith, D. and Potter, A. (2005) 'An exploratory study into airport choice factors for European low-cost airlines', *Journal of Air Transport Management*, Volume 11, Issue 6, pp. 388–392.

Windle, R. and Dresner, M. (1999) 'Competitive responses to low cost carrier entry', *Transportation Research Part E*, Volume 35, Issue 1, pp. 59–75.

York Aviation (2004) 'The social and economic impact of airports in Europe.'

5 Airline performance prediction

Sveinn Vidar Gudmundsson

Any form of life which insulates itself too successfully against pain fails to notice any change in its environment until it is too late.

Hermann Korn (in Martin, 1957)

1 Introduction

Over the last decade the airline industry has experienced extreme financial adversity. Whilst external low probability but high impact factors have been partially to blame some airlines have done worse than others. Predicting difference in airlines' financial performance is of interest for various stakeholders. A performance, distress or bankruptcy prediction model can be used by financial institutions to assess the financial health of a company in order to calculate the likelihood of recovering a loan or an investment. Such models can also be used as an early warning system in order to initiate change or proactive turnaround.

There are different definitions of distress, bankruptcy and performance relevant to what follows in this chapter. Using as an example the different types of bankruptcy under the US Bankruptcy Code[1] helps to clarify and distinguish between different types of prediction objectives. *Bankruptcy prediction* can be seen as the equivalent to predicting the probability of filing under Chapter 7 (total liquidation) of the US Bankruptcy Code; *distress prediction* can be seen as the probability of filing under Chapter 11 (reorganization); whilst *performance prediction* can be seen as the probability of a firm incurring *profit* or *loss* in a future year.

This chapter introduces a neural network approach to predict airline performance. Although much performance prediction research has focused on corporate distress[2] and bankruptcy, little has been done on *performance prediction* focusing on firms' operating profit or loss. Performance prediction is concerned with variation in performance, with or without distress, as defined before, since a firm can incur operating loss without being in immediate danger of not meeting obligations or heading for liquidation. Airlines are peculiar in that industry structure imposes strong downward pressure on margins, increasing vulnerability to changes, both internal and external, that affect productivity and utilization of resources, in other words profitability.

From a methodological consideration, focusing on performance opposed to distress, the concern is primarily with prediction accuracy and stability when using future data. Hence, the robustness of the model is based on its ability to detect subtle variations in airlines' operating characteristics that can cause shift from loss to profit or vice versa. To capture these variations the research presented in this chapter compares two approaches, namely a single year and a multi-year training set: a single-year training set is the tradition in distress prediction. Since a performance prediction model is not focused on bankruptcy (termination event) or distress (not meeting obligations) the performance prediction model has to capture the dynamism of airline operations from year to year and its influence on performance.

A failure prediction model based on financial ratios does not indicate "what" has gone wrong if a company fails, because financial ratios are symptomatic rather than causal by nature. Examples exist of managers trying to improve "the ratios" without addressing underlying problems (Altman, 1993). Hence, it is of interest to develop prediction models based on variables that reflect better operational decisions. Using non-financial variables can accomplish this to a degree.

Financial distress prediction models are generally considered of little use in multi-country samples due to differences in accounting laws, and differences in the business and political climate of different countries (ibid.). Again, national biasing factors can be partially controlled by focusing the models on non-financial variables. What is more, in the case of airlines often there is only one airline or a few airlines operating in a single country making an industry-specific prediction model for one country impossible.

Using multi-year data to construct prediction models is still relatively under-explored. Berg (2006) developed a multi-year model, and compared it with a one-year model and found that the multi-year model exhibited robustness to yearly fluctuations that was not present in the one-year model. Similar results were reported by Vieira *et al.* (2009) using three years of data applying several different methodologies including a multi-layered neural network. Consequently, a multi-year data model was expected to capture better the year-to-year changes causing fluctuations in airline profitability.

Therefore, the objective in this research was to construct a neural network *performance prediction* model, a *multi-country single industry* model and to compare *a multi-year* and *single year* model. The industry is international airlines, the data used is *non-financial*, and input parameters were selected on *significant difference of the means* between the two performance states. In the following sections an overview is given of performance measurement, distress prediction and airline industry-specific prediction models. Then the methodology is explained, followed by research findings, and conclusions.

2 Overview of performance measurement

Before introducing performance prediction it is necessary to introduce performance measurement at large. A number of studies have been conducted that cite management as the main contributor to corporate success or failure (Peters and Waterman, 1982; Kotter and Heskett, 1992; Collins and Porras, 1994; Foster and Kaplan, 2001; Joyce *et al.*, 2003). *In Search of Excellence* (Peters and Waterman, 1982) was the first popular book in a long stream of publications that followed, most of which have failed to come up with a plausible theory or sustainable prescription for business success. Varadarajan and Ramanujam (1990), criticized the Peters and Waterman book on various counts. They stated that the generalizations of the book were not timeless, that it omitted factors such as proprietary technology, market dominance and control of raw materials, and finally that the definition of "excellence" was faulty. Many of these studies lack rigour in research design, and employ faulty sampling techniques. Rosenzweig (2007) talks about a "halo-effect," the tendency of human beings to draw specific conclusions from general impressions, causing people to praise company management and strategy in good times, and by the same token find fault in bad times, without any major changes having taken place in the company in between the two states. Rosenzweig (2007, p. 15) asserts that company performance cannot be assumed to follow some law of physics, to be accurate and predictive, as most studies on performance have been shaped by the dependent variable they are supposed to explain. His observations cut at the root of positivism, the philosophical view holding that all areas of investigation, including the social sciences, can be explained by the methods of the natural sciences (see Hacking, 1981). The problem with this perspective, in the context of performance, is the interdependency of decisions of different companies competing within a restricted space of resources and clientele. What is important to grasp is that performance is relative and not absolute (Rozensweig, 2007; Buzzell and Gale, 1987). As a matter of fact, the authors of one of the more sensible books on business performance, *The PIMs Principle: linking strategy to performance*[3] (Buzzell and Gale, 1987) shy away from attaching to their findings an underlying theory or principles.

Despite the lack of plausible theory, businesses do go through a life-cycle, from birth to eventual demise. Several researchers have tried to explain what differs between succeeding and failing companies at different life-cycle stages. Flamholtz and Randle (2000) conclude that many firms develop an organizational development gap, "growing pains." The gap can occur for two reasons, namely too fast growth or poor adaptation of infrastructure to size increases. Miller and Friesen (1983) similarly find in a study, based on the life-cycle concept, that increases in information processing and decision-making sophistication occurred at early life-cycle stages, and that successful companies had more decision-making complexity, especially in analysis, multiplexity and integration. They also found that in successful phases companies tended to have higher level of innovation-related activity but not risk-taking. In fact greater risk-taking took place among companies surviving the birth-phase, but the opposite was true for the decline-phase when unsuccessful companies were more prone to risk-taking. Gudmundsson (1998) performed life-cycle analysis of airlines proposing seven phases based on revenue categories.[4] His findings had many similarities to Miller and Friesen's (1983) life-cycle phases, but differed by suggesting that new-entrant airlines operating in a deregulated environment were prone to collapse rather than decline, the latter being the case with the pre-deregulation/liberalization incumbent carriers. The reason for this phenomenon has been linked to "anchor mass," defined as investment and trading reputation necessary to buffer against sudden failure. A carrier that is overtrading does not build anchor mass as growth is pursued at the cost of profitability, draining investors' faith and reducing the financial flexibility necessary to reach the upper phases of the airline life-cycle (Gudmundsson, 1998). There are few exceptions to this phenomenon, Southwest Airlines being the most noteworthy, sticking hard to its controlled growth policy for most of its life-cycle, enabling the airline to edge itself slowly through to the *mega carrier phase*.

The life-cycle concept is important, primarily in demonstrating that fewer and fewer companies exist in a population established in a given year, as time passes. However, the theory does not substantiate that all organizations will eventually die. In fact a company having perfect ability to adapt to its environment will survive indefinitely. In other words, an adaptable company may be engaged in a totally different business 50 years from foundation.

3 Distress prediction: prior research

Four main categories of models have been used for the prediction task: univariate and multivariate linear models, probability models (Logit, Probit, Logistic Regression) and genetic models (Neural Networks, Genetic Algorithms, etc.).[5] The prediction methodologies have been in constant development although advancement has been mostly in the robustness of the models over longer time periods and in out-of-sample predictions.

3.1 Univariate analysis

The first notable application of univariate analysis (UVA) was by Beaver (1966). Using this approach the predictive ability of financial ratios is analysed on a one-by-one basis. Beaver used 79 industrial firms in his sample over a five-year period. Each non-failed firm was matched with a failed firm by industry and asset size. The data analysis proceeded in three steps: a comparison of means, a dichotomous classification test, and analysis of likelihood ratios. The comparison of means showed that the means of each ratio were significantly different for the failed and the non-failed firms. With the dichotomous classification, Beaver arrayed each ratio to a cut-off point. The best performing ratio was the ratio of *cash flow to total debt*, in that it showed the minimum per centage error in predicting the two groups in the sample studied. Although Beaver's predictors perform fairly well, the main difficulty with his approach is that the classification can take place for only one ratio at a time. The potential exists for finding conflicting classification of any given firm according to various ratios.

3.2 Multivariate linear discriminant analysis

Altman (1968) argued that the financial status of a firm is actually multidimensional, and no single ratio is able to capture those dimensions; thus, a multivariate approach would be necessary to capture the dimensions. Consequently, the largest body of the early academic failure prediction literature applied discriminant analysis (DMA). DMA works in the way that a linear discriminant function is used to distinguish between distressed and non-distressed firms. The discriminant function transforms the values of the individual variables of the firm into a single discriminant score (*z score*), which is then used arbitrarily to classify the firms into the failed or non-failed group (Frederikslust, 1978). In his pioneering DMA work, Altman used a sample of 33 manufacturers who filed for bankruptcy under Chapter X of the US National Bankruptcy Act during the period 1946–1965.

Altman included 22 ratios from which five were finally selected as the greatest discriminators of the dichotomous dependent variable. The model took the form,

$$Z = 0.021X1 + 0.014X2 + 0.033X3 + 0.006X4 + 0.999X5$$

where *Z* is the overall index and X1 is *Working Capital/Total Assets*, X2 *Retained Earnings/Total Assets*, X3 *Earnings Before Interest and Taxes/Total Assets*, X4 *Market Value of Equity/Book Value of Total Debt*, and X5 is *Sales/ Total Assets*.

The principal aim in failure prediction is to reduce the misclassification error of the models in order to increase the prediction ability of the model. This can be tested on a hold-out sample that represents similar characteristics to the sample on which the model is based. The accuracy of the original Altman model in the prediction of bankruptcy was 95 per cent one year prior to bankruptcy and 72 per cent two years prior to bankruptcy. In the third year prior to bankruptcy the accuracy fell rapidly to 48 per cent or no better than a flip of a coin. Most studies that followed attempted to improve the Beaver and Altman models in one way or another. Edmister (1972), for example, recognized that when many closely correlated variables are included, the resulting function is likely to be biased towards the sample from which it was developed. Thus, he eliminated highly correlated variables from the model. He also included in the study only those ratios that were found to be significant predictors of bankruptcy in previous empirical studies. The seven-variable discriminant function was accurate at an overall accuracy rate of 93 per cent one year prior.

Altman, Haldeman and Narayanan (1977) published an improvement of Altman's original model, where the new model had 53 bankrupt and 58 non-bankrupt firms, mixing two industries, a controversial practice in bankruptcy prediction. Classification accuracy of this new model rose considerably with overall classification accuracy of 93 per cent one year prior to failure, 89 per cent two years prior to failure, 83 per cent three years prior, 80 per cent four years prior, and finally 77 per cent five years prior to failure. Edmister (1972) also achieved quite good results in his model which utilized dummy variables to indicate upward or downward trend in ratios, a new methodology he proposed.

Other researchers have attempted to use different prediction techniques such as conditional probability models and neural networks.

3.3 Conditional probability models

Conditional probability models (Probit, Logit and LRA, etc.) are used to estimate the probability of occurrence of a choice or outcome. These models use the coefficients of the independent variables to predict the probability of occurrence of a dichotomous dependent variable. A cumulative probability distribution is needed in order to constrain the predicted values to comply with the limiting values (0 and 1) of probability distributions. Collins and Green (1982) find the logistic method more theoretically appealing in bankruptcy prediction than MDA, since it has few of the data requirements of MDA analysis. Another reason is that the logistic cumulative distribution function is a "sigmoid curve" (S-curve) that has the "threshold" trait that a bankruptcy forecasting problem logically requires. Furthermore, the LRA formulation is more robust to distribution assumptions being a "distribution free" methodology.

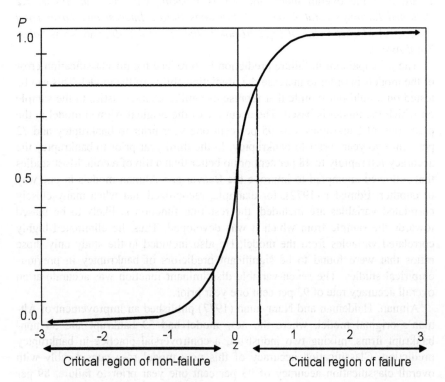

Figure 5.1 LRA S-curve.

In LRA the determination of the "threshold" is important because if the probability score falls along the lower bend of the curve, p (0 to 0.2), the probability of failure is practically 0. However, if the score passes the bend and falls along the growth section of the curve, p (0.2 to 0.5), the probability of failure increases dramatically. Hence, there is little increase in the probability of failure as the change in the ratio falls along the upper bend of the curve, p (0.8 to 1). Thus, the "breaking" point falls somewhere in the middle of the growth section of the curve, p (0.5). The logistic regression function produces a Z value that is transformed by a function into a probability. The Z is the linear combination of the resulting model, taking the form,

$$p(\text{failure}) = \frac{1}{1 + e^{-z}}$$

where,

$$Z = B_0 + B_1 X_1 + B_2 X_2 + \ldots + B_p X_p$$

$e = 2.718$ (the base of the natural logarithms)

Deakin (1972) introduced one of the first probabilistic bankruptcy prediction models reporting better results in terms of misclassification, more than one year from failure than the Altman model. Some other early applications of probabilistic methods in financial distress prediction are those of Ohlson (1980), Santomero and Vinso (1977) and Martin (1977). Probability models are also advantageous over discriminant models in that significant coefficients can be interpreted in terms of the relationship with the dependent variable.

3.4 Neural networks

The first application of neural networks to distress prediction occurred in the early 1990s (Tam and Kiang, 1992; Salchenberger, Cinar and Lash, 1992) on bank failures. Tam and Kiang (1992) reported in a misclassification test on a hold-out sample of 44 banks (22 failed and 22 non-failed) in one- and two-year periods, that the neural network remained the best classifier in terms of low type 2^6 error and overall classification. The neural network representing ten hidden units achieved the second highest accuracy rate of 89 per cent, compared to 92 per cent for the best performing model, a logistic regression model specified from the same data.

This study and most studies that followed using the neural network approach reported similar or better performance than other methodologies commonly used. It was especially in out-of-sample prediction the neural network models showed some promise (Udo, 1993; Lacher, Coats, Sharma and Fant, 1995).

A neural network is a computer-based computational model that simulates the functional aspects of biological neural networks. Artificial neurons are interconnected and process information using computation. A neural network is an adaptive system that changes connectors based on information processed during a learning phase. Neural networks are a statistical data modelling tool of non-linear nature that finds patterns in data to model complex relationships between inputs and outputs.

As shown in Figure 5.2, a feedforward multilayer neural network has an *input layer* of source nodes and an *output layer* of neurons (Huang *et al.*, 1994). The output layer, if a prediction task, will yield approximation scores that may or may not match the target due to error. Figure 5.3 shows a hypothetical output where two cases are obviously misclassified.

The input and output layers are therefore the interfaces with the external environment of the network. In addition to these two layers, there are usually one or more layers of hidden neurons that extract important information contained in the input data.

The neural network can be represented as a mathematical function (Rumelhart *et al.*, 1994),

$$I_i = \sum_j w_{ij} O_j + \phi_i, \text{ and } O_i = \frac{1}{1 + e^{I_i}}$$

where

$I_i =$ input of unit i,

$O_i =$ output of unit i,

$w_{ij} =$ connection weight between unit i and j,

$\varphi_i =$ bias of unit i.

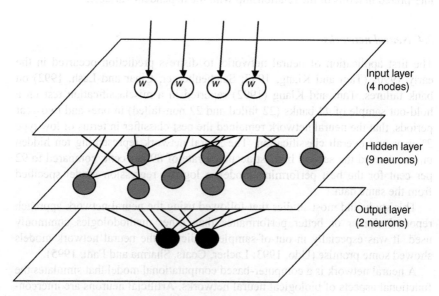

Figure 5.2 Three-layered neural network.

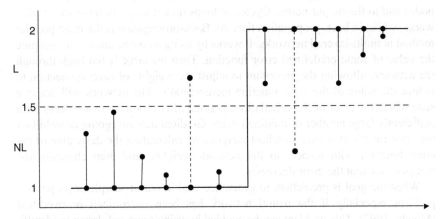

Figure 5.3 Neural network classification diagram.

The function works as follows (Tam and Kiang, 1992, p. 929): "A unit *i* receives input signals from other units, aggregates these signals based on input function I_i, and generates an output signal based on an output function O_i (sometimes called a transfer function). The output signal is then routed to other units as directed by the topology of the network."

Neural networks offer the possibility of learning if given a specific task to solve, in this research it is provided with a prediction target (1 = *profitable*; 2 = *unprofitable*), and a class of functions *F*, solving the task in some optimal sense. The function $f(x)$ is defined as a composition of other functions $g_i(x)$, further defined as a composition of other functions, hence the term *network*. This can be conveniently represented as a network structure, with lines depicting the dependencies between variables (*see* Figure 5.2). A widely used type of composition is the nonlinear weighted sum, or $f(x) = K\left(\sum_i w_i g_i(x)\right)$, where the activation

function *K* is a predefined function (hyperbolic tangent), and where collection of functions g_i is a vector $g = (g_1, g_2, \ldots g_n)$. The neuron outputs a signal if the activation is greater than the threshold value, otherwise it outputs zero.

The most important concept in neural network learning is the cost function, as it is a measure, for the problem to be solved, of how far a particular solution is from an optimal solution. Hence, the learning algorithm searches through the space of possible solutions to find an optimal function with the smallest possible cost. Thus, learning entails defining a cost function $C:f^*$ such that, for the optimal solution f^*, $C(f^*) \le C(f).\forall f \in F$, no solution has a cost less than the optimal solution.

There are two fundamental types of neural networks, feedforward and back-propagation. The earliest neural networks were feedforward and can be considered the simplest type of neural network. The information moves in only one direction, and in this type of network, from the input nodes, through the hidden nodes and to the output nodes. Cycles or loops do not occur in feedforward networks, whilst in back-propagation they do. Back-propagation is the most popular method in multi-layered networks. It works by using a correct answer to compute the value of some predefined error function. Then the error is fed back through the network, allowing the algorithm to adjust the weights of each connection to reduce the value of the error function incrementally. The network will detect a state where the error of the calculations is small after repeating this process for a sufficiently large number of training cycles. Gradient descent (going downhill on the error function) is used to adjust weights, by calculating the derivative of the error function with respect to the network weights, and then changing the weights such that the error decreases.

When the goal is prediction, to generalize well in out-of-sample cases poses a problem especially if the neural network has been overtrained or overfitted (Moody, 1992). This problem can be avoided by using cross-validation to identify whether overtraining has occurred and select hyperparameters[7] to minimize the generalization error. Another way is to use regularization, which in statistical learning theory implies a goal to minimize empirical risk and the structural risk, in other words to minimize the error in the training set and the predicted error in the unseen data due to overfitting. In the presence of noise[8] in the target values overfitting is more likely to occur (Moody, 1992). Similarly, measurement error in the inputs is also considered noise in the data. The greater the level of noise, in these two respects, the lower the accuracy of network generalization no matter how extensive the training that takes place. If cases have finite variance and noise is independent, a trained network using least-squares produces outputs that approximate the conditional mean of the target values (Bishop, 1995; White, 1990).

Certain assumptions about noise are necessary. Usually, the noise distribution is assumed to have a zero mean and finite variance. The noise present in different cases is assumed to be independent or to follow some known stochastic model, such as an autoregressive process. The more that is known about the noise distribution, the more effectively the network can be trained (McCullagh and Nelder, 1989).

In some cases neural networks are highly sample specific and generalization of the model on out-of-sample data consequently limited. In using a neural network, the purpose was specifically to achieve high generalizability. Thus, it is necessary to estimate the generalization loss, through a generalization loss algorithm (see Lehman and Casella, 1998); in other words to stop training early enough to avoid overfitting, given an acceptable generalization loss target to avoid underfitting of the network.

3.5 *Airline performance and distress prediction*

Bankruptcy and distress prediction for airlines was pioneered by two financially based DMA studies in the early 1980s (Gritta, 1982; Altman and Gritta, 1984). In these two studies generic bankruptcy models, not specifically developed for the airline industry, were applied on airline data to assess the risk of bankruptcy. Later a dedicated MDA model for the airline industry appeared, named AIRSCORE (Chow *et al.*, 1991), using three ratios: *interest/total liabilities, operating revenues per air mile*, and *shareholder equity/total liabilities*. This model was reported to achieve accuracy rates of between 76 and 83 per cent (cf. Gritta *et al.*, 2008). A comparison study of financial and non-financial bankruptcy prediction models for new-entrant airlines was performed by Gudmundsson (1999) who applied the LRA approach in comparing various models constructed on data derived from a qualitative survey among airline managers and a quantitative data source containing traffic and financial data of new-entrant airlines. His main finding was that non-financial models performed better two and three years prior to distress than financial models, while the latter performed better one year earlier. These models along with *P-Score* (Pilarski and Dinh, 1999) were the first probabilistic models specified for air carrier bankruptcy prediction. The next methodology leap was neural network models that appeared for air carriers in the late 1990s, one for major US airlines (Davalos *et al.*, 1999), another for smaller US carriers (Gritta *et al.*, 2000) and the third specified on a mix of large and small US carriers (Gritta *et al.*, 2002). These studies achieved 100 per cent (large carriers), 88 per cent (small carriers) and 77 per cent (small and large carriers) one year prior. In these three early studies generalization of the models was reported to be a problem using neural networks and out-of-sample testing was not performed (Gritta *et al.*, 2008).

Having covered the general and specific airline-related bankruptcy and distress models the following section will cover the methodology used to build a performance prediction model for international airlines.

4 Methodology

There are several methodology issues in using prediction models on performance data: first, the lack of theory guiding variable selection; second, data usually violates normality and other statistical assumptions; third, sampling design cannot meet randomness assumptions due to large proportionality differences between the two groups under observation; and fourth, the need to retain large enough hold-out sample for validating purposes (Huang *et al.*, 1994).

The first issue above cannot be directly addressed and has been explained in previous sections of this chapter. However, financial variables are inherently macro level, whilst non-financial variables applied in this research are micro level (Gudmundsson, 2004). We also established that the importance of relative performance rendered prescriptive accounts of success strategies useless or weak at best: improvement may be reflected in a positive change in a ratio for an individual carrier and still it may be a poor performer if other carriers improve faster. Development in relative performance can be partially captured by using a multi-year training set, as was done in this research. Using the neural network approach, data assumptions can be relaxed, especially if compared to DMA. For instance, a neural network does not require equal size of the two groups under observation. However, in the study, due to limited data availability, data gathering did not allow random sampling from the population as often recommended. The fourth issue mentioned, the use of a hold-out sample, was addressed by testing the neural network on future years, with new data. For example, the multi-year model was trained with three years of data, using results one year posterior to each year in the training set, then the network was tested one and two years into the future using operating results two years and three years posterior.

A good trait of the network is prediction stability, i.e. ability to predict future years with similar accuracy. Unlike distress and failure models, where an event takes place causing termination or major reorganization, a performance model is simply concerned with operating loss or profit. The event as such may or may not threaten the existence of the firm and may fluctuate from year to year depending on various internal and external factors. Hence there is not so much need or sense in predicting a loss several years before it occurs, unlike the case with failure prediction. Since airline performance is relative, affected by the performance of other airlines and technological advances, it is unlikely that a single static network will perform well over a long period, although it may perform well over several years before being updated. Again, a multi-year model should be more robust to changes in the efficiency frontier and consequently relative changes within an industry.

4.1 Data description

To this it is necessary to add that classification error of failure prediction models can be explained on the one hand by noise in the data, and on the other hand by the fact that companies are dynamic identities that can at any time return to profitability due to change processes, extraordinary circumstances or relative position in industry. In view of that there will always be misclassification.

The airline industry is in many respects convenient for non-financial distress prediction because of international data available through various statistical programs. The data-set used in this research consists of ratios, as well as continuous and nominal variables collected over a period of five years (t_{-2}, t_{-1}, t_0, t_{+1}, t_{+2}) for 41 commercial airlines worldwide, covering economic, fleet, traffic and government equity. Year t_0 is denoted as base year. In the base year there were 18 unprofitable (NP) and 23 profitable airlines (P). The operating profit and loss figures were derived from airline annual reports, and the *Airline Business* and the *Air Transport World* magazines. An airline was classified as unprofitable in any year (t_x), when showing operating loss the following year (t_{x+1}). The training was performed using data of the first three years (t_{-2}, t_{-1}, t_0); the base year (t_0) was used for training the single year network. The last two years (t_{+1}, t_{+2}) were used as hold-out sets to test the generalizability of the network.[9]

The data was gathered from airlines' annual reports, the *Air Transport World Airline Report*, *IATA World Airline Traffic Statistics* and the *ICAO Statistics*.

Table 5.1 shows how the sample is spread geographically in the base year (t_0). Most airlines in the study are from Europe (39 per cent), but fewest from Africa (4.9 per cent) and the Middle East (4.9 per cent). Most non-profitable and profitable airlines come out of Europe (33 and 43 per cent respectively) at base year (t_0).[10]

Table 5.2 shows the fleet size of the non-profitable and profitable airlines at base year (t_0). One can see that in the sample the non-distressed airlines have larger fleet size than the distressed airlines in the 26–50 seat category (*P* 33 per cent; *UP* 20 per cent) and the 101–250 seat category (*P* 29 per cent; *UP* 10 per cent); the non-profitable airlines have more frequency in the categories of fewer than 25 passenger (*P* 14.3 per cent; *UP* 20 per cent) and 51–100 passenger aircraft (*P* 29 per cent; *UP* 40 per cent).

Table 5.3 shows the sample airlines and the initial performance classifications in the base year as well as government equity in the airline (shown if greater than 25 per cent).

4.2 The choice of variables

In the study an initial set of 16 variables, ratios, continuous and nominal, were created. Then variables were selected for the training set based on a *t*-test (see Table 5.5) using a grouping variable for the dichotomous dependent variable revealing three ratios and one continuous variable having statistically significant difference between unprofitable and profitable airlines. These were: (1) *passenger average haul* (ratio); (2) *departures per aircraft* (ratio); (3) *average age of fleet* (continuous); and (4) *available seat kilometres per employee* (ratio).

Table 5.1 Geographic spread of airlines in base year (t_0)

Region	# UP	# P	Total
Africa	2	0	2
Asia and Pacific	4	7	11
Europe	6	10	16
Latin America	4	2	6
Middle East	0	2	2
North America	2	2	4
	18	23	41

Table 5.2 Size of fleet according to loss and non-loss in base year (t_0)

Fleet size	# UP	# P	Total
<25	4	3	7
26–50	4	7	11
51–100	8	6	14
101–250	2	6	8
>250	0	1	1
	18	23	41

Table 5.3 Airlines categorized as loss and non-loss in base year (t_0)

Unprofitable (UP)	Passengers (000)	GEQ	Profitable (P)	Passengers (000)	GEQ
Aerolineas Argentina	4,025	0	Aer Lingus	5,506	1
Air Afrique	996	1	Aeromexico	7,816	1
Air India	3,011	1	Air Canada	16,203	0
Canadian Airlines	8,169	0	Air China	6,454	1
Garuda Indonesia	6,623	1	Air Europe	2,565	0
Iberia	2,2259	1	Air France	33,498	1
Malaysian Airlines	13,654	0	Air Malta	1,159	1
Malev	1,749	0	Air New Zealand	6,426	0
Olympic Airways	6,403	1	Alaska Airlines	13,029	0
Philippine Airlines	7,405	0	All Nippon Airways	41,471	0
Sabena	8,749	0	Ansett Australia	11,970	0
South African Airw.	5,117	1	Austrian Airlines	3,234	1
Tarom	908	1	British Airways	36,593	0
Transbrasil	2,895	0	British Midland Airways	5,975	0
Turkish Airlines	9,949	1	China Southern Airlines	14,455	1
TWA	23,909	0	El Al	2,729	0
Varig	11,215	0	Emirates	4,057	1
VASP	5,387	0	Finnair	6,771	1
			Japan Air System	19,518	0
			Korean Airlines	19,605	0
			Lan Chile	2,998	0
			SAS	21,507	1
			TAP Air Portugal	4,681	1
N = 18			*N* = 23		

Notes
GEQ = 1, government equity (equal to or greater than 25%); 0, no government equity.

Tables 5.5 and 5.7 give a detailed statistical description of each of the variables, the mean, standard deviation (S.D.) and the significant difference of the means between unprofitable and profitable airlines. From the table we see that unprofitable airlines had *longer haul per passenger, fewer departures per aircraft,* higher *average age of the fleet* and fewer *available seat kilometres per employee.* All the variables were significant for the multi-year data (see Table 5.5) at $p > 0.05$, except *passenger haul* that was significant at $p > 0.1$. Tables 5.4 and 5.6 show the correlations of the five variables included in the model, including the dependent variable *performance* that was significantly correlated with all the variables in the multi-year model. *Average age of fleet* and *average number of departures per aircraft* were significantly correlated with *average passenger haul*.

4.3 Variable description

PASS_HAU (P 1860; UP 2160; $p = 0.06$) a ratio, measures the *average number of kilometres flown per passenger* with the airline. There are two factors influencing this ratio, namely connectivity offered by the airline online and

Table 5.4 Multi-year data correlations (t_{-2}, t_{-1}, t_0)

$N = 123$	1	2	3	4	5
1 PASS_HAU	1.00				
2 DEP_AC	−0.42	1.00			
3 AGE_FLT	0.34	−0.05	1.00		
4 ASK_EMP	0.16	0.14	−0.03	1.00	
5 DISTRESS	0.20	−0.23	0.29	−0.18	1.00

Notes
Table shows Spearman's rho correlations. All coefficients > |0.18| are significant at $p > 0.05$ level.

average length of haul. An airline having high online[11] connectivity may have low to medium average length of haul but high average number of kilometres flown per passenger. Surprisingly, however, the average is higher for non-profitable airlines in the sample, indicating that there may be some important trade-offs between longer average distance travelled per passenger online. This could be for instance lower average fares charged for connecting flights than direct origin destination flights, or less productivity of resources.

DEP_AC (P 1629; UP 1362; $p = 0.02$) a ratio, measures the *average number of departures per aircraft* in the fleet. This is a ratio that captures both route structure characteristics and effective utilization of aircraft. The utilization of aircraft, given the large associated cost and capital outlay, is of utmost importance in airline management. Higher performing carriers may have higher number of departures per aircraft as a consequence of better network management (aircraft acquisition and allocation, schedule planning, etc.). An expected intervening factor is *average stage length*, i.e. a good performing carrier operating mostly long-distance routes should have *fewer departures per aircraft*. However, there was weak correlation between these two variables so regardless of long stage lengths better performing carriers may still achieve higher fleet utilization measured as departures per aircraft than a comparable low performance carrier.

AGE_FLT (P 9.0; UP 12; $p = 0.00$) a continuous variable, measures the *average age of the fleet* employed. In general, newer aircraft are more efficient to run than older aircraft. Older planes have higher maintenance costs and fuel consumption. Thus, higher average fleet age can be a characteristic of poorer performing airlines. There can be two different reasons for this. First, the financial situation of the airline does not allow the acquisition or leasing of new equipment. Second, fleet acquisition decision is influenced by political forces due to a governmental stake in the airline or by aircraft import restrictions.

ASK_EMP (P 2139557; UP 1796292; $p = 0.03$) a ratio, measures the *average available seat kilometres per employee*. This ratio measures employee productivity in terms of seats offered and distance. With the advent of deregulation (USA) and liberalization (EU) we have understood that a large difference can exist, between airlines, in terms of employee productivity. This appears to be a function of a business model employed (low-cost vs. network model, short-haul vs. long-haul, etc.), management of tasks undertaken (what the airline should engage in and what it should not), and outsourcing (what the airline is good at doing and what can be better done by specialists). Even in countries where labour is cheap one may assume that excessive numbers of employees compared to world industry average may have a detrimental impact on airline performance for reasons of higher transaction costs, longer decision-making chains, stronger resistance to change and less overall competitive dynamism of the respective airline.

Performance ($P = 1$; $UP = 2$) is a dependent nominal variable.[12] In this research the concern was to predict operating profit and loss stemming from decisions pertaining to operating characteristics of airlines.

5 Results

When performing the neural network training session, back-propagation was used, maximum number of iterations 15,000 and the Average Mean Squared Error (MSE) < 0.05.[13] Furthermore, at the end of the training session the best network in terms of MSE was retained. Table 5.8 shows the predictive power of the single year and multi-year neural networks.

Table 5.5 Multi-year descriptives (t_{-2}, t_{-1}, t_0)

		N	Mean	S.D.	t	Sig. (2-tailed)
PASS_HAU	P	79	1860	842.2	−1.9	0.058
	UP	44	2160	822.8		
DEP_AC	P	79	1629	621.0	2.3	0.022
	UP	44	1362	593.4		
AGE_FLT	P	79	9	3	−3.7	0.000
	UP	44	12	4		
ASK_EMP	P	79	2139557	882378	2.2	0.029
	UP	44	1796292	704548		

Notes
t = significance test for difference of means.

Table 5.6 Single year data correlations (t_0)

N = 41	1	2	3	4	5
1 PASS_HAU	1.00				
2 DEP_AC	−0.43				
3 AGE_FLT	0.39	−0.08	1.00		
4 ASK_EMP	0.16	0.11	0.04	1.00	
5 PERFORM	0.12	−0.16	0.36	−0.18	1.00

Notes
Table shows Spearman's rho correlations. All coefficients > |0.30| are significant at $p > 0.05$ level.

The single year network has 102 hidden units and the importance of the inputs (see Table 5.9) ranged from 20 to 34 per cent. The Y1 performance was excellent, i.e. 0 per cent for type 1 and 8 per cent for type 2 error giving an overall classification accuracy of 96 per cent. Using the hold-out data, Y2 and Y3, the prediction performance deteriorated rapidly to 72 and 59 per cent respectively. In Y2 the type 1 error was 31 per cent and the type 2 error 24 per cent. In Y3 type 1 error was 42 per cent and type 2 error 41 per cent.

The multi-year model had 18 hidden units and the importance of inputs ranged from 20 to 30 per cent (see Table 5.9). Overall accuracy of the multi-year model was 91 per cent in Y1, 80 per cent in Y2 and 77 per cent in Y3. The model performed better on type 2 error than type 1 error, i.e. classifying profitable airlines correctly as profitable. In Y1, type 1 error was 7 per cent and type 2 error 10 per cent, in Y2 25 and 16 per cent and in Y3 32 and 14 per cent respectively.

6 Discussion

In this chapter it has been shown that a multi-year data set for performance prediction gives more robust and stable prediction accuracy on hold-out data two

Table 5.7 Single year descriptives (t_0)

		N	Mean	S.D.	t	Sig. (2-tailed)
PASS_HAU	P	25	1,946	889	−0.48	0.637
	UP	16	2,076	796		
DEP_AC	P	25	1,700	708	1.37	0.180
	UP	16	1,422	500		
AGE_FLT	P	25	10	3	−2.45	0.023
	UP	16	13	5		
ASK_EMP	P	25	2,283,721	953,289	1.21	0.232
	UP	16	1,935,940	794,248		

Table 5.8 Classification comparison of single and multi-year models

Single year model Hidden units = 102	Classification			
	% overall correct (Total error)	% correct UP (Type 1 error)	% correct P (Type 2 error)	N
Y1 NN$_{s1}$	96.0% (2)	100.0% (0)	92.0% (2)	41
Y2 NN$_{s2}$	72.4% (12)	68.8% (5)	76.0% (6)	41
Y3 NN$_{s3}$	58.5% (12)	57.9% (8)	59.1% (9)	41
Multi-year model Hidden units = 18				
Y1 NN$_{m1}$	91.2% (12)	93.2% (3)	89.9% (8)	123
Y2 NN$_{m3}$	79.5% (8)	75.0% (4)	84.0% (4)	41
Y3 NN$_{m3}$	77.4% (9)	68.4% (6)	86.4% (3)	41

Table 5.9 Variable importance in models

Input	Multi-year %	Single year %
pass_haul	19.8	24.1
dep_ac	28.4	19.8
age_flt	29.9	21.6
ask_empl	21.8	34.5

and three years into the future, than a single year model. A perfect prediction capability of a performance prediction model is unattainable due to noise that is usual in the data, i.e. carriers shifting from a non-distress state to a distress state and vice versa, showing the characteristics of one over the other in the short to medium term. However, the good generalization trait of the multi-year model shows that a performance prediction model for international airlines is attainable and perfectly comparable to single country, single industry financially based models reported so far (see Table 5.10).

The multi-year network demonstrated a fairly high prediction accuracy of 91 per cent overall and relatively stable prediction performance in Y2 and Y3, especially for type 2 error. Compared to other usual benchmark models (see Table 5.10) such as Altman (1968) the performance of the model was superior in Y3 and matching Beaver's (1966) results in Y3. Compared to airline models it had superior performance to Gritta *et al.*'s (2000) neural network model, one year previously. The same applied to the non-financial LRA model specified by Gudmundsson (1998) for US new-entrant airlines, which was outperformed in all three years.

An important feature of the models is the inclusion of effective prediction variables pertaining to productivity of the fleet and employees. Previous research, especially Oum and Yu (1998), demonstrated the importance of these measures to explain profitability differences among the world's airlines. Past research on failure prediction models has not improved the understanding of failure processes much, but rather has improved methodologies in segregating the two states in the dichotomous variable very slightly. Using a non-financial underpinning in a performance prediction model does cast more light on the underlying relationships, and leads to prediction results as good as in traditional financially based models. However, the neural network approach does suffer from the "black box" aspect of the hidden layer. If knowledge (theory) existed in how to connect the "hidden" units to the output units it would enhance interpretation, but since such knowledge does not exist the hidden units are fully connected usually in one or more layers (O'Leary, 1998). Nothwithstanding, it has been argued in the chapter that performance is a relative phenomenon that does not lend itself to prescriptions for success or avoidance of failure. That being said, performance, distress and bankruptcy prediction models do have their place, but with the understanding that their accuracy is far from being timeless.

Table 5.10 Comparison of misclassification rates of several prediction studies

Meth. Year[3]	Beaver (1966) Univariate		Altman (1968) MDA		Gritta et al. (2000) NN (US small airl.)		Gudmundsson (1998) LRA (US N.E. airl.)		Gudmundsson NN (I.A./M.Y.)[2]	
	Overall (%)	Type[1] I II (%)	Overall (%)	Type I II (%)	Overall (%)	Type I II (%)	Overall (%)	Type I II (%)	Overall (%)	Type I II (%)
1	87	17.4	95	6.3	88	9.3	83	17.17	91	7.10
2	79	26.6	83	28.6			75	22.28	80	25.16
3	77	28.6	48	na			72	28.28	77	32.14
4	76	29.2	29	na						
5	78	23.3	36	na						

Notes
1 Type I error is misclassifying a failed firm; Type II error is misclassifying a non-failed firm.
2 I.A. = international airlines; M.Y. = multi-year model.
3 The last model in the table predicts for years forward in time, whilst all the other models predict for years backward in time.

All in all, the international prediction model is promising and does lend confidence to the viability of a multi-country, non-financial performance prediction. It is evident that differences in economic and political environments do not interfere with the prediction capacity of the model and using multi-year data for network training captures to some extent the inherent dynamism of the industry.

Notes

1 There are two types of bankruptcy under the US Bankruptcy Code, Title 11 which concerns firms: Chapter 7 is basic liquidation, a straight bankruptcy; whilst Chapter 11 is reorganization, a form of corporate financial reorganization which typically allows companies to continue to function while they follow debt repayment plans. US airlines have used Chapter 11 bankruptcies extensively since deregulation. In Europe bankruptcy laws vary substantially from one country to another, too elaborate to cover in this chapter.

2 The Webster Dictionary gives a general definition of distress: "an acute financial hardship or being in great difficulty."

3 The PIMS methodology uses relative quality measurement, which is based on a questionnaire where respondents are led through a "quality profiling" where they identify the key product and service attributes that count in the purchase decision. These attributes are then rated by the subjects on an additive scale totalling 100, followed by rating of own performance compared to the performance of leading competitors for each attribute on a scale from 1 to 10.

4 There were seven stages in his airline evolution model: start-up, new entrant, transitional, interim major, modulation major, mega carrier and global carrier. Analysing new entrants in the US airlines in the first four stages tended to collapse rather than decline when facing financial adversity.

5 The resulting models can be based on financial ratios, non-financial ratios or a mixture of both.

6 *Type 1* error is classifying an unprofitable airline as profitable; *type 2* error is classifying a profitable airline as non-profitable.

7 A *hyperparameter* is a parameter of a prior probability distribution. A *prior probability distribution* means representing knowledge about an unknown quantity a priori before any data have been observed (Rubin *et al.*, 2003).

8 Noise is the presence of unpredictable variation in target values independent from the inputs of a network.

9 Operating results used were one year posterior to the annual training set.

10 These proportions in each group are not representative for the airline industry at large.

11 Online denotes a connecting flight with the same airline.

12 One can argue that as long as a non-profitable firm is not dissolved or liquidated it can be seen as lacking performance, because a turnaround is still possible. According to Asquith (1991) lacking performance can be associated with three main reasons: an industry downturn, high interest expense, or lack of performance relative to industry average.

13 Generalization loss level (set at 4 out of 10; 1 = low, 10 = high loss) was also specified to stop the network from overtraining. The generalization loss algorithm monitors validation error dynamics and training progress using several criteria.

References

Altman, E. I. (1968) Discriminant analysis and the prediction of corporate bankruptcy, *The Journal of Finance*, 23(4): 589–609.

Altman, E. I. (1993) *Corporate financial distress: a complete guide to predicting, avoiding and dealing with bankruptcy*, New York: John Wiley & Sons.

Altman, E. I. and Gritta, R. (1984) Airline bankruptcy propensities: a Zeta analysis, *Journal of the Transportation Research Forum*, 25.

Altman, Edward I., Haldeman, Robert G. and Narayanan, P. (1977) ZETA analysis: A new model to identify bankruptcy risk of corporations, *Journal of Banking and Finance*, 1: 29–54.

Asquith, P., Gertner, R. and Scharfstein, D. (1994) Anatomy of financial distress: An examination of junk-bond issuers, *The Quarterly Journal of Economics*, MIT Press, 109(3): 625–658.

Beaver, W. (1966) Financial ratios as predictors of failure, *Journal of Accounting Research*, 5: 71–111.

Berg, D. (2006) Bankruptcy prediction by generalized additive models, *Applied Stochastic Models in Business and Industry*, 23: 129–143.

Bishop, C. M. (1995) *Neural networks for pattern recognition*, Oxford: Oxford University Press.

Buzzell, R. D. and Gale, B. T. (1987) *The PIMS principles: Linking strategy to performance*, New York: The Free Press.

Chow, G., Gritta, R. and Leung, E. (1991) A multiple discriminant analysis approach to gauging air carrier bankruptcy propensities: The AIRSCORE Model, *Journal of the Transportation Research Forum*, 31(2): 371–377.

Collins, J. C. and Porras, J. I. (1994) *Built to last*, New York: Harper Business.

Davalos, S., Gritta, R. and Chow, G. (1999) The application of Neural Network approach to predicting bankruptcy risks facing the major U.S. carriers: 1979–1996, *Journal of Air Transport Management*, 5(2): 81–86.

Deakin, E. B. (1972) A discriminant analysis of predictors of business failure, *Journal of Accounting Research*, Volume 10, 167–179.

Edmister, R. (1972) An empirical test of financial ratio analysis for small business failure prediction, *Journal of Financial and Quantitative Analysis*, March: 1477–1493.

Flamholtz, E. and Randle, Y. (2000) *Growing pains*, San Francisco: Jossey-Bass.

Foster, R. and Kaplan, R. (2001) *Creative destruction*, New York: Doubleday.

Frederikslust, R. A. I. (1978) *Predictability of corporate failure*, Leiden/Boston: Martinus Nijhof Social Division.

Gritta, R. (1982) Bankruptcy risks facing the major U.S. air carriers, *Journal of Air Law and Commerce*, 48.

Gritta, R., Davalos, S., Chow, G. and Huang, W. (2002) Small U.S. air carrier financial condition: A back propagation neural network approach to forecasting bankruptcy and financial stress, *Journal of the Transportation Research Forum*, 56(2): 35–46.

Gritta, R. D., Adrangi, B., Davalos, S. and Bright, D. (2008) A review of the history of air carrier bankruptcy forecasting and the application of various models to the US airline industry: 1980–2005. In: Gratzer, K. and Stiefel, D. (eds) *History of insolvency and bankruptcy from an international perspective*, Huddinge: Södertörn högskola, pp. 193–214.

Gritta, R. D., Wang, M., Davalos, S. and Chow, G. (2000) Forecasting small air carrier bankruptcies, *Journal of Financial Management and Analysis*, 13(1): 44–49.

Gudmundsson, S. V. (1998) New-entrant airlines' life-cycle analysis: growth, decline and collapse, *Journal of Air Transport Management*, 4(4): 217–228.

Gudmundsson, S. V. (1999) Airline distress and failure prediction: a comparison of quantitative and qualitative models, *Transportation Research Part E*, 35: 155–182.

Gudmundsson, S. V. (2004) Management emphasis and performance in the airline industry: An exploratory multilevel analysis, *Transportation Research Part E*, 40: 443–463.

Hacking, I. ed. (1981) *Scientific revolutions*, New York: Oxford University Press.

Huang, C. S., Dorsey, R. E. and Boose, M. A. (1994) Life insurer financial distress predictions: A neural network model, *Journal of Insurance Regulation*, 13(2): 131–167.

Joyce, W., Nohria, N. and Roberson, B. (2003) *What really works*, New York: HarperCollins/HarperBusiness.

Keasey, K. and Watson, R. (1987) Non-financial symptoms and the prediction of small company failure: A test of Argenti's hypotheses, *Journal of Business Finance and Accounting*, Autumn, 335–354.

Kotter, J. P. and Heskett, J. L. (1992) *Corporate culture and performance*, New York: The Free Press.

Lacher, R. C., Coats, P. K., Sharma, S. C. and Fant, L. F. (1995) A neural network for classifying the financial health of a firm, *European Journal of Operational Research*, 85(1): 53–65.

Martin, D. (1977) Early warning of bank failure, *Journal of Banking and Finance*, 1: 247–276.

McCullagh, P. and Nelder, J. A. (1989) *Generalized linear models*, 2nd edn, London: Chapman & Hall.

Miller, D. and Friesen, P. H. (1983) Successful and unsuccessful phases of the corporate life cycle, *Organisational Studies*, 4: 235–236.

Moody, J. E. (1992) The effective number of parameters: An analysis of generalization and regularization in nonlinear learning systems. In: Moody, J. E., Hanson, S. J. and Lippmann, R. P. (eds), *Advances in neural information processing systems*, San Mateo, CA: Morgan Kaufmann, pp. 4, 847–854.

Ohlson, J. A. (1980) Financial ratios and the probabilistic prediction of bankruptcy, *Journal of Accounting Research*, 18(1): 109–131.

O'Leary, D. E. (1998) Using neural networks to predict corporate failure, *International Journal of Intelligent Systems in Accounting, Finance and Management*, 7: 187–197.

Oum, T. H. and Yu, C. (1997) *Winning airlines: Productivity and cost competitiveness of the world's major airlines*, Boston: Kluwer.

Oum, T. H. and Yu, C. (1998) An analysis of profitability of the world's major airlines, *Journal of Air Transport Management*, 4: 12–45.

Peters, T. J. and Waterman, R. H. (1982) *In search of excellence*, New York: Harper & Row.

Rubin, D. B., Gelman, A., Carlin, J. B. and Hal, S. (2003) *Bayesian data analysis*, 2nd edn, Boca Raton: Chapman & Hall.

Pilarski, A. and Dinh, T. (1999) Numerical scoring approach to credit risk analysis, *Handbook of Airline Finance*, 329–342.

Rosenzweig, P. (2007) Misunderstanding the nature of company performance: The halo effect and other business delusions, *California Management Review* 49(4): 6–20.

Rumelhart, D. E., Widrow, B. and Lehr, M. A. (1994) The basic ideas of neural networks, *Communications of the ACM*, 37(3): 87–92.

Salchenberger, L., Cinar, E. M. and Lash, N. (1992) Neural networks: A new tool for predicting thrift failures, *Decision Sciences*, 23(4): 899–916.

Santomero, A. and Vinso, J. (1977) Estimating the probability of failure for firms in the banking system, *Journal of Banking and Finance*, 1: 185–205.

Tam, K. Y. and Kiang, M. Y. (1992) Managerial applications of neural networks: The case of bank failure predictions, *Management Science*, 38(7): 926–947.

Udo, G. (1993) Neural network performance on the bankruptcy classification problem, *Computer and Industrial Engineering*, 25(4): 377–380.

Varadarajan, R. and Ramanujam, V. (1990) The corporate performance conundrum: A synthesis of contemporary views and an extension, *Journal of Management Studies*, 27(5): 463–483.

Vieira, A. S., Duarte, J., Ribeiro, B. and Neves, J. C. (2009) Accurate prediction of financial distress of companies with machine learning algorithms. In: *Adaptive and Natural Computing Algorithms*, Berlin/Heidelberg: Springer, pp. 569–576.

White, H. (1990) Connectionist nonparametric regression: Multilayer feedforward networks can learn arbitrary mappings, *Neural Networks*, 3: 535–550.

Wilson, N., Chong, K. and Peel, M. (1995) Neural network simulation and the prediction of corporate outcomes: Some empirical findings, *International Journal of the Economics of Business*, 2(1): 31–50.

6 World air cargo and merchandise trade

Franziska Kupfer, Hilde Meersman, Evy Onghena and Eddy Van de Voorde

1 Rationale and setting

Air cargo transport has developed very rapidly over the last couple of years. Some time ago, air cargo was considered as a by-product of passenger transport. Currently, however, a number of airlines specialize in the air cargo market. Also a number of (smaller) airports consider air cargo as their core business. At the same time, a number of industrial-economic evolutions took place in the sector, such as co-operation agreements.

As a product, air cargo is heterogeneous. There is the traditional air cargo on the one hand, transported in full freighters or passenger airplanes' belly, and express cargo on the other hand. Strictly separating both, however, is artificial, since there are overlaps. The increasing importance of full-freighter transport results from a combination of various factors: insufficient freight capacity linked to more severe security regulation aboard passenger planes, a tendency towards consolidation and scale increase, and the important imbalance between some incoming and outgoing air cargo flows.

For the volume of air cargo, measured in tonne kilometres, one can differentiate between potential and realized air cargo. Potential air cargo volumes can be seen as the demand for air cargo which is determined by economic activity and particularly by trade. Thus, when analysing the macro-economic characteristics of air cargo it is also necessary to get an insight into the relationship between air cargo, economic activity and trade, which is one of the objectives of this chapter. Next to the potential air cargo volumes, realized air cargo can be considered. Business economic facets determine the micro-economic environment which will affect the strategies of cargo airlines.

The supply of air cargo is influenced in particular by available capacity, competition from other modes, especially maritime container transport, and the costs and yields of the cargo airlines which are also determined by their competitive position in the sector. For airline companies, additional profit can be generated by filling unused belly capacity with cargo. Cargo yield, which traditionally has been below that of passenger transport, has improved over the last couple of years, approaching that of passenger transport. Guided by their profit opportunities, cargo airlines develop their network and choose their (cargo) airport.

However, external criteria concerning the geographical location, the infrastructure, the service quality, the tariffs and the (inter)national legal systems are also taken into consideration.

The previous observations combined with the predicted long-term growth in the air cargo sector indicate that air cargo can indeed influence airline companies' success. This chapter intends to deliver the economic rationality behind the air cargo market structure to lead to a better understanding of the air cargo sector.

Section 2 presents a general overview of the most important trends in the air freight market on an aggregated level, focusing on the evolution of traffic and the share of all-cargo and combi traffic. Moreover, the imbalances in air freight flows and the share of different commodities in air freight are analysed.

In section 3 the focus lies on the macro-economic aspect of air cargo and its potential volume. A regression analysis is carried out to discover the underlying factors that influence the development of air cargo. In the last section the overall conclusions are summarized and the agenda for further research is set up.

2 Trends in the air freight market

In this section, an insight is provided into the demand side of the air freight market on an aggregated level. More specifically, in the first place the evolution of worldwide air freight over the last 30 years is investigated. Second, the proportion between all-cargo and combi traffic and the evolution of both types of air cargo are examined. Third, an overview is given of the important imbalances between incoming and outgoing air cargo flows. Finally, an insight is gained into the most important commodities shipped by air freight for different geographical markets.

2.1 Evolution of worldwide air freight traffic

Figure 6.1 shows how worldwide air freight transport evolved from 1975 to 2008. It is clear from this figure that there was a strong increase in air freight during this period: from about 20 000 million FTKs in 1975 to 156 000 million FTKs in 2008.[1] This strong growth results from a number of crucial developments at the demand and supply side of the (liberalized) international air freight market: a growing world trade, technological progress, increasing value/weight rate of goods, downward pressure on air freight yields, changing production processes (e.g. JIT, Make to Order), strategic importance of e-services, etc. The graph also illustrates the traffic decreases in 2001 and 2008 due to the September 11 effect and the worldwide economic crisis respectively. In section 3, it will be investigated which factors in the global economy are driving the demand for air freight.

2.2 Share of all-cargo and combi traffic

Air freight can be transported in specialized freighter aircraft, in the belly hold of passenger aircraft or in combi aircraft.[2] In this section, the term all-cargo

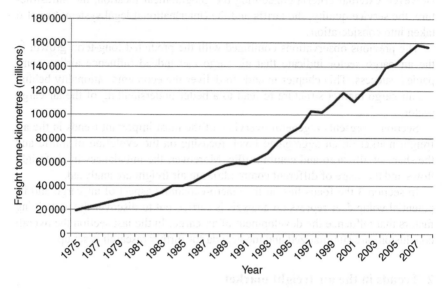

Figure 6.1 Evolution of worldwide air freight traffic in FTKs (millions), 1975–2008 (source: ICAO Journal, 1987–2006; ICAO Annual Report of the Council, 2008–2009).

traffic is used to designate all-cargo flights, i.e. air freight carried by specialized freighter aircraft. The term combi traffic comprises air freight traffic carried in the bellyspace of passenger aircraft or in combi aircraft. The distinction between all-cargo and combi traffic is not the same as the difference between all-cargo carriers and combination carriers, since the latter can also use full freighters (e.g. Cathay Pacific, Singapore Airlines, Korean Airlines, Lufthansa, Air France-KLM).

Figures 6.2 and 6.3 illustrate the evolution of the share of all-cargo and combi traffic from 1976 to 2008 in tonnage and tonne-kilometres. Both graphs concern data of the IATA members' air transport operations.[3] These figures show that all-cargo traffic has become more important over the last years. The proportion between all-cargo and combi traffic expressed in tonnage and tonne-kilometres has evolved from approximately 40–60 to 50–50 in 30 years. The growth of all-cargo services results from a combination of various factors: an insufficient cargo capacity on passenger flights linked to more rigorous security regulation aboard passenger aircraft, a tendency towards consolidation and scale increase, and the important imbalance between some incoming and outgoing air cargo flows (Herman and Van de Voorde, 2006, p. 17).

In order to gain an insight into the evolution of both traffic types, the annual percentage change of freight tonnes of all-cargo and combi traffic is depicted in Figure 6.4. It becomes clear from this figure that all-cargo traffic is more volatile than combi traffic. This is due to the fact that combi traffic involves more

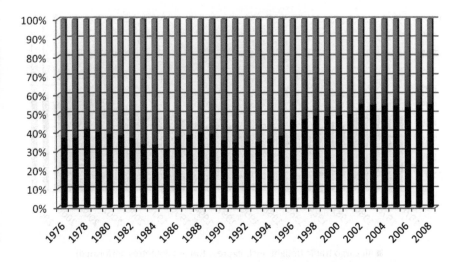

Figure 6.2 Evolution of the share of all-cargo and combi traffic (freight tonnes carried),
international and domestic, scheduled services, 1976–2008 (source: IATA
World Air Transport Statistics, 1981–2009, IATA Members' Air Transport
Operations).

traditional carriers and is related to passenger traffic. Moreover, in case of a
worsening economic climate, airlines will reduce their all-cargo capacity more
easily than their combined passenger-belly capacity. An example of this is the
period 1979–1983, in which the airline industry was in crisis as a consequence
of the increase in oil prices combined with a stagnating demand and decreasing
revenues. The figure shows a decrease in all-cargo traffic in this period, while
the change in combi traffic remains positive, with a sharp increase in 1983 as a
sign of recovery from the crisis. In the second half of the 1980s the airline
industry performed relatively well. However, this changed in 1990 due to a rise
in oil prices which induced a crisis in the period 1990–1993. A slowdown of
the economy in different countries but especially in the US and the UK, gave
rise to a decreasing demand. The first Gulf War in 1991 worsened the situation
even more and led to the bankruptcy of several airlines (Nolan *et al.*, 2004,
p. 240).

In 1991, all-cargo traffic as well as combi traffic decreased. The strong
growth of all-cargo traffic in 1994 indicates again a recovery from the crisis. The
combi traffic decrease in 1998 was a consequence of the economic crisis in East
Asia, resulting in a traffic decrease on intra-Asian routes and thus problems for
several Asian airlines. In addition, some European and North American airlines
saw a traffic decrease on their routes to and from East Asia. The figure also
shows a traffic decline in 2001 (all-cargo and combi) induced by the crisis in the
airline industry in the aftermath of 9/11. Rather remarkably, all-cargo traffic

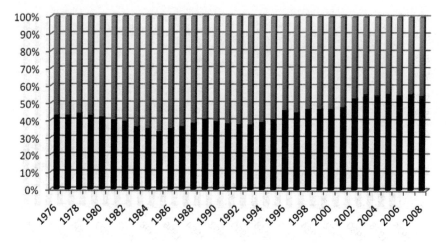

■ All-cargo traffic (freight, incl. express tonne-kilometres performed)

▨ Combi traffic (freight, incl. express tonne-kilometres performed)

Figure 6.3 Evolution of the share of all-cargo and combi traffic (freight, incl. express tonne-kilometres performed), international and domestic, scheduled services, 1976–2008 (source: IATA World Air Transport Statistics, 1981–2009, IATA Members' Air Transport Operations).

recovered well in 2002, while combi traffic still decreased. A final traffic decrease can be seen in 2008 due to the worldwide economic crisis. All-cargo traffic and combi traffic both decreased by about 5 per cent. However, as seen in 2001, combi traffic decreased slightly more than all-cargo traffic.

2.3 Air freight imbalances

While passengers normally make a two-way journey, air cargo is carried in only one direction: from production to distribution or consumption centres. This results in imbalances between incoming and outgoing cargo flows. These imbalances are influenced by export/import imbalances between regions or countries and may result in large variations in air cargo rates according to the traffic direction (Zhang and Zhang, 2002, p. 179).

Figure 6.5 gives an overview of imbalances in air cargo flows between selected regional markets in 2008. The imbalance from Europe to China is 1:2.6 and from USA to China 1:3.1. Between Europe and the US, there is no imbalance since the ratio is 1:1. The largest imbalance is found from the US to the Middle East (excl. Israel), namely 14.2:1. The main reason for this is the strong growth of this region, which imports many high-value goods by air freight. As its export mainly consists of oil which is transported over sea, the imbalance is very large.

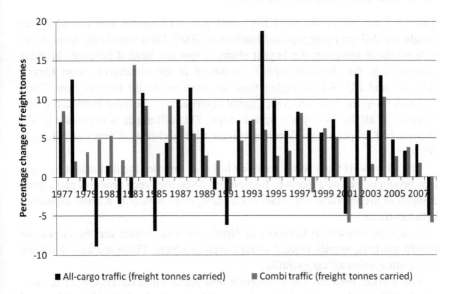

Figure 6.4 Annual % change of freight tonnes of all-cargo and combi traffic, 1977–2008 (source: IATA World Air Transport Statistics, 1981–2009, IATA Members' Air Transport Operations).

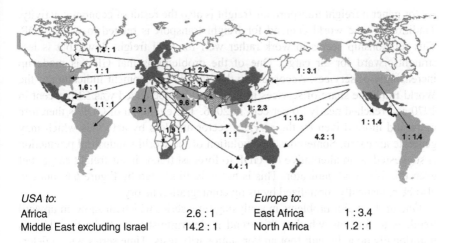

USA to:		Europe to:	
Africa	2.6 : 1	East Africa	1 : 3.4
Middle East excluding Israel	14.2 : 1	North Africa	1.2 : 1

Figure 6.5 Export/import air freight tonnage ratio[1] for selected regional markets in 2008 (source: YDL Management Consultants).

Note
1 Explanation of export/import tonnage ratio: e.g. USA to South America, 1:1.4 – for every tonne exported from USA, 1.4 tonnes are imported back via air freight.

2.4 Commodities shipped by air freight

Table 6.1 represents the most important goods categories transported by air freight for different geographical markets in 2007. On a worldwide level, high-tech products represent the largest share. There are large differences between markets, e.g. the share of capital equipment in the air exports from Europe (EU–AS and EU–NA) is higher than its share in the air exports from North America (NA–EU and NA–AS). Capital equipment is the most important goods category in all the air exports from Europe. This difference is explained by the strength of European manufacturers of industrial machinery (Clancy and Hoppin, 2006).

The air exports from North America to Latin America are dominated by high-tech products. For its exports to Europe and Asia, high-tech products and capital equipment are the most important goods categories with only a small difference between them.

Asia's air exports to Europe and North America, which are the largest air freight markets, mainly consist of high-tech products. These are also dominant in the intra-Asian air cargo traffic.

The market between Latin America and North America (LA–NA) is completely different from the other markets as it is largely dominated by refrigerated goods.

3 World air freight and merchandise trade

As for general freight transport, air freight is also the result of economic activity. Traditionally the world demand for freight transport is related to world GDP. This relationship seems to work rather well for total freight flows, but is less straightforward for air cargo. One of the problems is that GDP is made up increasingly of services. According to the World Development Indicators of the World Bank the share of services in total world value added was 53 per cent in 1970 and reached nearly 70 per cent in 2006. The evolution of GDP is therefore more and more driven by the services sector and less by activities which may generate air cargo. Sometimes the evolution of the world's industrial production is suggested as an alternative for GDP to forecast trends in air freight cargo, but even this is a weak indicator. This is not only illustrated by Figure 6.6, but can also be statistically formalized by using cointegration theory.

One of the major problems in analysing time series which all show an upward trend, is to find out whether this trend is deterministic or stochastic.[4] This is traditionally done by unit root and/or stationarity tests. Time series with a deterministic trend are stationary and can be related to each other by simple ordinary least squares regressions taking into account the deterministic trend. Time series with stochastic trends and which are therefore not stationary can only be related to each other by a regression equation if they are cointegrated, which means that they should have a common trend. The seminal work of Nobel Prize winners Engle and Granger treats this in detail and Granger's Representation theorem

Table 6.1 Commodity share of directional air freight markets in 2007 (share of FEU[1]-kilometres, billions of FEU-kilometres)

	World	AS–EU	EU–AS	AS–NA	NA–AS	Intra-Asia	EU–NA	NA–EU	LA–NA	NA–LA
Billions of FEU-km	15.24	2.79	1.53	2.98	1.13	1.60	0.80	0.67	0.42	0.39
Refrigerated foods (%)	5	1	3	1	4	5	3	3	41	2
Non-refrigerated foods (%)	1	0	1	0	1	1	1	1	8	0
Consumer products (%)	16	22	14	15	13	16	19	15	9	16
Apparel, textiles, footwear (%)	17	25	9	31	3	15	12	3	19	5
High-tech products (%)	27	32	19	36	28	35	18	24	10	36
Capital equipment (%)	19	10	37	11	26	15	32	27	6	24
Intermediate materials (%)	12	8	15	6	21	11	14	23	4	14
Primary products (%)	2	2	3	0	4	2	2	3	3	3

Source: Based on MergeGlobal world air freight supply and demand model, MergeGlobal Value Creation Initiative, 2008, p. 36.

Note
An FEU is a forty-foot equivalent unit (2 TEUs).

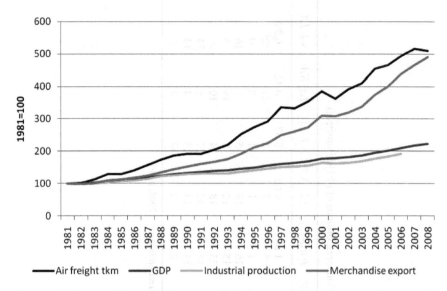

Figure 6.6 World air freight in tkm and world economic activity (sources: Air freight in tkm: ICAO; GDP in constant US$ of 2000: Worldbank; Industrial Production: industry value added in constant US$ of 2000: Worldbank; Merchandise exports in USD of 2000: Worldbank and IMF).

states that cointegrated series are related to each other by means of a very specific dynamic model, the error-correction model (ECM), which models the long run equilibrium relation between cointegrated series and the short run adjustments towards this equilibrium relationship. If nonstationary time series are not cointegrated, they cannot be represented by a simple regression and there is no long run equilibrium relation between them. Only their short-term behaviour can be modelled in a statistically reliable way.

The first step in the analysis is to discover whether the trend in the time series under consideration is stochastic or deterministic. Traditionally this is tested by means of the following tests: Dickey–Fuller (DF), augmented Dickey–Fuller (ADF), Dickey–Fuller with detrending (DFGLS), Phillips–Perron (PP), Kwiatkowski, Phillips, Schmidt and Shin (KPSS), Elliot, Rothenberg and Stock (ERS), and Ng–Perron (NP). If the time series have a stochastic trend, the next step is to test whether they are cointegrated or not. There are several tests for cointegration: Engle–Granger 2-step approach, Engle–Granger–Yoo 3-step approach, the dynamic ordinary least squares (DOLS) developed by Stock and Watson, the unrestricted ECM approach, and the Johansen cointegration test. Finally, if the series are cointegrated, their relation can be represented by an error correction model. If they are not cointegrated, there is no long run equilibrium relation which ties the series together.

Unit roots tests for world air freight in tkm (TKM), world GDP in constant prices (GDP), and world industrial production in constant prices (IP) revealed a

stochastic trend in the series whether they were measured in levels or in logarithms. Several cointegration tests were applied indicating no cointegration
between TKM and GDP, and between TKM and IP. This leads to the conclusion
that there is no long run equilibrium relation between world air freight on the
one hand and world GDP or world industrial production on the other hand.

As air cargo consists mainly of international traffic of high-value goods, the
evolution of world air freight can be better explained by an indicator for world
international trade in high-value goods. This is approximated by the volume of
world merchandise exports (MERCH) as a global indicator of international trade
in combination with the share of manufactures in the total value of merchandise
exports (SHAREMANU).[5] An increase of the latter can be the result of an
increasing share of manufactures in the volume of merchandise trade, an increase
of the value of the manufactures, or a combination of both. All cointegration
tests indicated that TKM, MERCH and SHAREMANU are cointegrated. For the
error correction specification, the best results were obtained with the logarithm
of TKM and MERCH and by adding a dummy variable for the crisis in 1991
induced by the higher oil prices and the Gulf War (DUM91) and a dummy variable for the structural impact of 9/11 (DUMBREAK).

This gives the following ECM model:

$$\Delta \ln TKM_t = \beta_1 \Delta \ln MERCH_t + \beta_2 \Delta SHAREMANU_t + \beta_3 \Delta DUM91_t + \beta_4 \Delta DUMBREAK_t$$
$$+ \delta(\ln TKM_{t-1} - \alpha_0 - \alpha_1 \ln MERCH_{t-1} - \alpha_2 SHAREMANU_{t-1} - \alpha_3 DUM91_{t-1}$$
$$- \alpha_4 DUMBREAK_{t-1}) + \varepsilon_t$$

with

TKM	world air freight in tkm (ICAO)
MERCH	world merchandise export in USD of 2000 (World Bank and IMF)
SHAREMANU	share of manufactures in the value of world merchandise exports
DUM91	= 1 in 1991
	= 0 in other years
DUMBREAK	= 1 from 2001
	= 0 before 2001

Δ are first differences, ln indicates logarithms, and ε is the stochastic error term.

The long run equilibrium relation is given by

$$\ln TKM_t = \alpha_0 + \alpha_1 \ln MERCH_t + \alpha_2 SHAREMANU_t + \alpha_3 DUM91_t + \alpha_4 DUMBREAK_t$$

As the sample is rather small, the long term cointegrating relation is estimated
using the Stock–Watson DOLS-method (Stock and Watson, 1988, 1993). The
results are reported in Table 6.2.

The short run adjustments are estimated given the DOLS-estimates for $\alpha_0, \ldots,$
α_4 and are reported in Table 6.3.

Table 6.2 DOLS estimation of the long run relationship between world air freight and world merchandise exports

Sample (adjusted): 1983 2006
Included observations: 24 after adjustments
Newey–West HAC Standard Errors & Covariance (lag truncation = 2)

		Coefficient	Std. Error	t-Statistic	Prob.
C	a_0	−0.348759	0.213602	−1.632749	0.1308
LNMERCH	a_1	0.986979	0.055337	17.83581	0.0000
SHAREMANU	a_2	0.936589	0.268378	3.489818	0.0051
DUM91	a_3	−0.065071	0.030437	−2.137904	0.0558
DUMBREAK	a_4	−0.075160	0.034519	−2.177367	0.0521
DSHAREMANU(1)		0.209563	0.766090	0.273549	0.7895
DDUM91(1)		−0.002301	0.017582	−0.130859	0.8982
DDUMBREAK(1)		−0.034809	0.049727	−0.700013	0.4985
DLNXMERCH(−1)		−0.056092	0.353517	−0.158669	0.8768
DSHAREMANU(−1)		0.005442	0.507549	0.010722	0.9916
DDUM91(−1)		−0.011760	0.021071	−0.558099	0.5880
DDUMBREAK(−1)		0.014882	0.034023	0.437394	0.6703
R-squared		0.997523	Mean dependent var		5.529040
Adjusted R-squared		0.994821	S.D. dependent var		0.453568
S.E. of regression		0.032641	Akaike info criterion		−3.703331
Sum squared resid		0.011720	Schwarz criterion		−3.065219
Log likelihood		57.43998	Hannan–Quinn criter.		−3.534040
F-statistic		369.1756	Durbin–Watson stat		1.821909
Prob(F-statistic)		0.000000			

Table 6.3 Error correction model for world air freight and world merchandise exports

Dependent Variable: DLNTKM
Method: Least Squares
Sample (adjusted): 1984 2007
Included observations: 24 after adjustments

		Coefficient	Std. Error	t-Statistic	Prob.
DLNMERCH	β_1	1.006034	0.073951	13.60399	0.0000
DSHAREMANU	β_2	0.553164	0.290538	1.903929	0.0722
DDUM91	β_3	−0.041447	0.017759	−2.333856	0.0307
DDUMBREAK	β_4	−0.060238	0.025114	−2.398598	0.0269
RESDOLS(−1)	δ	−0.943221	0.231856	−4.068135	0.0007
R-squared		0.787872	Mean dependent var		0.063426
Adjusted R-squared		0.743214	S.D. dependent var		0.049532
S.E. of regression		0.025100	Akaike info criterion		−4.348839
Sum squared resid		0.011970	Schwarz criterion		−4.103411
Log likelihood		57.18607	Hannan–Quinn criter.		−4.283727
Durbin–Watson stat		1.583792			

with
RESDOLS = lnTKM + 0.349 − 0.987lnMERCH − 0.937SHAREMANU
          + 0.075DUMBREAK + 0.065DUM91

The error correction model reveals that the change in world air freight is due to the current change in world merchandise exports, the current change in the share of manufactures and an error correction which is an adjustment to deviations from the long run equilibrium in the previous period. The adjustment speed, which is given by $\delta = -0.94$, is high as it is close to -1.

The elasticity of air freight with respect to merchandise exports is not significantly different from 1 either in the long run equilibrium relation, or in the short run adjustment. So a one per cent change in world merchandise exports will result in a one per cent change in air freight. An increase of the share of manufactures in the value of merchandise exports with one percentage point, will lead in the long run to a one per cent increase in air freight as α_2 is not significantly different from 1. In the short run the impact will be smaller than 1. There has clearly been a negative impact in 2001 as a consequence of 9/11 which has led to a structural downward shift in air freight.

Figure 6.7 gives the actual value of air freight (in logarithms) and the fitted values calculated with the estimated error correction model within the sample for the years 1984–2007 and outside the sample for the year 2008.

In a next stage a similar model can be applied to the major air freight markets of Table 6.1. Moreover, it might be worthwhile to include the transport price of the best alternative, i.e. maritime shipping, in the analysis. At the supply side there is room for investigating the effect of oil price changes and capacity adjustments, and the way individual airlines adjust their strategy in order to determine their competitive position.

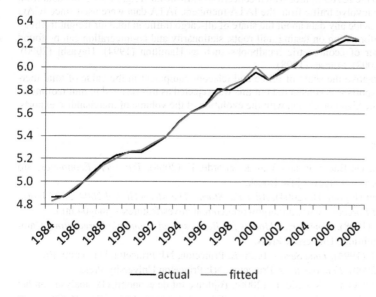

Figure 6.7 Actual and fitted air freight values.

4 Conclusions

Air freight transport has developed very rapidly over the last decade. While previously, air cargo was regarded as a by-product of passenger transport, a lot of traditional carriers consider it now as an instrument that adds positively to the ultimate goal of profit maximization. In addition, a number of carriers started to specialize in the air cargo market. Their success or failure depends on a number of factors. The future evolution of world merchandise trade is crucial and especially the trade in high-value goods needs close monitoring. Particular attention should be paid to the imbalances on trade routes, which results in imbalances between incoming and outgoing cargo flows.

Further research should aim at a study of the air cargo market on a disaggregate level, focusing on the different goods categories transported by air, the major routes and individual airlines. Concerning individual carriers, a more in-depth analysis at business economic level should be carried out, leading to a better understanding of the cost and organizational structure of individual cargo airlines.

The analysis done in this paper shows that the air cargo market is extremely volatile. The economic crisis of 2008–2009, with large traffic and turnover decreases on certain routes and in certain airports, illustrated this clearly. It is in these kinds of crisis that "air freight economics" is translated into "survival of the fittest."

Notes

1 An FTK is a Freight Tonne-Kilometre.
2 In combi aircraft, passengers as well as cargo are transported on the main deck.
3 Contrary to the ICAO figures which concern worldwide air freight traffic, the data from IATA only involve traffic from the IATA members. IATA data were used since ICAO does not provide any data about the share of all-cargo traffic in total air freight traffic.
4 Detailed information on testing unit roots, stationarity and co-integration can be found in a number of econometric handbooks such as Hamilton (1994), Hayashi (2000), Verbeek (2008), Franses (1998).
5 As an alternative the share of office and telecom equipment in the value of total merchandise exports was considered but this was rejected as this resulted in multicollinearity due to the high correlation with the evolution of the volume of merchandise exports.

References

Blauwens, G., De Baere, P. and Van de Voorde, E. (2008), *Transport Economics*, 3rd edn, Antwerpen: Uitgeverij De Boeck.

Clancy, B. and Hoppin, D. (2004), *After the Storm: The MergeGlobal 2004–2008 World Air Freight Forecast*, www.aircargoworld.com/archives/features/1_may04.htm.

Franses, P.H. (1998), *Time Series Models for Business and Economic Forecasting*, Cambridge: Cambridge University Press.

Hamilton, J.D. (1994), *Time Series Analysis*, Princeton, NJ: Princeton University Press.

Hayashi, F. (2000), *Econometrics*, Princeton, NJ: Princeton University Press.

Herman, F. and Van de Voorde, E. (2006), Bijdrage tot de economische analyse van het full-freighter luchtvrachtvervoer, *Tijdschrift Vervoerswetenschap*, 42 (4), 16–23.

IATA (1981–2009), World Air Transport Statistics.

ICAO (1987–2006), Annual Review of Civil Aviation 1994, in: *ICAO Journal.*

ICAO (2008–2009), Annual Report of the Council.

MergeGlobal Value Creation Initiative (2008), End of an era? Why the "super spike" in fuel prices may signal the end of "super growth" in air freight, *American Shipper*, 50 (8), pp. 32–47.

Nolan, J.F., Ritchie, P. and Rowcroft, J. (2004), September 11 and the world airline financial crisis, *Transport Reviews*, 24 (2), 239–255.

Stock, J.H. and Watson, M. (1988), Testing for common trends, *Journal of the American Statistical Association*, 83, 1097–1107.

Stock, J.H. and Watson, M. (1993), A simple estimator of cointegrating vectors in higher order integrated systems, *Econometrica*, 61, 783–820.

Verbeek, M. (2008), *A Guide to Modern Econometrics*, 3rd edn, New York: John Wiley & Sons.

Zhang, A. and Zhang, Y. (2002), A model of air cargo liberalization: Passenger vs. all-cargo carriers, *Transportation Research Part E*, 38 (3–4), 175–191.

7 Integrators in a changing world

Evy Onghena

1 Introduction

In our globalized economy, transport and logistics services are crucial to reduce cycle times and increase products' speed to market. Logistics service providers with an extensive network allow the transport costs of international trade to be kept down, while realizing a more efficient use of production factors.

However, during the past decade, the requirements for transport and logistics have become stricter and more numerous. The share of high-value and/or time-sensitive goods with a short economic life cycle has increased. Therefore, there is a growing need for fast and reliable transport that allows companies to gain access to global markets and supply chains.

Integrators are crucial for the delivery of those transport services. Since they are able to control the total supply chain ("one-stop shopping"), the strategic and operational importance of integrators for the commercial and production processes of shippers is extremely high. In addition, integrators enlarge companies' catchment area and their options for the location of production and assembly facilities.

Besides the importance of integrators for shippers, the competitiveness of a region is also partly determined by the presence of one or more integrators. This can be illustrated very well by the relocation of DHL's hub activities from Brussels National Airport to Leipzig in 2008, which have far-reaching microeconomic and macroeconomic consequences for the airport and for the Belgian economy in general.

Over the past decade, international express has grown at more than twice the rate of total worldwide air cargo[1] traffic, averaging 12.9 percent[2] annually (Boeing, 2006, p. 4). The integrators account for almost 85 percent of the world's express shipments (US–ASEAN Business Council, 2005, p. 6). Currently, only four players[3] are fully integrated across all transport modes, including air transport: UPS, FedEx, DHL and TNT.

Despite the importance of integrators for shippers and economic regions, the strategies of integrators are hardly examined. Insight into the market structure and the cost structure of these companies, as well as into the consequences of their expansion and cooperation strategies, is lacking.

This chapter deals with the integrator market, focusing on the market structure and the supply side of the market. More specifically, the objective is to position the integrators in the global air cargo business and to get an insight into their cost structure. In addition, some challenges and opportunities specific to the integrator market will be examined. Section 2 outlines the business positioning of integrators within the air cargo industry. In section 3, the cost structure of integrators is investigated. Section 4 points out the challenges and opportunities typical for integrators. Section 5 summarizes the main conclusions of this research.

Many definitions of integrators can be found in the literature. In this chapter, integrators are considered as "vertically integrated express companies that provide time-definite, door-to-door services and, for that purpose, perform their own pick-up and delivery services, operate their own fleet of aircraft and trucks and tie it all together with advanced information and communication technologies" (Zondag, 2006, p. XI).

2 Business positioning of integrators within the air cargo industry

The different actors in the air cargo industry can be categorized into three main sub-industries:

1   general or traditional air cargo industry;
2   air express industry;
3   postal services industry.

This categorization is presented in Figure 7.1.

The general air cargo industry consists of actors providing airport-to-airport services. General air freight companies focus on the transportation of specialized and/or consolidated freight, consisting of individual shipments from many different customers grouped together and transported as one large shipment in an air container (Pirenne, 2007). All-cargo carriers such as Cargolux, Polar Air Cargo and Nippon Cargo Airlines belong to the general air cargo industry.

The air express industry is described as "an industry of which the core business is the provision of value-added, door-to-door transport and deliveries of next-day or time-definite shipments, including documents, parcels and merchandise goods" (Oxford Economic Forecasting, 2004, p. 5). Typical characteristics of the air express industry are time-definite delivery of goods, door-to-door delivery and full tracking control of shipped goods. Two main types of players are part of the air express industry, namely couriers and express carriers. Examples are GeoPost, General Logistics Systems and Ziegler Express.

Combination carriers, air cargo forwarders and indirect air carriers are positioned at the intersection of the general air cargo and the air express industry. Due to the strong competition of integrators, some combination carriers try to stay competitive by offering time-definite, door-to-door services themselves and,

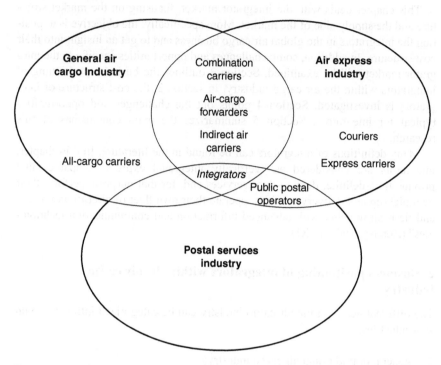

Figure 7.1 Categorization of the air cargo industry (source: own composition based on Zondag, 2006, p. 18 and Duponselle *et al.*, 2005).

thus, are entering the air express industry. An example of this strategy is Cathay Pacific, which expanded its services to the express industry by offering its Wholesale Courier and Cargo Express services. Despite the fierce competition between integrators and combination carriers, both types of market players can also be complementary to one another. This is illustrated by the case of Northwest Airlines, which lost DHL Express, its most important cargo customer, as from the end of 2008. Northwest Airlines was obliged to reconsider its cargo activities due to this loss.

Air cargo forwarders and indirect air carriers are also positioned at the intersection of the general air cargo and the air express industry since they are increasingly offering value-added, logistics services and door-to-door delivery. Whereas in the past they were merely considered as intermediaries between shipper and airline, they are increasingly acting as integrated logistics service providers. Examples of these market actors are Kuehne + Nagel, Schenker and Panalpina.

Public postal operators, which originally belonged only to the postal services industry, are currently positioned at the intersection of the postal services industry and the air express industry. The reason for this evolution is the entry of postal service providers (e.g. Deutsche Post World Net, TPG, La Poste, etc.) into the air express market.

Integrators are part of all three sub-industries since they are offering a broad service portfolio including general air freight services, express services and mail services.

The most important conclusion of this section is that the boundaries between the different segments of the air cargo industry are blurring since the services offered by the different players start to overlap. This intensifies competition and leads to various forms of cooperation. An example of the overlap between different segments of the air cargo industry is the case of Austrian Post, which is increasingly developing its B2B express parcels business by the acquisition of parcel carriers such as trans-o-flex (Germany, 2006), Merland Express (Hungary, 2007) and Road Parcel (Hungary, 2007). Austrian Post aims at becoming a niche player in the European B2B express market. Another example is Lufthansa Cargo, which created time:matters in 1992, a subsidiary specialized in same-day, door-to-door express transport.

3 Cost structure of integrators

3.1 Introduction

Whereas a lot of research is dedicated to the cost structure of the passenger airline industry, the scientific knowledge about the air freight industry's cost structure is limited. This is mainly due to the lack of structured air freight statistics. Moreover, the existing literature about the supply side of the air freight industry focuses mainly on non-integrated service providers. In the integrated express market, one service provider offers integrated, door-to-door transport from sender to receiver. The typical express delivery shipment cycle is depicted in Figure 7.2.

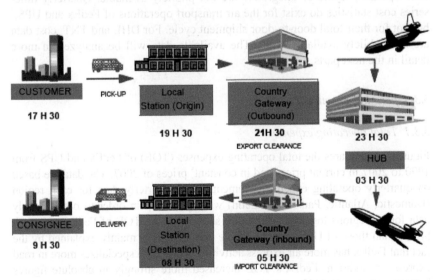

Figure 7.2 Door-to-door operating cycle (source: Oxford Economic Forecasting, 2004).

Figure 7.2 shows that an integrator offers multimodal transport, consisting of road and air transport, from sender to receiver. However, one needs to take into account that integrators do not always use air transport for the transport of packages. Local and access transport is always performed by ground vehicles, but long-haul transportation can be conducted by ground and air. In integrated express networks, the express items (overnight, next-day) are usually transported by air for long-haul trips due to tight delivery deadlines whereas the deferred products of integrators, also called economy products, may be sent by ground or air. Today's general economic climate and the sharp rise in fuel prices have impacted both integrators and their customers, resulting in a growing demand for economy instead of premium express products. To minimize costs, the deferred products are increasingly shipped by road instead of air transport.

To analyze the cost structure of an integrator, the total express delivery shipment cycle needs to be considered. Toward this end, a simulation model of the door-to-door operating cycle is being constructed. This model will allow understanding, explaining and forecasting strategic and operational behavior of the current market players. Finally, the model will be used to make forecasts about the future market structure and the economic consequences of strategic decisions. However, the development of the simulation model is outside the scope of this paper.

3.2 Data collection

As indicated in the previous section, the total express delivery shipment cycle needs to be taken into account to analyze an integrator's cost structure. Ideally, cost data of the total door-to-door shipment cycle will be used to study the cost characteristics of integrators. However, detailed cost data for the total door-to-door operating cycle of integrators are not publicly available. Quarterly time-series cost statistics do exist for the air transport operations of FedEx and UPS,[4] but not for their total door-to-door shipment cycle. For DHL and TNT, cost data are not publicly available at all. The available data will be analyzed in more detail in the next parts.

3.3 Operating expenses

3.3.1 Total operating expenses

Figure 7.3 compares the total operating expenses (TOE) of FedEx and UPS from 1990 to 2007 in current prices and in constant[5] prices of 2007. The data are based on quarterly operating expense statements.[6] The quarterly data for each region (Domestic, Atlantic, Pacific and Latin) were added up in order to obtain yearly data for all regions together. The figure shows that the TOE of FedEx are much higher than those of UPS over the whole period. This is mainly explained by the fact that FedEx has more air express activities, while UPS specializes more in road express. In addition, FedEx's TOE increased more strongly in absolute figures between 1990 and 2007 compared to those of UPS, which results in a larger difference between FedEx and UPS in 2007 compared to 1990. In 2007, FedEx incurred TOE of approximately $21.25 billion, while UPS's TOE amounted to approximately $4.61 billion. From 1990 to 2007, FedEx's TOE increased by approximately $14 billion, while those of UPS increased by approximately $3.7 billion. However, the relative growth of TOE in 2007 compared to the level of 1990 is higher for UPS (434 percent) than for FedEx (195 percent).

To have a clearer view on the growth differences, Figure 7.4 depicts the annual percentage changes of the integrators' TOE. The figure shows that the annual changes for UPS are much larger than those of FedEx. It is also clear from this figure that both integrators' TOE are increasing over the whole period, with the exception of FedEx's TOE in 2001. This decrease in 2001 is a result of the crisis in the air transport business which resulted in lower operating expenses due to lower volumes.

The integrators' TOE comprise three types of expenses:

• direct/aircraft operating expenses: expenses that are incurred directly in the in-flight operation of aircraft;
• indirect and other operating expenses: grouped together in P-7 as one category, namely "total servicing, sales and general operating expenses";
• transport-related expenses: all expense items applicable to the generation of transport-related revenues, which come from the US Government as direct grants or aids for providing air transportation facilities and all services which grow from and are incidental to the air transportation services performed by the air carrier. These are revenues and expenses that are not directly attributable to providing air transportation, e.g. if a carrier has a "sister" company that provides fuel services or catering services to other carriers, this would be considered transport related. In the case of FedEx vs. UPS, FedEx includes its ground operations/trucking in its reports and those

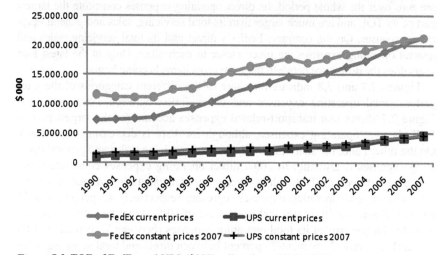

Figure 7.3 TOE of FedEx and UPS ($000), all regions, 1990–2007.

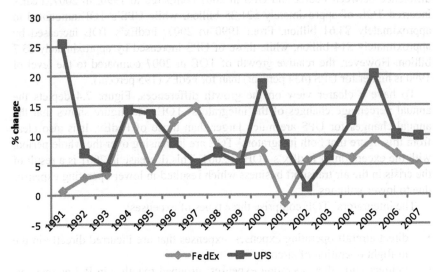

Figure 7.4 Annual percentage change of TOE FedEx and UPS.

are put into transport related. UPS's ground/trucking is considered a separate company and the airline contracts out to that company for the services. It is all done through their parent company.

Figures 7.5 and 7.6 present an overview of the different categories of the integrators' TOE and their evolution between 1990 and 2007. For FedEx, transport-related expenses (ground operations/trucking) represent the largest part of its TOE, followed by direct operating expenses. In the case of UPS, transport-related expenses are zero over the whole period. Its direct operating expenses constitute the largest part of its TOE and are much larger than its total servicing, sales and general operating expenses. On the contrary, FedEx's direct and its total servicing, sales and general operating expenses are much closer to each other. Only in the latest four years does the difference between those two cost items become larger.

Figures 7.7 and 7.8 indicate the share of the different categories of the integrators' total operating expenses and its evolution between 1990 and 2007. Figure 7.7 shows that transport-related expenses account for the largest part of FedEx's total operating expenses, although its share is decreasing since 2000. On the other hand, the share of direct and total servicing, sales and general operating expenses is growing. In 2007, direct operating expenses constitute about 34 percent of FedEx's TOE, while transport related expenses and total servicing, sales and general operating expenses represent respectively 43 percent and 23 percent. Figure 7.8 illustrates that in the case of UPS, direct operating expenses form the largest part of its total operating expenses (between 75 percent and 80 percent). The ratio 75 percent/25 percent between direct and total servicing sales and general operating expenses remains nearly constant over the whole period.

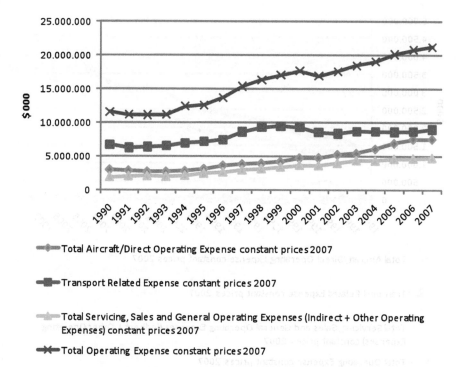

━◆━ Total Aircraft/Direct Operating Expense constant prices 2007

━■━ Transport Related Expense constant prices 2007

━▲━ Total Servicing, Sales and General Operating Expenses (Indirect + Other Operating Expenses) constant prices 2007

━✕━ Total Operating Expense constant prices 2007

Figure 7.5 Evolution of FedEx direct operating expenses, transport related expenses, servicing, sales and general operating expenses and TOE, all regions, 1990–2007, constant prices of 2007.

In the following section the integrators' direct operating expenses will be discussed in further detail. Total servicing, sales and general operating expenses as well as transport related expenses will not be analyzed in more detail in this chapter.

3.3.2 Direct/aircraft operating expenses

Aircraft or direct operating expenses are expenses that are incurred directly in the in-flight operation of aircraft. Schedule P-52 of the Form 41 Financial Reports provided by the BTS contains detailed quarterly aircraft operating expenses for large certificated US air carriers. It includes the following cost categories:

- flying operations expenses: expenses incurred directly in the in-flight operation of aircraft and expenses related to the holding of aircraft and aircraft operational personnel in readiness for assignment for an in-flight status;
- flight equipment maintenance expenses;
- net obsolescence and deterioration – expendable parts: provision for losses in value of expendable parts inventory;

120   E. Onghena

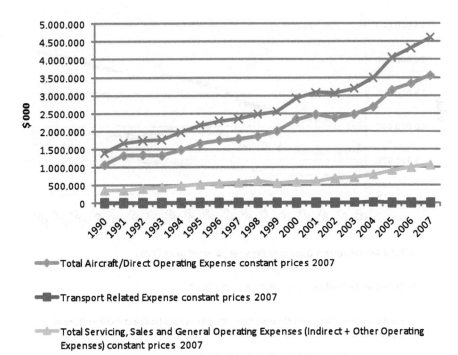

=◆=Total Aircraft/Direct Operating Expense constant prices 2007

=■=Transport Related Expense constant prices 2007

=▲=Total Servicing, Sales and General Operating Expenses (Indirect + Other Operating Expenses) constant prices 2007

=✕=Total Operating Expense constant prices 2007

Figure 7.6 Evolution of UPS direct operating expenses, transport related expenses, servicing, sales and general operating expenses and TOE, all regions, 1990–2007, constant prices of 2007.

- flight equipment depreciation expenses;
- flight equipment amortization expenses.

Figure 7.9 shows the annual percentage changes of total aircraft operating expenses of FedEx and UPS between 1990 and 2007. The annual changes for UPS are stronger than for FedEx, except in 1996, 1997, 2002, 2004 and 2006. The evolution of the annual changes is similar for both integrators, except in 1991, where the direct operating expenses of UPS show a very high growth compared to FedEx and in 2002, where the expenses of UPS even show a negative growth while FedEx's direct operating expenses grow more than 10%.

Figures 7.5 and 7.6 show that the evolution of total aircraft operating expenses for both integrators between 1990 and 2007 is quite similar, with a strong increase between 2002 and 2007. The direct operating costs of FedEx in 2007 amount to approximately $7.5 billion, which is more than twice the level of UPS in 2007, namely $3.5 billion. The main reason for this difference is the fact that FedEx is more active in air express than UPS. Therefore, FedEx is

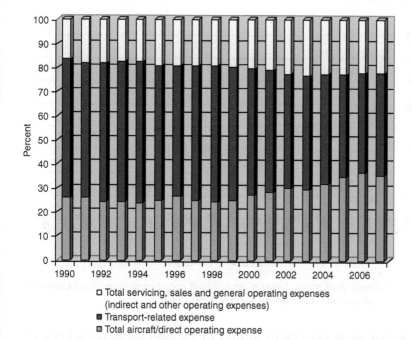

Figure 7.7 Share of different categories of FedEx TOE, all regions, 1990–2007.

- Total servicing, sales and general operating expenses (indirect and other operating expenses)
- Transport-related expense
- Total aircraft/direct operating expense

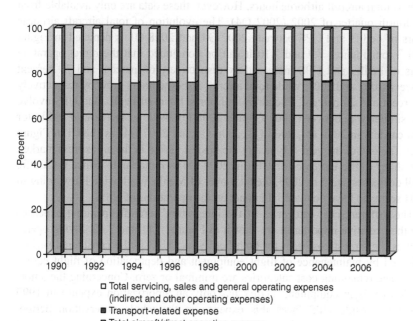

Figure 7.8 Share of different categories of UPS TOE, all regions, 1990–2007.

- Total servicing, sales and general operating expenses (indirect and other operating expenses)
- Transport-related expense
- Total aircraft/direct operating expense

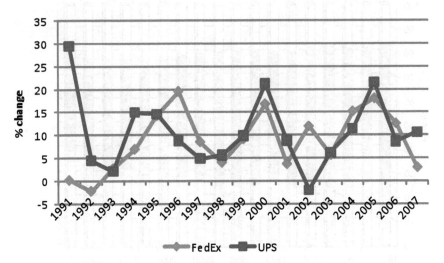

Figure 7.9 Annual percentage change of total aircraft operating expenses FedEx and UPS
– all aircraft types used, all regions, 1990–2007.

considered as an air cargo carrier whereas UPS is more considered as a ground-based express delivery company.[7]

It is interesting to compare the operating cost level with an output measure, such as total aircraft airborne hours. However, these data are only available from the fourth quarter of 2002 (2002 Q4). The evolution of total aircraft airborne hours of FedEx and UPS between 2002 Q4 and 2008 Q1 is depicted in Figure 7.10. From Figures 7.9 and 7.10 it can be concluded that the direct operating costs of FedEx and UPS increased by respectively 66 percent and 73 percent between 2002 and 2007, while total aircraft airborne hours grew by respectively 7 percent and 20 percent. The aircraft airborne hours of FedEx and UPS evolve in a similar way between 2002 Q4 and 2008 Q1, with an increase in traffic for both carriers in 2004 Q4, 2005 Q4, 2006 Q4 and 2007 Q4, as shown in Figure 7.10. The end of the year is typically the busiest period in the air express market. The sharp traffic increase for UPS in 2004 Q4 is remarkable. Since the traffic level decreases again in 2005, the take-over of Menlo Worldwide Forwarding in 2004 seems to have no material impact on the operations of UPS.

The different cost categories of the integrators' aircraft operating expenses and their relative importance are shown in Figures 7.11 and 7.12. Flying operations is the largest cost item for both FedEx and UPS in the considered period, followed by maintenance of flight equipment and depreciation of flight equipment. The remaining cost categories are minimal or zero. Concerning the amortization of flight equipment, FedEx has only an amortization expense in 1990 and 1991, while UPS faces this expense in the whole observation period. However, due to the small relative importance of this type of expense, it is not visible in the figures.

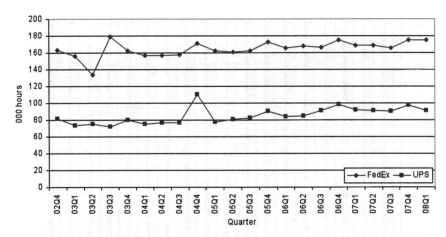

Figure 7.10 Total aircraft airborne hours (000) FedEx and UPS – sum of all regions, all aircraft types used, 2002 Q4–2008 Q1.

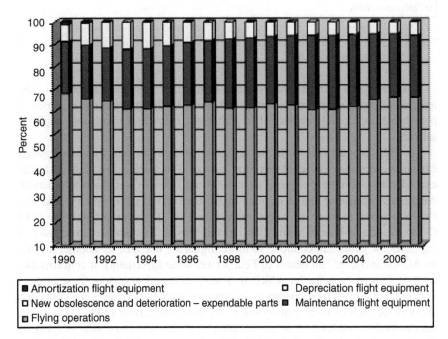

Figure 7.11 Share of different categories of FedEx total aircraft operating expenses, all regions, 1990–2007.

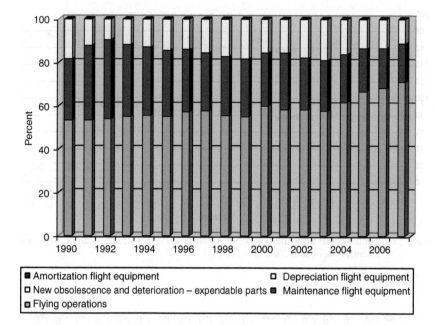

Figure 7.12 Share of different categories of UPS total aircraft operating expenses, all regions, 1990–2007.

In Figures 7.13 and 7.14 the evolution of the most important categories of the integrators' flying operations expenses is shown. The flying operations expenses of both integrators mainly consist of aircraft fuel, rentals and pilots' and copilots' salaries.

For UPS, aircraft fuel forms the largest expense in its total flying operations expenses over the whole observation period. For FedEx, the fuel cost was exceeded by the rentals expense from 1993 until 2002. Over the whole period, the rentals expense of FedEx is much higher than that of UPS, which means that FedEx outsourced more of its operations than UPS. For aircraft types Beech 18 C-185, Cessna 404[8] and Cessna 208 Caravan,[9] FedEx has rental expenses and no expenses for pilots and copilots, so these flights are operated by another airline, an ACMI-provider,[10] on behalf of FedEx (wet-lease agreement). It concerns aircraft of limited capacity for which it is more economical to hire these aircraft than to have it in its own operation. In contrast, UPS has expenses for pilots and copilots for each of its aircraft types. Comparing the current (2008 Q1) aircraft fleet of FedEx and UPS, it is remarkable that FedEx has more aircraft types of small capacity in its fleet than UPS. This results from the fact that FedEx has more domestic flying operations, while UPS is more active in road express for its domestic operations. The Airbus A 300–600 and the MD-11 are the only aircraft types that are used by both integrators. Figures 7.13 and 7.14 also show the strong increase in fuel expenses since 2000.

4 Challenges and opportunities for integrators

4.1 Cost control in a fixed cost environment

Integrators have to deal with very high fixed costs, e.g. to build and maintain their transport network, to set up new infrastructure worldwide, to maintain existing hubs and gateways, etc. An important question for an integrator nowadays is how to build in more flexibility in a fixed cost network. One way to do this is by choosing optimally between using their hub-and-spoke network or flying point-to-point. These two possible network structures are depicted in Figure 7.15. In the hub-and-spoke network in this figure, each plane stops twice (two sectors or segments), so 12 cities can be connected with six planes. However, there are not always two stops per plane in a hub-and-spoke network. During peak periods, an integrator will fly more point-to-point since the volume is high enough to fly directly. In times of recession, the hub-and-spoke network will be used more. In a point-to-point network, each plane normally stops four times. In Europe, DHL's network consists of one super-hub in Leipzig and several regional hubs (e.g. East Midlands, Bergamo, Copenhagen), while TNT only uses a single hub-and-spoke network (hub in Liège). A hub-and-spoke network involves more fixed costs than a point-to-point network, but it offers a high service level since many cities can be connected in a relatively short time period. Therefore, a hub-and-spoke network is also called a service model, whereas a point-to-point network is considered as a cost model. In general, the network and route structure chosen by the integrator depends on the existing demand per stretch.

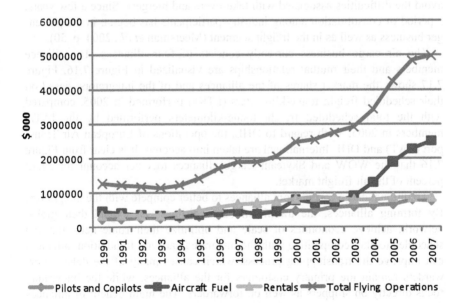

Figure 7.13 Evolution of the most important categories of FedEx flying operations expenses, all regions, 1990–2007.

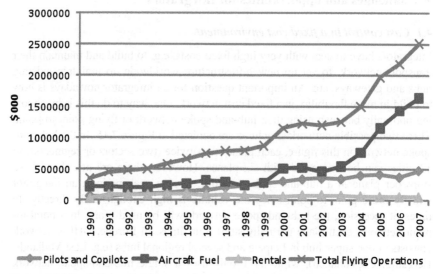

Figure 7.14 Evolution of the most important categories of UPS flying operations expenses, all regions, 1990–2007.

4.2 Concentration, consolidation and convergence

Since the beginning of the 1990s, multinational alliances are created in order to avoid the difficulties associated with take-overs and mergers. Since a few years, a period of consolidation among industry participants has begun, in the passenger business as well as in the freight segment (Meersman *et al.*, 2004, p. 50).

The air cargo business currently consists of four alliances. The alliance members and their mutual relationships are visualized in Figure 7.16. Figure 7.17 shows the market shares of the alliances and of the integrators, based on their scheduled freight tonne-kilometers (FTKs) performed in 2005, compared with the total scheduled freight tonne-kilometers performed by the IATA members in 2005. With regard to DHL, the operations of European Air Transport (EAT) and DHL International are taken into account. It is clear from Figure 7.16 that the WOW and Skyteam Cargo alliances together account for 27.42 percent of the air freight market.

Traditional cargo carriers join alliances to better compete with the integrators. By forming alliances, the traditional cargo airlines can extend their global network, achieve economies of scale and optimize their route networks and schedules to stay competitive with the integrated carriers. In addition, alliances can improve the transhipping process, which causes many of the delays. Forwarders remain the primary customers for the alliances, while the integrators focus directly on shippers as well on forwarders. The main benefit of alliances for forwarders is the access to a single network with a single point of contact. The airlines benefit most from the cost savings achieved as a result of alliances.

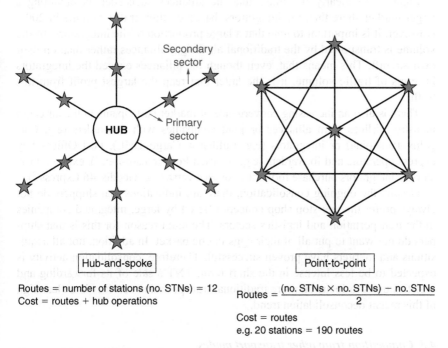

Figure 7.15 Overnight network structures of integrators (source: own composition based on presentation "DHL Global & European Networks" by MacBeth, M. (1 December 2008)).

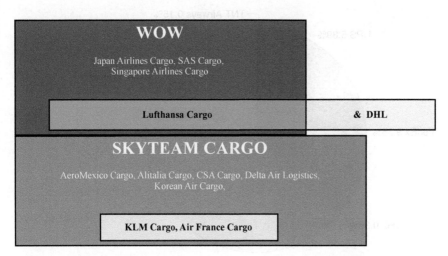

Figure 7.16 Air freight alliances (source: own composition based on Duponselle *et al.*, 2005).

Figure 7.17 clearly illustrates that the alliances succeeded in obtaining a larger market share than the integrators, based on their traffic volume in 2005. However, it is important to note that a large proportion of the integrators' traffic volume is transported by the traditional air freight alliances rather than on their own aircraft. This means that, even though the alliances exceed the integrators in terms of traffic volume, it is the latter that reap the largest profit from this traffic.

There is also an increasing convergence of market participants in the air cargo industry: airlines form alliances or joint companies with forwarders (e.g. Cargolux–Panalpina) or integrators (e.g. Lufthansa Cargo–DHL), Post Offices buy express operators and forwarders (e.g. Austrian Post–trans-o-flex[11]), express operators or integrators purchase forwarders or vice versa (e.g. Geodis–46 Express[12]).

Despite the ongoing consolidation, there are indications that shippers do not always prefer the one-stop shop concept offered by large, integrated companies in the transportation and logistics sectors. The main reason for this is that shippers do not want to put all of their eggs in one basket. In addition, not all acquisitions and mergers have proven successful. Therefore, consolidation activity is expected to be less intense in the short term. TNT's sale of its forwarding and logistics units to focus on more traditional transportation services is a clear sign of this recent deconsolidation trend.

4.3 Competition from other transport modes

An integrator's line-haul operations are carried out by air or by road: air express or road express. The choice depends primarily on the willingness to pay of the

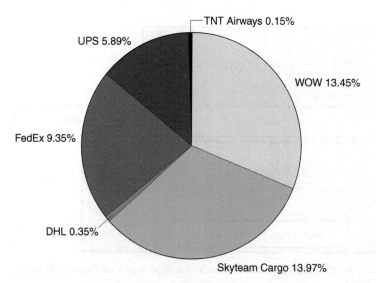

Figure 7.17 Market share of air freight alliances and integrators, based on scheduled FTKs performed in 2005 (source: own composition based on IATA, 2006).

customer. Starting from 2002, a modal shift from air to road is taking place, which is driven by three factors (MacBeth, 2008):

- increasing aircraft fuel prices;
- higher quality of road services;
- better logistics organization of the shipper.

The current economic crisis that started mid-2008 stimulates the shift from air express to road express even more. Of course, the choice for road express is only possible for e.g. intra-European or intra-US transport and not for intercontinental goods flows (ibid.).

In addition, the air freight industry is facing increasing competition from the rail sector on short-haul routes and the ocean sector on long-haul, intercontinental routes. Some of the integrators are planning to use high-speed trains for the pre- and post-carriage of air freight through Europe. The combination of rail and air makes it possible to lower costs and delivery times and to reduce the impact on the environment.

Regarding the intercontinental air freight market, a shift from air freight to ocean transport for some high-value goods has been noted, due to the high cost of air freight as a result of the continuing high prices for aviation fuel. According to Ken Choi, head of Korean Air Cargo, only 70 percent of mobile phones are currently moved by air, versus 99 percent in the past. Even though air freight is more expensive than ocean freight, it has a higher certainty of delivery on a predetermined schedule (ACMG, 2006).

4.4 Continued growth of e-commerce

Since 1990 the Internet has changed the air cargo industry substantially. One of the reasons for this change is the increasing number of firms investing in e-commerce. This enables them to expand their market reach. Since the cost of gaining an on-line sales presence is remarkably low and advances are made in global low-cost shipping, even a small firm can deliver goods to a worldwide customer base at a minimal cost. In addition, e-commerce typically leads to more sales in small quantities. Air transport is the ideal mode of transport for the worldwide delivery of small shipments. Although it is more expensive, it can guarantee a faster and more frequent delivery compared with other transport modes (Zhang *et al.*, 2007).

Although the Big Four integrators focus on the B2B market, they are developing their presence in the B2C market. While the B2B market has matured, the B2C market still has a high growth potential and involves many opportunities for integrators. It is necessary to build on B2C to stay sustainable. However, serving the B2C market is also challenging since it requires more flexibility compared to B2B. Therefore, it is impossible to use the B2B network to serve the B2C market. The integrators need to develop a special network for home delivery and have to deal with Last Mile logistics.

4.5 *Regulations and trade barriers*

Another possible threat to the integrator business are regulations, e.g. noise regulations. Restrictions on noise and night-time flying are increasing, which makes the choice of airports for integrators to develop their operations more complex. Next to other choice criteria such as good road connections and available space for warehouses, integrators require unrestricted night flights, since their activities typically take place at night.

5 Conclusions

The aim of this chapter was to get an insight into the cost structure of integrators and, hence, to analyze the industrial economic structure of the integrated express market. Due to the multimodal door-to-door operating cycle of integrators and the scarcity of useful cost data of the integrators' entire shipment cycle, the focus lies on the analysis of cost data about the air transport related operations of FedEx and UPS. In a next phase, a simulation model will be developed, which will be used for scenario-based analysis and modeling of the operational and strategic decisions of integrators. Supplementary to the simulation tool, the cost data may be used to estimate a cost function of these two integrators, which will be compared with that of non-integrated service providers. The industrial economic analysis of the market, combined with the investigation of the market, the major actors and their strategies, will lead to an understanding and forecasting of the expansion and cooperation strategies of integrators. Considering the enormous market power of integrators, an insight into the market structure is of high importance for shippers, economic regions or potential competitors.

Notes

1 According to Boeing, air cargo consists of freight, express and air mail. In some publications, air cargo is used as a more general term than air freight. In this thesis, however, both terms will be used without any distinction.
2 Measured in revenue tonne-kilometers (RTK).
3 The integrator market is an oligopolistic market since only a few sellers account for a substantial proportion of total sales. The main challenge for the analysis of an oligopoly is strategic behavior or strategic interdependence between competitors, which means that each firm's optimal behavior depends on its assumptions about its rivals' likely reactions (Lipczynski *et al.*, 2005).
4 Form 41 Air Carrier Financial Data provided by US Department of Transportation – Bureau of Transportation Statistics (BTS).
5 The constant prices of 2007 are based on inflation rates calculated from the Consumer Price Index, which is compiled by the Bureau of Labor Statistics (US Department of Labor). Since FedEx and UPS are multinationals offering servicing in different countries with different price evolutions, it is difficult to find a correct deflator.
6 Schedule P-7 of the Form 41 Financial Reports provided by the BTS was used. This database contains quarterly operating expense statements, by functional grouping, for large-certificated US air carriers.
7 This even has legal consequences since the labor relations law that governs the operations of FedEx and UPS is determined by two statutes: the Railway Labor Act (RLA)

and the National Labor Relations Law (NLRL). The RLA covers employees in the railroad and airline industries, while the NLRA governs most other private sector employees. As UPS was originally organized as a trucking company, its drivers are governed by the NLRA. FedEx drivers are governed under the RLA as the company was originally organized as an airline. The RLA makes unionization much more difficult than the NLRA. This difference is used by FedEx as a competitive advantage (Kearns, K.L., 2009).

8 The Cessna 404 exists in a pure cargo version, the Titan Freighter.

9 The Cessna 208 Caravan, also known as the Cargomaster, is a pure cargo, short-haul regional aircraft that was developed with FedEx. The integrator uses that aircraft for cargo feederline operations.

10 An ACMI-provider provides Aircraft, Crew, Maintenance and Insurance freighter leasing services. This means that an ACMI-provider wet-leases its aircraft to other airlines or freight forwarders against a fixed rate per hour. An ACMI contract usually involves a minimum number of block hours per month, which makes the risk/reward profile of an ACMI-provider relatively low.

11 Austrian Post acquired a 74.9 percent stake in trans-o-flex at the end of 2006. This acquisition enabled Austrian Post to considerably strengthen its Parcel & Logistics Division (Hitziger, 2007).

12 Geodis acquired 46 Express, a French courier company, to strengthen its domestic express business (CEP Research, 2007).

References

Air Cargo Management Group (2006), "International Air Freight and Express Industry Performance Analysis 2006."

Boeing (2006), *World Air Cargo Forecast 2006/2007*, www.boeing.com/commercial/cargo/wacf.pdf.

CEP-Research (2007), *Geodis Plans French Express Acquisition*, www.cep-research.com/cepresearch/respository/news/2007/august/news020807.html.

Coelli, T., Estache, A., Perelman, S. and Trujillo, L. (2003), *A Primer on Efficiency Measurement for Utilities and Transport Regulators*, Washington, D.C.: The World Bank.

Duponselle, D., Meersman, H., Van de Voorde, E. and Vanelslander, T. (2005), *Air Transport Colloquium, Critical Issues in Air Transport Economics*, Antwerp: Universiteit Antwerpen.

Falkner, J. (2007), DHL Feeling Pangs of Indigestion? *International Freighting Weekly*, Issue 1, 959.

Hitziger, W. (2007), *Austrian Post Building a European Niche Player*, Presentation held at Courier and Parcel Logistics Summit 2007, 2 and 3 October 2007, Barcelona.

IATA (2006), *World Air Transport Statistics Volume 1 – World Air Transport Digest*, Montreal/Geneva.

Kearns, K.L. (2009), *FedEx: Through the Looking Glass*, American Economic Alert, www.americaneconomicalert.org/view_art.asp?Prod_ID=3256.

Lipczynski, J., Wilson, J. and Goddard, J. (2005), *Industrial Organization, Competition, Strategy, Policy*, Harlow: Pearson Education.

MacBeth, M. (2008), "Cost structure of Integrators," interview with Network Planning Director Network Europe at DHL Aviation, 17 December 2008, DHL Aviation, Brussels Airport.

Meersman, H., Roosens, P., Van de Voorde, E., Witlox, F. and Vanelslander, T. (2004), *Optimising Strategies in the Air Transport Business: Survival of the Fittest?* Antwerp: Garant.

Onghena, E. (2008), "The Integrator Market: Actors and their Strategies," Proceedings of the 12th ATRS World Conference, Athens.

Oxford Economic Forecasting (2004), "The Economic Impact of Express Carriers in Europe," www.oef.com/Free/pdfs/euroexpressfinal091104.pdf.

Pirenne, M. (2007), "Worldwide Express Transport," guest lecture for the course Van Breedam and Van de Voorde, academic year 2006–2007, Logistiek en Expeditie, Universiteit Antwerpen, Antwerp.

US–ASEAN Business Council (2005), *Express Delivery Services: Integrating ASEAN to Global Markets*, www.globalexpress.org/doc/EDS_Report.pdf.

Zhang, A., Lang, C., Hui, Y.V. and Leung, L. (2007), "Intermodal Alliance and the Rivalry of Transport Chains: The Air Cargo Market," *Transportation Research Part E*, Vol. 43, no. 3, pp. 234–246.

Zondag, W.J. (2006), *Competing for Air Cargo, A Qualitative Analysis of Competitive Rivalry in the Air Cargo Industry*, www.fapaa.org/pdf/News/Jun06_Competingfor AirCargoThesis.pdf.

8   Airports of the future
Essentials for a renewed business model

Rosário Macário

1 Looking back

On 8 February 2003 we could read in the text of an air transport article of The *Economist* magazine the following sentence: "The key to flying is to defy gravity." Indeed this has been an aerodynamic challenge highlighted since the days of Leonardo da Vinci, and even before. However, in 2003, the newspaper used the old postulate to present the evidence that, by then, the challenge was as much financial as physical.

In 1997, according to the survey made by Pat Hanlon (2004, p. 5) there were already approximately 1,200 scheduled airline companies around the world, of which around 300 were operating on international routes. Diversity was wide and dimensions were in line with it, from airlines carrying over 80 million passengers annually and operating fleets of more than 600 aircraft, to airline companies that carry less than 10,000 passengers and operate only one or two aircraft. Ownership was also diversified, although government participation is reducing intensity of its role all over the world. Worth noticing is the fact that in the top 100 companies (revenues ranking) we can find only ten cargo airlines, although Federal Express is reported as the largest in terms of employees, with more than 114,000 employees. No doubt air transport business has seen plenty of growth and creativity in the last 30 years, and this is today the challenging set of clients that form the first line market for airports.

It is generally recognized by many authors that air transport is a growing industry and very few industries, if any, have enjoyed such a performing profile for long periods. Looking back we see that since 1945 world passenger traffic grew at an average annual rate of 12 percent (Hanlon, 2004, p. 13); since 1960 a 9 percent annual growth is reported in general with freight growing at an annual rate of 11 percent and mail at 7 percent. As the industry gets larger and more mature we observe also a decrease in the rate of growth, although we can still register a growth of 5 percent per annum in passenger traffic in the decade 1985–95, with the first historical decline in 1991, due to the Gulf War, and a consecutive slowdown in the years that follow as a consequence of the economic recession. Between the years 1992–3 the rate of growth was only 2.3 percent and it was only in 1997–8 that the industry returned to a 7 percent annual growth rate. Several forecasts are available (e.g. IATA, ICAO, Boeing, Airbus, etc.) and most predictions point to growth rates of around 5 percent in the years to come, although there is still not enough observation on how the industry will receive the impacts caused by recent (2007/8) turmoil in financial markets. It is likely that these will produce negative effects at least on the short-term growth rates, since it is clear that incomes, fares and service level are among the main factors responsible for travel demand.

Traditionally, airports, just like all transport infrastructure, have looked at airlines as their primary customers, due to their legally binding agreements and because airlines pay for several charges, such as landing and parking fees, charges per passenger or tonne of freight handled, etc. Airlines, in turn, have legally binding agreements with passengers and look at passengers as their primary clients. In their traditional passive management approach airports used to see themselves as providers of a highly technological demanding infrastructure, of national strategic interest, for very sophisticated operations where safety played both a very distinguished and distinct role.

Today, in a more commercial and private environment, with an increased pressure on having an awareness of the meaning of a business model for airports, these complex infrastructures are increasingly dependent on non-aeronautical revenues, and thus perceive passengers as another segment of their primary customers. So far there has been little vertical integration between airports and airlines but partnerships seem to be tightening up as airline–airport–passenger relationships becomes more complicated. Airports depend on airlines to bring passengers and the more the airport enlarges its retail or other (business centres, health care, etc.) activities the more risk exists that this dual role may well lead to conflict of interests, with flights often being delayed by passengers who spend increased time shopping or else without hearing boarding gate announcements.

According to ICAO reports (2002) there are 1,192 airports with international scheduled services but the world's top 25 airports are handling 32 percent of the traffic. This is consistent with the evidence provided in several studies (e.g. Graham, 2001) that there are significant economies of scale in airport activities, with costs falling rapidly per passenger handled, until around a million passengers, and continuing to fall, up to around three million passengers per annum, after which they level off. This cost profile has long been recognized as posing cost recovery difficulties and, together with the more recent airport evolution, justifies rethinking airports' business models, meaning:

> the set of which activities a firm performs, how it performs them, and when it performs them as it uses its resources to perform activities, given its industry, to create superior customer value (low cost or differentiated products) and put itself in a position to appropriate the value.
>
> (Afluah A., 2004, p. 9)

2 Drivers of the industry evolution

For a better discernment of the interactions between airlines and airports we must understand the market environment under which change has occurred and shaped the evolutionary stages of the industry. Globalization and international-ization are, of course, two major industrial trends of the twentieth century that are strongly reflected in the growth of trade and there are very consistent indica-tions that this has changed the way production and trade are done ever since (Thurow, 1996, p. 26; Giddens, 1999, p. 9).

In parallel with this phenomenon there was a profound change in the regula-tory and institutional organization of the air transport industry. The world-wide air transport reform entailed a movement that evolved from west to east and from north to south, very likely in a close relationship with the degree of devel-opment of the different societies, although there is as yet no scientific evidence to support this hypothesis of correlation. Table 8.1 below summarizes the main changes in the factors that characterize the industry and confront the market environment before and after the 1970s and in Table 8.2 we provide the main features of each evolutionary stage of the industry since the 1970s.

The US deregulation of air transport started in 1977 in its domestic markets for air freight and in 1978 extended to passengers, in articulation with Open Skies commitments as an approach to international markets in 1979. The European market moved rapidly towards a similar situation, with some countries taking the lead in the liberalization of their domestic market, while the European Union initi-ated in 1988 (so, ten years after) its movement towards economic deregulation which was achieved by mid 1997, by means of three regulatory packages of direc-tives for implementation in the different member states. The creation of a Single European Market within Europe from 1993 also meant that air transport was essentially moving towards more market liberalization from that date.

Table 8.1 Elements of differentiation of the industry before and after the 1970s

Past characteristics	Present characteristics
Air Transport seen as a national strategic asset – a public service	Air Transport seen as corporate commercial asset with alternative business models
Markets closed with bilateral exclusivity agreements	Open markets. Interline agreements lost "raison d'être"
Companies closed in their own networks with interline agreements	Productive and commercial assets shared for cost-cutting purposes. Multi-company networks become a valuable asset
Sharing only some productive assets (e.g. maintenance pools; handling agreements)	Strong willingness to involve private finance partners in several business areas
Modal superiority and non-cooperative attitude	Modal humbleness develops attitude in favour of intermodality (or co-modality)
Strong political support for subsidization	Flag carriers without meaning

Almost in parallel, in South America, several privatization programs were also implemented for liberalization of domestic markets and Australia and New Zealand soon followed the US movement (Button and Stough, 2000, pp. 59–83). Later, air transport issues also gained a position on the agenda of the Asian Pacific Economic Council (APEC), and in Japan the domestic airline All Nippon Airways was allowed to operate on international routes for the first time in 1986, by which time other companies had emerged in the Asian market, such as EVA Air in Taiwan, Asiana in South Korea, etc. (Doganis, 2001, p. 5).

Button and Stough report how frantic the deregulation movements have been across the world in those decades:

> By 1982, the US had signed 23 liberal air service agreements, mainly with smaller nations, in pursuit of its Open Skies agenda. This was followed in the 90s by a burst of agreements with European states including those with Switzerland, Luxembourg, Iceland, Sweden, Norway, Belgium, Denmark, Finland and the Czech Republic in 1995, Jordan in 1998 and Singapore, Brunei, Taipei, Panama, Guatemala, El Salvador, Honduras, Costa Rica, Nicaragua, New Zealand, Malaysia, Aruba, Chile, Romania and the Netherlands Antilles in 1997. More major agreements with the Netherlands and Germany came as a result of agreements on airline alliances between KLM and Northwest Airlines and Lufthansa and United Airlines, respectively.
>
> (Button and Stough, 2004, p. 64)

However, they have been followed by alliance movements which in fact tend to reduce competitive pressure.

Looking back, what we observe is that from an economic perspective sound theories advocate the liberalization of markets and the increase of competition as more effective tools to achieve market efficiency and consumer welfare, and regulatory policies all over the world have followed this recommendation. However, the selfish strategy of each agent leads to survival action, which counteracts those policies and finds market solutions to achieve a higher degree of dominance and to maintain prices at a convenient level in a profit-oriented perspective. As a response to these individual actions, governments attempt to control possible abuses of such dominance through enforcement of competition rules. This purpose is also pursued through convergence of competition rules of major regions (e.g. USA, EU) and/or countries.

Several authors agree about the prospects for the years to come, largely supported by the agents' behaviour in the last decades, pointing out that:

• Growth rates will differ between market segments, suggesting that Customer Resource Management might become an indispensable tool for airlines and airports. A good example is the dramatic decline of premium traffic, in particular in the intra-european routes where it virtually disappeared (Doganis, 2001).

- Diversification of ownership will place airlines and airports in a position of greater sensitiveness to the turmoil of financial markets. This is the more true, the more yields will stretch under scenarios of overcapacity and high fuel prices (Morrel, 2007).
- Strong downward pressure on fares and cargo tariffs is likely to continue as the threat of the low-fare (or no-frills) phenomenon develops in passenger transport and eventually extends also to freight transport (Macário *et al.*, 2007).
- Liberalization, together with abandonment of ownership restrictions and privatization of airlines hitherto government-owned, will contribute to accelerating the industrial concentration within global alliances creating dominant market positions (Doganis, 2001) and severely hindering the envisaged competitive environment.
- Falling yields will lead to cost-cutting pressure envisaging financial success, with a strong emphasis on labour costs (Button and Stough, 2000).
- In order to reduce costs and improve service to customers, airlines will intensify the use of electronic communications both on business-to-customer and business-to-business relationships, putting travel agents and freight forwarders under strong pressure to regenerate their business models (Doganis, 2001).
- Air traffic services and airports will be under severe pressure, in what concerns slot management, the main competitive instrument of the airport, very likely accelerating the privatization of air traffic control worldwide as a solution to ensure the required investments for modernization of the sector.

In general these prospects reflect an interaction between agents and governments that results in what we can call regulatory waves shifting the market from one evolutionary phase to the next as a consequence of the action/reaction of the different agents, as illustrated in Table 8.2. The key question is whether regulatory competencies can be enhanced to the point that regulation drives the market instead of simply policing it. In an industry as complex as the one we have in air transport neither one nor the other role is easy. But it seems that the twenty-first century requires also some reform in the way regulatory roles are played, increasing the leading role and, consequently, decreasing the policing one, towards a more efficient and effective industry.

3 Interaction between airlines and airports

The evolution of the industry shows evidence that airlines and airports work on interactive markets where service quality plays an important role. Airports must compete among themselves for transfer of passengers while developing attractive facilities for specific customer segments. Key features to increase demand seem to be convenience, materialized in available slots and convenient facilities for non-aeronautical activities, network connectivity and more recently brand development.

Table 8.2 Features of the different evolutionary phases of air transport industry

Regulation	Deregulation	Reshaping	Consolidation	Regeneration
Stabilized capacity	Increased capacity	Cost reduction, increased efficiency	Industry consolidation (alliances) Contestability reaches labor structures	Loss of stability, trend towards increased capacity
Market captured	New entrants	Restructuring operations to improve performance, use of network effects	Market loses contestability and gains discipline	Unbundling services by market segment
Bundled services	Unbundling of services	New service growth	Networks extend to airports and airlines	Activity-based cost specialization
Low diversity offer	Reduction of prices	Weak players out	Fortress Hubs emerge as structurally secure positions	Network fragmentation
Slot distribution based on grandfather rights	Slot as a competitive instrument	Slots commercially driven, network approach and partnership dependency	Slot trading emerges	Big airports move to slot auctions
Airports as strategic infrastructure	Airports start tackling competition	Airports as intermodal nodes of a chain	Airports as multifunctional logistic platforms	Airports move toward business diversification, emergence of concepts like airport-city. Shareholders' value concept becomes determinant
Regulation focused on enhancing competition	Regulation focused on safety/security	Regulation focused on quality of service and customer welfare	Regulation focused on enhancing competition	Regulation focused on safety/security, need for cross-sector regulation emerges
Current positions		→ ASIA	→ EU	→ USA

The business slightly shifted from service focus to process focus, giving priority to seamless flows of passenger and freight, with intermodality (or co-modality) playing an important role in cost efficiency of the services provided and obtaining enhanced effectiveness through economies of scope, offering an increased number of destinations without any burden on the productive structure.

As Button and Stough (2001, p. 204) state, airports represent a multi-service networked industry with significant monopoly control in the provision of many of its services. In fact, as we have already mentioned, in recent decades the evolution of the air transport industry shifted away from the traditional view of the airport as a facility where aircraft operate and passengers and freight transit, giving place to a more encompassing business model where parallel to the aeronautical activities most airports incorporate a wide variety of other activities that fit smoothly into the process flow of passenger and freight, increasing the value of the use of the infrastructure for its customer, resulting in:

• retail mall concepts merged into passenger terminals;
• airport property beyond the terminal encompassing development of hotels, entertainment facilities, conference and exhibition complexes, office buildings, logistics and free trade zones;
• complementary sets of facilities for airports and airline employees (e.g. day care centers, health clinics, etc.).

This corresponds to looking at the infrastructure with stakeholders' eyes and including all services that can bring value to the stakeholders' processes, being external or internal clients of the airport. That is passengers, freight forwarders, accompanying persons (external customers) and employees of the many services, whether aeronautical or non-aeronautical, suppliers, etc. (internal customers). Small airports include only retail activities while larger airports may reach the point of taking features of metropolitan business districts, becoming significant employment, shopping, business meeting and entertainment destinations in their own right. Figure 8.1 below presents a list of activities that can be developed within the inner operational perimeter of the airport (i.e. inside the fence), and others that can be developed in the outer perimeter (i.e. outside the fence), adding value to the first and generating additional demand.

The Airport Council International (ACI), based on the information registered in their data bases estimates that in 1990 about 30 percent of airport revenues resulted from non-aeronautical activities. In 1995 the weight of non-aeronautical revenues increased to 41 percent, in 2001 to 51 percent and in 2005 to 54 percent. Worth noticing is the airport of Atlanta, Hartsfield-Jackson, that in 2005 registered about 60 percent of non-aeronautical revenues.

The increasing importance given to this wide concept of airport business, also known as industrial airport or city airport, is reflected in the following examples reported by John Kasarda (2000) (www.airportinnovation.com) to whom the concept of airport city has been assigned:

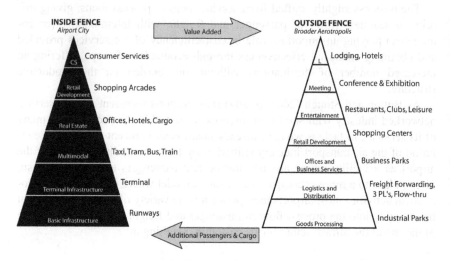

Figure 8.1 Added value activities in a wider airport concept (source: Schiphol Airport and John Kasarda (2000)).

- Aeróports de Paris established a real estate division in 2003 to act as the developer, general contractor and construction project owner and manager of landside commercial properties at Paris.
- Beijing Capital Airports Holding, whose master plan takes an expansive definition of airport functions including, among others, shopping, entertainment, education, sports and leisure, logistics, light manufacturing, finance, trade and housing.
- Dallas-Fort Worth's management is leasing its vast airport land to a wide variety of commercial tenants, including oil and natural gas exploration.
- Hong Kong International Airport's SkyCity is a one-million-square-meter retail, exhibition, business office, and hotel and entertainment complex near its passenger terminal.
- Kuala Lumpur International Airport's new airport city is commercially anchored by its large Gateway Park that, in addition to retail and office development, includes motor sports, an automotive hypermarket and leisure venues drawing on the local as well as aviation-induced market.
- Incheon's "AirCity" encompasses international business areas, logistics zones, shopping and tourism districts, as well as housing and services for airport city workers and residents.
- Dubai World Central is a $32 billion airport city under development (first runway open in December 2007), 25 miles south of downtown Dubai. Cornerstoned by a massive multimodal air logistics hub, the airport city will include office towers, hotels, a mega mall, golf course and housing for 40,000 on-site workers. Its airport, commercial and residential zones will be connected by an internal light rail system.

- Amsterdam Schiphol, through its Schiphol Real Estate Group, has been involved for two decades in landside commercial development. These developments include office complexes, hotels, meeting and entertainment facilities, logistics parks, shopping and other commercial activities branded under the AirportCity name. Nearly 58,000 people are employed at Schiphol, which integrates multimodal transportation, regional corporate headquarters, shopping, logistics and exhibition space to form a major economic growth pole for the Dutch economy.

In all these cases a positive synergy is established between the non-aeronautical activities that offer added value to the stakeholders of the airport, and return value to aeronautical activities through the increased demand generated.

4 New paradigm I: quality management

Stakeholders are thus composed of internal and external customers. The former group includes any entity that is part of the production process, and so internal to the airport system (the inner perimeter), who have to rely on the good performance of the suppliers of the system's components placed upstream and downstream of its own contribution. This interdependence highlights the process orientation of the functional organization underlying the interaction between airports and airlines and, consequently, underlying air transport.

Entities which are not part of the production process are considered as external customers, just like the users who are the "raison d'être" of the air transport system. An exception to this definition occurs when either the traveling process or the technological devices require the user of the air transport system to be involved in the productive process through any sort of "self-service" action (e.g. self-ticketing, paying the parking station, etc.) in which the user takes an active role, usually in the last part of the service. Nonetheless, in general we consider the individual and collective user of the airport systems as external customers.

Indeed, quality definitions may differ substantially when switching from the internal to the external customer perspective. In the diagram presented in Figure 8.2 (Macário, 2003) we break down the quality concept into the following four sub-concepts or elements:

- Expected Quality (Q1) – This is the level of quality which implicitly or explicitly is required by the customer. The level of quality is understood as a composition of a number of criteria, not all related to the travel itself but, instead, encompassing other attributes connected with the added value activities the airport offers. Qualitative analysis on customer profiles and preferences can assess the contributions of these criteria, which may change from one airport to the other or even between segments of clients of the very same airport.
- Targeted Quality (Q2) – This is the level of quality which the service provider or manager of an airport system is aiming to provide to the customers

as a consequence of his/her understanding of the customer's expectations and of the capabilities of the productive side of the system. Targeted quality must be set in an objective way and decoupled through the different services available within the airport and within the several sub-processes encompassed within the travelling process. For this, there is the need to identify for each perceived quality element which variables are meant to be kept constant across the whole system, which ones depend on geographical incidence, and also which is the decision level and the agent responsible for each variable, so that the corresponding decision-maker can be identified.

- Delivered Quality (Q3) – This is the level of quality effectively achieved in the provision of air transport services by the different components of the system, which does not necessarily coincide with what is visible to the customers. Delivered quality must also be measured from the customer viewpoint and not only from the supply-side perspective; that is, it should be assessed against the client's criteria.

- Perceived Quality (Q4) – This is the level of quality perceived by the user-customer. This is influenced by several factors, such as their personal experience of the service or from associated or similar services, the information received about the service, from the provider or other sources, the non-direct service elements (e.g. convenience), or even the personal environment and needs. In the more recently explored domains of marketing (in its different approaches: mass, one-to-one, relational, affluent) this concept is very close to the one of "customer experience."

The operational materialization of these concepts differs from one airport to another and even within the same airport, whenever assessed under different circumstances or for different types of services. However, we can group these concepts in two different categories: one represents the production perspective – targeted and delivered quality; and the other represents the consumption perspective – expected and perceived quality.

The relationship between these four concepts is of utmost importance to adjust the service both to the stated and to the real (revealed) needs of the external customer. These relations can also be observed on the service and organizational scale, but their complexity increases substantially when we consider the air transport system as a whole, as the quality gaps identified in Figure 8.2 result from the interaction of several agents and processes at the different decision (or planning) levels. Two good illustrations of this logic are the delay of a flight, caused by the action or inaction of different agents that intervene in the dispatching process, and the delay caused by the customer him/herself who may have spent more time than allowed enjoying non-aeronautical service offers of the airport. In the former case there is a performance gap in the service delivered while in the latter it is a market misreading that led to the misunderstanding of clients' priorities.

The difference between expected quality (QE) and targeted quality (QT) reveals the existence of deficiencies in the process of identifying the needs of external customers and sometimes in distinguishing between stated needs and real needs, that is, difficulties in reading market signs. These deficiencies can be caused by problems at the observation or at the decision levels: in the former case, this means lack or poor effectiveness of the mechanisms for observation and study of customers' perceptions and needs; in the latter it will be either the malfunction of the strategic or tactical level of decision or the non-existence of one of these levels, which is a common situation. Together these decision levels and the intertwining of agents are responsible for the service definition, irrespective of the number of agents involved in the process.

Deviations between targeted quality and delivered quality can be caused by several reasons that might be related either with the service design or production, that is any situation of underperformance related to the provision of the services. This performance gap is either a measure of the effectiveness of one (or more) of the several service providers in achieving their own targets or of the effectiveness in breaking down targeted quality into the different service components.

Perceived quality often bears little similarity to delivered quality. This dissonance has several causes. It can result from a customer's accumulated knowledge about the service delivered and of personal or reported experiences with the service under assessment or with similar ones, and of personal background and environment, which create an expectation of the service provided. Consequently, perceived quality is assessed having an expectations scale as a filter

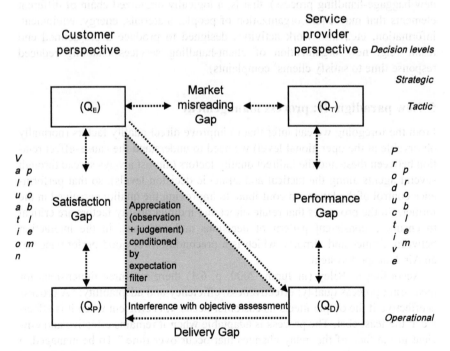

Figure 8.2 Quality gaps (source: Macário (2003)).

for this assessment. Marketing strategies and tactics (e.g. brand management) play a key role in the manipulation of expected quality and consequently in the satisfaction gap, which is the difference between expected and perceived quality.

A particular case of the application of these four quality concepts to air transport that serves to highlight the complexity of the interactive product and business model at stake is the case of the electronic check-in, used by the external customers on a self-service base. This case is particularly difficult in terms of quality management since the perceived quality is very much influenced by the good use that the customers make of the facility. That is, in these cases customers' education and training is fundamental for the overall quality perception of the service.

There is an implicit cause–effect logic underlying the quality approach. In a context-independent interpretation this means that there should be a permanent understanding between the cause and effect, i.e. between the transformation process and the desired outcomes. This is clearly reflected in the decomposition of the quality concept into the productive and consumption side as well as in the relation between direct and indirect quality factors.

Indirect quality factors are elements not directly observable by the air transport customer that are capable of tweaking the system in order to improve the perception of customers of the observable quality elements. These can be isolated elements (e.g. a new baggage track computer system) or processes (e.g. a new baggage-handling process), that is, a logically organized chain of different elements that may entail organization of people, materials, energy, equipment, information, etc., into work activities designed to produce a pre-defined end result (e.g. new organization of client-handling services enabling reduced response time to satisfy clients' complaints).

5 New paradigm II: process management

From the foregoing we can infer that to improve direct quality factors (normally observable at the operational level) we need to understand the cause–effect relation between these and the indirect quality factors (almost always spread through several agents along the tactical and strategic decision levels), so that performance control of the latter can contribute to improving the quality perceived in the former. So the processes that relate direct and indirect quality factors are critical to ensure a consistent pattern of decisions and activities, in the interaction between airlines and airports, which is a precondition for good performance of an Air Transport system.

According to Riley (in Juran, 2000, p. 6.1) there are three dimensions for measuring process quality: effectiveness, efficiency and adaptability. "A process is effective if the output meets its customer needs. It is efficient when it is effective at the least cost. The process is adaptable when it remains effective and efficient in the face of the many changes that occur over time." To be managed, a process must fulfil certain minimum conditions, such as:

- it should have an owner, for easier accountability;
- it should be fully defined (inputs, resources to be used, activities to be developed, outputs, and objectives to be achieved) to enable its control;
- its management infrastructure should be in place;
- its measurements and control points should be defined;
- it should be able to demonstrate stable, predictable and repeatable performance.

To define which aspects of a process should be measured, knowledge of the process mission and customer (internal and external) needs is required. For example, process measures based on customer needs are suitable to measure process effectiveness, while process measures based on cost, cycle time, labor productivity, etc., are more adequate to measure process efficiency. Simultaneous maximization of process effectiveness and efficiency, if successful, will very likely lead to service production of higher quality at lower cost. That is, it will increase value for customer and owner.

However, performance measurement is closely related to the direct quality factors selected and to the structural organization of the air transport system. Indeed, when designing the organizational structure of the airport's business model some of the following aspects should be considered:

- the process flow, patterns of which are achieved by understanding the way activities are structured and agents are engaged on it;
- and how the process interacts with each decision level and agent. The latter is largely conditioned by the design of the institutional network where agents interact, the span of control and accountability of each decision level and of each agent.

Span of control is defined by the number and diversity of processes that an agent has under his/her direct control. Span of accountability is defined by the number and diversity of functions that each agent is expected to develop and the performance standards that are required to be met. Processes and span of control and accountability converge to define span of attention, which refers to the number of activities that are within the two previous aspects. As Simons notes (2000, p. 54) in his analysis of organizational performance, span of attention is a concept with a different nature since it is defined by the agent itself, while span of accountability and span of control are always defined by an upper decision level; in other words, they are top-down defined concepts, while the former is set by the agent to enable better correspondence with the responsibilities received from the upper decision levels.

The good performance of the airport system largely depends on the capacity to control the critical quality criteria. For this it is fundamental to understand the (rather stochastic) cause–effect relation in the chain of activities (or processes) that leads to those quality outputs, in order to know what should be controlled, when to do it and which performance measures should be used.

As quality criteria differ between airports, since they result from a local interpretation of stakeholders' needs and expectations, no universal set of measures can be recommended. However, it is possible to identify some categories of performance measures that should accompany the development of airport-specific performance goals according to the quality criteria selected and the respective cause–effect relation with indirect quality factors.

Performance goals, if well communicated and appropriately deployed, which can be done through fora like the airline operating committees (AOC) that gather representatives from all airlines' agents, and possibly also through incentive mechanisms, set out guidance for each agent to contribute to the achievement of the strategic objectives of the system.

For goal deployment a sound measurement mechanism is needed, aligned with the consistency requirements illustrated in Figure 8.3, where a goal represents a formal general aspiration that defines purpose or expected levels of achievement (e.g. improved productive efficiency), and objectives are measurement standards and time frames to gauge progress and/or simple success (e.g. reduce the waste and scrap in maintenance departments by 5 percent each semester over next year) that are made operational through targets, that is concrete values attributed to objectives. As Simons also states, "goals and objectives can be made actionable only when a measurement is attached to any set of aspirations" (2000, p. 231).

The following categories of the largely complementary performance measures have been systematized by (Harbour, 1997, pp. 9–19) through the formulation of the following questions that represent a logical sequence of analysis for a given performance goal/objective:

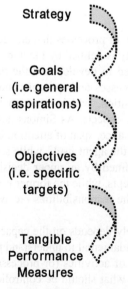

Strategy

Goals
(i.e. general
aspirations)

Objectives
(i.e. specific
targets)

Tangible
Performance
Measures

Figure 8.3 Strategic nature of performance goals (source: Macário (2005)).

- *What is the current performance level?*
  - Baseline measures establish the current performance and form the basis for all subsequent measures. Collecting initial data to feed baseline measures usually requires intensive work. The basic rule of thumb is that absence of baseline measures means there is no performance measurement system and consequently what is not measurable can not be improved.
- *How is a specific performance level changing over time?*
  - Trend measures show the evolution of a performance indicator with time and enable the provision of preventive actions whenever progress evaluation results are negative or too slow, when compared with what was planned.
- *Is performance staying within some predetermined boundary or tolerance level?*
  - Control measures are feedback measures and like trend measures provide early warnings when some activity or process is straying from a predetermined performance level.
- *What is causing a specific problem and where is the problem area located?*
  - Diagnostic measures provide orientation to a specific problem area and have a preventive character, as they can avoid the first occurrence of a problem.
- *Given past and current performance levels, what levels should be planned for in the future?*
  - Current and past performance can and should be used to support the development of future scenarios and as feeders of future strategies and subsequent plans.

6 Conclusions and recommendation for a renewed business model

From what we have said in the previous sections of this chapter it is demonstrated that airport activity is a complex set of interactions between agents of diversified interests that have to work together in a well-articulated chain of processes. So, airport performance depends on the quality management of these processes so that effective value can be offered to the different market segments.

It has also been made evident that airports have tremendously broadened the scope of their activities and services offered to the external customers. Besides, with the enlargement of activities and associated complexity, employees and suppliers have become internal customers.

By shifting the airport management logic toward a business-oriented focus we must keep in mind that the goal of any business model is to make money and like any other business, the airport makes profits if its revenue model considers:

- offering products or services at a lower cost than its competitors do (e.g. office rentals); or,

- offering differentiated products at premium prices that more than compensate for the extra cost of differentiation (e.g. conference center, logistic parks); and,
- discovering whether there are enough customers that want the product or service and can afford it (e.g. spa facilities, restaurants).

In this new paradigm for the airport business model the airport management has to address three new concerns. The first is to undertake a transversal management process that enables the definition of sustainable ways for staying in business and developing it successfully, knowing that potential competitors are the other airports and also the interchange stations of some land-based modes (e.g. TGV for European distances below 500 km), or even some industrial parks. This means defining the business, setting the scope of activities, i.e. "knowing yourself" and adjusting the capabilities according to opportunities and threats of the external environment, which entails the setting of the possibilities frontier over which the performance gap will occur. The second is to identify customer expectations and adjust the product or service to them, meaning market reading and preventing the respective gap; in other words "knowing your customer" and setting up the processes that enable the management of the marketing cycle; perceive the customer – conceive the service – deliver it with envisaged quality. The third is to maintain a vigilant attitude that enables a business to pursue evolutionary change while preserving stability and avoiding stalling risks, meaning "knowing your path" while interacting with markets and competitors.

In brief, long-term business stability in the future airport business is achievable through a business model that offers: clear mission; thorough strategy; effective marketing; and efficient and accountable management.

References

Afluah, A. (2004) *Business Models: A Strategic Management Approach.* New York: McGraw-Hill.

Button, K. and Stough, R. (2000) *Air Transport Networks: Theory and Policy Implications.* Cheltenham, UK: Edward Elgar.

Doganis, R. (2001) *The Airline Business in the 21st Century.* London: Routledge.

Giddens, A. (1999) *Runaway World.* London: Profile Books.

Graham, A. (2001) *Managing Airports: An International Perspective.* Oxford: Butterworth Heinemann.

Hanlon, P. (2004) *Global Airlines.* Oxford: Elsevier Butterworth-Heinemann.

Harbour, J. L. (1997) *The Basics of Performance Measurement.* New York: Productivity Press.

Juran, J. M. (1990) *Planning for Quality.* Wilton, CT: Juran Institute Inc.

Kasarda, J. D. (2000) "Aerotropolis: Airport-Driven Urban Development in the Future: Cities in the 21st Century," working document from UDL (Urban Land Institute), at Washington, D.C

Macário, R. (2005) "Quality Management in Urban Mobility Systems: An Integrated Approach," PhD Dissertation, Instituto Superior Técnico, Lisboa, Portugal.

Macário, R. and Lopes, D. (2003) "Quality Service Perception as a Planning tool," 4th National Congress of Rail Transport, organised by ADFER (Association for the Development of Railways), Lisbon, Portugal.

Morrel, P. (2007). *Airline Finance*. Aldershot: Ashgate.

Riley, J. F. (2000) "Process Management," in Juran, J. and Godfrey, A. B. (2000) *Juran's Quality Handbook*, New York: McGraw-Hill, pp. 6.1–6.21.

Simons, R. (2000) *Performance Measurement and Control Systems for Implementing Strategy*. Upper Saddle River, NJ: Prentice Hall.

Thurow, L. (1996) *The Future of Capitalism: How Today's Economic Forces Will Shape Tomorrow's Future*. New York: William Morrow.

9 The airport city

A new business model for airport development

Douglas Baker and Robert Freestone

1 Introduction

The airport city concept has been embraced by many airports of different scales and in varied ways around the world. Airports everywhere have diversified their landside revenues with non-aviation commercial and industrial development in order to increase revenues and spread risk in the notoriously volatile aviation market. As intermodal hubs in a connected, globalised world, airports have evolved from transportation nodes into multi-faceted business enterprises. They have assumed a critical role as 'transactional' spaces in the global economy (Gottdiener, 2001).

This evolution in the role of airports, non-traditional business strategies, and a new focus in non-aviation commercial development is reflected in both the transformation of the terminals into designer spaces of consumption and the commodification of surplus land within the airport fence. In some cases, greenfield opportunities on under-developed airports have fostered large-scale property development. The rise of non-aeronautical uses is a defining element of the new airport, leading to one caricature of the modern British airport as 'a runway with a shopping mall beside it' (Graham and Guyer, 2000, p. 253). Non-aviation commercial revenues (notably, retailing and car parking) on average now account for half of all airport income worldwide (Graham, 2009). These trends are challenging conventional wisdom about the very nature of airports (Morrison, 2009).

These trends pose considerable challenges for stakeholders. As airport needs expand beyond purely technical aviation concerns, their operations and planning intersect with the surrounding urban environment across a variety of economic, environmental, infrastructural, social and institutional interfaces (Stevens *et al.*, 2010). The airport city can no longer function solely under the direction of the airport; the city and the airport become more interdependent whilst their interests do not necessarily converge (Güller and Güller, 2003).

This chapter provides an overview of the issues that have arisen as a result of the changing role of airports in the development of land for non-aeronautical uses. The analysis will focus on two mid-sized airports, Athens and Brisbane, with specific reference to issues around land use planning, infrastructure and governance. The aim is to provide a descriptive review of each case to provide insights into how two airports have embraced the airport city concept to develop lands within their boundaries. Our two cases are chosen because they are contextually different and offer diverse development approaches. However, the land use choices and challenges faced by the airports have similarities that are shared around the world. Although there has been growing interest in the importance of non-aeronautical revenues at airports (for example, Graham, 2009), little empirical research has focused on real estate development within airport boundaries.

2 The airport city in context

As airport and city become increasingly implicated in each other's affairs, the notion of an airport city defies easy categorisation, especially when the term is used liberally and loosely for marketing purposes. Table 9.1 provides a summary of key concepts in the area to help situate the airport city concept against related phenomena of vastly different scales.

The baseline entity is the airport itself. In traditional mode this is a 'monomodal' airside operations-minded facility generating most of its economic revenue from aviation-related activities (passenger and freight) with airlines as the major client (Jarach, 2001). This airport type is disappearing even in regional areas. Extended terminal offerings and some retail and general employment-related uses have become the norm. The customers of the modern airport are more diverse than just air passengers and air transportation employees.

We will expand on the nature of airport cities below, but for now we accept the definition of them as 'the more or less dense cluster of operational, airport-related activities, plus other commercial and business concerns, on and around the airport platform' (Güller and Güller, 2003, p. 70). The other 'concerns' can be

Table 9.1 A hierarchy of airport spaces

Airport spaces	Character	Type/model	Planning
Airports	Specialist aviation-focused facility	Hub Secondary Regional Freight	Airport master planning
Airport cities	Planned mixed-use development of airport site	Hospitality Retail Cargo Offices	Local/city planning
Airport regions	Airport and environs	Airfront Airport corridor Airea	Sub-regional/precinct/corridor planning
Airport metropolis	Time-sensitive metropolitan distribution of airport-oriented uses	Aerotropolis	Regional/metropolitan planning

classified in different ways. They are variously passenger-directed (terminal retailing, hotels, parking), aviation-oriented (maintenance, cargo, logistics) and revenue-driven (entrepreneurial non-aviation uses, e.g. production and consumption). The expansion of retail offerings in terminal buildings to capture discretionary spending in passenger 'dwelltime' marked the beginnings of the airport city concept. The science of maximising concession revenues has been developed incrementally through trial and error (Doganis, 1992). The injection of retail planning techniques has seen airport retailing become a lucrative niche with sales and rents per area frequently above the metropolitan norm (Kasarda, 2008).

The wider airport zone has been described and commodified by various terms including aeroville, aeropark and aeropolis. Most airport-oriented development has been spontaneous and ill-planned or at best imperfectly micro-regulated between jurisdictions with systemic regional intervention noticeably lacking. Three substantive conceptual interpretations can be noted. The 'airfront' denotes the 'myriad of commercial, industrial, and transportation facilities and services intrinsically tied to the airport' yet 'of the region'. The characteristic land use mix of these airport fringe zones include car rental facilities, hotels and meeting facilities, freight and cargo services, manufacturing and warehousing, all requiring or dependent upon frequent air connections, and sometimes down at heel (Blanton, 2004). The 'airport corridor' links airport and central city as a band of integrated road/rail infrastructure and development opportunities. This zone is often 'the city's backyard, a governmental vacuum of small municipalities and weak regional authorities, out of reach of the city or metropolitan authorities and neglected by the urban planners because it is neither city nor airport' (Schaafsma, 2008, p. 83). The corridor as a normative concept envisages this space as an integrated economic zone. The 'airea' concept picks up the interrelationship of otherwise various fragmented islands of development within a 'space of opportunity in relation to the airport'; defined by isochrones, marketing coherence, and stage of developmental interactions (Schlaack, 2009).

The 'aerotropolis' idea jumps another notch by situating the 'airport city' at the epicentre of the wider metropolis and interconnected by dedicated motorways ('aerolanes') and high-speed rail links ('aerotrains') with outlying clusters of aviation-oriented businesses such as e-commerce fulfilment centres, business and logistic parks, retail complexes, hotels and free trade zones. This recognises the significance of airports as drivers of local and regional economic development in their attraction of directly aviation-linked activity and more indirectly (through accessibility, agglomeration and prestige economies) aviation-oriented land uses both in the immediate airport environs and along radiating transportation corridors.

3 Airport cities

The notion of the airport as a city in microcosm has been noted and explored by cultural theorists. The modern air terminal in particular reads as an urban entity: accommodating an anonymous mass of pedestrians and users, a commuting labour force, rush hours, 'main street' concourses, distinctive governance structures, and omnipresent commercialisation of parking, shopping and food services (Gottdiener, 2001). But the analogies are more than sociological. The airport city has become a propulsive business concept for not only enhancing the passenger experience and maximising revenues from their stays and transfers within terminals but also providing a guiding principle for spatial development on the airport's landside. Nonetheless a certain hybridity persists (Güller and Güller, 2003). An airport is no longer a mere traffic machine but nor is an airport city just another urban development. The intersection takes a variety of different forms, not simply or singly conceptualised.

Just as cities can be categorised as a hierarchy, airport cities fall into a similar spectrum as integrated business enterprises. At one end are the relatively small-scale 'airparks' organised around aviation-related business parks. Alliance Texas exemplifies the high physical and infrastructure standards of a master planned community, minus the housing. Conway's (1993) model of the 'decoplex' (development-ecology complex) synthesised this urban form with fly-in residential communities to constitute a complete community with an economic base. Trends at major commercial airports have further lifted the bar. Kasarda (2000) likens the commercial offerings at major hub airports as akin to that of central business districts. Asian master planned airports purposefully plan to capture upscale, mixed development.

The industry journal *Global Airport Cities* published by British-based Insight Media carries regular news stories of innovative activities around the world. The relentlessly optimistic tone has an emphatic 'build it and they will come' conviction and while it lacks critical analysis of implementation strategies and broader business and spatial planning contexts, the coverage nevertheless conveys the remarkable appeal and adaptability of the concept. Two airport city developments always feature prominently: Amsterdam and Beijing.

Amsterdam claims to be the original airport city from the 1980s but this evolution built upon a longer history of catering for air-minded sightseers as a potential source of revenue (Adey, 2006). Its transformation into an icon for diversified commerce over the last quarter century has proceeded through four phases: the merging of retail mall concepts into passenger embarking and disembarking areas, the commercial development of airport property beyond the terminal, involvement in land development off the airport platform, and direct ownership stakes and management contracts in airports around the world. Immediately before the GFC, aspirations were raised a notch with three projected developments: Transfer City (an integrated parking, hotel and airport function complex), Chinamex (trade centre for manufactured goods), and Dreamport, an aviation theme park (Schiphol's Long-Term Vision, 2007). The current rubric has shifted towards a policy of sustainable growth and the ambition of a 'green' airport city (Rutten, 2009).

The emergent airport to watch is clearly Beijing, like all things in modern urban China an outsized project driven by global economic competition. Over the last decade growth in traffic movements has seen a revamped Beijing move into the top 20 world airports. In 2004 the Airport City Development Co. Ltd was formed as a public corporation to undertake associated property development (Bates, 2009b). The flagship project is the Airport City Logistics Park as a gateway to the capital region and northern China offering 'one-stop customs clearance'. It forms the first stage of an economic cluster envisaged in time as comprising high-tech manufacturing, shopping malls, tourism and leisure centres.

The potential list of revenue-generating terminal and landside commercial activities in airport cities is expansive. Kasarda (2006) develops a long inventory: duty-free shops; restaurants and speciality retail; cultural attractions; hotels and accommodation; business office complexes; convention and exhibition centres; leisure, recreation and fitness; logistics and distribution; light manufacturing and assembly; perishables and cold storage; catering and other food services; free trade zones and customs-free zones; golf courses; factory outlet stores; and personal and family services such as health and child day care. The 'conceptual forms of activity in an airport city' reproduced in Williams (2006) also include high-technology research and development centres and 'supply chain key locations'. Schaafsma et al. (2008) distils such lists into four comparable development clusters: airside terminal passenger facilities (duty-free, shopping malls), commercial offices, air cargo facilities, and tourism, leisure and health facilities. These are given different weights in various airport-specific 'product market combinations' depending on market opportunities.

Identifying a 'silver bullet' model for the airport city is chimerical. Betz (2009) reports on a study of 12 international airports in terms of their approaches to airport city ideas and identifies no less than seven different models in terms of integration of airport functions, terminals, cargo, retail, non-aeronautical and relation to residential areas. There appears to be no one single formula or blueprint for an airport city; indeed one of the hallmarks of the concept is specialisation to meet competitive economic opportunities (Beck, 2007; LeTourneur, 2002). Characteristically, the most extensive documentation comprises vignettes and case studies (Siebert, 2008). Prins (2008) concludes that the creation of airport cities in the search for the optimal mix of airport uses is ultimately 'a local affair'.

4 Airport land development

The transformation of airports from transportation facilities into more broadly based activity centres is driven by multiple factors. These include the inexorable rise in passenger numbers; the emergence of more entrepreneurial airport owners and managers; the airports' need to create additional revenue streams beyond traditional aeronautical sources (e.g. landing fees, gate leases, passenger service changes) for profit-seeking, infrastructure investment and counter-cyclical business reasons; the ability of some airports to supply conveniently located serviced land for relatively footloose businesses; the increasing role of e-commerce and logistics, and the globalisation of supply chain management and rise of 'just in time' manufacturing and delivery (LeTourneur, 2002; Schaafsma *et al.*, 2008). The process began with international airports and is now trickling down into the strategic development plans of regional facilities. It has been stimulated by airport corporatisation and – in most countries other than the US where a different, light-handed regulation has prevailed – privatisation. The airport is no longer a government department but a commercial enterprise and there have been massive changes 'as the close ties between governments and airports have been progressively loosened' (Doganis, 1992, p. xii).

The nature of these trends is incontrovertible but uneven, being played out with different vigour and character depending on the scale and mix of airport activity in its metropolitan context. Not one size and type fits all cases, with varied responses according to geographical, institutional and economic context. Different airports have been able to exploit comparative advantage reflecting their regional economic settings. The relative 'success' of commercial diversification strategies is ultimately attributable to a variety of elements including responsive corporate leadership and organisational responsiveness, infrastructure provision, planning and development regulations, and the balance of development opportunities and constraints bestowed by metropolitan context (Betz, 2009).

As airports evolve towards marketing-oriented multi-service providers, the non-aviation activities which previously played a secondary role have become core revenue generators (Jarach, 2001). The traditional focus on airside layout, aviation engineering, and operational growth and efficiencies has shifted towards business-to-consumer (B2C) priorities in which landside operations can become a primary source of income (Williams, 2006). Both public and private-sector-operated airports have established either commercial or property divisions to develop their landside areas (Kasarda, 2007). A range of business models has been adopted usually involving a variety of leasehold arrangements. Reiss (2007) identifies four main development strategies in the Australian context: englobo leasing of large land parcels to major users, long-term ground leasing of fully-serviced individual lots, joint venture projects sharing profits and risks with third party developers, and direct property investment.

Airports are changing urban form by virtue of their choices of developing land within airport boundaries, where both aviation and non-aviation land uses are strategically developed and integrated according to new business models. There is a significant difference from traditional airport development plans. How do airports develop commercial real estate and how is this staged into master planning? Is the master plan developed in conjunction with surrounding land uses and within a regional metropolitan planning context? We explore these more specific questions with reference to two case study airports.

5 Case studies

Brisbane (Australia) and Athens (Greece) airports have actively developed commercial real estate over the past five years and have marketed themselves as airport cities. Both airports are mid-sized: in 2008, Brisbane airport accommodated approximately 18.5 million passengers, and Athens handled approximately 16.5 million passengers. Figure 9.1 provides a spatial comparative analysis of each airport. Each airport is a greenfield airport, with both having considerable vacant land for development. However, underlining the importance of local factors, the relative locations of the airports have given rise to different business strategies, land use development practices, and types of commercial land use development. In addition, the ownership structure affects how the management and strategic business plans are developed.

5.1 Brisbane Airport

Brisbane Airport is an important domestic hub for the state of Queensland with direct international connections to Asia, the Pacific and the United States. The airport in its current configuration dates from the 1980s but the site was first established as an aerodrome in the late 1920s. It now consists of approximately 2,700 hectares, of which 1,000 hectares are suitable for land use development, one of the largest landbanks of any major Australian airport (Brisbane Airport Corporation, 2009a). The airport is located approximately 15 kilometres from the CBD, and once was separated from the city; however, much of the airport is now flanked by urban development.

Brisbane Airport Corporation Pty. Ltd. (BAC) secured a long-term lease (50 + 49 year option) from the Commonwealth (federal) Government in 1997 for the rights to develop and manage Brisbane Airport. BAC is a private sector company that is a part of a corporate group, of which the ultimate holding company's shareholders consist of predominantly (greater than 80 per cent) major Australian

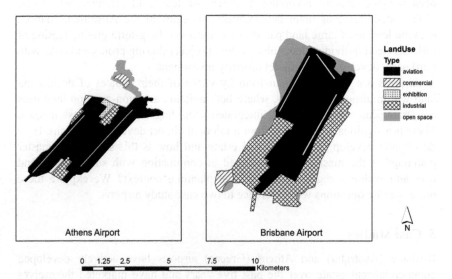

Figure 9.1 Land uses at Athens and Brisbane airports.

financial institutions such as superannuation funds. The remaining shareholding is held by Schiphol Australia Pty. Ltd., a wholly owned subsidiary of Schiphol Airport, Amsterdam. The crucial stakehold of Schiphol underlines the globalisation of airport ownership and operations (Graham, 2003). Schiphol culture has decisively shaped Brisbane's overall business model strategy of an airport city, that is a connected, integrated hub of commercial, industrial, leisure, retail and services driving regional growth. The vision works as an holistic notion operationalised by the executive team according to roles and responsibilities (Timbrell *et al.*, 2006).

The airport has developed non-aviation property in defined precincts within the context of the airport master plan required by the federal aviation authority. The master plan outlines nine precincts that are zoned to suit prescribed uses. The airport has undertaken a well-defined prescriptive framework to allocate land uses and has adopted a zoning approach to control land uses within precincts. Table 9.2 outlines the nine precincts and the relevant zones; six of the precincts are zoned for commercial and industrial real estate development. For each of the zones, such as Special Purpose Centre Mixed Industry and Business (SPCMIB), performance zoning outcomes are matched with prescribed 'intended uses'. For example, the intended uses for the SPCMIB zone comprise business premises, entertainment facility, freight-handling facility, function centre, general store, industrial retail outlet, medical centre or self-storage units. Thus, the zoning flexibility outcomes allow for a wide range of land uses that are deemed a compatible mix of uses that enhance site opportunities.

The innovative approach Brisbane Airport takes in zoning is similar to the performance-based planning approach required of local authorities by the state government (Baker *et al.*, 2006). Although the zoning classifications are different, the adoption of performance-based planning introduces an assessment

Table 9.2 Brisbane Airport Precincts and Land Use Zones

Airport Precincts	*Brisbane Airport Land Use Zones*
Brisbane International	Special Purpose Centre Airport
Brisbane Domestic	Special Purpose Centre Airport
Future Aviation Facilities Area	Special Purpose Centre Airport
The Airport Village	Major Centre
	Sport and Recreation
Export Park	Special Purpose Centre Mixed Industry And Business
Da Vinci	Special Purpose Centre Mixed Industry And Business
Banksia Place	Special Purpose Centre Mixed Industry And Business
Airport Industrial Park	Light Industry
	General Industry
	Conservation
Aerotech Park	General Industry

Source: Brisbane Airport Corporation (2009a).

regime based upon design and infrastructure standards (Mactaggart, 2008). For example, criteria for development assessment may consist of energy use (building orientation, life cycle costing, technology), water (rain-water harvesting, water polishing, minimise irrigation), waste (recycling), and biodiversity (landscape masterplan, species selection, maintaining native remnant species).

BAC has taken a diverse approach to property development, embracing a range of development and profit-sharing strategies. In addition to developing property through its own real estate department, the airport has entered into joint ventures to minimise risk. For example, in the Airport Village precinct a diverse range of property development has occurred over the last five years that includes a 24,000 m^2 Direct Factory Outlet, a supermarket, a daycare centre, a liquor store outlet, a data centre, a wide range of office buildings and a new 157-room Novotel, the first hotel at the airport. The development of a speculative 5,300 m^2 industrial/office project in late 2006 was conducted under a profit-sharing partnership with Ray White Real Estate. Within this context the risk for development was shared by the partners. The real estate firm managed the funding, construction, marketing and leasing of the buildings; the airport was involved in the design and tenant inquiries, project aspects, and managed the approvals process; and both parties share in the ground lease (Pearson, 2007).

5.2 Athens Airport

Athens Airport, the home base for Olympic Air and Aegean Airlines, was developed to replace the older Hellinikon Airport and is located approximately 25 kilometres northeast of Athens. It was opened in March 2001 in advance of the 2004 Olympic Games under a BOOT (build, own, operate, transfer) agreement with a 30-year concession running to June 2026. The airport is located in Spata with approximately 16.5 km^2 of land. It is a considerable distance from the surrounding communities and highway, metro and railroad infrastructure provide convenient access to Athens.

The airport operates as a private company under a public–private partnership scheme with the Greek state owning 55 per cent of assets shared with Hochtief Airport (26.67 per cent), Hochtief Airport Capital (13.33 per cent) and Copelouzos (4.99 per cent). The airport is one of the largest recent greenfield projects in Europe, costing €2.2 billion and funded 60 per cent by commercial debt under a user recovery principle (Paraschis, 2009). Determined to lessen the vulnerability of dependence on aeronautical charges, the new airport consciously followed the 'inspiring models' of major hubs like Amsterdam, Frankfurt, Hong Kong and Dallas in line with an airport master plan (Arend, 2009).

Following the development of commercial space in the terminal buildings and the construction of a hotel in 2001, the airport turned to exploitation of its real estate assets in two phases: first, the Airport Retail Park, and most recently the Metropolitan Exposition and Conference Centre. The Airport Retail Park is located approximately 2 kilometres south of the main terminal and is separated by the Attiki Odos highway, the main link to Athens. It consists of an IKEA (26,000 m^2),

Factory Outlet fashion centre (13,000 m²), Leroy Merlin home improvement DIY (do it yourself) store (10,000 m²), Electronics and Appliances Centre (5,000 m²), and gas station/food outlet (2,000 m²). The Retail Park was developed in conjunction with other infrastructure on the airport such as the train station (2004). The second phase of development, the 50,000 m² Exposition and Conference Centre, was opened in 2009. The Centre has a car parking capacity of 3,500 spaces and is also connected to the airport station by shuttle bus. Future phases of development within the airport usufruct consist of a second hotel, sports/leisure and entertainment park, a business park, and a warehouse and logistics park. In addition, other types of new business development are being considered, including those in the field of renewable energy sources such as a photovoltaic park and geothermal energy. The airport is also making available their management expertise in the areas of assets and facilities holistic management (Gyftakis, 2010).

The Athens Airport land development strategy was developed based on the strengths – and weaknesses – of the BOOT model (Paraschis, 2009). The limited usufruct period of the concession (30 years) before the property could be given back to the state at no residual value (or to be re-concessed) re-leased, added considerable risk in lacking exit value for both developers and the airport as well as making it difficult to attract investing developers (Bates, 2009a). In addition, a considerable amount of upfront capital had to be forwarded for infrastructure to service the greenfield site. On the other hand, the strengths of the airport's position consist of marketable land uses, flexible development methods, simple licensing, and fast-track implementation (Paraschis, 2009). Based on this, the airport's business approach was to develop business cases incrementally for infrastructure and utilities, minimise development risk by securing tenancies in advance, and ensure returns on investment through minimum guarantees and sharing of incremental turnovers (Gyftakis, 2009). The business case for property development is constantly customised through real estate market assessment, special projects and updates to the master plan (Gyftakis, 2009).

5.3 Discussion

Both Athens and Brisbane airports have aggressively embraced the airport city model, using aviation traffic and regional accessibility to leverage ancillary commercial uses and promoting their airports as 'destinations' in their own right for a non-aviation clientele. The ownership and institutional setting of the two airports is different, and each has taken a distinctive approach to developing non-aviation properties to minimise risk and ensure return on investment. While specific development strategies are tied to the ownership structure and to the governance arrangements, they are similar in terms of tenancy security and risk averse methods. Both airports have developed a significant amount of non-aviation land uses over the past five years. The most recent revenue generated from the non-aviation land development for each airport is summarised in Tables 9.3 and 9.4.

Both airports have had the advantage of considerable institutional autonomy in their development planning. Planning laws designed to prevent out-of-town commercial development and national aviation regulations requiring reinvestment in airport infrastructure that have dampened the prospects for on-airport commercialisation in other jurisdictions did not apply. But the larger issue confronting both airports in implementing their airport city strategies has been enhanced interaction and potential conflict with the city proper in relation to competitive commercial developments, infrastructure provision, transport connectivity, and the enduring issues of noise and amenity. At Athens the economic spin-off associated with the new international airport was anticipated by a spatial development plan prepared by the Ministry of Environment, Land Planning and Public Works in 1997 (Christofakis, 2004). The on-airport real estate development strategy was coordinated with the surrounding communities and with the city of Athens, with the airport professing a desire not to compete directly with the city (Bates, 2009a). But the 'big box' style of development adopted has only encouraged further auto-based suburbanisation on the American model and inevitably development is creeping towards the airport perimeter.

In Brisbane, the relationship between the airport and the surrounding Brisbane City Council has had its ups and downs, despite the Council being a shareholder in BAC. The tensions which have arisen relate primarily to disagreements

Table 9.3 Revenue sources for Athens International Airport

Revenue sources (2009)	Euros
Aviation-based revenue	375,066,164
Non-aviation activity revenue	82,427,549
commercial	44,142,961
parking	18,160,053
advertising	4,951,424
railway station commercial	383,332
building rental	957,895
ground rental and concessions	7,018,018
building services	2,098,358
It&T charges	4,515,093
other	200,416

Source: Athens International Airport (2009).

Table 9.4 Revenue sources for Brisbane International Airport

Revenue sources (2009)	Australian dollars
Aeronautical revenue	135,767,000
Security mandated revenue	26,681,000
Retail	50,234,000
Landside transport	73,997,000
Operating property	32,246,000
Investment property	39,367,000
Other	21,054,000

Source: Brisbane Airport Corporation (2009b).

between inclusive (city) and exclusive (airport) planning paradigms. While the Council has necessarily adopted a synoptic all-of-city approach using planning instruments sanctioned by the Queensland state government, the privatised airport's planning decisions have been governed solely by federal legislation, the *Airports Act* 1996. Traffic congestion near the airport has been a major headache, with some critics blaming new commercial development at the airport. Major motorway upgrades, a new airport access road, and a city–airport link underground toll road project are currently in train with the airport making a multi-million dollar financial contribution. In 2005 the major retailer Westfield Management Ltd. lost a Federal Court case against BAC's right to undertake non-aeronautical development. Since that time the city and airport have enjoyed a stronger relationship underpinned by a set of protocols and planning agreements in relation to local land taxes, payment of infrastructure charges and sharing of information. A new national aviation policy for Australia from 2010 affecting all major airports will mandate new planning forums, consultative committees, and closer scrutiny of non-aeronautical development (Australian Government, 2009).

6 Conclusion

The airport city phenomenon is the product of global shifts in modes of commerce, travel activity, and new governance structures intersecting to produce greater possibilities for commercial activity. The airport is a node of high accessibility simultaneously in both aviation networks and metropolitan space and is thereby shaped by both global and local forces. In these terms the airport city represents an instructive exemplar of 'glocalisation' manifested by considerable variety in the scale and forms of development (Swyngedouw, 2004).

Freathy and O'Connell (1999, p. 595) identified the commercial turn for airports as both 'a predictable and a systematic response to changes in the external environment'. A decade on from their analysis, many of the emergent trends which they identified have become far more entrenched: airport managers are less suspicious of commercial activities, airport management structures have been comprehensively reconfigured to accommodate real estate divisions, and a new planning paradigm sensitive to design and market opportunities has taken hold. Non-aeronautical sources look set to become the major growth vector in airport economies. The barrier to development posed by restricted terminal space in the 1990s has been breached not only by larger facilities but by the development of diverse revenue-generating activities on airport land beyond the terminal (Kasarda, 2007).

LeTourneur (2002) identifies several major challenges associated with the development of airport land. These include striking the right balance between aviation and non-aviation uses, inter-jurisdictional issues relating to land use and infrastructure, responding to the concerns of both adjacent communities and airport tenants, maintaining efficient ground transportation, and market caution to leasehold development on restricted time frames. There are also longer-term questions to confront about the future of airport cities in an era of peak oil (Charles *et al.*, 2007) and climate change (Gössling and Upham, 2009).

Our case studies of airport city development highlight the commercial land use development initiatives and challenges for two medium-scale international airports enjoying strong metropolitan economic monopolies. Both have considerable land capacity for future expansion. Like comparable airports elsewhere, their future trajectories will be increasingly and inextricably linked to their respective urban settings. Problems of airport-centric development are inevitable as the territories of airport and city increasingly negotiate their interface and complex land use planning arrangements evolve to mediate the different roles and expectation of airport authorities, the various tiers of government, and wider community interests (van Wijk, 2007).

Acknowledgements

The authors would like to thank Thanassis Gyftakis from Athens airport and Dr. Brad Bowes from Brisbane Airport Corporation for their comments in this chapter.

References

Adey, Peter (2006) Airports and Air-mindedness: Spacing, Timing and Using the Liverpool Airport, 1929–1939, *Social and Cultural Geography*, 7: 343–363.

Australian Government (2009) Flight Path to the Future. National Aviation White Paper. Canberra: Department of Infrastructure, Transport, Regional Development and Local Government.

Arend, Mark (2009) *Final Approach: Athens International's Emerging Airport City*. Site Selection (online at www.siteselection.com; accessed December 2009).

Athens International Airport S.A. (2009) Financial statements as at 31 December 2008 in accordance with the international financial reporting standards.

Baker, Douglas, Neil Sipe and Brendan Gleeson (2006) Performance-based Planning: Perspectives from the United States, Australia and New Zealand, *Journal of Planning Education and Research*, 25: 396–409.

Bates, Joe (2009a) CEO Vision: Interview with Yiannis Paraschis, *Global Airport Cities*, 4(1): 6–11.

—— (2009b) Build and Supply, *Global Airport Cities*, 4(1): 23–24.

Beck, Paul (2007) Integral Planning of Airports Cities. Paper presented to the Global Airport Cities Conference, April, Frankfurt.

Betz, Stephanie (2009) Managing Airport Cities: Benchmark Study 2008, Paper presented at 'From Airport City to Airport Region?' 1st Colloquium on Airports and Spatial Development, University of Karlsruhe, Germany, July 2009.

Blanton, Whit (2004) On the Airfront, *Planning*, 70(5): 34–36.

Brisbane Airport Corporation Pty. Ltd (2009a) Brisbane Airport 2009 Master plan.

—— (2009b) Brisbane Airport Corporation – Financial Report 2009.

Charles, Michael, Paul Barnes, Neal Ryan and Julia Clayton (2007) Airport Futures: Towards a Critique of the Aerotropolis Model, *Futures*, 39: 1009–1028.

Christofakis, Manolis (2004) Athens Metropolitan Area: New Challenges and Development Planning. City Futures Conference, Chicago, July.

Conway, McKinley (1993) *Airport Cities 21: The New Global Transport Centers of the 21st Century*, Atlanta: Conway Data Inc.

Doganis, Rigas (1992) *The Airport Business*, London: Routledge.

Freathy, Paul and Frank O'Connell (1999) Planning for Profit: The Commercialization of European Airports, *Long Range Planning*, 32: 587–597.

Gössling, Stefan and Paul Upham, eds. (2009) *Climate Change and Aviation: Issues, Challenges and Solutions*, London: Earthscan.

Gottdiener, Mark (2001) *Life in the Air: Surviving the New Culture of Air Travel*, Lanham, MD: Rowman and Littlefield.

Graham, Anne (2003) *Managing Airports: An International Perspective*, Oxford: Butterworth-Heinemann.

Graham, Anne (2009) How Important are Commercial Revenues to Today's Airports? *Journal of Air Transport Management*, 15: 106–111.

Graham, B. and C. Guyer (2000) The Role of Regional Airports and Air Services in the United Kingdom, *Journal of Transport Geography*, 8: 249–262.

Güller, Mathis and Michael Güller (2003) *From Airport to Airport City*, Barcelona: Editorial Gustavo Gill.

Gyftakis, Thanassis (2009) Airports under the Perspective of 'Real Estate Business Development'. Airport Cities World Conference and Exhibition. Athens, 29 April.

—— (2010) The Importance of Asset Management. Airport Cities World Conference and Exhibition. Beijing, 22 April.

Jarach, David (2001) The Evolution of Airport Management Practices: Towards a Multipoint, Multi-service, Marketing-driven Firm, *Journal of Air Transport Management*, 7: 119–125.

Kasarda, John D. (2000) *Aerotropolis: Airport-driven Urban Development. In ULI on the Future: Cities in the 21st Century*, Washington, DC: Urban Land Institute, pp. 32–41.

—— (2006) The New Model, *Airport World Magazine* (online at www.aerotropolis.com; accessed December 2009).

—— (2007) Airport Cities & the Aerotropolis: New Planning Models. An interview with Dr. John D. Kasarda, Airport Innovation, April 2007, 106–110.

—— (2008) Shopping in the Airport City and Aerotropolis, *Research Review*, 15(2): 50–56.

LeTourneur, Christopher (2002) The Bricks and Mortar of Global Commerce, *Airport World*, 6(6): 36–40.

Mactaggart, Rob (2008) Brisbane Airport Property Development. Ray White real estate seminar, Brisbane, Australia, 21 July, 2008.

Morrison, William G. (2009) Real Estate, Factory Outlets and Bricks: A Note on Non-aeronautical Activities at Commercial Airports, *Journal of Air Transport Management*, 15: 112–115.

Paraschis, Yiannis (2009) The Development of the Airport City and the Economic Impact of Athens International Airport. Airport Cities world conference and exhibition, Athens, 28 April.

Pearson, Hans (2007) Innovative Airport Development Partnerships. Aviation Business Airport Development 2007 Conference, Sydney, Australia, 16–17 August.

Prins, Mariëlle (2008) Landing an Airport? Airport Development and Strategic Land Use Planning in the EU, Real Corp Conference Proceedings, Vienna, May 2008, pp. 47–56.

Reiss, Brett (2007) Maximizing Non-aviation Revenue for Airports: Developing Airport Cities to Optimize Real Estate and Capitalize on Land Development Opportunities, *Journal of Airport Management*, 1: 284–293.

Rutten, Ad (2009) Blazing the Trail, *Global Airport Cities*, 4(2): 30–33.

Schaafsma, Maurits (2008) Accessing Global City Regions: The Airport as a City. In *The Image and the Region: Making Mega-city Regions Visible*, eds Alain Thierstein and Agnes Forster, Baden: Lars Muller, pp. 69–79.

Schaafsma, M., J. Amkreutz and M. Güller (2008) *Airport and City. Airport Corridors: Drivers of Economic Development*. Amsterdam: Schiphol Real Estate.

Schiphol's Long-Term Vision (2007) *Global Airport Cities*, 2(2): 5.

Schlaack, Johanna (2009) Defining the Airea: Evaluating Urban Output and Forms of Interaction between Airport and Metropolitan Region, Paper presented at 'From airport city to airport region?' 1st Colloquium on Airports and Spatial Development, University of Karlsruhe, Germany, July 2009.

Siebert, Lucy, ed. (2008) *Airport Cities: The Evolution*, London: Insight Media.

Stevens, Nicholas (2006) City Airports to Airport Cities, *Queensland Planner*, 46: 37.

Stevens, Nicholas, Douglas Baker and Robert Freestone (2010) Airports in their Urban Settings: Towards a Conceptual Model of Interfaces in the Australian Context, *Journal of Transport Geography*, 18: 276–284.

Swyngedouw, Erik (2004) Globalisation or 'Glocalisation'? Networks, Territories and Rescaling, *Cambridge Review of International Affairs*, 17: 25–48.

Timbrell, Greg, Marcus Foth and Greg Hearn (2006) Towards Knowledge Management for Explorers: The Case of the Brisbane Airport Corporation, *International Journal of Knowledge, Culture and Change Management*, 6(6): 97–104.

van Wijk, Michel (2007) Airports as Cityports in the City-region, *Nederlands Geographical Studies*, 53, Utrecht.

Williams, Alan (2006) *Developing Strategies for the Modern International Airport: East Asia and Beyond*, Aldershot: Ashgate.

10 The economics of airline alliances

Martin Dresner

1 Introduction

Oliver Williamson, the Nobel laureate and Berkeley University economist, developed a theory to explain the choice of organizational form. Basing his theory on Coase (1937) and others, Williamson (1979) finds that companies organize their activities in order to minimize transaction costs. When transaction costs are high, for example due to supply uncertainties, companies may choose to combine operations under one corporate umbrella. This internal organization reduces transaction costs (e.g., by decreasing search costs), thus lowering total operating costs and increasing profits. However, when transaction costs are low, companies may retain separate corporate identities and transact over the market. By transacting through market exchanges, companies avoid costly capital investments in suppliers and other supply chain partners. In some cases, companies may choose "intermediate" forms of corporate organization; that is, they can maintain their independence from other entities, but enter into long-term contracts with these firms. Intermediate organizational forms both act to reduce potential uncertainties in supply chain relations and to lower transaction costs through contract provisions. In addition, they conserve corporate capital since equity investments in trading partners are not required. An "alliance" is one type of intermediate organizational structure.

Perhaps more than any other industry in the world, the airline industry is characterized by the presence of alliances. Airlines form alliances to transact and cooperate with other airlines. No one carrier is able to satisfy all of the world's passenger demand since individual airlines serve limited numbers of destinations. If a passenger wishes to travel on a route requiring use of two carriers, Airline 1 can sell the passenger a ticket for the entire trip and purchase space at the market rate on Airline 2 for the portion of the trip not covered by Airline 1. Or, the two airlines can enter into an alliance that can result in reduced operating costs on the route, and deliver a better traveling experience for the passenger.

Morrish and Hamilton (2002, p. 401) define an airline alliance as, "any collaborative arrangement between two or more carriers involving joint operations with the declared intention of improving competitiveness and thereby enhancing overall performance." Iatrou and Alamdari provide a definition of an airline alliance derived from the International Air Transport Association as "airlines participating in a commercial relationship or joint venture, where a joint and commonly identifiable product is marketed under a single commercial name or brand" (2005, pp. 127–128).

The origins of airline alliances can be traced back at least as far as the early 1980s. At that time, a number of major U.S. carriers entered into alliances with smaller regional airlines to provide services on lower density routes and to supplement services on major routes. The regional carriers operated small aircraft – initially turbo-propeller airplanes and later regional jets – and had lower cost structures than the major carriers.[1] The alliances allowed the major carriers to market flights to smaller cities served by the regional carriers. Thus, a passenger could fly with a Delta ticket from the carrier's Atlanta hub to Pensacola, Florida, for example, even though the actual flight was offered by a regional affiliated carrier. In addition, Delta could add mid-day frequencies and late-night frequencies to its schedules on major routes (e.g., Atlanta–New Orleans) by relying on its commuter affiliates when demand might not justify the use of its own larger jet fleet.

The alliance concept spread to international agreements by the late 1980s. These global agreements make use of a common feature of many airline alliances, code-sharing. A code-sharing arrangement permits carriers to jointly market a single product, namely an airline flight, under the brand names, or codes, of allied carriers. Code-sharing arrangements facilitate carriers to expand their route networks without committing additional resources. In addition, they allow carriers to expand onto routes which, due to legal restrictions, they may be constrained from serving. In this regard, a European carrier, for example Air France, may fly from Paris to the Atlanta hub of Delta Air Lines, its code-share partner. From Atlanta, Delta serves a large number of domestic U.S. points. Air France can enter into a code-sharing arrangement with Delta to put its own airline code on flights to many of these domestic U.S. destinations served by Delta. Although Air France may have the legal authority to serve these "beyond gateway" destinations in the U.S., it would have to serve them as part of a route originating in Europe since, as a non-U.S. carrier, Air France does not have the right to operate purely domestic routes in the U.S. For practical purposes, therefore, code-sharing with an allied U.S. carrier is the only way for Air France to serve a widespread network in the U.S. Likewise, Delta can code-share with Air France on its intra-European routes from Air France's hub in Paris, thus enabling the U.S. carrier to expand its European network, despite restrictions on non-European carrier operations of intra-European routes.

As the network of global code-sharing arrangements has grown, airline alliances have expanded and became more formalized. The first global alliances typically included one U.S. airline and one European airline operating a number of code-share flights in the U.S. and Europe. However, as the alliances have expanded, they have incorporated additional U.S. and European carriers, as well as carriers from other parts of the world. By the early 2000s, many of the global airlines had entered into one of four global alliances, each headed by at least one

U.S. carrier and one European carrier. The merger of Air France and KLM triggered a consolidation of the global alliances, leaving three major alliance groups – Star Alliance, oneworld, and Sky Team. Each of these alliances includes major carriers from Europe, Asia, and North America. According to Wan *et al.* (2009), the three major alliance groups now account for over three-quarters of the world's aviation market based on revenue passenger-kilometers flown.[2]

In addition to code-sharing, alliance airlines often engage in other joint or coordinated activities for the benefit of their member carriers and their passengers. For example, airlines in an alliance may use common check-in counters and gates at airports, thus allowing the carriers to share airport-related expenses. Allied carriers may also coordinate purchases from suppliers, thus allowing the airlines to benefit from quantity discounts. Allied carriers may operate from the same terminal at an airport, thus reducing connecting times for code-share passengers. Operations from the same terminal may also decrease the potential for baggage loss or delays. Alliances generally allow passengers to accumulate frequent flier miles on flights from any of the airlines in the alliance and to apply these points to their own frequent flier plans. Thus, for example, a United Airlines' frequent flier can accumulate points for the United Mileage Plus plan while flying on alliance partner Lufthansa, thus allowing the flier to more easily achieve "elite" status with United. Business travelers and elite members of allied frequent flier plans typically have access to the airline lounges of all members of the alliance, a benefit to those passengers flying internationally. Alliances may convey competitive advantages to member carriers. Since code-sharing arrangements allow allied airlines to market flights operated by partner carriers, allied airlines can market increased frequencies on key routes, thus making them a more popular choice for time-sensitive travelers. Finally, as is discussed in more detail below, code-sharing alliances allow carriers to achieve lower costs through economies of density and to offer lower fares to their customers by cooperating in scheduling.

Many of the consumer benefits from alliances are derived due to their complementary aspects. A complementary alliance is one where passengers may travel for part of a trip on one allied carrier and the rest of the trip on another (see, for example, Park 1997). Passengers gain from reduced connection time at gateway or hub airports due to coordinated operations among allied carriers. On the negative side, alliances may reduce the level of competition on "gateway-to-gateway" or "parallel" routes. For example, for Delta Air Lines and Air France, a gateway-to-gateway route is Atlanta–Paris where, as non-aligned carriers, the two carriers would compete for passengers. However, as allied carriers, they may jointly set prices and capacities, thus reducing the level of competition. As discussed below, the potential for reduced competition and higher prices is greatest when governmental authorities grant carriers antitrust immunity, thereby allowing allied carriers to jointly set prices and capacities.

In this chapter, we provide a comprehensive examination of the economic impacts of airline alliances, with an emphasis on the role that code-sharing agreements play in determining costs and benefits to carriers and passengers. In the following section, we examine more closely the potential impacts of alliance code-sharing on airfares and traffic on complementary routes. Section 3 reviews the potential effects from alliance code-sharing on fares and traffic on parallel routes. Section 4 presents a number of other potential economic impacts from alliances. Section 5 examines the special case of U.S. domestic airline alliances, and how they impact fares and traffic. Finally, Section 6 concludes this chapter by providing a summary of the economic impacts from airline alliances.

2 The impact on airfares and traffic from airline alliances in complementary networks

As outlined by Whalen (2007), passengers traveling with non-aligned carriers may face a "double marginalization" problem. Double marginalization exists when two companies, both with market power, offer a joint product. The product may be marketed by one firm, but both firms have input into the product. An example in the airline industry is an interline ticket with service provided by two carriers. If a passenger wishes to fly from A to C, and no airline flies between these two cities, then the passenger will have to fly on two (or more) carriers. Suppose Airline 1 flies from A to B and Airline 2 from B to C. If Airline 1 sells the passenger a ticket from A to C, it must buy the BC portion of the trip from Airline 2. Airline 2 will incorporate a profit into its price, thus charging Airline 1 a price exceeding marginal cost (given some monopoly power). Airline 1 must incorporate Airline 2's price (and profit) into its own cost function when it sells the complete interline ticket to the passenger. Therefore, Airline 1's price includes both the profits earned by Airline 2 as well as its own profits – thus, the double marginalization.

Based on this rationale, Brueckner (2003a) develops a theoretical model to illustrate how cooperation within a complementary alliance reduces prices. Brueckner's (2003a) simple complementary airline network is presented in Figure 10.1. Airline 1 flies between cities A and B while Airline 2 flies between cities B and C. Neither airline provides service from A to C. In order to simplify the analysis, Brueckner (2003a) assumes that the two routes are of equal length, the airlines exhibit economies of scale, and that the costs per passenger are equal to a constant, c, for both carriers. Two types of fare-setting are defined – cooperative and non-cooperative. In the non-cooperative case, each airline chooses fares for the segment it operates, with the fare for a traveler wishing to go from A to C equal to the sum of the AB and BC fares. In the cooperative fare-setting arrangement, the two carriers set fares to maximize their total profits.

As shown in Brueckner (2003a, p. 107), Airline 1's profits in the non-cooperative case are given by the following:

$$(s_{ab} - c)D(s_{ab} + s_{bc}) \tag{1}$$

where s_{ab} and s_{bc} are the fares for Airlines 1 and 2 on route segments AB and BC, respectively and D is demand for the route AC. As outlined by Brueckner

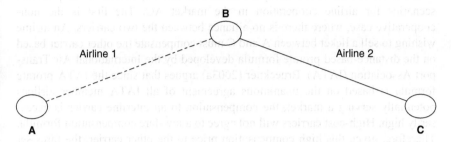

Figure 10.1 Complementary airline network (source: Brueckner (2003a, p. 106)).

(2003a), Airline 1 will choose s_{ab} to maximize its profits with a first order condition viewing s_{bc} as a constant. Likewise, Airline 2 will choose s_{bc} to maximize its profits viewing s_{ab} as given. The first order condition for Airline 1 can be derived as follows:

$$D/D' + s_{ab} = c. \tag{2}$$

The first order condition for Airline 2 can be similarly derived. Due to the symmetry assumptions, the fares on each of the route segments, AB and BC, will be equal to $p_{ac}/2$. Given this assumption, as outlined by Brueckner (2003a), Equation 1 can be rewritten as follows after making the substitution for the inverse demand slope, $(\partial p_{ac}/\partial q_{ac}) = 1/D'$:

$$2q_{ac}(\partial p_{ac}/\partial q_{ac}) + p_{ac} = 2c. \tag{3}$$

Under a cooperative arrangement, Brueckner (2003a) assumes that the carriers engage in joint profit maximization. Their combined profits can be written as follows:

$$2 (p_{ac}/2 - c) D(p_{ac}) \tag{4}$$

with a first order condition given by the equation:

$$q_{ac}(\partial p_{ac}/\partial q_{ac}) + p_{ac} = 2c. \tag{5}$$

As outlined in Brueckner (2003a), given that $(\partial p_{ac}/\partial q_{ac})$ is necessarily negative, the left-hand side of Equation 3 will be smaller than the left-hand side of Equation 5 for a set number of passengers. Given that marginal revenue from an additional passenger should equal marginal cost, the non-cooperative situation must be satisfied at a lower traffic level, and hence, a higher airfare, than the cooperative situation. Therefore, fares must be lower in a complementary alliance than when the two carriers do not cooperate.

Based on his theoretical analysis, Brueckner (2003a) outlines three potential scenarios for airline cooperation in the market AC. The first is the non-cooperative case, where there is no alliance between the two carriers. An airline wishing to sell a ticket between A and C must compensate the other carrier based on the distance-based prorate formula developed by the International Air Transport Association (IATA). Brueckner (2003a) argues that since the IATA prorate formula is based on the unanimous agreement of all IATA member airlines potentially serving a market, the compensation to an interline carrier is necessarily high. High-cost carriers will not agree to a low-fare compensation formula. Therefore, given this high compensation price to the other carrier, the fares set by either Airline 1 or Airline 2 are necessarily high.

The second scenario outlined by Brueckner (2003a) is one where the two carriers have a code-sharing alliance for the market AC, but do not have governmental permission to jointly set fares in that market. This is the non-cooperative case outlined in the theoretical model. Brueckner (2003a) argues that the carriers will agree on a compensation formula below the prorate tariffs set by IATA. This lower level of compensation will allow the allied carriers to undercut non-cooperating airlines, thus allowing the alliance to gain market share. Finally, the third scenario is an alliance with antitrust immunity, equivalent to the cooperative case in the theoretical model. This third scenario will produce the lowest fares in the market AC, since the double marginalization problem is eliminated.

Brueckner (2003a) uses a dataset consisting of over 50,000 ticketed passengers from the third quarter of 1999 to estimate an empirical model based on his theoretical construct. The base case is Scenario 1 – interline tickets issued by non-aligned carriers without code-sharing agreements or antitrust immunity. Compared to this non-cooperative situation, Brueckner (2003a) finds that when an itinerary involves code-sharing, airfares are 8 to 17 percent lower, depending on the estimation procedure used. The presence of antitrust immunity in a market lowers fares an additional 13–21 percent. For flights that involve code-sharing between two immunized carriers (i.e., both code-sharing and antitrust immunity), fares are 17–30 percent lower than the base case. Thus, Brueckner (2003a) concludes that there are substantial consumer benefits to permitting airline alliances, and to granting antitrust immunity for complementary airline networks.

A number of other research efforts have also examined, empirically, the impact of complementary airline networks. Brueckner and Whalen (2000) use a 1997 dataset to examine the impact of alliances on airfares. Based on fares paid by approximately 47,000 international ticketed passengers (with either an origin or destination in the United States) in close to 17,000 city-pair markets, the authors find that code-sharing passengers pay approximately 25 percent lower fares than do passengers traveling on itineraries issued by non-aligned carriers. The authors attribute the lower fares provided by code-sharing partners to such factors as lower operating costs due to economies of density, as well as the elimination of double marginalization.

Brueckner (2003b) separates out the impact of alliance membership from code-sharing. Although code-sharing is an integral part of alliances, allied carriers typically do not code-share in all possible markets. Using data similar to Brueckner (2003a), Brueckner (2003b) finds that interline tickets offered by carriers belonging to the same alliance are 4 percent lower than fares offered by non-aligned carriers (the base case). Code-sharing reduces airline fares by 17 percent compared to the base case, while antitrust immunity reduces airfares by 16 percent compared to the base case. In total, a passenger traveling on a code-share ticket offered by two carriers in the same alliance with antitrust immunity could be expected to pay 27 percent less than a passenger traveling on a pair of non-aligned carriers in the same market.

Following the work by Brueckner, and based on his own theoretical model,[3] Bilotkach (2007) examines the impact of alliance membership, code-sharing, and antitrust immunity using a 1999 data sample similar to Brueckner (2003a). He adds value to the previous work by incorporating an additional variable for markets covered by "open skies" agreements.[4] Although his results show some variation depending on the empirical model estimated, in general, Bilotkach (2007) finds results similar to Brueckner (2003a); that is for complementary networks, alliance membership, code-sharing, and antitrust immunity all act to reduce airfares, even after controlling for the impact of open skies agreements (which also reduce fares).

Whalen (2007) extends previous work by estimating a panel dataset on international routes, rather than a cross-sectional set as used for previous analyses, and provides an estimation of the impact of alliances on passenger traffic as well as on airfares. In addition, Whalen (2007) compares his estimations to the "online" case, where passengers travel on a single carrier without code-sharing or interlining. If pure interline tickets (i.e., no alliance and no code-sharing) can be thought of as a high-price base comparison, then online tickets can be viewed as a low-price base comparison. It would be reasonable to assume that code-sharing and alliances reduce tickets from the high-price base, approaching the low-price base as cooperation intensifies. Whalen (2007) uses transatlantic data from 1990 to 2000, with a final sample consisting of over 100,000 observations to estimate his models. Whalen (2007) finds, as expected, that online tickets (i.e., the low-fare base case) are significantly lower than tickets offered by non-aligned carriers (i.e., the high-fare base case), by a magnitude of 16–22 percent, depending on the model estimated. Interestingly, in some of his regressions, Whalen (2007) finds that fares offered by aligned carriers with antitrust immunity are not statistically different from online fares. (In other cases, they approach online fares but are slightly higher.) Whalen (2007) also finds that immunized alliances contribute to large increases in passenger traffic, from 52–88 percent greater than the traffic for non-aligned carriers, after controlling for other variables that might influence traffic.

Finally, Park and Zhang (2000) find that the impact of alliances on fares and traffic may vary considerably among alliances. The authors gather data on transatlantic fares and traffic for the years 1990–1994. Four alliances that existed at the time are considered – British Airways/USAir, Delta/Sabena/Swissair, KLM/Northwest, and Lufthansa/United. Interestingly, the authors find that three of the alliances lead to increased traffic, the exception being the Delta/Sabena/Swissair grouping. The authors attribute the decline in traffic for this latter alliance to member airlines not feeding passengers to gateway cities.

In summary, the impact of complementary alliances on lowering fares and increasing traffic is quite strong. Allied carriers gain from the elimination of double marginalization, by entering into code-sharing agreements, and by seeking antitrust immunity from governments. Immunized carriers can coordinate route capacity and fare-setting through their alliances, leading to cost and fare reductions, and to increased passenger traffic.

3 The impact on airfares and traffic of airline alliances in parallel markets

Although the theoretical rationale and the empirical evidence for benefits to both carriers and passengers from complementary alliances are quite evident, the same is not true for alliances covering parallel or gateway-to-gateway routes. The routes are called "parallel" since two or more allied carriers may operate on the route. For international alliances, these routes typically are between international gateway cities; that is hub-to-hub routes for the allied carriers. For example, Frankfurt–Chicago is a parallel Star Alliance route, since Frankfurt is the hub for German-based Star Alliance carrier, Lufthansa, and Chicago is a hub for U.S.-based Star Alliance carrier, United. The term "parallel" is used even if only one alliance carrier actually operates on the route, since other allied carriers have the *potential* to operate on the route, and can also market tickets on the route through code-share arrangements with their allied partners. As Wan *et al.* state, the concerns with alliances on parallel routes relate to possible harm to passengers:

> Since alliance airlines may be granted antitrust immunity from regulatory authorities, they can cooperate in price-setting on these "parallel" routes operated between alliance hubs. Even if immunity is not granted, the alliance may contribute to tacit cooperation in price-setting on the parallel route. Cooperative, rather than competitive price-setting, may lead to higher airfares.
>
> (Wan *et al.* 2009, p. 627)

Regulatory authorities have long recognized the possibility of anticompetitive actions of allied airlines operating on parallel routes. Brueckner and Proost (2009) describe what they term as "carve-outs" under alliance agreements, whereby antitrust regulators exclude hub-to-hub routes from antitrust immunity. Under these carve-outs, carriers are not allowed to jointly set prices or capacities on specific routes. For example, the U.S. Department of Transportation imposed carve-outs on the Star Alliance's hub-to-hub routes, Chicago–Frankfurt and Washington–Frankfurt, when it granted United Airlines and Lufthansa antitrust immunity to cooperate in other markets.

Wan *et al.* (2009) develop a theoretical model that illustrates the impact of alliances on parallel routes. As indicated by the authors, the impact is not straightforward. As illustrated in Figure 10.2, alliances that cover parallel routes may also cover complementary routes. In addition to the hub-to-hub parallel route, HK, an alliance between Airlines 1 and 2 may cover complementary markets, such as AK and BC. Given the benefits of complementary alliances to passengers, the initiation of an alliance between Airlines 1 and 2 (as shown in Figure 10.2) will likely generate traffic in the complementary markets. Since the generated passengers must travel on the parallel route segment, HK, the alliance will lead to increased densities on this route. These increased densities will allow the allied carriers to achieve economies of density on the parallel route, for example through the operation of larger aircraft with lower per-passenger costs, or perhaps through the shared operation of flights.[5] So, even if the alliance allows Airlines 1 and 2 to exert market power on the parallel route, HK, the upward impact on airfares from this monopoly power may be offset by the downward effects from density economies. The net impact of the alliance on airfares on the parallel route is, therefore, not certain.

In developing their theoretical model, Wan *et al.* (2009) create four scenarios. The first scenario is the case of two non-allied carriers operating on the hub-to-hub route, HK. The second scenario is an alliance between Airlines 1 and 2 with interline coordination, but without joint price-setting. This scenario is equivalent to Brueckner's (2003a) non-immunized alliance. The authors assume that operational improvements undertaken by the allied carriers stimulate traffic, for example through joint operations in common airport terminals. In addition, passengers may prefer to travel with the aligned carriers in order to better accumulate frequent flier points. The third scenario is an artificial creation, where the two airlines do not engage in interline coordination but do engage in joint price-setting. This scenario is introduced in order to separate out the effects of joint price-setting from interline cooperation. Finally, Scenario 4 allows both interline

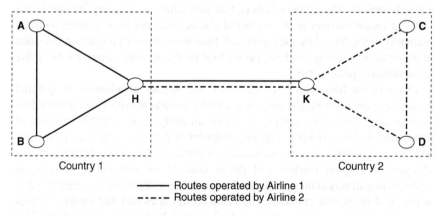

Figure 10.2 Alliance network including parallel and complementary markets (source: Wan *et al.* (2009) adapted from Brueckner and Whalen (2000)).

cooperation and joint price-setting (equivalent to the immunized alliance in Brueckner 2003a). Based on their analysis, Wan *et al.* develop the following three propositions:

Proposition 1: With the presence of an alliance, increased traffic and economies of density result in a downward impact on the airfares in the nonstop hub-to-hub market.

Proposition 2: When the traffic in the interline markets is held constant, the anti-competitive effects from airline alliances through joint pricesetting will result in higher airfares on the nonstop hub-to-hub route.

Proposition 3: The formation of airline alliances will increase (decrease) the airfares in the nonstop hub-to-hub market when the price raising effects from joint price-setting are greater (less) than the price reduction effects from economies of density; the net effect is uncertain.

(Wan *et al.* 2009, p. 633)

In order to test their propositions, Wan *et al.* (2009) gather data, collected in 2007, on 113 nonstop transatlantic routes. Their key variable, *Alliances*, is coded 1 if both the U.S. route endpoint and the European route endpoint are hubs for airline members of the same alliance. The dependent variable is a measure for route airfares. Their model estimations reveal little impact of alliances on route airfares, which the authors attribute to the offsetting effects described above; that is, lower prices due to economies of density but higher prices due to cooperative price-setting. The only significant result obtained by the authors is when separate dummies are used for the three major alliances. In this estimation, the authors find lower business class ticket prices on the hub-to-hub routes for the oneworld alliance carriers, compared to business class tickets between the hubs of nonaligned carriers. The authors believe that this latter finding may be due to the fact that major carriers in the oneworld alliance had not been granted antitrust immunity at the time data were gathered; thus the downward impact on fares due to traffic densities may not have been offset by the upward impact on fares due to cooperative price-setting.

Other researchers who have examined the impact of alliances on parallel routes have obtained results that are generally consistent with those obtained by Wan *et al.* (2009). For example, based on an analysis of their 1997 dataset of international airline tickets (with one endpoint in the United States), Brueckner and Whalen (2000) find no statistically significant difference between prices charged by aligned carriers and prices charged by nonaligned carriers on gateway-to-gateway routes, although the authors term their findings tentative due to potential estimation concerns. Bilotkach (2007) does find that antitrust immunity leads carriers to charge fares up to 7 percent higher than fares charged by carriers without immunity on nonstop trips between alliance hubs. However, this upward impact on prices from antitrust immunity will be offset by the downward impact on allied fares due to cost efficiencies derived from code-sharing and other alliance economies.

In summary, economic theory predicts that on parallel routes, cooperation between allied carriers will result in higher airfares. However, allied carriers will also benefit from density economies on these routes leading to lower costs and lower airfares. Empirical evidence indicates that these two effects tend to offset, leaving the fares charged by allied carriers on parallel routes not significantly different from the fares charged by non-aligned carriers on similar routes.

4 Other impacts from alliances

As indicated in the previous two sections, much of the work on the economic effects of airline alliances has examined the impact of alliances on airfares and traffic. However, there have been a number of other papers that assessed other impacts from alliances. These papers are reviewed in this section.

Oum et al. (2004) collected a panel dataset on thirty international airlines for the years 1986–1995 in order to examine the impact of alliances on airline productivity and profitability. Alliance activity for each airline is measured using two variables: The first variable is a count of the number of alliances in which an airline has entered for a given year. The second variable measures the level of cooperation in each of these alliances. All alliances are calculated as low-level cooperative or high-level cooperative. Low-level alliances cover code-sharing on individual routes, while high-level alliances cover code-sharing on a network of routes. For each airline, the percentage of alliances classified as high-level is calculated for each year and entered into the model as the second alliance variable. Two dependent variables – one for productivity and the second for profitability – are estimated. Productivity is measured by dividing an output index by an input index, and thus is an assessment of total factor productivity. Profitability is measured by dividing total revenues by total input costs. Strong support is found for the positive impact of the number of alliances on productivity. The impact of the level of cooperation on productivity is significant and positive, but only at the 10 percent level. The level of cooperation is found to have a more significant (and positive) impact on profitability, while the number of alliances is only marginally significant in some of the regressions on profitability.

Goh and Yong (2006) examine the impact of code-sharing alliances on airline costs. The authors estimate a translog cost function using data on ten U.S. airlines for the time period from the first quarter of 1994 to the first quarter of 2001. The authors differentiate between "large" and "small" code-share partners. Three of the carriers in the dataset are classified as large – United Airlines, American Airlines, and Delta Air Lines – while the other seven carriers are categorized in the small category.[6] The authors find that alliances have likely resulted in cost savings for the airlines, although the magnitude of these savings appears to be small. They also find that the impact of alliances on cost reduction is greater for the smaller carriers than for the larger carriers. The authors believe that this differential impact may arise because alliances are more important for smaller carriers in allowing for the expansion of networks than they are for larger carriers.

Chen and Chen (2003) investigate the impact of code-sharing on airline load factors, defined as the percentage of seats occupied on a route. The authors hypothesize that code-sharing on parallel routes can be viewed as a risk-pooling activity among carriers. By pooling capacities on a parallel route, airlines can decrease the risk of unsold seats, thereby increasing load factors.[7] On the other hand, the authors hypothesize that complementary alliances may not necessarily lead to increases in load factors. The authors use *Traffic by Flight Stage* data from the International Civil Aviation Organization for the years 1988–1998 to test their model. A before-and-after analysis is conducted for each code-sharing alliance; specifically, load factors are examined for the three years before and the three years after the conclusion of an alliance to examine the impact on load factors. Support is found for both of the authors' hypotheses; parallel alliances lead to increases in load factors but complementary alliances do not.

Czerny (2009) examines the welfare implications of code-sharing agreements. In particular, Czerny (2009) is interested in the impact of code-sharing agreements on passengers using carriers outside of an alliance. Although a complementary alliance may have positive impacts on passengers traveling within an alliance, the same may not be true for passengers who do not make use of the alliance. In his theoretical model, Czerny (2009) shows that complementary alliances may encourage carriers to engage in price discrimination, and that this discrimination can work to the detriment of non-alliance passengers. For example, Airline 1, which flies route AB, may enter into a code-share alliance with Airline 2, which flies route BC, in order to transport passengers from A to C. Without an alliance, if Airline 1 wants to increase traffic on AB, it will likely reduce fares for all of its passengers; that is, not discriminate between passengers flying AB or ABC. However, with an alliance, Airline 1 may choose to target this reduction only to the passengers flying from A to C. Thus, passengers wishing to fly only from A to B may be worse off with the alliance.

Park *et al.* (2003) examine the impact of airline alliance developments on the stock value of rival airlines. If positive announcements are made about an alliance (e.g., the alliance is granted antitrust immunity) then the announcement can be expected to have detrimental impacts on rival airlines since they will now be worse off competitively. Following these announcements, rival carriers should realize lower-than-expected stock returns (i.e., abnormal negative returns). On the other hand, if negative announcements are made regarding alliances (e.g., antitrust immunity is denied), then rivals should experience higher-than-expected stock returns (i.e., abnormal positive returns) following the announcements. The authors examine six announcements (three classified as positive and three classified as negative) that preceded a 1993 alliance between British Airways and USAir. Using standard "event study" methodology, the authors find that, as expected, rival carriers generally experience negative abnormal returns following positive announcements and positive abnormal returns following negative announcements. The authors also examine the stock returns for the two alliance carriers and find positive abnormal returns following the positive announcements (ranging from 1.2 percent to 4.9 percent, on average, for the two carriers) and negative abnormal returns (from –0.6 percent to –2.9 percent) following negative announcements.

Finally, Zhang *et al.* (2004) examine air cargo alliances using a theoretical model. The authors find that airlines that enter into cargo alliances can increase not only their cargo traffic, but also their passenger traffic. Since many airlines carry both passengers and cargo, the two revenue streams can be viewed as complementary. An increase in cargo traffic can reduce the break-even cost of carrying passengers. The authors conclude that a cargo alliance will lead to an increase in the joint profits of the allied carriers while reducing the profits of competitors.

In summary, there have been a number of empirical and theoretical studies into various impacts of airline alliances. Alliances have been found to have positive impacts on productivity, cost reduction, profits, and load factors. They have also been found to have negative impacts on rival carriers and on non-alliance passengers.

5 Airline alliances in the U.S. domestic market

As outlined above, alliances are prevalent in the international airline industry in large part because international airlines are prohibited from merging due to national ownership restrictions imposed by governments.[8] As a result, most of the research work in the alliance field has examined the impacts of international alliances. However, there is a significant body of work that has researched the impact of alliances within the U.S. domestic market.[9] Although there are no strict prohibitions on mergers within this market, U.S. airlines may choose to enter into alliances with other U.S. domestic carriers because they desire cooperative agreements short of merger, because they believe that antitrust authorities would not support a merger but would support an alliance, or because union agreements or other contract provisions make mergers difficult to consummate.

Ito (2007) states that U.S. domestic code-sharing is, in practice, significantly different from code-sharing on international routes. Most international code-sharing arrangements involve complementary routes, a type of arrangement that the author terms "traditional" code-sharing. The vast majority of U.S. domestic code-sharing (85 percent according to the author), however, occurs when a customer purchases a ticket from Airline 1 and travels entirely on Airline 2. The route networks of the two airlines may not be complementary; indeed the airlines need not share any common route endpoints. Ito (2007) calls this type of arrangement "virtual" code-sharing. Virtual code-sharing has a marketing carrier (Airline 1) and an operating carrier (Airline 2). The ticket is issued by the marketing carrier, but the passenger is carried only by the operating carrier. All the ticket revenues flow to the operating carrier, save for a commission to the marketing airline.

In assessing antitrust concerns, the U.S. government typically examines the overlap among routes between the airlines wishing to enter into an alliance. Support for the alliance is more likely to be forthcoming if the airlines have little overlap. In this case, the potential for diminished competition due to the alliance is low. In fact, the alliance will likely result in benefits to consumers since, for example, customers of Airline 1 will be able to buy tickets from that airline, earn frequent flier points from that airline, but travel on routes operated by Airline 2. In other words, a domestic alliance with little route overlap expands the market for an allied airline's customers without diminishing competition. On the other hand, if the allied carriers do have significant route overlap, then the alliance has a greater chance of being challenged by the government due to competitive concerns.

Currently, in the U.S., many of the domestic code-share alliances correspond to membership in the three major international alliances. United Airlines, an original Star Alliance carrier, has had a code-share agreement with Star Alliance partner US Airways since 2003. United also entered into a code-share arrangement with Continental Airlines when Continental joined the Star Alliance in 2009. Delta Air Lines and Northwest Airlines, two Sky Team members, had a code-share arrangement before their merger in 2008, and, in fact, continued to operate code-share flights under the two carriers' codes following the merger.[10] However, U.S. domestic alliance partners do not necessarily have to be members of the same global alliance. For example, American Airlines and Alaska Airlines have had an alliance since 1999, with only American being a member of the oneworld grouping.

One of the first major empirical studies on U.S. domestic airline alliances was conducted by Bamberger et al. (2004). The authors examine the impacts on fares and passenger traffic of two code-sharing alliances formed in the mid-1990s – one between Continental Airlines and America West Airlines, and a second between Northwest Airlines and Alaska Airlines. For both alliances, the authors find that fares fell and traffic increased following the formation of the alliance. They attribute consumer benefits arising from the alliance to greater competition between the alliance carriers and other, rival carriers.

Armantier and Richard (2008) investigate a code-share alliance between Continental Airlines and Northwest Airlines and arrive at different results than Bamberger et al. (2004). Armantier and Richard (2008) find that the Continental/ Northwest alliance had no significant impact on the average passenger. Using data from 1998–2001 on over 1,000 markets, the authors find that there was no significant change in consumer surplus following the creation of the alliance. The authors do find that the consumer surplus of nonstop passengers in the code-share markets declined by 5.9 percent. However, this decline is offset by an increase in surplus of 2.45 percent to the connecting passengers in the code-share markets; the net effect on passengers – about zero.

Ito (2007) collected data from the year 2003 on 37.5 million passengers traveling over approximately 15,000 city pairs. Using his dichotomy between traditional and virtual code-share itineraries described above, the researcher finds that traditional code-share itineraries are priced about 11.6 percent lower than interline itineraries offered by non-allied carriers, but are 6.4 percent higher than online itineraries. These results are consistent with the results reported for international code-sharing; that is, online itineraries are the lowest priced and non-aligned itineraries are the highest priced, with alliance itineraries falling in between these two extremes. A surprising finding, however, is that virtual code-share itineraries are priced 5–6 percent lower than online itineraries. Since both virtual code-share itineraries and online itineraries are flown by a single carrier, it is not immediately evident why this should occur. Ito (2007) argues that a virtual code-share ticket is an imperfect substitute for an online ticket. Although an Airline 1 customer obtains certain benefits by flying on alliance partner, Airline 2, the customer does not obtain as many benefits as he/she would obtain by flying on his/her own carrier. For example, the virtual code-share customer may not have the same chance to be upgraded from economy to business class as would the online customer. Therefore, Ito (2007) argues that passengers view the virtual code-share tickets as "less desirable" than online tickets, and that the virtual code-share tickets are thus discounted compared to online tickets.

Following Ito (2007), Gayle (2008) classifies code-sharing itineraries into either the traditional or the virtual category. He then uses a before-and-after comparison to analyze the impact of the 2003 Delta/Continental/Northwest alliance. Based on data on nearly 27,000 city pairs, the author finds that the alliance is associated with a small overall (up to 4.8 percent) increase in prices on over three-quarters of the city pairs. Gayle (2008) also finds that the alliance helped to generate traffic on the routes served by member carriers. Overall traffic in the markets served by alliance code-shares rose by about 10 percent, with alliance partner traffic up by about 20 percent. In contrast to Ito (2007), Gayle (2008) finds that virtual code-share itineraries are associated with significant price increases, while traditional code-share itineraries are not. Although Gayle (2008) finds that the increases in prices on virtual code-share are consistent with collusive behavior, he claims that since traffic also increases on these routes, it is not clear whether effective collusion actually takes place.

In summary, the empirical evidence on the costs and benefits of U.S. domestic code-share alliances is mixed. Some results point to higher prices while others point to lower prices resulting from the domestic alliances. Although most of the evidence indicates that connecting passengers on complementary routes who take advantage of traditional code-share flights achieve benefits from the alliances, the evidence on benefits to passengers on nonstop routes from virtual code-sharing is decidedly mixed. Finally, the research does seem to indicate that domestic alliances generate traffic for their member carriers.

6 Conclusions

Alliances are viewed as "intermediate" forms of organizational structure, with many of the advantages of hierarchical organization, but without some of the costs. Companies that enter into alliances can achieve transaction cost economies by contracting with other firms. In addition, they do not have to undertake the capital expenditures that would be required through acquisitions.

In the global airline industry, alliances are a common form of association in part because nearly all governments prohibit mergers between international carriers that would result in foreign control. Alliances have been shown to reduce operating costs and generate passenger demand for their partner carriers. They allow airlines to reduce operating costs through the achievement of economies of density, and induce passenger demand by making the flying experience more favorable, for example by offering lower connection times at hub airports.

The empirical evidence is quite strong that global alliances reduce prices for passengers flying on complementary routes, in part, due to the elimination of double marginalization. There is also evidence that they lead to increased passenger demand for allied carriers. Parallel alliances have offsetting effects on prices – they reduce competition leading to upward pressures on prices, but also reduce costs contributing to lower prices. Empirical findings show that, on average, parallel alliances have little impact on airfares, likely due to these offsetting effects.

Alliances in the U.S. domestic market are characterized by a large percentage of "virtual" code-share routes. With virtual code-share itineraries, a passenger buys a ticket on one airline (i.e., the marketing carrier) but travels exclusively on another carrier (i.e., the operating carrier). The evidence on virtual code-sharing is mixed, with one study showing an upward impact on airfares (Gayle 2008) and another a downward impact (Ito 2007). It is clear that additional research needs to be undertaken to further explore the impact of virtual alliances on competitive outcomes.

Until governments are willing to allow for the consolidation of the airline industry across national borders, there will continue to be a place for global alliances. It is evident that they have been advantageous to their member carriers and have produced a number of positive outcomes for passengers. However, global alliances also act to reduce competition. Although the empirical evidence to date does not appear to support the view that airfares have increased due to alliance activity, it is important to keep monitoring the industry to ensure that alliance activity continues to produce more benefits than costs.

Notes

1 Typically, labor rates were considerably lower at the regional carriers than at the major airlines.
2 Information on the airline members of the three alliances can be obtained at the following websites: Star Alliance – www.staralliance.com/en/; oneworld – www.oneworld.com/; Sky Team – www.skyteam.com/.
3 See Bilotkach (2005).
4 Open skies agreements are intergovernmental regulatory agreements that promote competition in international markets. As opposed to traditional air transport bilateral agreements, open skies agreements allow carriers more competitive opportunities, notably fewer restrictions on access to routes and airport facilities. In addition, the governmental role in approving or prohibiting international fares is strictly limited with open skies agreements.

5 For example, Airline 1 could operate on the route Monday, Wednesday and Friday, while Airline 2 could operate Tuesday, Thursday and Saturday. The shared operations will allow the carriers to use larger aircraft than would be the case if both of the carriers operated six times per week.
6 The authors acknowledge that these other carriers may not be considered to be small by world standards, but show that as measured by revenue passenger-miles, they are significantly smaller than the "big three."
7 Risk-pooling has been closely examined in the operations management literature. For example, a distributor can reduce required safety stocks of inventory by pooling inventory in a central warehouse.
8 Although the European Union allows carriers from any member country to operate without discrimination anywhere within the Union, non-Union airlines are not granted this right.
9 The discussion in this section is confined to alliances between two or more network carriers and does not apply to alliances between network carriers and their regional feeder carriers.
10 This alliance also included Continental before it switched from the Sky Team Alliance to the Star Alliance.

References

Armantier, O. and Richard, O. (2008) "Domestic Airline Alliances and Consumer Welfare." *RAND Journal of Economics*, Vol. 39(3), pp. 875–904.

Bamberger, G. E., Carlton, D. W., and Neumann, L. R. (2004) "An Empirical Investigation of the Competitive Effects of Domestic Airline Alliances." *Journal of Law and Economics*, Vol. 47, pp. 195–222.

Bilotkach, V. (2005) "Price Competition Between International Airline Alliances." *Journal of Transport Economics and Policy*, Vol. 39(2), pp. 167–189.

Bilotkach, V. (2007) "Price Effects of Airline Consolidation: Evidence from a Sample of Transatlantic Markets." *Empirical Economics*, Vol. 33, pp. 427–448.

Brueckner, J. K. (2003a) "International Airfares in the Age of Alliances: The Effects of Codesharing and Antitrust Immunity." *The Review of Economics and Statistics*, Vol. 85(1), pp. 105–118.

Brueckner, J. K. (2003b) "The Benefits of Codesharing and Antitrust Immunity for International Passengers, with an Application to the Star Alliance." *Journal of Air Transport Management*, Vol. 9, pp. 83–89.

Brueckner, J. K. and Proost, S. (2009) "Carve-Outs under Airline Antitrust Immunity." Unpublished working paper.

Brueckner, J. K. and Whalen, W. T. (2000) "The Price Effects of International Airline Alliances." *Journal of Law and Economics*, Vol. 43(2), pp. 503–545.

Chen, F. C.-Y. and Chen, C. (2003) "The Effects of Strategic Alliances and Risk Pooling on the Load Factors of International Airline Operations." *Transportation Research Part E*, Vol. 39, pp. 19–34.

Coase, R. H. (1937) "The Nature of the Firm" reprinted in O. E. Williamson and S. G. Winter, eds., *The Nature of the Firm: Origins, Evolution and Development*. Oxford, UK: Oxford University Press, pp. 18–74.

Czerny, A. I. (2009) "Code-Sharing, Price Discrimination and Welfare Losses." *Journal of Transport Economics and Policy*, Vol. 43(2), pp. 193–210.

Gayle, P. G. (2008) "An Empirical Analysis of the Competitive Effects of the Delta/Continental/Northwest Code-Share Alliance." *Journal of Law and Economics*, Vol. 51, pp. 743–766.

Goh, M. and Yong, J. (2006) "Impacts of Code-Share Alliances on Cost Structure: A Truncated Third-Order Translog Estimation." *International Journal of Industrial Organization*, Vol. 24, pp. 835–866

Iatrou, K. and Alamdari, F. (2005) "The Empirical Analysis of the Impact of Alliances on Airline Operations." *Journal of Air Transport Management*, Vol. 11, pp. 127–134.

Ito, H. (2007) "Domestic Code Sharing, Alliances, and Airfares in the U.S. Airline Industry." *Journal of Law and Economics*, Vol. 50, pp. 355–380.

Morrish, S. C. and Hamilton, R. T. (2002) "Airline Alliances – Who Benefits?" *Journal of Air Transport Management*, Vol. 8, pp. 401–407.

Oum, T. H., Park, J.-H., Kim, K., and Yu, C. (2004) "The Effect of Horizontal Alliances on Firm Productivity and Profitability: Evidence from the Global Airline Industry." *Journal of Business Research*, Vol. 57, pp. 844–853.

Park, J.-H. (1997) "The Effects of Airline Alliances on Markets and Economic Welfare." *Transportation Research Part E*, Vol. 33(3), pp. 181–195.

Park, J.-H. and Zhang, A. (2000) "An Empirical Analysis of Global Airline Alliances: Cases in North Atlantic Markets." *Review of Industrial Organization*, Vol. 16, pp. 367–383.

Park, J.-H., Park, N. K., and Zhang, A. (2003) "The Impact of International Alliances on Rival Firm Value: A Study of the British Airways/USAir Alliance." *Transportation Research Part E*, Vol. 39, pp. 1–18.

Wan, X., Zou, L., and Dresner, M. (2009) "Assessing the Price Effects of Alliances on Parallel Routes." *Transportation Research Part E*, Vol. 45, pp. 627–641.

Whalen, W. T. (2007) "A Panel Data Analysis of Code-Sharing, Antitrust Immunity, and Open Skies Treaties in International Aviation Markets." *Review of Industrial Organization*, Vol. 30, pp. 39–61.

Williamson, O. E. (1979) "Transaction-Cost Economics: The Governance of Contractual Relations." *Journal of Law and Economics*, Vol. 22(2), pp. 233–261.

Zhang, A., Hui, Y. V., and Leung, L. (2004) "Air Cargo Alliances and Competition in Passenger Markets." *Transportation Research Part E*, Vol. 40, pp. 83–100.

11 The transmogrification of hub-and-spoke airline networks

Kenneth Button

"Economic progress, in capitalist society, means turmoil."

Joseph Schumpeter, Harvard economist, 1942

1 Introduction

Air transportation from the 1970s has proved to be a highly adaptive industry once freed from a labyrinth of economic regulations that had encumbered most markets since the initiation of commercial airline services. Prior to 1977, when the first major "deregulation" of air transportation occurred in the domestic US air cargo market, an extensive system of economic regulations, largely on a bilateral basis, saw governments negotiate international air-fares and award market access rights. In the larger domestic markets, such as within the United States, fares and service providers were institutionally determined by the national government. This command and control approach to the sector had stymied the development of efficient airline networks. It had resulted in artificially high fares and widespread static and dynamic X-inefficiency in the supply of services.

The regulations had also almost universally limited the development of the most economically efficient networks; essentially each service, whether within a domestic market or internationally, was treated as a peculiar product and regulated in isolation. The particulars of network economics were lacking within the policy-making frameworks and synergies between services and routes were given little attention in fare setting and licensing decisions. Despite this, there were extensive hub-and-spoke networks in existence, although restricted in their form, and certainly not optimal in their nature.[1]

In particular, hub-and-spoke operations[2] had developed in international air transportation as a result the bilateral air service agreement system that emerged after the Chicago Convention,[3] but they were limited in the sense that the flag carriers at major "gateway" airports could never exceed 50 percent of the capacity. The constraint was that, with some notable exceptions, most countries limited their international services to a monopoly "flag carrier," with the national airline services being matched by those of the carrier of the partner country. Bilateral agreements invariably divided traffic equally, or in some agreed proportion, between the local flag carrier and the foreign flag carrier.

The system was thus not nearly as refined as in subsequent deregulated markets where carriers sought to benefit from economies of scope and density on the cost side, and to gain from greater market presence on the demand side. The simple economics of the situation often led to carriers having much more than 50 percent of traffic at their hubs. The gradual emergence of "Open Skies" agreements, effectively from the early 1990s although they did exist earlier, in international markets, and the growth in strategic alliances between airlines reinforced a trend towards hub-oriented networks.

As with any business model, success depends upon context. The hub-and-spoke structure grew following a long period of regulation, and experiences with market conditions were virtually non-existent when liberalization came. The emergence of the new airline business models from the late 1980s, together with changes in technology and demand patterns, and more generally in public policy concerns over environmental matters, have shifted the parameters in the world in which hub-and-spoke networks exist, and with this has come new thinking about the optimal way air services should be delivered. Not surprisingly, this has affected the role of hub structures in individual airlines' networks, and in the larger air transportation value chain.

This chapter looks at the factors that initially stimulated the growth of airline hub-and-spoke networks, the forces that have subsequently led to their being modified, and the forms that they now take. The examination not only looks at underlying economic forces involved, but also at the political economy of such things as the emergence of mega-trade blocks, attitudes towards anti-trust and merger activities, and increasing amounts of environmental regulation. Markets for air services, and with them the relevance of hubs, are not independent of the institutional structures in which they function, and changes in these institutions, along with new technologies and innovations in management, inevitably affect the types of service networks airlines offer.

2 The economics of the hub-and-spoke concept

2.1 The emergence of competitive markets

As the Nobel Prize-winning economist Oliver Williamson (2000) pointed out in the context of the New Institutional Economics, markets do not exist in a vacuum but function within legal boundaries and society's approaches to governance. The United States' air transportation market prior to 1977 was under the direction control of the Civil Aeronautics Board, but was perhaps more nuanced than those within other countries because of the explicit separation between the regulatory agency and political involvement. The strict forces of supply and demand did not determine prices and output in this situation, but unlike most other countries there were strict rules governing how fares and routes were regulated, and the airlines providing the air services were unsubsidized commercial companies. Elsewhere, airlines such as British Airways, Air France, and Alitalia tended to be largely state-owned entities with the regulations governing their actions determined by politically controlled bodies. But even for countries such as the United States, international services involved government agreements, and the situation was almost universally one of political manipulation.

The result of these structures was large-scale capture of the system by airlines,[4] and possibly the regulators, and, concomitantly, extensive Tullock and X-inefficiencies. The widespread use of rate-of-return regulation in countries such as the US, which allowed airlines to pass on in higher fares and cargo rates any cost increase they incurred, as well as extensive subsidies, were used to support mainly state-owned and largely international flag carriers elsewhere. This limited allocative efficiency pushed up the costs of services, and offered little incentive for innovation in the way services were supplied. In terms of hub-and-spoke systems, there was little incentive for airlines to press for them and, in any case, the institutional structure was unlikely to optimize them. In addition, because there was limited fare competition and costs could be passed on to users there was considerable gold-plating of services to attract customers.[5]

The removal or reform of many of the institutional constraints has seen significant efficiency gains in the provisions of airline services, many of which have been passed on to customers in the form of lower fares and freight rates, and more market-responsive service levels.[6] Some of this may be attributable to the simple advent of competitive and, perhaps to a lesser extent, contestable forces, but there were also significant changes in the nature of the air services that were provided. Further, not all markets were subjected to the same institutional changes, and even when they were, the timing was often different.

Despite the use of the term "deregulated" in the United States, the markets for air transportation services are not entirely free of economic regulation although they have certainly been extensively liberalized (in the English sense of the term) over the past quarter of a century. There are still restrictions governing many international markets, and within some of the smaller domestic ones. In addition while economic regulations have retreated, there have been significant increases in the level of social or quality regulation covering such things as safety and the environment. The latter have an impact on the costs of airlines and other elements of the air transport supply chain and this, in turn, has had an increasing influence on the way airline networks have been evolving. Further, the nature of reforms has varied with different markets being liberalized in a variety of sequences. Perhaps the most transparent of these is seen in the "big bang" approach adopted within the United States whereby regulations were relaxed in one short, sharp act, compared to the European Union approach that was one of gradualism with changes coming over a period through a sequence of "Packages" (Button and Johnson, 1998).

One of the major changes that the reforms have brought about has been the greater consolidation of traffic through large airports rather than having a multiplicity of individual point-to-point services. At its simplest, this hub-and-spoke structure allows all points on a network to be serviced using a small number of routes, albeit with a combination of direct and one-stop services rather than with all direct services between all origins and destinations.[7]

2.2 The pot-pourri of economies

In more detail, and from a wider commercial perspective, the economic rationale for hub-and-spoke services is that they can generate a variety of economies for the airlines offering them that in aggregate, and when passed on to passengers or consignors of freight, outweigh their additional costs. In welfare economic terms, this increases the combined consumer and producer surpluses associated with air travel.

By combining services, airlines may gain from economies of scope – the costs of providing services in combination being lower than offering them separately.[8] For example, rather than linking up $i \rightarrow j$, $i \rightarrow k$, and $j \rightarrow k$, but instead offering services linking $i \rightarrow k$ and $j \rightarrow k$ with passengers going $i \rightarrow j$ going via k, the airline is combining the latter flow with those individually going $i \rightarrow k$ and $j \rightarrow k$, and thus the airline saves on aircraft. Further, because the services offered will be more intensively used, there are potential economies of density to be reaped. There may also be other economies if the airline can maximize the use of its ground facilities – checking, baggage handling, etc. – and spread what are in effect fixed costs.

By effectively serving larger markets on the retained routes, the hub-and-spoke structure allows more intensive use of capital because of the higher load factors enjoyed and, hence, lowers unit cost per passenger. But there are also potential benefits on the revenue side from the hub-and-spoke structure. It may make it viable to serve more markets by combining flows from otherwise uneconomic markets and, thus, generating more traffic because of the range of destinations that can be served via a hub. There are so-called economies of market presence. It is a little like supply creating its own demand; more frequent services, even if involving a change at a hub, can attract customers that may not otherwise have made a trip.

2.3 The downside of hub-and-spoke economics

Hub-and-spoke operations require the concentrated arrival and departure of services to allow the transshipment of passengers to take place. This leads to the "banking of flights" with a large number of passengers arriving at once and then, after changing planes, leaving at about the same time. This inevitably leads to problems of peaks and with them come congestion issues.

Congestion is in economic terms a "club good" problem whereby there is a need to ensure a club's facilities, in this case airport capacity, are optimally allocated to a limited group of users. The problem is that one member's use interferes with the use of others (it is difficult for two aircraft to land on a runway at the same time). There is thus the need to limit the use of the infrastructure to those that gain the most from it. If there is a single user – one airline using the airport – then it can be argued that the facility will be used optimally and a network carrier will schedule services so that its banks of flights optimize congestion, although this is often far from perfect given the complexities involved (Brueckner, 2005).[9] In other cases, with a multiplicity of users measures such as slot auctions can make better use of capacity, but they do require some notion of what the optimal capacity is (Button, 2008a).

More germane in a way is the fact that there is a need to define what the capacity to allocate should be. In economic terms, one is seeking a capacity beyond which additional flights push up net costs. An issue that has become more important in recent years is the matter of which costs to include. Figure 11.1 provides a simplification. On the vertical access, costs per passenger are measured, and the horizontal measures load factors of aircraft. (For simplicity we assume a single type of plane.) With fully efficient hubbing and no congestion, the load factor for an airline should be 100 percent.

In terms of the flight costs borne by an airline, these continually fall as the load factor rises as the various fixed costs of a flight can be spread across more fare passengers. The terminal costs of the service will rise with passenger numbers as congestion increases and this is seen additively in the figure. The costs to passengers of making trips will also rise with hubbing because it entails layover times at the hub airport. Finally, the environmental costs per passenger of higher load factors will fall as load factors rise because there are fewer empty seats to be transported.

These varying costs imply that there are a number of possible optimum levels of hubbing. The airlines may wish to maximize it but the airports would opt for a level of L_p that takes into account the amount airlines would be willing to pay for a high level of hubbing but offsets that against the airports' own congestion costs. The passengers would prefer a little more hubbing, L_e, because they take into account the time and inconvenience of changing planes. If the environment is taken into account an even higher load factor is desirable because it reduces wastage of natural resources. In broad terms, if the air transportation system does

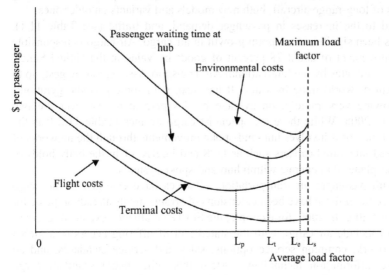

Figure 11.1 The notion of optimal hubbing.

not take into account environmental factors, in most circumstances, one would anticipate larger hubs in terms of flights, involving smaller aircraft.

Congestion in any network can also result from what traffic engineers refer to generically as "incidents." While the congestion associated with volume and banking of flights is largely volume based and may be controlled to some extent at dominated hubs, congestion due to incidents has associated problems of uncertainty. Incidents in aviation are not always accidents but can be weather related or to do with a mechanical or communications malfunctioning; e.g. a problem with an aircraft or air traffic control computers. The difficulty with interconnecting services, such as those passing through a hub, are the inevitable knock-on effects that a relatively small delay caused by an incident can set in motion. With point-to-point services there are few passenger connections and an incident is thus basically contained, but if a flight has problems in a hubbed network there are implications across the system and throughout the day.

3 The changing model

3.1 The global air services market

Much of the increase in air travel has involved international markets.[10] This may in part be attributable to increases in income in many parts of the world, such as China, but also more leisure time has become available in more established market-based economies and populations have aged and this has led to more tourism. Added to this has been the push since the late 1970s from the United States towards Open Skies bilateral agreements that have liberalized many of the important international air transportation markets. Stimulated by these trends, the major aircraft manufacturers, Airbus and Boeing, have produced increasing numbers of long-range aircraft; both new models and variants on older ones.

Added to the increases in passenger demand, and traffic (see Table 11.1), there has been significant temporal growth in air cargo. Air cargo is responsible for the movement of about 28 percent of goods by value in the United States, and some estimates by the International Air Transport Association suggest, up to 40 percent of world trade by value. It has also, with some periodic gyrations, been growing very rapidly; on average by 4.8 percent a year over the two decades to 2008. While there are specialist cargo airlines (Table 11.2 lists the largest), much of it involves hub-and-spoke movements through the networks of specialized integrated carriers such as UPS and FedEx, or in the belly holds of passenger planes that operate within hub-and-spoke systems.

As with passenger air transportation, alliances have emerged in the cargo market. Some of these have been extensions of arrangements already in place for passenger traffic. In 2000, for example, the SkyTeam alliance extended its cooperation to include air cargo, with the stated aim of offering access to a global route network, common service options, sales and service standards, and an interfaced information technology system that will ensure seamless cargo coordination and delivery throughout SkyTeam's global network.[11]

Alliances have also formed between cargo airlines, such as that of WOW Alliance, SkyTeam Cargo and ANA/UPS Alliance. The WOW Cargo Alliance, formed in 2000, currently includes JAL Cargo, Lufthansa Cargo, SAS Cargo Group and Singapore Airlines. SkyTeam Cargo includes Aeroméxpress, Air France Cargo, CSA Cargo, Delta Air Logistics, KLM Cargo, Korean Air Cargo, NWA Cargo and Alitalia Cargo. There is also a more limited agreement between All Nippon and United Parcel Services that have a code-share to transport each other's cargoes.

Although some of the expansion into international markets has involved relatively short-haul movements, there have been significant increases in both long-haul passenger and freight traffics. This has led to an increase in multiple-hubbing of airline services.[12] What has happened in recent years has been the emergence of "dog-bone" or "dumb-bell" hub-and-spoke configurations as seen in Figure 11.2.

Taking our original purely domestic case, for a country with a large airport at **A** as seen in the left of the figure, then a full network of services offered by a carrier would have to link all the cities (n = i) in that country (x ⇔ y, x ⇔ z; y ⇔ z, x ⇔ **A**; y ⇔ **A**; and so on). Clearly this would lead to numerous separate

Table 11.1 International air transportation

Year	Passengers	Freight (tonnes)	Passenger kilometers	Freight (tonne-kilometers)
1996	412	13.6	1,380,680	75,510
1997	438	15.7	1,468,150	87,740
1998	458	15.8	1,512,040	87,050
1999	493	17.3	1,622,250	93,280
2000	542	18.8	1,790,370	101,560
2001	536	18.0	1,726,580	95,950
2002	547	18.8	1,736,070	101,590
2003	561	19.6	1,738,510	103,133
2004	647	21.8	2,015,070	115,120
2005	704	22.6	2,197,360	118,480

Source: International Civil Aviation Organisation.

Table 11.2 2004 international scheduled cargo tonne-kilometers flown

1	Korean Air	8.164 million
2	Lufthansa Cargo	8.028 million
3	Singapore Airlines Cargo	7.143 million
4	Cathay Pacific	5.876 million
5	China Airlines	5.642 million
6	FedEx Express	5.595 million
7	Eva Airways	5.477 million
8	Air France	5.384 million
9	British Airways	4.771 million
10	Cargolux	4.670 million

Source: International Air Transport Association and only includes member airlines.

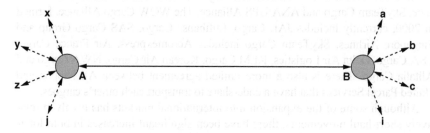

Figure 11.2 The dumb-bell pattern of international hub-and-spoke operations.

services and the probable inability to use larger aircraft. Hub-and-spoke operations would funnel traffic through **A** where there is consolidation of consignments from various origins that are going to a variety of destinations that can be
combined (hence traffic would be of the form x ⇒ **A** ⇒ y; x ⇒ **A** ⇒ z; and so
on). The ability to combine passengers or consignments reduces costs by both
exploiting economies of scope (e.g. in the case of cargo, carrying shipments with
multiple final destinations on each aircraft) and density (e.g. making for larger
payloads on each route).

We can take this further in larger, international markets. For longer routings
there may be several consolidations of passengers or cargo (for example passengers from origin x to destination c, may be routed x ⇒ **A** ⇒ **B** ⇒ c). To allow
for this type of structure to work at maximum efficiency requires large volumes
of traffic and numerous origins and destinations. Sophisticated booking and
information systems are also needed. Additionally, while there are significant
economies associated with suppliers of network services combining their traffic,
there are also transaction costs at the hubbing points; travel time costs for passengers and inventory holding costs for cargo.

3.2 Competition between hubs with strategic airline alliances

The spread of Open Skies agreements, especially since the 1990s, has not only
allowed airlines to modify their network structures, but also in many cases to
combine and coordinate their activities through strategic alliances (Table 11.3)
and thus to push more feed through their major hubs.[13]

Competition in this system is largely between interconnected airline networks,
often involving strategic cargo airline alliances. Figure 11.3 again takes the long-
distance movement x ⇒ c but now looks at the options that may be available when
comparing different air cargo or passenger alliances rather than just looking at the
services of a single airline. The routing x ⇒ **A** ⇒ **B** ⇒ used in Figure 11.2 is
retained as the base case, but the airline offering this may also have alliance ties
with other carriers and push traffic through one or more of their hubs (**C, D,** etc.);
this may make x ⇒ **C** ⇒ **A** ⇒ **B** ⇒ c an option, or x ⇒ **C** ⇒ **D** ⇒ c. A competitive alliance may also offer x ⇒ **F** ⇒ **G** ⇒ c. And so on.[14]

Figure 11.3 Network competition in the air transportation sector.

Depending on schedules and routes served there are thus numerous possibilities for moving cargo or passengers from x to c. From a costing perspective, these various options will differ for the combinations supplying airlines involved. The cheapest route, because of various cost economies of scope and density, may transpire to be physically longer than x $\Rightarrow$ **A** $\Rightarrow$ **B** $\Rightarrow$ c. A major difference between the networks of the cargo providers and passenger airlines in this case would be the length of stay at the various hubs. Packages and freight are much less sensitive to layovers at hubs provided they reach their destinations on schedule; especially if just-in-time production is involved. There is ample evidence that individuals are averse to having to change aircraft at hubs – they value travel time in the air differently to the value they give to waiting for flights – and thus optimization involves different weightings of service elements.[15]

What this means from the perspective of hub development, is the increased coordination of services (including those within the airport, such as check-in facilities, information systems, lounge, and gate use) between members of strategic alliances to reap the maximum benefits from their union. It would also logically mean the more widespread creation of countervailing power by airlines to combat the often monopolist situation of airport authorities – effectively more bilateral-monopoly, or at least oligopoly relationships (Button, 2010).[16] This leads to gaming on the part of the airports when they have mixed low-cost, non-hubbing airlines and traditional carriers using their capacity. The services demanded are different and the airport must allocate its scarce capacity between the various user groups.

3.3 The non-aviation elements of hub economics

Large passenger airport hubs, by definition, have extensive transit traffic flows often leaving individuals with long layover times.[17] There are also periods where passengers are in limbo between checking and boarding. Airports, and particularly hub airports, have increasingly been using this time to sell non-airport goods and services. In the case of international services this has, since its initiation in 1947 at Shannon Airport, Ireland, often been linked to duty-free sales, although these have vanished on many routes, such as within the European Union, and free trade groupings have emerged.

Table 11.3 The main strategic airline alliances

	Star Alliance	SkyTeam	Oneworld	Rest of industry
Passengers per year	499.90 million	462 million	328.63 million	489 million
Destinations	912	905	673	
Revenue ($ billion)	141.71	97.9	99.78	113
Market share	29.3%	20.6%	23.2%	26.9%
Participants	(JP) Adria Airways (AC) Air Canada (CA) Air China (NZ) Air New Zealand (NH) ANA (OZ) Asiana Airlines (OS) Austrian Airlines (KF) Blue1 (BD) BMI (OU) Croatia Airlines (MS) EgyptAir (LO) LOT Polish Airlines (LH) Lufthansa (SK) SAS (FM) Shanghai Airlines (SQ) Singapore Airlines	(SU) Aeroflot (AM) Aeroméxico (UX) Air Europa (AF) Air France (AZ) Alitalia (CZ) China Southern (CO) Continental (switching to Star Alliance as of October 27, 2009) (CM) Copa Airlines (OK) Czech Airlines (DL) Delta–Northwest (Merged) (KQ) Kenya Airways (KL) KLM (KE) Korean Air	(AA) American Airlines (BA) British Airways (CX) Cathay Pacific (AY) Finnair (IB) Iberia (JL) Japan Airlines (LA) LAN (MA) Malév (QF) Qantas (RJ) Royal Jordanian (MX) Mexicana (S7) S7 Airlines (to join 2010)	(EI) Aer Lingus (AB) Air Berlin (AI) Air India (switching to Star Alliance) (AT) AirTrans Airlines (AS) Alaska Airlines (AV) Avianca (BA) Bahamasair (SN) Brussels Airlines (joining Star Alliance) (5J) Cebu Pacific (MU) China Eastern Airlines (U2) easyJet (LY) El Al Airlines (EK) Emirates Airlines (EY) Etihad Airways

(SA) South African Airways
(JK) Spanair
(LX) Swiss International Air Lines
(TP) TAP Portugal
(TG) Thai Airways International
(TK) Turkish Airlines
(UA) United Airlines
(US) US Airways

(VN) Vietnam Airlines (to join 2010)

(FR) Frontier Airlines
(G3) GOL Airlines
(GF) Gulf Air
(HA) Hawaiian Airlines(9W) Jet Airways
(B6) JetBlue Airways
(IT) Kingfisher Airlines
(MH) Malaysia Airlines
(PR) Philippine Airlines
(QR) Qatar Airways
(FR) Ryanair
(SV) Saudi Arabian Airlines
(WN) Southwest Airlines
(JJ) TAM Airlines (joining Star Alliance)
(VS) Virgin Atlantic Airways
(DJ) Virgin Blue
(WS) WestJet Airlines
(OA) Olympic Airlines
(many others)

Sources: http://skyteam.com/downloads/news/facts/skyteamFactSheet.pdf; www.staralliance.com/int/press/facts_figures/star_alliance_facts_and_figures_dec2008_final.pd; www.oneworld.com/content/factsheet.

The importance of these commercial activities for the financial viability of airports can be significant, and most now have de facto shopping centers in them and around them. Revenue flowing from two major sources inevitably affects the economics of running large airports; it impacts on the ways fixed costs are allocated and thus on pricing, and on decisions regarding investments. In a way hub airports are providing joint products. In some cases this has posed problems in the formulation of appropriate regulatory structures for large hubs.

Because of their natural advantages of scale and scope economies there is a concern that airlines using hub airports can reap economic rent from some groups of passengers; they have a degree of quasi-monopoly power and are able to charge passengers flying directly to and from the airport a premium. The evidence on the extent of such power, and the degree to which hub airports exercise it, is open to some dispute. Numerous studies in the United States have come up with a range of figures for rent extraction through hub premiums.[18] Besides the challenges of calculating premiums, there are also issues concerning whether they are really exploitive or simply charging users a premium because of the availability of a wide range of routes and for more extensive airport facilities.

The ability of congested hub airports to extract some of the hub premiums has been a further concern for the authorities and countries such as the United Kingdom have got mired in debates over the dual role of airports as air service hubs and retail centers;[19] namely whether price capping should be based on a single till or a dual till (Starkie, 2001). The intention is not to dwell on these debates – that is outside of our remit – but rather to highlight the fact that the nature of many major hubs has changed with liberalization and the changing incentives that are engaging their management as they seek ways to diversify their income portfolios.

4 The economic challenge of keeping airlines

Airlines have choices of which airports to serve and they do switch their hubs. Airports essentially have to sell their services to the airlines. The success of hub-and-spoke operations and the size of hub airports, however, depend largely on the cost structures not only of the airports themselves but also of those that use them; namely the passengers and the airlines

Scheduled airlines have historically found it difficult to recover their full costs; indeed globally over the past quarter of a century they have earned a zero operating margin, much below that required to cover their capital investments. The problem is one common to many service industries providing a guaranteed product in advance of delivery in a competitive market; airlines schedule their services and collect fares well in advance of take-off. The difficulty is that if there are several carriers offering similar services then they will compete their fares down to their marginal costs. They will not be able to cover the full costs of the service and thus there will be continual entry to and exit from the market.[20]

If there is volatility of this type in the airline market, or at least large parts of it, then notions of optimal size and capacity constraint are flexible. Airlines, as they seek to minimize the problems of market stability, essentially use the ability to move services between airports as part of their on-going business strategies. If airports do have capacity constraints, and these may be at particular times of the day or elements in their offering (e.g. slots, gates, or fees) that are unattractive, then a carrier can move capacity on either a long- or short-term basis. This raises issues about what exactly capacity means and what hubbing means from a temporal perspective.

Most hub-and-spoke airlines have found it difficult to make a normal profit over the past 20 years or more, and this has been particularly so for the American carriers whose viability has often only been made possible by periodic bouts of Chapter 11 bankruptcy[21] and mergers. The evidence is, however, that the airports themselves are doing less badly, unless they lose a major client (e.g. Pittsburgh Airport's loss of US Airways). The length of leases and agreements made by the airlines with the airports has offered something of a short-term cushion, and airports do enjoy supplementary revenues for concessions and car parks.

In the United States, the airlines' approach has been to focus on their core airports and to seek longer routes with less competition from low-cost carriers. This has been leading to concentration of hubs, a trend that has been reinforced as airlines have merged in both the United States and Europe.[22] These larger airlines and their alliance partners have different needs to their predecessors and offer different challenges to the airports. For example, airport lounges provide revenue to airports, but there are economies in providing these and merged/allied carriers save money at the airport's expense by consolidation.

5 Hubs and the low-cost airlines

5.1 Competition through cost

So far little has been said about the low-cost airlines[23] that play significant roles in many short-haul markets; Southwest carries more domestic passengers in the US market than any traditional carrier, and Ryanair enjoys a similar position in Europe. The low-cost model is the opposite approach to success in a competitive market highlighted by Michael Porter (1985). Porter argues that you can get a competitive advantage by product differentiation that customers are willing to pay a premium for, for example the variety of service options offered by traditional carriers and their use of convenient airports, or you can get an advantage by offering a standard service at a lower cost than other suppliers. In the former case, it may be possible for several suppliers, airlines in our case, to compete in a market if consumers perceive their services to be different but valuable, but there can only be one successful low-cost carrier in a market.

The low-cost airlines' networks are often described as linear; functioning a little like a bus services by maintaining their load factors by picking up and dropping off passengers as an aircraft makes a series of relatively short flights.

This is, however, misleading in most cases. Ryanair and to a lesser extent many of the other low-cost airlines do have hubs but not in the sense normally associated with the legacy airlines. They offer limited or, for example Ryanair, no on-line services; Southwest Airlines have about 30 percent of its passengers on-lining.

In the Ryanair case the planes and crew are based at airports and fly in and out of that airport on a series of radial routes throughout the day. This makes it easy to switch bases if, for example, there are disputes over landing fees or it proves uneconomical. It also means there is no down time for crew – pilots fly the maximum 900 hours a year permitted – or wasted seats as personnel are repositioned. It also keeps labor costs down by maximizing the flying hours of crew; there is no repositioning; and capital costs are contained by having a common fleet that not only allows crew flexibility and a strong bargaining position when buying hardware, but also a smaller reserve fleet to deal with aircraft failures.

5.2 The failure of the low-cost model

While there are several highly visible success stories regarding low-cost airlines with Ryanair and Southwest Airlines being the prime examples, the business model has not proved to be universally profitable as the list of failed European low-cost carriers in Table 11.4 illustrates. Many of these carriers were manifestly unprepared for the rigors of any market – air transportation has that sort of veneer of romance associated with it – but others did survive for a period, and other carriers assimilated some.

Table 11.4 European low-cost carriers that ceased to exist (2003 to 2005)

Aeris	BuzzAway	Hellas Jet
Agent	Dream Air	Hop
Air Bosnia	Duo	Jet Magic
Air Andalucia	Europe DutchBird	Jetgreen
Air Catalunya	EastJet	JetsSky
Air Exel	EU Jet	JetX
Air Freedom	Europe Exel Aviation Group	Low Fare Jet
Air	Fairline Austria	Maersk Air
Air Littoral 15Feb	Fly Eco	Now
Air Luxor	Fly West	Silesian Air
Air Madrid	Flying Finn	Skynet Airlines
Air Polonia	Free Airways	Spirit Of Balkan
Air Wales	Fresh Aer	Swedline Express
Airlib Express	Germania Express	V Bird
BasiqAir	GetJet Poland	VolareWeb
BerlinJet	Go Fly	White Eagle
Bexx Air	Goodjet	Windjet

Note
Most of these airlines operated for a period and then went into bankruptcy. Some such as Go Fly and BuzzAway merged with successful low-cost airlines. In a few cases, the airline was registered but never offered actual services.

The difficulty from a business perspective is that pursuing a low-cost model involves an all-or-nothing market share – the lowest cost airline basically takes all. This means that there inevitably tends to be hub domination, albeit for offering radial services rather than a connected network of services. If this hub domination is eroded, either by other low-carriers moving directly into the market or by competitive low-cost centers being developed, then market instability results.

Given the differing business models, the Porter dichotomy, associated with traditional carriers and low-cost carriers, some airports have sought to meet the needs of both by having two sets of facilities; often different terminals. The aim is often to ensure that one composite, although divided hub, caters for a region's air transportation rather than having a competing low-cost hub away from the established airport (as is the case in places like Frankfurt where there are Hahn and Main airports). In 2006 Aéroport de Marseille Provence, for example, opened terminal MP2 specifically for budget airlines, but the efforts at separation of hubs at one location can also be found at places like Paris Charles de Gaulle where terminal T3 handles charter and low-cost carriers.

These dual operations are clearly somewhat different in their nature from the conventional idea of a hub that focuses primarily on the interchange of passengers. Even in Europe when there was a significant and discrete charter market, these services were mainly segregated from the flag carriers and were served by secondary airports.[24] Whether these dual role facilities have a long-term future is uncertain and may well depend on the degree to which competition between the low-cost carriers makes that end of the business successful for the airports.

6 Other factors

Other factors have influenced the development of hub airports and are likely to continue to play a role. We briefly focus on two.

6.1 Air traffic control

Air traffic navigation systems direct traffic flows and have all the features of a private good; they are both excludable and rival. In some parts of the network the crossing of airways combined with traffic descending to and ascending from a major airport can lead to major issues of congestion that is independent of the capacity of the airport itself to handle this traffic. In Europe there is de facto cap and trade at many airports stemming from the allocation of runway capacity and airlines trading in these slots. But the ability to use these slots effectively even within this structure depends on available airspace. In the United States, with a few exceptions, there is no capping of slots and in this case, air traffic control capacity can be even more of a constraint at certain airports and times of the day.

Air traffic systems in many parts of the world are being upgraded to meet the growing demand for air travel. There are, for example, the Single European Skies initiative in Europe and the Next Generation Air Transportation System in the United States. The ways this is done and the capacity provided will inevitably influence the nature of airline networks. While much of the effort is concerned with flow capacity, this, together with new approach and terminal control technology and procedures, will affect the capabilities of large hub airports to handle increases in traffic volumes.

6.2 *The environment*

The market for air transportations services, even under the largely liberalized conditions of the early twenty-first century, is far from perfect. While the traditional microeconomic issues of market power – lack of homogeneity in the product, the "club good" nature of airports, and indivisibilities – have been a traditional concern of regulators, there has been an increasing focus on the externalities of air travel. Environment costs are the main concern.

While much of the historical focus was on noise issues around airports, which continues to influence the ability to expand both operations and physical infrastructure at many major hub airports,[25] there have been more recent concerns about the greenhouse gas emissions, such as CO_2 and water vapor, associated, with flight itself. Airlines, for example, are estimated to be responsible for about 2 percent of global CO_2 emissions and some 3 percent of climate change gasses.

It is clear that the constraints imposed by noise restrictions have physically limited capacity expansions at many large airports, and delayed investments even when finally adopted. They also affect how they may be used (e.g. the imposition of night curfews and temporal limitations on runway use as at Heathrow). Both have affected the economics of hub-operations for airlines, essentially restricting infrastructure availability and the way they can manipulate their service networks. This has been a long-standing issue and partly explains such things as the use of more remote airports for cargo activities rather than the use of large passenger facilities at off-peak times, and the use of more remote airports by European charter operators in the past and more recently some low-cost airlines.[26]

The introduction of new policies to reduce the carbon footprint of air travel, which are mooted for the future and seem likely to be based on a form of cap and trade structure, will affect the relative costs of different forms of airline networks. Aircraft consume more fuel in take-offs and landings than when cruising and a fully loaded large aircraft of a similar technology uses less fuel per passenger kilometer than a small one. This tends to make the costs of moving large numbers of passengers, or tons of cargo, over longer distances cheaper. Thus, it would seem that with higher fuel costs when environmental costs are included, traditional airlines would have an advantage over low-cost counterparts if they can generate enough feed to their hubs. This, however, ignores the potential cost advantages of the low-cost airlines that may not be completely dissipated by carbon dioxide emission costs being internalized and the need for the hub-and-spoke operators to have sufficient demand to fill their planes. Added to this, the feeder services for long-haul flights are themselves often short haul and these would be affected by higher fuel costs in the same way as their low-cost competitors.

7 Conclusions

There is no such thing as a "hub-and-spoke network" for airline services, but rather there are a variety of different hub-and-spoke structures that have emerged over time to meet changing market and technological conditions. The simple economic idea that there are commercial costs and benefits associated with particular degrees of hubbing that define the extent to which airlines focus their business on transfer hubs has intellectual value, but putting hard numbers into the concept at any one time, and arriving at the "optimum" is more difficult. Hubs are not independent entities but compete with each other in an imperfect gaming environment, and the airports are not themselves passive, neutral entities that simply let airlines use them to their commercial advantages. Rather, large airports are involved in bilateral oligopolistic games along with the large airlines under which deterministic solutions are not easily arrived at.

Notions that there are limits to the size of hubs may have some contextual usefulness, but as Joseph Schumpeter points out, they are enmeshed in a world of destructive competition as innovation makes existing business models obsolete, and new forms come along. The idea of the hub airport and hub-and-spoke airline networks espoused not long after the deregulation of the US airline market now seems simplistic and dated. The fortress hubs of the traditional carriers have been undermined by point-to-point hub-busting services and the rent extraction of hub operators has more generally been eroded by low-cost carriers. Technology, rising global income, and growing international trade has seen an increase in multi-hub networks. In other words, the simple idea of hub airports, while perhaps meaningful at one point in aviation history, is now rather *passé*.

Notes

1 There was no agreement on what deregulated networks, and thus the role of hubs, would be post-deregulation in the US. Alfred Kahn (1988), for example, who as head of the Civil Aeronautics Board, was responsible for the deregulation in the US was surprised at the degree of competition that emerged in the market.

2 Hub-and-spoke networks have a long history in transportation and go back at least as far as the first seaports when goods were consolidated for sailings. In modern times, the post offices have perhaps exemplified their most extensive use. While the term is often used differently in specific contexts, we simply define a hub-and-spoke system as a network of services that allows inter-operability and inter-modality for users at some point in a person or goods movement.

3 The Convention on International Civil Aviation in 1944 – the Chicago Convention – established the International Civil Aviation Organization (ICAO), an agency of the United Nations charged with coordinating and regulating international air travel. The Convention established rules of airspace, aircraft registration, and safety, and details the rights of the signatories in relation to air travel.

4 This was because the airline had control over the information flows on such things as unit costs required for their regulation. It was perhaps a classic case of regulatory capture (Stigler, 1971).

5 This may be seen as a particular case of the Averch–Johnson (1962) effect with the gold plating being the excess use of capital.

6 Because of the quality of the data that is available, the US domestic market reforms have been most rigorously studied – e.g. see Morrison and Winston (1995).

7 When there are *n* cities, only *n* − 1 routes are necessary to connect all nodes in a hub-and-spoke network. This compares to the routes $\{n(n - 1)/2\}$ that would be required to connect each node to every other node in a point-to point network

8 Technically, economies of scope are assessed when

$$S = \{[C(Q1) + C(Q2)] - C(Q1 + Q2)\}/\{C(Q1 + Q2)\}$$

where: $C(Q1)$ is the cost of producing $Q1$ units of output one alone; $C(Q2)$ is the cost of producing $Q2$ units of output two alone; and $C(Q1 + Q2)$ is the cost of producing $Q1$ plus $Q2$ units together. Economies of scope exist if $S > 0$. There are economies of scale if C/Q falls as Q expands.

9 Some studies have shown no indication of congestion internalization at congested airports (Harback and Daniel, 2007).

10 The annual global revenue passenger-kilometers done, including international movements, rose from 3,381 billion in 2000 to 4,621 in 2008 despite the difficulties of the aftermath of the attack on the United States in 2001 and the onset of global recession in late 2007, and Boeing forecast a level of 12,090 in 2028. The major international flows are between Europe and North America, Central America and North America, China and Europe, and Africa and Europe.

11 www.skyteamcargo.com/en/about/press_room/pr_releases/pr_28092000.htm.

12 In some cases with longer trips, the feed and distribution functions may be served by non-aviation modes, especially if they are relatively short distances. As examples, Lufthansa offers seemless services with inter-city rail at its Frankfurt-Main hub, and there is a TGV station under Paris Charles de Gaulle airport. Hence some of the spokes may not be by air.

13 In some cases airlines have modified their use of hubs to focus on markets that they retain a degree of market power after confronting competition on international routes that now come under Open Skies agreements (Button *et al.*, 2005).

14 The evidence is somewhat mixed as to whether strategic alliances and competition between large networks benefits passengers and consignors of cargo (Morrish and Hamilton, 2002).

15 This is one reason why alliances tend to provide common lounge facilities to their higher fare-paying passengers; it reduces the disutility of waiting time.

16 While the focus here is largely on trends in the ways that airlines have changed the structures of their networks over time, with a focus on airline management and regulation, there has also been significant change in the way that infrastructure is now supplied and regulated (Button, 2007) and this can affect the outcome of the games that are played in bilateral monopoly situations and, *ipso facto*, the development of hubs.

17 Although hubs have large transit flows there is evidence that success also depends on having a reasonably sized local market. The attempt in Canada to hub traffic through a new airport, Montreal–Mirabel Airport, failed badly because it was too far from both Montreal and Toronto. Transit movements were not sufficient.

18 Many of these have been done by government agencies (such as the Government Accountability Office). A useful summary of results and methods is in Lee and Luengo-Prado (2005).

19 Retail activities at Heathrow Airport amounted to £206.5 million in revenue in 2005/6.

20 This is the well-known problem of an empty core – there is no stable equilibrium because of the existence of indivisibilities and fixed costs. While traditionally applied to industries with large physically fixed infrastructure, it would also seem relevant to service industries like airlines where there are fixed and indivisible costs of meeting a schedule.

21 Under US Chapter 11 bankruptcy, in most instances the debtor remains in control of

its business operations as a debtor in possession, and is subject to the oversight and jurisdiction of the court.

22 Major mergers in recent years include KLM and Air France (2004), SWISS and Lufthansa (2005), Delta and Northwest (2008), and British Airways and Iberia are to merge in 2010. There are also major cross share holdings – e.g. Air France has 25 percent of the shares of Alitalia.

23 Often called "no-frills carriers" in Europe.

24 The charter carriers also seldom provided anything like the radial spread of services that the larger low-cost airlines do.

25 The noise nuisance associated with aircraft movements around airports varies somewhat by country, but measures of its impact on adjacent house prices is significant (Nelson, 2004).

26 For more details of recent analysis of air transportation and the environment see the 2010 Special Edition of *Transportation Research D, Air Transport, Global Warming and the Environment*.

References

Averch, H. and Johnson, L.L. (1962) Behavior of the firm under regulatory constraint, *American Economic Review*, 52, 1052–70.

Brueckner, J.K. (2005) Internalization of airport congestion: a network analysis, *International Journal of Industrial Organization*, 23, 599–614.

Button, K.J. (2007) The implications of the commercialization of air transport infrastructure, in D. Lee (ed.) *The Economics of Airline Institutions, Operations and Marketing 2*, Oxford: Elsevier.

Button, K.J. (2008a) Issues in airport runway capacity charging and allocation, *Journal of Transport Economics and Policy*, 42, 563–85.

Button, K.J. (2008b) Auctions: what can we learn from auction theory for slot allocation? in A. Czerny, P. Forsyth, D. Gillen and H.-M. Niemeier (eds) *Airport Slots International Experiences and Options for Reform*, German Aviation Research Seminar Series No. 3, Burlington: Ashgate.

Button, K.J. (2010) Countervailing power to airport monopolies, in P. Forsyth, D. Gillen, J. Müller and H.-M. Niemeier (eds) *Competition in European Airports*, German Aviation Research Seminar Series No. 4, Burlington: Ashgate.

Button, K.J. and Johnson, K. (1998) Incremental versus trend-break change in airline regulation, *Transportation Journal*, 37, 25–34.

Button, K.J., Costa, A. and Reis, V. (2005) How to control airline routes from the supply side: the case of TAP, *Journal of Air Transportation*, 10, 50–72.

Harback, K.T. and Daniel, J.I. (2007) (When) do hub airlines internalize their self-imposed congestion delays? *Journal of Urban Economics*, 63: 613–30.

Kahn, A.E. (1988) Surprises of airline deregulation, *American Economic Review, Papers and Proceedings* 78, 316–22.

Lee, D. and Luengo-Prado, M.J. (2005) The impact of passenger mix on reported "hub premiums" in the US airline industry, *Southern Economic Journal*, 72, 372–94.

Morrish, S.C. and Hamilton, R.T. (2002) Airline alliances: who benefits? *Journal of Air Transport Management*, 8, 401–8.

Morrison, S.A. and Winston, C. (1995) *Evolution of the Airline Industry*, Washington, DC: Brookings Institution.

Nelson, J.P. (2004) Meta-analysis of airport noise and hedonic property values: problems and prospects, *Journal of Transport Economics and Policy*, 38, 1–28.

Porter, M.E. (1985) *Competitive Advantage: Creating and Sustaining Superior Performance*, New York: Free Press.

Starkie, D. (2001) Reforming UK airport regulation, *Journal of Transport Economics and Policy*, 35, 119–35.

Stigler, G.J. (1971) The theory of economic regulation, *Bell Journal of Economics and Management Science*, 2, 3–19.

Williamson, O.E. (2000) The new institutional economics: taking stock, looking ahead, *Journal of Economics Literature*, 38, 595–613.

12 The impact of airline network strategies for service quality of airports

The case of Amsterdam Schiphol and Paris Charles de Gaulle

Jan Veldhuis

1 Introduction

Along with the liberalisation process that has already been continuing in aviation for more than two decades, a concentration process among airlines has been going on. Although in the short haul intra-continental markets, new entrants – mostly low-cost carriers – have come up, long-haul aviation is now dominated by three large alliances: SkyTeam, STAR and oneWorld. Most alliances are in effect joint network integration strategies between independent airlines, being members of a particular alliance. There are moreover distinct degrees of network integration. Airlines may limit integration to *code share agreements* on one or more single routes only, but there are also examples of integration of complete networks. The oldest example is the network integration between KLM and Northwest Airlines: the *Wings alliance,* from 1989. This network integration has linked KLM flights to the Northwest hubs, Detroit and Minneapolis, with the dense network of Northwest within the USA. At the other side, Northwest flights from the USA to Amsterdam have got access to the dense KLM network within Europe. The advantage is that significantly more city-pairs can be served with single-transfer connections and hence the share of the Wings alliance in the North Atlantic market could increase significantly.

Today, in all three alliances, airlines have to a large degree integrated their networks. However, in most cases the member airlines have stayed independent entities. A main event in this context was the merger between Air France and KLM in 2003. At that moment, KLM (as well as Northwest) not only joined the SkyTeam alliance, but at the same time KLM took another unprecedented step: a merger with Air France. This not only entailed network integration, but together an integration of the two entire companies. Although airline mergers had been seen earlier, this was the first transnational merge between two main global airlines.

The advantages of the 'traditional alliances' without a merger are generally limited to the revenue side. Covering a maximum number of markets with the intention of increasing market share is a main element of their strategy. Within the traditional alliances, there is, however, limited scope for cost cutting, as the member airlines stay independent entities. The merger between Air France and

KLM enables the new (and larger) airline to reach additional economies of scale and hence to reduce unit costs. Hence, there is additional scope for revenue management.

This chapter addresses the impact of network changes for the users (passengers) of the two airports Amsterdam Schiphol and Paris Charles de Gaulle. The content of this chapter is as follows. First, in the second section, the possible effects of the merger are introduced, followed by a brief theoretical introduction on the methodology of the assessment of consumer benefits changes in the third section. We will for this purpose show the effects of network integration on the route between Amsterdam and Dallas. Thereafter, we will show similar effects on other routes as well as other possible effects of the merger. The final paragraph will include some conclusions on the results found.

2 Effects of the Air France/KLM merger

This paragraph introduces the possible impacts of the Air France/KLM merger. In this context, we will explicitly distinguish the two elements of the merger:

- network integration effects, KLM and Northwest giving up Wings and joining SkyTeam
- effects of the merger between Air France and KLM: further scope for cost reduction

While the merger between Air France and KLM has undoubtedly benefited the airline, the question is to what extent the consumers (i.e. the passengers) have benefited. Over time, in most aviation markets, consumers have clearly benefited from increasing service levels in aviation: more destinations, more frequencies. Possible decreasing real airfare levels may have further contributed to consumer benefits, unless in particular markets real fares have increased.

These consumer benefits are measured by comparing the *generalised travel costs* between two networks over time (for example over the five-year period between 2003 and 2008). For this purpose the NetCost model[1] is used. For each relevant connection, direct as well as indirect, the model determines the *generalised travel costs*, being a representation of all inconveniences the traveller is confronted with at that specific connection. The model that is used here builds on earlier work (Veldhuis (1997), Burghouwt (2005) and Burghouwt *et al.* (2009), where airline networks are analysed, not only direct connections, but also indirect connections.

Generalised travel costs include not only airfares, but also the perceived costs of travel time and waiting time for the next flight. These costs are translated into an indicator, expressing the perceived value for the consumer (passenger). By determining this indicator between two subsequent periods, such as 2003 and 2008, conclusions can be drawn to which extent passengers, particularly those using Amsterdam Schiphol and Paris Charles de Gaulle, have benefited from the network changes in this period.

By comparing two subsequent years only, one may draw conclusions on the overall benefits over time, but not on the specific benefits due to the network integration in SkyTeam and the merger in 2003. More network changes have occurred than the Air France/KLM integration/merger alone. Other airlines have joined (and left) alliances and there was the market and frequency growth in general. Therefore we will evaluate the effects of three scenarios:

1   network of September 2003 (KLM and Northwest still in Wings);
2   network of September 2003 (with joining KLM/Northwest SkyTeam);
3   network of September 2008.

The first scenario refers to the airline networks of 2003, before KLM and Northwest joined SkyTeam. It assumes that KLM is still joined with Northwest in the Wings alliance. The second scenario has the same network as 2003, but with a different alliance configuration: KLM and Northwest have given up Wings and joined the SkyTeam alliance of Delta and Air France (together with others). This specification enables us to isolate the network integration effects of joining KLM and Northwest to the SkyTeam alliance.

It has been observed above that giving up the Wings alliance by KLM/Northwest and joining to SkyTeam is a different thing than the merger of Air France and KLM. This in fact is a step further. Both carriers joining SkyTeam show the effects of network integration only. The advantage of the merger is a scope for further cost reduction and hence the possibility of lower airfares, with the corresponding gains in market shares but also consumer benefit. While network integration is a strategy that can be realised within a relatively limited time scope, the realisation of cost reduction takes more time. However, it is realistic to assume that five years after the merger, in 2008 significant cost reductions could have been achieved.

Therefore, a fourth scenario is assumed, which shows the effect of cost reduction and lower airfares for Air France/KLM specifically.

4   network of September 2008 (with lower fares assumed for Air France/KLM specifically).

The network integration effects can now be seen by comparing Scenario 1 with Scenario 2. The additional (potential) effects of the merger can be seen by comparing Scenario 3 with Scenario 4.

The question is, however, whether the full effects of the merger can be seen from these scenarios. In this context it is relevant to observe that in 2003 KLM's partner Northwest was considering joining Delta Airlines and Air France in the SkyTeam alliance. At the same time KLM's financial reserves were declining. For KLM there was in effect a choice between joining Delta and Air France in the SkyTeam alliance as well or becoming a stand-alone carrier without major partners. KLM took the first option: joining the alliance and merging with Air France. KLM concluded that Scenario 1 was in fact an unsustainable option:

Northwest was about to join SkyTeam, which in effect would be the end of the Wings alliance. To assess the full effects of the Air France/KLM scenario, a fifth scenario would certainly need to be included:

5   network of September 2003 (with KLM as stand-alone carrier, without Northwest).

In summary, there are now five scenarios, which are illustrated in Figure 12.1 below. There are the following relevant comparisons:

*   Scenarios 1–2: Network integration in SkyTeam
*   Scenarios 3–4: Potential merger effects
*   Scenarios 1–4: Overall consumer benefits over time
*   Scenarios 4–5: Potential benefits of merger in comparison with 'worst case' KLM stand-alone

3 Consumer benefits of network changes

The consumer benefits of network changes are estimated with the NetCost model. This model determines the extent to which passengers have benefited from network changes due to specific events (such as the KLM and Northwest joining the SkyTeam alliance) or over time. There are two variables determining this:

*   The changes in number of weekly travel options to a particular destination (direct and indirect frequencies). Not only direct frequencies count here, but

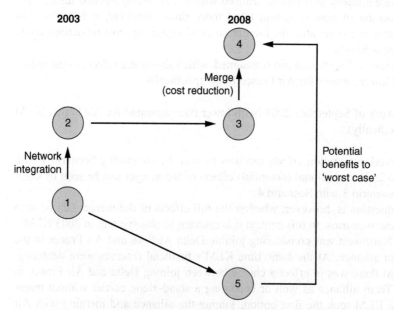

Figure 12.1 Scenarios, illustrating effects of merge between Air France and KLM.

also the number of indirect connections that can realistically be made. This number is in the model derived from the number of direct frequencies from the origin to the intermediate hub and from the intermediate hub to the final destination.

- The average (generalised) travel cost of these travel options.

The consumer benefit of these network changes are determined as:

$$CB_{x,y,0}^{x,y,1} = \frac{LN(F_{x,y,1}) - LN(F_{x,y,0})}{\vartheta} + GC_{x,y,0} - GC_{x,y,1} \qquad (1)$$

where:

$CB_{x,y,0}^{x,y,1}$: the changes in consumer benefits (measured in €) between Scenario 1 and Scenario 0.

$F_{x,y,0}$: the number of weekly direct and indirect travel options between origin x and destination y in Scenario 0.

$F_{x,y,1}$: the number of weekly direct and indirect travel options between origin x and destination y in Scenario 1.

$GC_{x,y,0}$: the average (generalised) travel costs between origin x and destination y in Scenario 0.

$GC_{x,y,1}$: the average (generalised) travel costs between origin x and destination y in Scenario 1.

ϑ: coefficient, expressing the consumer benefit effect of frequency changes.

This consumer benefit is decomposed into a 'frequency' and a 'cost' effect. The left part of the equation represents the frequency effect and represents the benefit due to changes in the number of frequencies (or travel options), irrespective of their travel costs. The right part is the cost effect and represents changes in average travel costs, irrespective of the frequency level. A similar approach is applied in the aviation forecasting model system for the Netherlands, assessing market share changes of airlines as well as consumer welfare impacts of network changes [4].

3.1 Network integration

Table 12.1 summarises the changes in these variables resulting from the network integration in the market between Amsterdam (AMS) and Dallas (DFW). There were no direct connections between these two airports[2] in 2003. Nevertheless, there were 120 weekly indirect travel options via hubs such as London, Frankfurt, Chicago, Detroit, etc. The integration of KLM and Northwest into SkyTeam has linked the flights of these airlines to the flights of other SkyTeam members. The most relevant one is Delta Airlines, who had in 2003 flights between Detroit and Dallas as well as between Memphis and Dallas. As the KLM/Northwest combination had flights between Amsterdam and both hubs (Detroit and Memphis), the integration increased the number of indirect travel options via Detroit and Memphis. Other new options arose via Mexico, where the KLM flights from Amsterdam to Mexico could connect to the flights of Aeromexico (another SkyTeam member) from Mexico to Dallas. This increased the total number of indirect travel options from 120 to 127.[3] This makes a positive contribution to the consumer benefits. According to the above specification, the average passenger perceives this increase with a value of €4.06 (per one way trip).

Another effect results from the changes in average generalised costs. In fact these increase by €3.86, which has an equivalent negative effect on consumer benefits. The major part of this change results from the competition level, which has decreased in that specific market. The number of competing airlines (alliances) decreased, as the Wings alliance integrated its network with SkyTeam, which has increased the dominance of SkyTeam somewhat. This – in turn – increases expected airfares with an inherent effect on consumer benefits. The two effects are to a large extent compensating each other, resulting in an overall consumer benefit of €0.20 per passenger (one way).

Table 12.2 below shows similar effects for a selected number of other destinations. Taking London Heathrow as a destination, the integration of KLM in SkyTeam has changed nothing to the consumer benefits on that route. There are – as the distance is short – no realistic indirect connections and hence there are no new indirect connections that could arise, as was the case on the route to Dallas. The table shows also the competition level: 67 per cent.[4] There are also no other SkyTeam members than KLM on that route and hence the competition level – and so the expected airfares – remained unchanged.[5] The other route where no changes in consumer benefits are seen is the route to Frankfurt. Similar arguments as used for the route to London Heathrow hold here, although the competition level is lower (48 per cent).

Consumer benefits on the route to Paris Charles de Gaulle decrease, however, by little over €15 per passenger (one way). There are – as with London and Frankfurt – no new indirect connections, and hence no benefits from increased frequency levels. Nevertheless, competition level has decreased significantly. The route had two competitors (Air France and KLM) before entering the SkyTeam alliance, but after entering the alliance it changed to what was in practical terms a monopoly.[6] Similar effects are seen on the routes to Lyon, Malpensa and Prague, as there was not only a network integration with Air France, but also

Table 12.1 Effects of network integration in SkyTeam in the market between Amsterdam (AMS) and Dallas (September 2003)

	Scen1	Scen2	CB
Frequency per week	120	127	4.06
Average gen. costs (€)	1.121,57	1.125,44	–3.86
Total			0.20

Table 12.2 Effects of network integration in SkyTeam in the market between Amsterdam (AMS) and selected destinations (September 2003)

	Cons. benefit from		CB total	Compet. level	
	Freq'cy	Costs		Scen1 (%)	Scen2 (%)
LHR London Heathrow				67	67
CDG Paris Ch. de Gaulle		−15.52	−15.52	56	12
LYS Lyon		−13.94	−13.94	50	−
FRA Frankfurt				48	48
MXP Milan Malpensa		−15.33	−15.33	49	−
FCO Rome Fiumicino		−13.42	−13.42	59	22
PRG Prague		−13.65	−13.65	48	−
JFK New York Kennedy	6.20	−6.15	0.05	74	64
ATL Atlanta	9.63	−39.41	−29.79	72	50
DFW Dallas	4.06	−3.86	0.20	74	71
IAH Houston	3.33	−14.85	−11.53	75	67
LAX Los Angeles	3.59	−7.62	−4.03	70	66
ICN Seoul Incheon	2.09	−46.16	−44.07	67	40

with the other SkyTeam members Alitalia and Czech Airlines, resulting in decreasing competition levels on these routes as well. Only on the route to Rome, there remained some competition, as there was the daily flight of Virgin Express at that time.

Next, Table 12.3 represents the overall effects of the network integration for OD-passengers using both Amsterdam and Paris Charles de Gaulle airports. Except for the routes between France and the Netherlands, no effects are seen on the short-haul destination regions from the airports, which is explained above. To longer haul destinations there are positive consumer benefits from increased number of travel options. These benefits occur from new connections that arise from linking KLM flights to the new SkyTeam partner hubs (such as Paris, Milan, Prague, Atlanta, Mexico and Seoul) and linking Air France flights to the new SkyTeam partner hubs (such as Amsterdam, Detroit and Minneapolis). It appears that – regarding the benefits of new connections – the value added for the Dutch OD-market of the network of Air France and its 'old' SkyTeam partners is much higher than the value added for the French OD-market of the network of KLM and its 'old' Wings partners, in effect only Northwest. This means that the typical KLM and Northwest destinations throughout the world were before the integration to a large extent already covered by Air France and its old SkyTeam partners. The value added of the Wings network for the French OD-market is therefore limited and is – on average – estimated at €0.18 per passenger movement. Much more significant is the value added for the Dutch OD-market of the Air France (and its old partners) network, which is estimated at €0.88 per passenger movement. This indicates that the Dutch market has got (better) access to destinations that were before integration not (or only at low service levels) covered by KLM and Northwest.

Table 12.3 Effects of network integration in SkyTeam in the market between AMS/CDG and selected destination regions (September 2003)

| | AMS Amsterdam | | | | CDG Paris Ch. de Gaulle | | | |
| | Weight (%) | Consumer benefit from | | | Weight (%) | Consumer benefit from | | |
		Frequency	Costs	Total		Frequency	Costs	Total
TOTAL	100	0.88	-2.35	-1.47	100	0.18	-1.36	-1.18
Benelux	6				9	0.00	-7.78	-7.78
UK/Ireland	22				24			
France	7		-11.29	-11.29	3			
Germany	19				13			
Switzerland/Austria	4				5			
Scandinavia	5				4	1.41	0.79	2.20
Spain/Portugal	5	2.60	-0.66	1.94	7			
Italy	5	4.21	-8.41	-4.19	6			
Rest South Europe	1	3.70	0.95	4.65	1			
Central Europe	2	0.10	-4.43	-4.33	2			
Rest Europe	2	0.44	0.42	0.86	2	0.11	0.20	0.31
North America	10	2.02	-7.66	-5.64	11	0.70	-5.27	-4.57
Latin America	2	5.40	0.54	5.94	2	0.23	-2.40	-2.17
Africa	2	2.94	-1.50	1.44	2	0.36	-1.23	-0.87
Middle East	3	0.89	0.27	1.16	1	0.69	1.19	1.88
Asia/Pacific	6	2.23	-4.06	-1.83	6	0.29	-1.79	-1.51

While the consumer benefit from more travel options is – by definition – positive, there is generally a negative consumer benefit from the increased average travel costs. There are, however, more components in this increasing average travel costs: those related to travel time, to waiting time (for the next flight) and to airfares. Travel time is not changing and hence its corresponding costs. The average waiting time between two subsequent frequencies is decreasing, at least to the final destinations beyond the new SkyTeam hubs with the increased number of travel options. Hence the travel costs related to waiting time are decreasing with positive effects on consumer benefits. The final component of the travel costs is related to airfares, which are generally increasing by the concentration effects and decreasing competition levels. The negative effects of changing airfares are generally stronger than the positive effects of decreasing waiting times, except to some regions, such as Latin America (in the case of AMS) and the Middle East.

Table 12.4 provides a summary of the above described effects. At both airports the overall effects are negative if measured in consumer benefits. There are clearly positive benefits from more (indirect) connections, but these benefits are more than compensated by the concentration: fewer competitors and hence higher airfares. Such concentration effects are confirmed by Brueckner and Pels (2005), who conclude mergers and alliance consolidation harm consumers as their effects are anti-competitive.

Most of the effects are concentrated at the intercontinental final destinations. Most of the short-haul routes are not affected anyway, except the routes between the SkyTeam hubs (such as from Amsterdam to France and Italy). Finally, it appears that the negative effects of concentration are stronger for the Dutch market using Amsterdam than for the French market using Paris. While the concentration effects take place at both airports, it appears that this has had a more limited effect in the French market, where the dominance of Air France/KLM is smaller and competition level is, on average, higher.

The overall negative effect on consumer benefits of the network integration is €1.47 in the Dutch market and €1.18 in the French market. These are, however, still the effects per (average) passenger movement. If these effects are multiplied by the number of OD-passenger movements (24 million in Amsterdam and 32 million in Paris Charles de Gaulle in 2003) the total negative effect of network integration is therefore about €35 million on a yearly basis in the Netherlands and slightly more in France: €38 million.

3.2 Developments between 2003 and 2008

Looking to all network developments between 2003 and 2008 one can observe that frequency levels from both airports have increased in these five years, which has obviously had its own impacts on consumer benefits. Table 12.5 below shows the changes between 2003 and 2008

There has been a moderate increase from both airports, looking to frequency levels, 8.8 and 10 per cent from AMS and CDG respectively, being less than 2

Table 12.4 Effects of network integration in SkyTeam in the market between AMS/CDG and selected destination regions (September 2003)

	AMS Amsterdam				CDG Paris Ch. de Gaulle			
	Weight (%)	Consumer benefit from			Weight (%)	Consumer benefit from		
		Frequency	Costs	Total		Frequency	Costs	Total
TOTAL	100	0.88	-2.35	-1.47	100	0.18	-1.36	-1.13
Europe	78	0.46	-1.68	-1.22	77	0.08	-0.80	-0.72
Intercontinental	22	2.36	-4.56	-2.20	23	0.51	-3.26	-2.75
	OD-passengers (*million, 2003) 24		Total effect (*mln. €) -35		OD-passengers (*million, 2003) 32		Total effect (*mln. €) -38	

Table 12.5 Weekly frequency from AMS and CDG, by carrier group, September 2003 and September 2008

	AMS Amsterdam			CDG Paris Ch. de Gaulle		
	2003	2008	% growth	2003	2008	% growth
Total	**3.836**	**4.172**	**8.8**	**4.886**	**5.376**	**10.0**
SkyTeam	2.289	2.653	15.9	3.080	3.339	8.4
Other network carriers	1.078	1.008	−6.5	1.561	1.624	4.0
Point-to-point carriers	469	511	9.0	245	413	68.6
Europe	**3.080**	**3.325**	**8.0**	**3.850**	**3.962**	**2.9**
SkyTeam	1.806	2.023	12.0	2.478	2.513	1.4
Other network carriers	875	847	−3.2	1.141	1.092	−4.3
Point-to-point carriers	399	455	14.0	231	357	54.5
Intercontinental	**756**	**847**	**12.0**	**1.036**	**1.414**	**36.5**
SkyTeam	483	630	30.4	602	826	37.2
Other network carriers	203	161	−20.7	420	532	26.7
Point-to-point carriers	70	56	−20.0	14	56	300.0

Source: OAG.

per cent yearly. There are, however, significant differences seen between the two airports as well as between the airline groups.

Looking to service levels at European destinations, SkyTeam (practically all Air France/KLM) has increased frequencies considerably more from Amsterdam than from Paris (12 and 1.4 per cent respectively). The other network carriers have – in contrast to SkyTeam – decreased frequency levels from both airports, from Paris even more than Amsterdam. The advantage for the consumer of other European network carriers is that they give indirect access via their European hubs to other destinations. If SkyTeam does not serve these destinations, this is obviously a considerable added value, but even if SkyTeam does serve these destinations it may also be an added value as it brings more competition and hence lower expected airfares. Whereas Paris has developed more slowly than Amsterdam when network carriers are concerned (SkyTeam plus the others), it has, to a greater extent than Amsterdam, developed its network of the point-to-point carriers (mainly 'low-cost', but also charters), although Paris is still behind Amsterdam where total frequency level of this group is concerned (357 and 455 respectively).

On the intercontinental routes, SkyTeam has developed more strongly at Amsterdam as well as Paris, albeit at Paris even a bit stronger (about 37 and 30 per cent respectively). Significantly larger differences are seen within the other network carriers group. While this group has also developed strongly from Paris (more than 26 per cent), it has shrunk its network from Amsterdam by little over 20 per cent. This has significant implications for consumer benefits at both airports. The added value of this carrier group is that they give access via their overseas hubs to secondary destinations all over the world, destinations that are unlikely to be served by the other carrier groups.

These changing frequency levels have obviously had impacts on consumer benefits. Overall, frequency level has increased at both airports and hence it is expected that there have been positive consumer effects from this. Nevertheless, it is not only overall frequency level that counts here; the overall consumer benefits is a mixture of other developments, including:

- higher frequency levels from general market growth, as described above;
- changes in alliance composition (except the merger of Air France and KLM);
- changes in code share agreements between carriers;
- changes in competition level by new entrants;
- further penetration of low-cost carriers on intra-European routes.

The overall effect on consumer benefit is indeed significant and even similar at both airports. Consumer benefit per passenger movement has increased at Amsterdam by €10.06 and at Paris a little more, by €11.66. Nevertheless, there are differences, as Table 12.6 shows.

Looking again to European destinations, the positive effect per passenger at Paris has been significantly smaller (€2.03) than at Amsterdam (€9.67). This is mainly due to the relatively slow development of network carriers at Paris (SkyTeam as well as the others). The main difference is, however, seen at intercontinental destinations, where the consumer benefits at Paris have increased much more strongly than at Amsterdam (€44.91 and €10.26 respectively). This is not so much related to SkyTeam, which has developed at both airports with growth rates of the same order of magnitude. It is mainly related to the other (at these routes also the non-European) network carriers, who have shrunk their networks at Amsterdam, but increased strongly at Paris. The changing consumer benefits on intercontinental routes resulting from travel costs are notable: a net benefit at Paris of €16.71, but a net dis-benefit at Amsterdam of €6.93. This difference may be related to the increased dominance of SkyTeam on intercontinental routes at Amsterdam, with a negative impact on airfares. The frequency share of SkyTeam on intercontinental routes from Amsterdam has increased from 64 to 74 per cent, while the same share at Paris has remained practically stable at 58 per cent.

Multiplying the described effects with the actual OD-passenger numbers, result in total consumer benefits at both airports: €241 million for passengers using Amsterdam and €373 million for passengers using Paris.

3.3 Potential merger effects

The earlier paragraphs have shown that between 2003 and 2008 considerable positive consumer effects have taken place. The main effects came from developments not related to the network integration of Air France and KLM. The network integration has even led to limited decreases in consumer benefits, mainly caused by increased dominance and hence decreasing competition and an upward pressure on airfares.

Table 12.6 Effects of network integration in SkyTeam in the market between AMS/CDG and selected destination regions (September 2003)

	AMS Amsterdam				CDG Paris Ch. de Gaulle			
	Weight (%)	Consumer benefit from			Weight (%)	Consumer benefit from		
		Frequency	Costs	Total		Frequency	Costs	Total
TOTAL	100	6.56	3.50	10.06	100	5.57	6.09	11.66
Europe	78	3.44	6.22	9.67	77	-0.95	2.98	2.03
Intercontinental	22	17.19	-6.93	10.26	23	28.19	16.71	44.91
	OD-passengers (*million, 2003) 24		Total effect (*mln. €) 241		OD-passengers (*million, 2003) 32		Total effect (*mln. €) 373	

However, Air France and KLM have not only integrated their networks, but even merged. Network integration is seen at all major alliances, but Air France and KLM have gone a step further: a full merger. The advantage of the merger is a scope for further cost reduction and hence the possibility of lower airfares, with the corresponding gains in market shares but also consumer benefit. While network integration is a strategy that can be realised within relatively limited time scope, the realisation of cost reduction takes more time. However, it is realistic to assume that five years after the merger, in 2008 significant cost reductions could have been achieved.

It is uncertain how much this possible cost decrease between 2003 and 2008 has been. Hence it is also uncertain what the benefits have been from such cost decreases. Another effect may be that Air France/KLM may not always translate lower costs into lower fares. In markets where it is dominant, it may even not decrease fares at all and use the resulting savings either to increase profits or even decrease fares stronger in competitive markets.

The effect that airfares are changing according to changing competition levels has already been taken into account in the paragraphs above. For instance, network integration may generally lead to increasing airfares, as is shown in section 3.1. Also, insofar as the other developments have led to changing competition levels, this has been translated into changing relative airfares and the corresponding consumer benefits from this. The question remains whether eventual cost savings from the Air France/KLM merger will lead to additional changes in relative airfares. This cannot be excluded, but the simplified assumption has been made here that cost savings are directly translated into lower airfares, irrespective of the competition level in the market.

The other assumption is that Air France/KLM has achieved a cost saving of, say, 10 per cent. This leads then to 10 per cent lower fares, only for Air France/KLM. The fares of the other carrier groups are left unchanged. This is a working hypothesis, acknowledging that cost savings of 5 or 15 per cent are equally realistic as well. Further research could be done into this, but this chapter stays with this working hypothesis. The assumption of 10 per cent cost savings leads to particular consumer benefits, to be discussed below. Should other percentages of cost savings be considered as more realistic, the resulting consumer benefits are easily determined as they are directly proportional to the cost savings. Table 12.7 below summarises the consumer benefits of 10 per cent lower fares for Air France/KLM.

The table shows that all benefits can be attributed to cost changes and obviously not to frequency changes. This is the other implicit assumption of the working hypothesis, that these cost changes have not led to network changes. The table shows also that the benefits on intercontinental routes are higher than on European routes. As intercontinental fares are higher than European fares, the (absolute) changes of a 10 per cent reduction are clearly also bigger. Finally, the benefits resulting from the airfare reduction are slightly higher at Amsterdam than at Paris, particularly on intercontinental routes, which is related to the

Table 12.7 Effects of 10% cost savings in Air France/KLM in the market between AMS/CDG and selected destination regions (September 2003)

	AMS Amsterdam				CDG Paris Ch. de Gaulle			
	Weight (%)	Consumer benefit from			Weight (%)	Consumer benefit from		
		Frequency	Costs	Total		Frequency	Costs	Total
TOTAL	100		13.96	13.96	100		12.05	12.05
Europe	78		9.32	9.32	77		7.92	7.92
Intercontinental	22		30.28	30.28	23		25.73	25.73
	OD-passengers (*million, 2003) 24		Total effect (*mln. €) 335		OD-passengers (*million, 2003) 32		Total effect (*mln. €) 386	

higher dominance of Air France/KLM at Amsterdam and therefore the higher proportion of passengers using Air France/KLM.

The overall effect of this cost saving is on average €13.96 for passengers using Amsterdam and slightly less (€12.05) for passengers using Paris. Higher or lower cost saving percentages will lead to proportionally higher or lower consumer benefits. Multiplying these figures with the total number of OD-passengers will result in total benefits of €335 million and €386 million for Amsterdam and Paris respectively.

3.4 Overall consumer effects between 2003 and 2008

The previous paragraphs have shown potential consumer benefits between 2003 and 2008, broken down to effects related to the Air France/KLM merger (network integration and cost savings) and to all other network changes between the two years. Table 12.8 summarises the potential consumer benefits per passenger.

The table shows that the total consumer benefits at Amsterdam and Paris over these five years are practically equal, little over €22.50 per passenger movement. It also shows that almost half of these effects can be attributed to the Air France/KLM merger and the related cost savings, at Amsterdam a little more than at Paris. There is a slightly negative effect if only network integration is considered (€1.47 at Amsterdam and €1.18 at Paris), mainly caused by the increased dominance of the alliance.

But there are high potential benefits from cost savings, that can – in contrast to other alliances – be attributed to the actual merger, not only integrating networks, but entire companies. The overall benefits of the merger are therefore €12.49 and €10.87 at Amsterdam and Paris respectively per passenger movement.

The question is, however, whether one can see here the full effects of the merger. In 2003 KLM's partner Northwest was considering joining Delta Airlines and Air France in the SkyTeam alliance. At the same time KLM's financial reserves were declining. For KLM there was in effect a choice between joining Delta and Air France in the SkyTeam alliance or becoming a stand-alone carrier without major partners. KLM took the first option: joining the alliance and merging with Air France. It realised that the stand-alone option was in fact not

Table 12.8 Summary of consumer benefits between 2003 and 2008 from AMS and CDG (in € per passenger)

	Actual development 1 → 4	
	AMS	CDG
1–2. Network integration	−1.47	−1.18
2–3. Developments 2003–8	10.06	11.66
3–4. Potential merger effects	13.96	12.05
Overall development	22.55	22.53

sustainable: Northwest was about to join SkyTeam, which in effect would be the end of the Wings alliance. It would in fact mean a stand-alone KLM.

The other question would then be whether KLM would be able to survive in this stand-alone scenario. Already in 2003 the financial reserves were declining and it was probably not realistic to assume that it would in 2008 have the same network as it had then. It would be equally realistic to assume that a stand-alone KLM would in 2008 have had a considerably smaller network. It cannot be excluded that it would have degraded from a major world airline with an intercontinental network, comparable with the other majors, into a middle-range European airline, focusing mainly on European connections, with still a limited intercontinental network.

Assumptions have been made for such a stand-alone network. Today, most of the European destinations are served by KLM four or five times daily. This high-frequency level exists partly to support the hub-and-spoke system, which is focused on connecting European with intercontinental destinations. Frequency levels of KLM are therefore much higher than can be justified on the local market alone. However, if it degraded into a middle-range European airline, it is assumed that this 'Euro-intercontinental' hub-and-spoke system would degrade to a large extent and that frequency levels would be more in accordance with the local market alone. The assumption is therefore that most of the European connections are served 'double daily', being particularly the preferred service levels in the business market. The other assumption is that only few intercontinental destinations would be left, however, still at once-daily service levels. Looking back to Figure 12.1, this would not imply a development from Scenario (1) via (2) and (3) into Scenario (4), but instead of this a development from Scenario (1) into Scenario (5), the worst case.

Table 12.9 shows these effects by contrasting the development from (1) to (4) with the other 'worst-case' development from (1) to (5). The latter development scenario obviously does not have the network integration effects, nor the merger effects. But still this development includes all other developments between 2003 and 2008, which were not related to the integration and merger between Air France and KLM, of which the overall consumer benefits were estimated at €10.06.

Should a development have taken place from Scenario (1) into (5), the overall consumer benefits from the networks out of Amsterdam would have decreased by €29.03. The reason is not only the overall lower frequency of KLM, with longer waiting times for the next flight, but also the longer travel time at intercontinental destinations, as in more cases a connection at another hub is necessary, rather than flying directly to the intercontinental destination. In this decrease of €29.03, the increase of €10.06 is still taken into account and therefore the effects of a stand-alone KLM can be estimated at a negative benefit for the average passenger of €39.09. The overall effects of the merger, as also was argued in section 1, can best be assessed by observing the difference between Scenario (4), the full merger effects and Scenario (5), the 'worst case'. This difference is therefore estimated at a net benefit of €51.58. The main components of this net benefit are that the 'worst case' could be avoided (€39.09) and the

Table 12.9 Summary of consumer benefits between 2003 and 2008 from AMS and CDG (in € per passenger)

	Actual worst-case scenario		Difference
	$1 \rightarrow 4$	$1 \rightarrow 5$	
1–2. Network integration	−1.47		−1.47
2–3. Developments 2003–8	10.06	10.6	
3–4. Potential merger effects	13.96		13.96
Stand-alone KLM		−39.09	39.09
Overall development	22.55	−29.03	51.58

additional potential cost savings (€13.96). The only minor disadvantage is the increased dominance of SkyTeam, leading to higher expected airfares and possible decreasing consumer benefits (€1.47)

Multiplying this overall benefit with the total OD-market of 24 million passengers, one can estimate that the potential benefits of Air France/KLM for the local market at Amsterdam Airport can be estimated at more than €1.2 billion every year.

4 Concluding remarks

The above description illustrates that network integration is not necessarily in the interest of the consumers. While integration obviously provides more connections and better access by air, it is also conceived that in some markets competition level may increase with an upward pressure on airfares. Air France and KLM, however, have taken further steps by not only integrating their networks, as many alliances have done, but even by integrating the two companies. This has considerably increased the scope for further cost savings, clearly to the benefit of the airlines, but potentially also for the consumer.

In assessing the effects of the Air France/KLM merge, one must bear in mind that a stand-alone KLM would probably not have been sustainable. If KLM had not survived or had degraded to a 'middle-class' airline, the network quality would also have degraded significantly. Compared to this 'worst case' it is clearly concluded that particularly the Dutch consumers are better off with the merger.

Notes

1 See www.aaeconomics.com. 'Tools'.
2 KLM has opened a daily connection in the summer schedule of 2008.
3 The methodology for determining the number of indirect travel options is also described in the description of the NetCost model.
4 The methodology for determining the competition level is also described in the description of the NetCost model. In case of monopoly the competition level is 0 per cent. The competition level is 50 per cent in case of two competitors with equal frequencies. The

competition level approaches 100 per cent when the number of competitors increases. Only in the case of an infinite number of competitors is the competition level 100 per cent. This of course is only a theoretical case. In reality the maximum competition level is 80 per cent.
5 Airfares are also estimated in the NetCost model. Airfares are defined as a function of great circle distance between origin and destination, the type of connection (direct or indirect) and competition level. Hence, if competition level is unchanged, airfares also stay unchanged. This obviously ignores other factors which have an impact on airfares.
6 Only Varig had a daily flight as Paris was used as a stop-over in its connection from Amsterdam to Brazil.

References

Brueckner, J. and Pels, E. (2005) 'European airline mergers, alliance consolidation and consumer welfare', *Journal of Air Transport Management* 11, 24–41.
Burghouwt, G. (2005) *Airline Network Development in Europe and its Implications for Airport Planning*, Aldershot: Ashgate.
Burghouwt, G., de Wit, J.G., Veldhuis, J. and Matsumoto, H. (2009) 'Airline Network performance and Hub Competitive Position: Evaluation of Primary Airports in East and Southeast Asia', *Journal of Airport Management* 3, 384–400.
Veldhuis, J. (1997) 'The Competitive Position of Airline Networks', *Journal of Air Transport Management* 3, 181–8.
Veldhuis, J. and Kroes, E. (2005) 'Modelontwikkeling ACCM en kwantitatieve verkenning WLO-luchtvaartscenario's', *SEO Economic Research, Amsterdam/RAND Europe, Leiden* (in Dutch only).
Zhang, Y. and Round, D.K. (2009) 'The effects of China's airline mergers on prices', *Journal of Air Transport Management* 15, 315–23.

13 Congestion and air transport
A challenging phenomenon

Paul Roosens

1 Introduction

Congestion in transportation occurs when demand for infrastructure exceeds capacity, causing delays in travel time as one of the main symptoms.

Door-to-door travel time in air transport is subdivided in three parts: the time to travel to and from the airport, the time needed in the passenger terminal before and after the flight, and the airside travel time once boarded. Airside travel time depends on many variables, but in this chapter only the airport and airspace (en route)-related congestion problems and delays will be discussed. The immediate challenge is to decrease congestion but to keep the highest safety levels as traffic increases (FAA, 2005).

Although the capacity shortage in the US and the EU was expected to become worse after the implementation of the recent Open Skies agreement (Turner, 2007a), this problem was neutralized since 2008 by the lower demand for air travel in the wake of the financial and economic crisis. One of the symptoms is the dramatic increase of the parked airliner fleet in the deserts of the US. Over the last year, airlines, lessors, banks and hedge funds were responsible for a 49 per cent increase in stored aircraft (Bonnassies, 2009).

Fewer aircraft and flights result in less passenger and cargo traffic at airports, even amounting to a double digit drop in 2008 at some European airports (Dunn, 2009). However, as soon as the world economy and air travel demand eventually recover, the capacity problem will appear again. In this scenario capacity is even expected to lag demand by as much as 11 per cent in 2030 (Kaminski-Morrow, 2009).

Solutions for airport capacity enhancement have been discussed extensively already by air transport economists analysing mainly pricing strategies for congestion costs and airport slot allocation solutions. The focus in this chapter will be primarily on operational practices for airport congestion, such as runway occupancy time minimisation, and management of typical airport capacity problems such as caused by heterogeneous traffic, wake turbulence, noise problems and adverse weather.

En route congestion is caused by crowded airspace and several solutions will be discussed, such as Reduced Vertical Separation Minima (RVSM), the mandatory use of 8.33 kHz, the Single Sky project of the European Union, and the use of satellite navigation.

Most of the congestion issues discussed in this chapter rely on the vast European and US experience. Many of the available European and US solutions are as well adopted elsewhere in the world or are in the stage of being introduced.

2 Airport congestion

A proxy to indicate airport congestion is given by airport departure delays. Congestion indeed causes delays, but not all delays are caused by congestion. There are primary and secondary delays. Secondary or reactionary delays account on average for slightly less than 50 per cent of all delays and are typically caused by late arrival of aircraft. The airline companies themselves are by far the main contributors to primary delays, causing in Europe approximately 50 per cent of late departures (Murillo and Carlier, 2006). Airports and en route problems are considered to be the second factor for delays followed by adverse weather and security.

All these factors are variable in time and can cause major temporary problems, like the security terror alert in the UK in August 2006 (Sobie and Field, 2006). The relative share of airport-related delays is over the years more important than en route delays (Murillo and Carlier, 2006).

Most delays in the period 2007–2008 at European airports (CODA, 2009c) were limited to a maximum of four minutes. About 5.3 per cent of all flights were affected by delays of between five and 15 minutes, delays between 16 and 30 minutes were experienced by 3.75 per cent of the flights, 1.5 per cent of all flights had delays between 31 and 60 minutes and 0.3 per cent more than one hour. These numbers are averages, and hide substantially more serious problems at many European airports. The 20 worst performers for 2008 are listed in Table 13.2.

The high number of delays of these airports, however, do not consistently match the most busy departure airports. From the list of the 20 most busy departure airports in Europe (STATFOR, 2007), only seven airports are listed as well in Table 13.2: Paris CDG, London Heathrow, London Gatwick, Amsterdam, Rome, Milan and Manchester. This refers again to the observation that airport density and congestion is not the only variable that causes delays.

Table 13.1 Percentage share of primary departure delays in Europe

	2007	2008	January 2009	July 2009
Airlines	56	54	47	50
Airport	17	17	16	18
En route	10	13	6	15
Weather	10	10	25	8
Security	4	3	3	4
Miscellaneous	3	3	3	5

Source: CODA, 2008; CODA, 2009a; CODA, 2009c.

Table 13.2 Average delay in minutes per movement (2008)

1	Larnaca	22.9	11	Antalya	16.1
2	Iraklion	19.0	12	Malaga	15.9
3	Tenerife Sur	18.8	13	Dublin	15.9
4	Faro	17.9	14	Catania	15.5
5	Manchester	17.4	15	London/City	15.1
6	Las Palmas	16.9	16	Amsterdam	14.6
7	Rome	16.6	17	Bristol	14.6
8	London Heathrow	16.6	18	Paris/Charles de Gaulle	14.5
9	London Luton	16.4	19	Milan/Malpensa	14.5
10	London Gatwick	16.2	20	Venice	14.2

Source: CODA, 2009b.

Nevertheless, airports make the second largest contribution to congestion and delays and airport congestion is predicted to become worse in the period up to 2020 (Goold, 2005). It is consequently an absolute necessity that airport operators focus on sufficient capacity and appropriate operational procedures to use the available capacity as efficiently as possible.

2.1 Capacity

Although a major capacity crunch is expected in the longer run (European Commission, 2006), still sufficient overall capacity is currently available at most airports if flight departures and arrivals could be distributed evenly over the operational hours of the airport. Most runways can handle up to 30 to 50 movements per hour, which means approximately 250,000 movements per year per runway if the airport is fully operational during 18 hours a day. Operational and legal constraints often reduce airport capacity to lower levels, as is illustrated in Table 13.3.

The main congestion problems at most major airports are caused by peak hour traffic, which typically causes delays in the morning, around noon and during the evening. Delays during morning peaks can even cause a cascade impact and additional reactionary (Eurocontrol, 2007c) delays for the full day or even more when international connecting flights are involved (Murillo and Carlier, 2006).

Peak-related delays should not be solved primarily by expanding airport infrastructure, but by optimising operational practices, which is the responsibility of airport operators, airlines and air traffic control (Eurocontrol, 2007b).

2.2 Surface management

By law, runways are not allowed to be used for takeoff and landing as long as the runway is not vacated by another airplane. Consequently aircraft should minimise runway occupancy time (ROT) in order to make the departure or landing of another aircraft possible. Estimates have been made that reducing ROT can

Table 13.3 Airport capacity (IFR movements/year × 1,000)

Airports	Number of runways	Capacity*
London Gatwick	1	278
London Heathrow	2	484
Brussels Airport	3	470
Frankfurt Main	3	530
Paris CDG	4	680
Amsterdam Schiphol	5 (6**)	600

Notes
*Eurocontrol, 2006a, DAP/DIA/STATFOR Doc. 179.
**The Schiphol-East runway 04–22 is less important and primarily used by general aviation (www.schiphol.nl).

increase runway capacity between 5 per cent for single runway airports and 15 per cent in the case of multiple runway airports (Eurocontrol, 2003).

For the departure ROT, the pilot reaction time to takeoff clearance can be up to 11 seconds at some European airports. By reducing this to seven seconds, two extra departures per hour are possible (Eurocontrol, 2003). An airport with 18 operational hours could handle 36 extra flights a day, or 13,140 flights per year, or about 1.3 million extra passengers when each aircraft carries an average of 100 passengers.

A technical constraint is the spool-up time that aircraft engines need between idling and takeoff power. Especially the large turbofan engines of twin wide bodies, such as the Boeing 777 and the Airbus 330, need more spool-up time than narrow bodies, such as the Boeing 737 and the Airbus 319/320/321. Priority takeoff clearance should be given to aircraft with lower spool-up times.

Consistent data about surface management practices are hardly available for most airports. Tables 13.4 and 13.5 below, however, provide a good case example for three major London airports.

The delay variables between the three London airports are close to each other. Most striking are the higher takeoff ROTs for Heathrow, followed by Gatwick and Stansted with the lowest ROT. A simple explanation is the difference in runway length between the three airports. Longer runways can accommodate larger aircraft which require more takeoff distance and more time on the runway. At Heathrow, runway 09L/27R has a length of 3,902 m and runway 09R/27L is 3,658 m long. Runway 26L/08R at Gatwick is shorter with 3,316 m and the shortest runway is at Stansted with 3,048 m.

Landing ROT refers to the time an aircraft needs between touchdown and vacating the runway via the taxiway system. The configuration of the taxi exits affects airport capacity (Mohleji, 2001). Right-angle exit taxiways require slow groundspeeds for safety reasons (Eurocontrol, 2003). A Boeing 747 for instance needs to slow down to 5–10 knots to vacate the runway, becoming 5–6 knots in wet conditions.

A solution for this is offered by the rapid exit taxiways (RETs), with angles of exit between 30 and 60 degrees. Exit speeds are much higher, which reduces

Table 13.4 Key data for three London airports (2008)

Airport	Passengers	Main operators	Share (%)
London Heathrow (2 runways)	67.056 million	BA	41.3
		bmi	11.2
		Lufthansa	4.1
London Gatwick (1 runway)	34.214 million	easyJet	29.6
		BA	20.7
		Flybe	8.6
London Stansted (1 runway)	22.355 million	Ryanair	63.0
		easyJet	21.8
		Air Berlin	3.1

Source: The World's Top Airports, 2009.

Table 13.5 Delay variables in seconds for takeoff at the London airports

Period	ROT takeoff			Pilot reaction time			Line up time		
	H	G	S	H	G	S	H	G	S
Summer 2005	38.3	36.0	34.8	6.1	5.8	6.2	47.0	44.2	43.6
2006	35.1	33.4	34.1	6.4	3.6	–	46.2	42.7	47.8
2007	37.7	34.7	33.6	–	6.1	–	49.6	45.1	47.5
2008	41.0	36.4	34.0	6.9	–	–	46.1	44.4	49.6
2009	40.7	38.2	35.0	–	8.3	7.9	44.9	42.5	45.5

Source: Airport Coordination Limited.

Notes
Heathrow (H), Gatwick (G) and Stansted (S).

landing ROT. A Boeing 747 needs to slow down to only 30–40 knots, and to 20–30 knots in wet conditions.

Most runways on major congested airports in the world are nowadays already equipped with RETs or are in the process of implementing new ones. Recent examples are the RETs on the landing runway 33 of Madrid-Barajas and on the runways 07 and 25 of Barcelona El Prat. Most busy airports are able to keep the landing ROT at values lower than 60 seconds, which is illustrated for the London airports in Table 13.6. The shorter runway of Stansted explains the low landing ROTs compared to Gatwick and Heathrow.

Aircraft on the ground can be subject to additional delays caused by numerous non-runway factors (Eurocontrol, 2007b). Typical delays can happen already at the gate because of late gate announcements and gate openings, slow ground-handling activities such as cleaning, refuelling, boarding of catering, and late push back clearance received from ATC.

Start up and taxi clearance should be given by ATC before push back is terminated. Where multiple push backs are scheduled at the same time, priority should

Table 13.6 Landing ROT in seconds for London Heathrow, Gatwick and Stansted

Period	Heathrow	Gatwick	Stansted
Summer 2005	53.1	53.8	47.3
2006	52.8	54.5	47.2
2007	53.0	55.3	46.4
2008	53.3	53.5	46.6
2009	54.3	56.8	46.4

Source: Airport Coordination Limited.

be given to aircraft that can vacate the airport environment in less time, for instance by using shorter runways, intersection takeoffs, early turns after takeoff, etc.

During taxi, and definitely before reaching the holding point, cockpit crew should have received and copied the IFR (instrument flight rules) clearance, including the SID (standard instrument departure) and the en route clearance.

2.3 Homogeneous traffic and wake turbulence

When aircraft fly at similar speeds in final approach, less spacing between approaching aircraft becomes possible and this increases runway capacity. It is therefore not advisable to mix approaching jet aircraft with slower turboprops and general aviation. Most major hubs have strict limitations on general aircraft activity, and there are even airports that impose restrictions on carriers using turboprops. For each country this information can be found in the national Aeronautical Information Publication (AIP) which is a legal document issued by the national aviation authorities. The principle of sovereignty of individual countries in their own airspace is based on article 1 of the Convention of Chicago, but article 15 excludes discrimination based on the nationality of the carrier.

This type of discrimination is not acceptable in the European Union either. The flexibility of the airport operator towards heterogeneous traffic increases when multiple runways and intersection takeoffs are available.

To increase departure and landing capacity, the distribution of aircraft type should be as homogeneous as possible (Mohleji, 2001). An airplane needs aerodynamic lift to become and stay airborne, and this causes some adverse aerodynamic side effects. Vortexes are created at the wing tips, causing a phenomenon which is known as wake turbulence. Airplanes following the flight path of another aircraft at the same altitude or even 1,000 feet lower can encounter wake turbulence and in some cases could become uncontrollable. The most dangerous stages are approach and departure.

The Airbus A 300 of American Airlines Flight 587 that in 2001 fatally crashed after take off in New York was hit by wake turbulence of a preceding JAL Boeing 747. Consequently strict separation minima should be maintained for approaching and departing aircraft. These minima are higher behind heavy jets such as the Boeing 747 and the Airbus 380 and for aircraft with a typical adverse vortex pattern, such as the Boeing 757.

Typical separation minima are in the range between 4–6 nautical miles (7.5 to 11 km) for the approach and 2–3 minute time intervals for takeoff (FAA, 2009a, *AIM*). Research is going on to reclassify these minima, as well because there are too many variations between countries (Learmount, 2007c).

2.4 Adverse weather management

Low cloud ceilings and visibility can reduce runway capacity to zero. Landings could be more adversely affected than takeoffs. Runways can be provided with instrument landing systems (ILS) that allow approaches and landings with specified cloud ceilings and visibility (see Table 13.7).

Approaching airplanes only can enjoy the lower minima if they are properly equipped and if the cockpit crew is rated to perform the approach.

Microbursts and wind shear are typical weather phenomena caused by convective activity and occur frequently for instance in the US during the summer season. Approaching airplanes could face sudden changes in wind direction, even up to 180 degrees. Resulting loss of critical minimum airspeed can result in accidents. When wind shear is reported in the vicinity of airports, approaches will be abandoned or delayed. The worst case is a general wind shear alert around an airport, because this can adversely affect approaches on all runways. If the precise position of a microburst can be detected, for instance in the axis of a particular runway, there is a higher probability that the operations on other runways can continue as usual. By using such a system, safety and capacity are improved on many US airports based on the FAA Integrated Wind Shear and Detection Plan (FAA, 2009, *AIM*).

2.5 Noise abatement management

Noise abatement is frequently based on restrictions resulting in less available runway capacity. During sensitive periods, operations on some runways can be restricted or prohibited. A relevant example is Schiphol Amsterdam

Table 13.7 ILS minima for decision height (DH) and runway visual range (RVR)

Categories	DH (feet)*	RVR (feet)**
I	200	1,800
II	100	1,200
IIIa	none	700
IIIb	none	150
IIIc	none	none

Source: aviationglossary.com; FAA, 2009b.

Notes
*Decision height (DH) is "the height at which a decision must be made during an instrument approach to either continue the approach or to execute a missed approach".
**Runway visual range (RVR) is "the range over which the pilot of an aircraft on the centreline of a runway can see the runway surface markings".

(www.schiphol.nl). Night flight restrictions can even be extended to the entire airport, reducing capacity to zero during these times. Standard arrival routes (STARS) and standard instrument departures (SIDs) can become subject to changes because of noise concerns.

A relatively new procedure is the continuous descent approach. Approaching airplanes fly in a minimum drag configuration, using less or even idle power. This causes the lowest practicable noise level given the type of aircraft, and as well the lowest fuel burn and engine emissions.

The capacity of handling noisy aircraft like those of the ICAO noise Category 2 – called Chapter 2 – and hushkitted airplanes has been drastically affected in the European Union by Regulation 925/1999/EC (*Official Journal*, L115) and other noise operating restrictions at Community airports have been implemented since the introduction of Directive 2002/30/EC (*Official Journal*, L085).

Airports that opt for noise quota limitations impose a yearly maximum amount of noise production, and on many airports these noise quotas tend to become more restrictive. The only way to keep up sufficient capacity at these airports is the transition by the airline operators to airplanes of the lowest noise category. Airline operators can be encouraged to expedite this transition by being forced to pay higher landing fees on noisier aircraft.

The transition to quieter aircraft contributes at the same time to a cleaner environment, as less noisy engines generally produce cleaner exhaust gases.

3 En route congestion

Congested airspace ranks as the third most important factor for delays (Murillo and Carlier, 2006). Airborne airplanes need a minimum horizontal and vertical separation distance for safety reasons. Many solutions have already been initiated to deal with en route congestion. Separation distance in controlled airspace is managed by air traffic control (ATC).

ATC services between countries should be as homogeneous as possible in order to optimise the capacity of airspace. The optimum situation in the EU would be the existence of a very limited number of functional blocs of airspace (Turner, 2007b,), controlled by ATC using identical radar and communication equipment, and mandatory standardised English phraseology. Although ATC in the US is outdated and did not change significantly after its design in the 1950s (Air Transport Association of America, 2008), it has the advantage of being a homogeneous system. In the EU, however, the impact of member states on ATC is still high by tradition, which makes airspace control more fragmented than in the US. European airspace is still controlled by too many separate national air navigation service providers, causing approximately 250,000 hours of flight delay per year (Learmount, 2007b).

The EU – in cooperation with Eurocontrol – developed in recent years a strategy to set up the Single European Sky project, but still a lot of time will be needed before the final goal will be reached. The practical implementation has been given into the hands of SESAR, the Single European Sky ATM Research

Programme (www.sesar-consortium.aero). All major stakeholders of the air transport industry are participating in this consortium, which is co-financed by the European Union (www.europa.eu).

SESAR is actually beyond its definition phase (2005–2008), which is followed by the development phase (2008–2016) and finally the deployment phase which should be ready in 2020.

Reduced vertical separation between aircraft at high altitude (FL 290[1] and higher) has already been introduced by RVSM. These reduced vertical separation minima allow 1,000 feet vertical separation minima instead of the previous 2,000 feet. Airplanes making use of RVSM should have the appropriate cockpit equipment. Non-compliance with the new equipment forces these airplanes to fly at altitudes lower than FL 290, which is not compatible with economical fuel burn conditions for turbine aircraft. RVSM is in the process of being implemented on a worldwide scale.

Vertical and horizontal separation between traffic in European airways is managed by the Control Flow Management Unit (CFMU) of Eurocontrol (www.cfmu.eurocontrol.int). There is close coordination between airport ATC and CFMU. The clearance to join an airway at a specific altitude and time is communicated by CFMU to ATC of the departure airport. The cockpit crew finally gets the consolidated takeoff and airway clearance from ATC at the airport of departure.

Communication between cockpit crew and ATC is vital to ensure the safe operation of air traffic. The Very High Frequency Band (VHF) is used worldwide in the range from 118 to 137 MHz. The available frequencies were already doubled decades ago by reducing the 50 kHz channel spacing into 25 kHz. Increasing traffic, however, requires the additional availability of new frequencies. VHF communication is only possible on a one-to-one basis. When VHF communication is going on between an aircraft and ATC, all other airplanes have to wait before transmitting to ATC or receiving ATC messages. In this way a VHF frequency can be overloaded, very soon resulting in delays when airplanes are not able to contact ATC. The cost per year of these delays to passengers and airline companies is estimated by Eurocontrol to reach €450 million in 2010 and up to €6 billion in 2020 (Eurocontrol, 2006b).

The solution worldwide and in Europe is the use of a narrower channel spacing of 8.33 kHz. The deadline in Europe for implementation above flight level 195 was 15 March 2007, and probably 2010 for the lower altitudes (Eurocontrol, 2007a).

The traditional navigation system used by aircraft relies on ground-based VOR (Very High Frequency Omnirange) stations. Airplanes fly from one VOR to another, and this explains why airways have been centred along these VOR stations. Very often airplanes have to use multiple airways before ending up at the final destination. Consequently straight line navigation between departure and arrival airport is hardly possible. As airplanes flying between busy hubs have to use the same routings, airway congestion and delays are very common. Straight line navigation would take away the congestion from airways, shorten up flying distances, and reduce fuel consumption and emissions.

This solution can be offered by satellite navigation systems, such as the Wide Area Augmentation System (WAAS) in the US (FAA, 2009b) and by the plans for the European Geostationary Navigation Overlay System (EGNOS) based on the EU Galileo Project (Regulation 876/2002). Galileo has been delayed many times and will probably not be implemented before 2011 (ASD Media, 2007).

Another new system for the future will be ADS-B. This Automatic Dependent Surveillance-Broadcast system (Learmount, 2007a) will give pilots better traffic situational awareness, and consequently can accept more airplanes in the same blocs of airspace. Shorter and more efficient routes will become possible in the same airspace (Norris, 2007).

4 Conclusion

Many congestion problems in the air transport sector are caused by airports, ending up with more frequent delays than those caused by en route congestion.

Although airport capacity can be increased in the long run by building new infrastructure, short-run solutions should be adopted first to optimise the use of existing capacity. The possible actions are based on a differentiated mix of operational practices. Runway capacity can be increased by minimising runway occupancy time (ROT), by concentrating on homogeneous traffic with similar approach and departure speeds and same wake turbulence category. Adverse weather can be managed by more sophisticated instrument landing systems and microburst detection equipment. Noise congestion can be caused by legally imposed quotas per airport, involving maximum yearly amounts of noise production. In this case, more capacity is only possible when airline operators shift to airplanes producing less noise.

As airports are heterogeneous in nature, caused mainly by practical differences such as runway length, or more generally by geographical location and differences in national and local legislation, the positive impact of the operational actions on capacity and delays can vary depending on the airport.

En route congestion enhancement requires primarily an efficient air traffic control (ATC) system. Europe suffered traditionally from a heterogeneous ATC system, but is actually working towards a solution with the implementation of the Single European Sky project.

More airplanes can fly safely in the same airspace with the introduction of reduced vertical separation minima (RVSM), and the 8.33 kHz expansion programme will open up more VHF frequencies, allowing more airplanes to communicate with ATC.

The development of satellite navigation systems will allow straight line navigation, while in the long run the automatic dependent surveillance-broadcast (ADS-B) system will allow airplanes to fly more direct and efficient routes.

As most en route solutions for more capacity and less delays are relatively recent or still in the initial stage of implementation, hard conclusions on the real impact are not possible yet.

Note

1 Flight level (FL) 290 indicates 29,000 feet related to the reference datum of 29.92 inches of mercury or 1013.2 hPa.

References

Airport Coordination Limited (2009) *Capacity Declarations*, www.acl-uk.org.

Air Transport Association of America – ATA (2008). *ATC System Modernization, 8 April*, Washington, www.airlines.org/operationsandsafety/atc/atcsystemmodernization.

ASD Media (2007) Power struggle jeopardises EU Galileo satellite system, *Aerospace & Defence News*, 15 March, www.asd-network.com, pp. 1–2.

Bonnassies, O. (2009) Parked airliner fleet swells. *Flight International*, vol. 175, no. 5185, p. 15.

CODA (Central Office for Delay Analysis) (2008) *Digest – Annual 2008 Delays to Air Transport in Europe*, Eurocontrol, pp. 25, 36 and 38.

CODA (Central Office for Delay Analysis) (2009a) *Digest – January 2009 Delays to Air Transport in Europe*, Eurocontrol, p. 33.

CODA (Central Office for Delay Analysis) (2009b) *Digest – March 2009 Delays to Air Transport in Europe*, Eurocontrol, pp. 18 and 25.

CODA (Central Office for Delay Analysis) (2009c) *Digest – July 2009 Delays to Air Transport in Europe*, Eurocontrol, p. 32.

Convention of Chicago (7 December 1944), consulted in Luchtwetboek, Belgium.

Directive 2002/30/EC. *Official Journal*, L085, 28 March.

Dunn, G. (2009) Airports go on the offensive. *Airline Business*, vol. 25, no. 10, p. 16.

Eurocontrol (2003) *Enhancing Airside Capacity*, 15 September, edition 2, pp. 2.3–3.20.

Eurocontrol (2006a) *Eurocontrol Medium Term Forecast: IFR Flight Movements 2006–2012*, DAP/DIA/STATFOR Doc. 179, p. 25.

Eurocontrol (2006b) *8.33 kHz Expansion Programme*, edition 0.3, pp. 10–12.

Eurocontrol (2007a) *Europe tunes 8.33 kHz above FL 195*, press release, 5 February, pp. 1–2.

Eurocontrol (2007b) *ACE – Airside Capacity Enhancement*, vol. 1–8.

Eurocontrol (2007c) *ATFCM and Capacity Report 2006*, 12 February, p. 17.

European Commission (2006) *An Action Plan for Airport Capacity, Efficiency and Safety in Europe*, COM (2006) 819, 15 pages.

FAA (2005) *Moving America Safely*, Federal Aviation Administration Air Traffic Organization, 2005 Annual Performance Report, p. 15.

FAA (2009a) *Aeronautical Information Manual – AIM*, Aviation Supplies & Academics, Chapter 7 – Safety of Flight, § 7–1–26.

FAA (2009b) *Pilot/Controller Glossary*, www.faa.gov/air_traffic/publications, 27 August.

Goold, I. (2005) The capacity crunch. *Eurocontrol and ACI Europe: A vision for European aviation*, Newsdesk Communication Ltd, London, pp. 46–50.

Kaminski-Morrow, D. (2009) Gloomy outlook on airport capacity. *Airline Business*, vol. 25, no. 1, p. 18.

Learmount, D. (2007a) Eurocontrol readies ADS-B for EASA certification. *Flight International*, vol. 171, no. 5073, p. 10.

Learmount, D. (2007b) Single Sky is the holy grail. *Flight International*, vol. 170, no. 5067, p. 13.

Learmount, D. (2007c) Wake vortex rules set for shake-up. *Flight International*, vol. 171, no. 5074, p. 10.

Mohleji, S. C. (2001) *Terminal Airspace/Airport Congestion Problems in US and FMS/ RNAV Applications to reduce Delays*, The MITRE Corporation, pp. 9–10.
Murillo, A. and Carlier, S. (2006) *Flight Prioritisation Prototype*, Eurocontrol, EEC/ SEE/2006/002, p. 3.
Norris, G. (2007) ADS-B: the way forward. *Flight International*, vol. 171, no. 5075, p. 36.
Regulation 925/1999/EC. *Official Journal*, L115, 29 April.
Regulation 876/2002/EC. *Official Journal*, L138, 28 May.
Sobie, B. and Field, D. (2006) Terror alert: the aftermath. *Airline Business*, vol. 22, no. 9, p. 11.
STATFOR (2007) *A Place to Stand: Airports in the European Air Network*, Eurocontrol, Sept. 2007, p. 57.
The World's Top Airports (2009) *Airline Business*, vol. 25, no. 6, p. 58–62.
Turner, A. (2007a). Open Skies rewrites rules. *Flight International*, vol. 171, no. 5078, p. 16.
Turner, A. (2007b). Single Sky demands strong leadership. *Flight International*, vol. 171, no. 5068, p. 7.
www.aviationglossary.com.
www.cfmu.eurocontrol.int.
www.europa.eu.
www.schiphol.nl.
www.sesar-consortium.aero.

14 Towards a more efficient use of airport capacity at Europe's hubs

Jaap de Wit and Guillaume Burghouwt

1 The airport congestion problem

The current situation in the airline industry may postpone the problem of airport congestion in Europe for a while, but irrespective of the temporary reduction in aircraft movements substantial shortages of airport capacity are foreseen in the long run.

In the short run the recession is affecting air traffic in Europe on three broad fronts according to Eurocontrol (2009): reduced demand for air travel due to lower output and income; bankruptcies due to credit difficulties and, thirdly, a reverse in the growth of recent migration flows within Europe. Such weakness in air travel markets has usually lasted three years in earlier recessions before they returned to the former growth trend (IATA, 2008).

Also this recession will not affect the basic growth drivers of air travel such as price, income and international trade. Specific factors will continue to play their role too. The on-going market liberalization for example, such as stage two for the EU–US open sky agreement, will generate new growth. As a spin-off of this market liberalization, low-cost carriers continue to unbundle the airline product and create an unprecedented price competition in short to medium-haul markets. The low fares generate new demand and divert existing demand from other transport modes. Furthermore international travel will be stimulated in the longer run by the new economic growth of the BRIC countries (Brazil, India and China). Such strong upward trends can partly be countered by cap and trade measures to limit greenhouse gas emissions and by renewed oil price rises. Also improvements in the European high-speed train network will reduce air traffic growth in Europe.[1]

All in all, growth in air travel demand is here to stay. Recent Eurocontrol forecasts indicate a 1.5 per cent growth in European air traffic for 2010 before returning to more typical rates of between 3.5–4.5 per cent per year. In combination with the slow growth in 2008, at 0.4 per cent, and a reduction of 4.9 per cent in 2009, Eurocontrol's new medium-term forecasts reach the same traffic volumes around four years later than the earlier forecasts of 2004.

However, the further growth in the downstream market of air travel and the slow developments in the upstream market of airport capacity contrast remarkably. Many reasons can be furnished why the supply of infrastructure capacity fails to keep pace with the demand for capacity: time-consuming planning procedures (Werson and Burghouwt 2007), environmental concerns of noise abatement, political whims and the inability to start up new green field projects in the densely populated Western European region. The difference in growth between air travel demand in the downstream market and the supply of airport capacity in the upstream market will inevitably result in a capacity crunch. Eurocontrol (2004) estimates that more than 60 airports in Europe will be congested in 2025. The top-20 airports will become saturated for at least 8–10 hours per day. The seven largest airports will need an hourly capacity of 201 IFR movements on average, whereas they can only handle 110 movements.

Therefore, in the next two decades the European air transport industry will show a growing need for more efficient allocation methods with regard to increasingly scarce airport capacity. This chapter addresses the market-based options which may satisfy that need. After discussing the current slot allocation system in Europe and its inefficiencies, various market-based options will be compared and contrasted with the US experience. Thereafter special attention is paid to the question whether secondary slot trading as a market-based option at European hubs such as Amsterdam airport will result in more concentrated downstream air transport markets at these hubs.

2 The current EU slot allocation system

The EU slot regulation on common rules for the allocation of slots at Community airports (Council Regulation No 95/93 amended by Regulation 793/2004) provides an instrument that intends to create a more efficient allocation and use of scarce airport capacity and a better market access for new entrants. In other words, the EC acknowledges that the upstream market issue of airport capacity allocation is closely related to the downstream market issue of market access and airline competition. However, the Tinbergen principle basically states that for each policy objective only one instrument should be applied. In other words, it is likely that one and the same slot allocation mechanism can not reconcile two conflicting objectives in two different markets. The next sections will illustrate this in more detail.

2.1 The IATA scheduling guidelines

The current EU system of allocating scarce airport capacity is broadly based on the IATA Worldwide Scheduling Guidelines.[2]

If airport congestion becomes structural, the aviation industry has to find solutions through the airline scheduling process. For this purpose, the IATA Guidelines distinguish three types of airports (IATA, 2005, p. 3):

- At *level 1 non-coordinated airports* airport capacity adequately meets demand of the users.

- At *level 2 schedules facilitated airports* demand is approaching the capacity limitations at some periods. At level 2 airports airlines submit schedules to a schedules facilitator appointed by the airlines. The facilitator seeks cooperation and voluntary schedule changes to avoid congestion. The main forum for the interaction between the airlines and the schedules facilitator is the twice yearly Schedules Conference. Prior to the conference, airlines submit their schedules.

- If congestion worsens the government must decide on a change from self-regulation to an explicit government regulation as a *level 3 coordinated airport*. Based on the specific capacity bottlenecks, the annual and hourly declared capacity have to be established in terms of available slots.[3] Each airline needs a slot to operate an air service at the coordinated airport. The coordinator allocates the slots each season to the airlines in an independent, neutral and non-discriminatory way. The slot coordinator is appointed by the government.

It should be noted here that congestion and slot allocation at level 3 airports can be a seasonal affair. For example Salzburg and Innsbruck will be coordinated during the winter season, whereas a number of Spanish and Greek airports are subject to slot allocation during the summer season.[4] Slot allocation may play a role at either partially congested airports during specific periods of the day, such as Amsterdam Airport, or fully congested airports during the whole day, such as London Heathrow. Slot allocation is not exclusively based on runway congestion but may reflect other operational or environmental capacity dimensions. For example, Rotterdam Airport has been coordinated due to an apron capacity shortage. Amsterdam Airport's declared capacity is based on the maximum allowable noise levels.

2.2 The EC slot regulation

At Europe's coordinated airports the slots are allocated according to the EC Regulation mentioned earlier, in compliance with the IATA guidelines. Additionally, the EC Slot Regulation defines some specific provisions to protect for PSO routes and to encourage new entrants on intra-Community routes. The general principles of the slot allocation process in the EU can be summarized as follows.

Under the EC Slot Regulation slots can only be allocated to and held by operators[5] (air carriers as well as general aviation). The primary allocation[5] of the slots is made by the slot coordinator, subject to historical precedence – so-called grandfather rights – and retimings of historical slots for operational reasons. Obviously, the allocation in this system is dominated by the grandfather rights: if the series of slots (a minimum number of 5) are used in the previous equivalent season for at least 80 percent of the time the incumbent carrier has the right to use that slot in the next season as well (the 'use it or lose it' rule).[6]

A slot pool is created by the slots remaining after this initial allocation and by newly created slots as a result of extra available capacity. These slots are allocated free of charge by the slot coordinator in a twice yearly coordination process of the IATA slot conferences. In order to encourage competition and new entry, up to 50 per cent of the slot in the pool is set aside for new entrant airlines.[7] However, one should be aware of the fact that usually the slots pool is very small. As a result, the objective of encouraging competition and new entry appears to be quite severely constrained by the other objective of a more efficient use of airport capacity. In the allocation of the remaining slots, priority is given to year-round commercial air services. If air carriers do not need an allocated slot any more they can return their slots at the so-called slot return dates (31 January and 31 August) as that date is the baseline for the calculation of the 80/20 rule. Returned slots can be reallocated to air carriers that still have outstanding requests. Thereafter and during the actual season available slots are mostly allocated on an ad hoc basis.

2.3 *Slot mobility under the regulation*

Under the EC Slot Regulation, exchange and transfer are allowed under specified circumstances:

- Slots may be transferred by an air carrier from one route or type of service to another route or type of service operated by the same air carrier.
- Slots may be transferred unilaterally within the same 'commercial family', i.e.

  - between parent and subsidiary companies;
  - between subsidiaries of the same company;
  - as a part of acquisition or control over capital of an air carrier;
  - in the case of a total or partial take-over when the slots are directly related to the air carrier taken over;
  - in franchise or code-sharing operations carriers involved can use each others' slots.

- Slots may be exchanged one by one, subject to confirmation by the slot coordinator.

With respect to this definition of a slot exchanges, the question may arise whether either an illegal unilateral slot transfer or a legal slot exchange is involved if a valuable slot is exchanged for a so-called 'junk slot' in an 'artificial exchange'. A junk slot concerns a slot at a commercially less attractive time, for which there is no demand and which is allocated by the slot coordinator to an airline on request. After the exchange the other airline involved in the exchange will return this slot to the slot coordinator. The question about the legality of this artificial exchange played a role in the Guernsey case.[8]

The English High Court held that the artificial exchanges were exchanges in the ordinary meaning of the language and not unilateral slot transfers and this meaning was not qualified by the provisions of the Regulation, in spite of Art 14.3. 'The coordinator is not in a position to judge whether to what extent such an exchange is "artificial",' as the Court stated.

Artificial exchanges are believed to be often accompanied by monetary compensation. The EC Regulation remains silent as to monetary consideration and in the Guernsey case the Court found that there was nothing to prohibit monetary compensation accompanying slot exchanges and transfers. Therefore, the Guernsey case is said to have further encouraged the 'grey market' for secondary trading at the London airports.

In a reaction to the Court's decision in the Guernsey case the Commission proposed amendments of the Slot Regulation in 2004 that exchanges should only be permitted where each party to the exchange intends to use the slots it receives from the other. This proposal was not adopted by the Council. Due to the Commission's opinion the uncertainty about the legality of these artificial exchanges continued to exist until the end of April 2008. Then the Commission clarified that instead of persisting in its earlier opinion the Commission now 'does not intend to pursue infringement proceedings against Member States where such exchanges take place in a transparent matter respecting all the other administrative requirements'.[9] Allowing for secondary slot trading implicitly also addresses the key issue of the property rights of slots, which we discuss later.

3 The need to change the current slot allocation system

3.1 Inefficiencies

Pursuant to the Regulation 95/93, the current EU slot allocation system applied by the slot coordinator at a coordinated airport takes into account the principles of transparency, neutrality and non-discrimination as well as historic precedence of the slots, public service obligations, market access opportunities for new entrants, the IATA guidelines and possible local rules.

It is quite obvious that under these conditions existing airport capacity will not be allocated efficiently. Although grandfather rights and the 'use it or lose it' rule create the advantage of schedule continuity in successive schedule seasons, these elements are also strong incentives for airlines to hold on to slots. The result is slot immobility as reflected in 'slot babysitting', i.e. poorly using the slots by operating low load factors and/or small aircraft at a highly congested airport.[10] Sometimes an alliance partner 'baby sits' the slots for example in order to keep out newcomers.

Furthermore, if the slot coordinator is able to allocate a limited number of commercially attractive slots, he/she can hardly take into account the question of which airline can make the most valuable and beneficial use of the slot to be allocated. He/she can mainly prioritize the category of scheduled year-round services on a first-come, first-served basis.

From the point of view of efficient allocation it can also be doubted whether a new entrant as defined by the Commission[11] will have any serious impact on competition at a congested airport. DotEcon (2001), Matthews and Menaz (2003) and Starkie (1998) expect mid-sized incumbents to be a stronger competitive threat to the dominant carrier than these smaller start-ups.

3.2 Market-based efficiency

In theory an efficient allocation of scarce airport capacity would require charges to airlines that are set equal to marginal social cost (MSC), i.e. the sum of the marginal operating cost of the airport operator – which is relatively small – and the marginal cost of delay to the airline and its passengers. In this approach, all airlines are assumed to operate no more than one flight in each time period without considering whether an aircraft operated by a given airline was delaying other flights operated by the same operator. This results in so-called atomistic tolls comparable to road congestion pricing.[12]

More recently it has been questioned to what extent such pricing would reduce delays. Brueckner (2002) has pointed out that because an air carrier bears the cost of delay that it imposes on its other flights, it should be charged only for the delay it imposes on other carriers' flights and not for the delay they impose in themselves. For example, a dominant carrier with a 75 per cent share of the operations at an airport should only be charged for 25 per cent of the delay costs. At a hub, this percentage of the delay costs may even become negligible for the hub carrier, since it clusters its operations in connection waves and fully internalizes the delay costs whereas the non-dominant carriers operate their flights at off-peak times. Brueckner's approach fully focuses on the efficiency of scarce airport capacity and not on the distributional aspects it creates. Should, for example, operators with a small share of flights pay higher tolls than those with a large share, even if both operated during the same time period? However, Morrison and Winston (2007) find small differences between the net welfare gains of the atomistic and optimal congestion pricing policies. So, taking into account both efficiency and equity aspects of congestion tolls, implementation of the atomistic tolls seems to render a more feasible solution without substantially infringing efficiency objectives.

Another market-based approach to allocating scarce airport capacity among the users concerns the capping of airport capacity through a declaration of the total number of slots and pricing them through secondary trading. The MSC of a slot is expected to reflect the opportunity costs of the service provided by the selling air carrier. Only those air carriers will buy such a slot if their willingness to pay is high enough to compensate for the price.

Mott MacDonald (2007) stresses that the introduction of a market-based approach results in an economically efficient slot use in an allocative as well as a productive way. Allocative efficiency means that slots are used for those destinations that provide the highest social value in terms of generalized travel costs. Productive efficiency means that the total number of slots at an airport is maximized and that each slot is being used by moving the maximum amount of passengers (aircraft size) and maximum route distance possible. However, allocative and productive efficiency are not such straightforward concepts if secondary slot trading is introduced at a congested hub airport, as we will discuss later in this chapter.

It should be emphasized here that efficient slot use can be affected by the number of available slots, i.e. by the capping of the available slots through a capacity declaration. Since it is likely that declared capacity will usually be determined below the level of economic capacity, this opens up the possibility of extra scarcity rents. Probably, these rents primarily materialize in the hub carrier's operations, so it may be in the hub carrier's interest to keep the declared capacity lower than optimal. Therefore, an efficient use of the slots at least requires a neutral and transparent determination of the declared capacity.

4 Towards an amended allocation system

4.1 Primary auctioning and/or secondary trading

The current slot allocation system in Europe can be made more efficient in either a more rigorous or a more adaptive way with respect to the existing IATA Scheduling Guidelines applied world wide.

The rigorous way implies the one-off suspension of all grandfather rights and the new entrants rule, i.e. returning all slots into the slots pool. From the slots pool all slots are then allocated through a market-based system. For example an auction is used for this primary allocation.[13] Different types of auctions have been proposed in the literature, ranging from a simple clock auction or sealed-bid auction (NERA, 2004) to a simultaneous ascending auction including package bidding (NERA, 2004), or even a Simultaneous Multiple Round Auction (SMRA) (DotEcon 2001; Sickmann 2006). Gruyer and Lenoir (2003) prefer an even more advanced combinatorial bidding procedure based on the Vickrey–Clarke–Gooves mechanism. However, especially in a one-off event auction design should be made as simple as possible in order to enable bidders to apply the auction rules correctly.

A more advanced auction design can only be applied if a less rigorously different allocation system is chosen that requires an annual auction-based primary allocation. Such an approach can be effectuated by limiting the life time of the grandfather rights and by introducing a rolling programme in which a fixed percentage of the grandfather rights is being withdrawn annually while the reclaimed slots are auctioned each year.[14]

More recently Levine (2009) has pointed at the allocation problem of the revenues from these auctions and congestion pricing systems. If the revenues from prices or auctions are kept by the airport operator, static efficiency within a fixed capacity may be maximized, but it impairs dynamic efficiency through investing in new capacity and capacity-enhancing techniques. In order to simultaneously improve slot use decisions of aircraft operators and to enable airport operators to determine whether capacity expansion is economically worthwhile, he proposes a simplified version of the FAA's auction rule[15] as a second-best solution compared to congestion pricing. A more adaptive approach implies that the historical precedence of the allocated slots is maintained but that only secondary trading of grandfathered slots between airlines is allowed for. In that case it is expected that an air carrier may decide to sell slots to other airlines willing to pay the price involved if one is confronted with the opportunity costs of the slots in comparison with the value derived from operating these slots. In this way the efficient use of airport capacity will increasingly improve, be it at a slower pace than in a one-off auction.[16] This increased efficiency is expected to be reflected in a switch from short-haul to long-haul services, a switch from smaller to larger aircraft and correspondingly an increase in the average number of passengers per slot as well as a marginally improved utilization of the number of available slots with fewer slots remaining in the slots pool (NERA, 2004; Mott McDonald, 2007).

4.2 The choice of a market-based option and the issue of the slot property rights

Taking into account the recent publications of the EC and the US DoT/FAA[17] it seems that the European Commission and the US DoT/FAA are at a crossroads now where each of them is pointing in a different direction with respect to the fundamental issue of the slot property rights and the related market-based allocation mechanisms.

Although from the beginning the EC slot regulation was based on the IATA principle of the incumbent airlines' grandfathering rights, the EC has also continually emphasized that slots neither belong to airlines nor to airports. According to the latest EC definition[18] a slot is not a property right but a permission to the airline to use the airport infrastructure. However, the recent Commission's decision in COM(2008)277 to tolerate secondary trading at coordinated airports implicitly confirms the indefinite slot property rights of the airlines.

The US DoT/FAA on the contrary has chosen a different approach for LaGuardia Airport, by more explicitly defining the property right of a slot as the government's.[19] Instead of revitalizing the old Buy–Sell Rule at the High Density Airports, US DoT/FAA proposes to grant access to the public facility of the airways via a slot lease for a defined period. In other words, each year a limited number of slots – 10 or 20 per cent – is intended to be auctioned off by a Package Clock auction or a single Sealed Bid, Second Price auction (see Berardino, 2008).[20]

These EU and US approaches reflect substantially different appreciations of the downstream market effects of secondary slot trading. The EC now points at the 'grey' slot trading market that, according to the Commission, would have enabled new levels of competition at the London airports after the coming into force of the EU–US aviation agreement (at the same time ignoring the increased dominance of the incumbents). In the USA secondary slot trading under the High Density Rule is diagnosed as encapsulation of the incumbents that value their slot holdings much higher as a means of precluding entry by competitors onto high-yield routes (Berardino, 2008).

If this diagnosis is correct, the size of the secondary slot market in Europe may rapidly shrink after the initial trading stage. This corresponds with the figures of NERA (2004) that estimated 5–10 per cent of slots at coordinated airports in Europe to be traded each year based on an extrapolation of the initial stage of trading at Heathrow. More recently Mott McDonald (2006) even identified only 499 slots traded at Heathrow (some of them more than once) between 2001 and 2006 or an average fraction of around 1.2 per cent per year of the total operations. According to Mott McDonald (2006) a major part of these slots were sold as a result of the demise of Sabena and Swiss Air. The main buyers were the incumbents BA and Virgin (73 per cent and 13 per cent of the slots traded). This increase was also driven by British Airways' de-hubbing of Gatwick. Slot consolidation among major hub carriers corresponds with the findings of the GAO (1999) at the four High Density Airports in the US, where slot trading has been allowed since 1986 for domestic operations.

4.3 Secondary trading and downstream market concentration concerns

The position of the dominant carrier as a net slot buyer at a congested airport will result in a further slot concentration. This may result in an efficient capacity use providing new travel opportunities, if the dominant carrier launches new destinations and increases frequencies on existing routes. However, increased airport dominance also gives greater scope for anti-competitive behaviour by the dominant carrier. The carrier may engage for example in predatory bidding for slots, pre-empting competition in downstream origin-destination markets and pursuing discriminatory practices among potential slot buyers (see for example CAA/OFT (2005) and European Competition Authorities (2005)).[21]

The diagnoses of the consequences of this slot concentration are quite different. Kleit and Kobayashi (1996) concluded from their analysis of slot use at the most slot concentrated airport in the US (Chicago O'Hare), that the slot concentration more likely resulted from efficient airport use rather than from anti-competitive behaviour. In that respect higher fares mainly reflect the scarcity rents of congestion which are necessary to clear the market.

Borenstein (1989) and the GAO (1999) relate the higher fares at congested US airports to hub premiums as the dominant carriers exploit their dominance at individual routes. Starkie (2007), on the contrary, points out the possibility that, since the airports do not apply efficient charging schemes, the airlines are keeping their fares at market clearing levels. In other words, these fares do not reflect monopoly rents but scarcity rents (and these rents can be manipulated through a tighter declared capacity, as indicated earlier). Furthermore, it is the hub-and-spoke system that provides the origin-destination market at the hub with an excellent accessibility product of direct connections to a disproportionate set of worldwide destinations compared to the size of the local demand. These higher fares may correspond with a differentiated and more costly network quality. The higher costs of such a network may be the net result of the diseconomies of scale in hub operating costs (baggage handling systems, peak capacity of ground staff, check-in facilities, long turn-round times of aircraft, etc.) on the one hand and the benefits of hub-and-spoke network economies (i.e. economies of size, density and network scope) on the other hand.[22] Furthermore, De Wit and Burghouwt (2007) doubt whether the relationship between secondary slot trading and concentration at 'high-density' airports in the US is a causal one: other factors such as the consolidation in the US airline industry may also be at stake here.

Anyhow, the level at which overall airport dominance is passed on to consumers strongly depends on the interaction between airport dominance and route dominance as well as the presence of inter-airport competition. Abuse of monopoly power at the route level can be countered by adequate EU competition policy and close market investigation on a case-by-case basis.

Although it is obvious that slot concentration at congested airports is likely to occur if secondary slot trading is introduced, it is also important to take account of the fact that the congestion patterns at individual airports can be very different. For example, at London Heathrow carriers have to cope with continuous congestion all through the day, whereas other major airports in Europe operate as traffic pumps to provide connections between incoming and outgoing traffic waves in a hub-and-spoke system of the hub carrier. Congestion at these hub airports is a discontinuous phenomenon of alternating peak and off-peak periods. So the question in the final section is whether the dominant carrier at a hub such as Paris CDG or Amsterdam will behave differently from a dominant carrier such as BA at Heathrow with regard to the concentration of slots

5 Secondary slot trading and hubbing: the Amsterdam airport case

5.1 Scarce airport capacity at London Heathrow and Amsterdam

The question is whether the lessons learned from the grey slot market of London Heathrow (LHR) are fully applicable at, for example, the KLM hub in Amsterdam (AMS) and the Air France hub in Paris CDG. The continuous congestion at British Airways' home base Heathrow also partly reflects the focus of BA on the high-yield O-D market of the London metropolitan area itself. The primary role of LHR as a gateway is reflected in the low dominance level in Table 14.1 compared to the other three hub airports.

Table 14.1 Concentration at selected European hubs (% in total scheduled flight movements) in 2004

	KLM at Amsterdam	*Air France at Paris CDG*	*Lufthansa at Frankfurt*	*British Airways at Heathrow*
Home carrier (H)	46.9	56.4	57.7	39.7
H+Regionals (R)	49.4	63.2	59.9	41.3
H+R+Global Partners	62.0	70.9	71.1	51.3

Source: OAG data (2004).

The substantially lower transfer rates of London Heathrow in the range of 30–35 percent contrast with the 40–45 percent range at Amsterdam and the transfer rate at Frankfurt even over 50 percent. A hub such as Amsterdam shows successive periods of slot scarcity during the day due to the connection traffic peaks of the hub carrier, whereas Heathrow demonstrates a continuous excess demand of capacity during the whole day. Figure 14.1 illustrates this process of alternating peaks of connecting arrivals and departures for the KLM operations at Amsterdam.

The symptoms of productive efficiency in slot use to be expected after the introduction of slot trading discussed earlier are not so self-evident in this setting anymore. For example, the hub carrier cannot simply continue to substitute short-haul narrow-body flights by long-haul wide-body flights in the scarce peak slots. Both types of operations are indispensable in the hubbing process. On average, 75 percent of the seats on KLM's intercontinental flights is fed by European operations and vice versa. So the question rises how European hub carriers may react on secondary slot trading at their hub airport.

5.2 Hubbing and secondary trading at Amsterdam

First of all, it remains likely that the hub carrier will show a higher willingness to pay for scarce peak slots than low-cost carriers, charter airlines or freighter carriers. However, it is not likely that this will be the case for the slots of foreign European hub carriers. Their opportunity costs derived from their peak slots at Amsterdam are connected with the opportunity costs of the related slots that fit into their own hub-and-spoke system at their respective home bases.

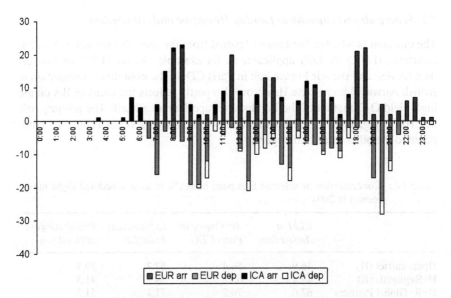

Figure 14.1 European and intercontinental movements of KLM per half hour at Amsterdam (OAG, 20–09–2006, local time) (source: OAG (2006)).

Figure 14.2 provides more information on the composition of the traffic peaks. The scarcity in the arrival and departure peaks is predominantly caused by the hub carrier and its alliance partners at Amsterdam. However, even in the peaks a number of slots are used by low-cost carriers as well as charter airlines. These carriers will be willing sellers of peak slots if the opportunity costs appear to be high. The question is whether the hub carrier is the obvious willing buyer.

This is not self-evident, when secondary slot trading starts to reveal the opportunity costs of peak slots. This information will primarily stimulate the hub carrier to optimize its traffic peak pattern of connecting waves. This may imply that monopoly routes operated by the hub carrier will be reallocated from the peak centre to the peak shoulders without substantial revenue loss. Although total travel time for transfer passengers increases due to longer transfer times at the hub, this is hardly reflected in the airline revenues since the passengers involved have not got an alternative travel option. In contrast, competitive spokes will be better centred within the peaks.

The introduction of secondary slot trading may not only stimulate adaptations within the existing waves but also be an extra incentive to reconsider the design of the existing wave system.

5.3 Optimizing the wave system

Although economies of scope in hub-and-spoke systems have often been identified as strong incentives to expand the connecting traffic peaks, hubbing comes at a

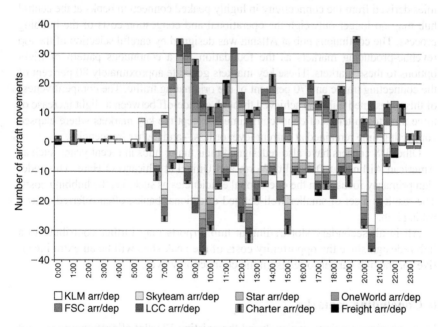

Figure 14.2 Total numbers of arrivals and departures per half hour and per traffic category at Amsterdam (OAG, 20–09–2006, local time) (source: OAG (2006)).

rapidly increasing cost of idle capacity in the off-peak periods at the hub. If the introduction of secondary slot trading also adds the growing opportunity costs of the peak slots in expanding peaks to these operational hubbing costs the sum of both costs may start to outweigh the scope economies of ever-growing peaks.

In other words, the opportunity costs of the peak slots will increase disproportionately with the height of the peaks. In addition, this will further aggravate the diseconomies in the hubbing costs. Since the slot prices are only one component in the total hubbing costs, the decreasing returns to scale in the hubbing costs as such are probably reflected already in several hubbing restructuring projects initiated by various hub carriers. Slot trading can be expected to further stimulate peak stretching. The internal delay costs and operational peak costs as such have already been sufficient triggers for stretching the connection waves in the examples discussed below. A secondary slot trading system would become an additional trigger for hub redesign.

Frank *et al.* (2005) describe the 'depeaking' of Lufthansa operations at Frankfurt airport using Lufthansa's own schedule to adapt the overall declared capacity as well as the declared capacity for arrivals and departures in such a way that the daily variability of operations can be adequately handled and the past flight delays are no longer incorporated in the constantly lengthening of planned inbound block times.

Another example is the further-reaching transformation of Delta's banked hub at Atlanta into a continuous hub that combines the revenue-generating power of the traditional banked hub with the operational efficiencies from a smooth continuous schedule, as described by Petroccione (2007). In other words, the network economies derived from the connectivity in highly peaked connection banks at the central hub may no longer outweigh the operational and congestion costs of the hubbing process. The continuous hub at Atlanta was designed by careful selection of the top revenue-producing markets as the foundation for a continuous pattern of flight options to these markets. These key markets generate approximately 80 per cent of the connecting traffic and 70 per cent of the originating traffic. The competitiveness of this redesigned hub was achieved through a trade-off between a slight increase of three minutes in terms of connecting time – except the key markets where elapsed connecting time remained at current level or less – and higher frequencies.

Other US carriers have also redesigned their major hubs in recent years, such as American Airlines at Dallas Ft. Worth and United at Chicago O'Hare. This redesign primarily focused on the operational efficiencies as such, i.e. the hubbing costs. The result is a set of smaller well-defined directional banks, often referred to as a rolling hub.

All in all secondary slot trading at hub airports may further contribute to a hub redesign since the opportunity costs of the peak slots will be an extra incentive for the hub carrier to redesign the connection waves.

6 Concluding remarks

In the previous sections, we analysed the existing EU slot allocation system and the need to introduce market-based approaches such as primary slot auctioning and/or secondary slot trading to enable an efficient use of slots at congested airports. The tension between the two objectives of the slot allocation, i.e. efficient use of scarce airport capacity and sufficient competition in the downstream air transport markets, cannot easily be resolved if slot concentration is inevitable after the introduction of secondary slot trading The slot trading results at Heathrow might point in this direction. However, this is not a straightforward consequence of slot trading at other congested airports in Europe due to different behaviour of the respective hub carriers and the different congestion characteristics at these hubs.

Secondary slot trading primarily seems to become an incentive to restructure the connection wave systems at these hubs.

Whereas the EC has indicated its willingness to tolerate slot trading at other coordinated airports in Europe according to the London model, this appreciation of secondary slot trading appears to be fundamentally different from the US experience with slot trading under the High Density Rule during the last few decades. Due to the resulting slot concentration and its impact on downstream markets, secondary trading is no longer seen as a viable market-based option for congested airports. The fundamental difference between the US and EU views on slot property rights also plays a role in US DoT/FAA's preferred slot auctioning with regard to the highly congested New York airports.

Acknowledgements

The authors would like to express their gratitude to the Dutch Slot Coordinator, Michiel van der Zee, and two unknown referees for their useful comments. The usual caveat remains applicable.

Notes

1 Eurocontrol (2009) estimates a 0.5 per cent reduction in growth for European air traffic in total over a period of seven years.
2 Airports in the USA are not subject to these IATA Guidelines: the 'first come, first served' principle is being maintained even for highly congested airports. Scarcity of airport capacity is mainly reflected in waiting queues during starts and landings. Only four 'high-density' airports were coordinated, i.e. subject to slot allocations based on declared capacity, whereas in Europe 73 airports are indicated as part-time or full-time coordinated based on IATA guidelines.
3 A slot is 'the scheduled time of arrival or departure available for allocation by a coordinator for an aircraft movement on a specific date at a coordinated airport. An allocated slot will take account of all the coordination parameters at the airport, e.g. runways, aprons, terminals, etc.' (IATA, 2005, p. 11). A slot allocated at the so-called US High Density Airports only refers to runway use. At US airports separate negotiations are necessary to acquire gates, check-in desks, baggage-handling systems, etc.
4 Summer peak airports like Kos are also nicknamed as hedgehog airports due to the traffic pattern which is a combination of a summer peak and a regular peak on one or two particular days of the week (Eurocontrol, 2007).
5 The primary allocation of the slots concerns the vertical allocation by the coordinator to applicants for slots or slot holders, whereas the secondary (re)allocation concerns

the horizontal transfer of allocated slots among air carriers without interference of the slot coordinator. Secondary trading concerns the transfer of slots including a monetary compensation between the carriers involved.

6 The 'use it or lose it rule' has been suspended by the EC during the 2009 summer season, as was the case in 2001–2002 and 2003, in order to enable airlines to cope with decreasing demand. The conflicting interests clearly emerged after this measure: the AEA applauded the measure, the ACI regretted the measure because of their short-term income reduction, like the budget airlines did due to further limitations on airport access. At the same time the EC referred to the environmental disadvantage of (almost) empty flights.

7 The definition of the term 'new entrant' has been revised in Regulation 793/2004 so as to increase potential competition on intra-Community routes. This did, however, not solve the problem of the small size of the slot pool, mentioned earlier.

8 In the Guernsey case Air UK ceased to serve the Heathrow–Guernsey route as from the end of the Winter season 1997/1998. It exchanged its historic Summer 1998 slots with slots from British Airways, which it then returned to the slot pool. The Guernsey government then brought judicial review proceedings in the English High Court against the Heathrow slot coordinator.

9 COM (2008) 227, 31–4–2008.

10 KLM for example operated Fokker 50s on the Rotterdam–Heathrow and Eindhoven–Heathrow routes. KLM has transferred these slots to Northwest to start up new Transatlantic routes from Heathrow after the coming into force of the EU–US Open Sky Agreement on 30 March 2008.

11 See also footnote 8.

12 See for example Brueckner and Van Dender (2008).

13 Such a one-off event also manifests itself when a new runway is opened at a congested airport where excess demand is not dissolved by the extra capacity.

14 Each of these two approaches would be incompatible with the current IATA guidelines in which the continuity of airline schedules is a key issue.

15 See for this rule section 4.2.

16 From the optimal efficiency point of view the difference between primary and secondary trading is only gradual and not fundamental: primary trading will bring forward the long-run effects of secondary trading. It should be kept in mind, however, that primary trading of all slots as a one-off event also requires secondary allocation rules like secondary trading as a follow-up for slots returned.

17 COM(2008)277 and the supplemental notice of proposed rule making on the congestion problems at New York's LaGuardia Airport (Docket No. FAA-2006–25709; Notice No. 08–04).

18 According to the EC Regulation 793/2004 a slot means 'a permission given by the coordinator ... to use the full range of airport infrastructure necessary to operate an air service at a coordinated airport on a specific date and time for the purpose of landing or take-off'.

19 The US DoT/FAA has always claimed a residual right to withdraw and reallocate slots at any time they think fit. However, Levine (2009) suggests to allow for an unrestricted slot use period unless the slot is withdrawn in a lottery in advance of the next scheduling season. In his opinion airlines should be compensated for the value of the slots withdrawn and airport operators for the new slots provided to the slot pool.

20 A blind auction is proposed to force bidding airlines to value the slots independently of knowledge of the competitive impact of the slot transfer.

21 Examples are: reluctance to sell slots to competing carriers; selling only at excessive prices; with non-compete clauses, only to certain airlines; at higher prices to stronger competitors; tying the buying airline to other services as well.

22 See also Bilotkach and Pai (2009) who were able to split up the well-known airport dominance effect into a significant quality and a market power-based component.

References

Berardino, F. (2008) Market pricing of airport access and the EU–US liberalization. Paper presented at the Airneth Conference, April 2008. Available at: www.airneth.com/index2. php?option=com_docman&task=doc_view&gid=608&Itemid=15 (accessed May 2008).

Bilotkach, V. and Pai, V. (2009) *Hub versus Airport Dominance.* Available at: http://ssrn.com/abstract=1349381.

Borenstein, S. (1989) Hubs and high fares: dominance and market power in the U.S. airline industry. *Rand Journal of Economics*, vol. 20, pp. 344–365.

Brueckner, J.K. (2002) Airport congestion when carriers have market power. *The American Economic Review*, vol. 92, no. 5, pp. 1357–1375.

Brueckner, J.K. and Dender, K. Van (2008) Atomistic congestion tolls at concentrated airports? Seeking a unified view in the internalization debate. *Journal of Urban Economics*, 64: 288.

CAA/OFT (2005) *Competition Issues Associated with the Trading of Airport Slots.* OFT832.

De Wit, J. and Burghouwt, G. (2007) The impact of secondary slot trading at Amsterdam Airport Schiphol. SEO Economic Research. Report Number 957. Available at www.seo.nl/binaries/publicaties/rapporten/2007/957.pdf (accessed May 2008).

Commission of the European Communities on the application of Regulation (EEC) (2008) No. 95/93 on common rules for the allocation of slots at Community airports. As amended, Brussels COM 227.

DotEcon (2001) Auctioning airport slots. A report for HM Treasury and the Department of the Environment, Transport and the Regions, January 2001.

Eurocontrol (2007) A place to stand: airports in the European air network. *Eurocontrol trends in air traffic*, Volume 3.

Eurocontrol (2009) *Medium-Term Forecast, Flight Movements 2009–2015, volume 1.*

European Competition Authorities (2005) Progress report of the Air Traffic Working Group on slot trading. Updated 17 June 2005.

Frank, M., Mederera, M., Stolz, B. and Hanschke, T. (2005) Depeaking-economic optimization of air traffic systems. *Aerospace Science and Technology*, vol. 9, no. 8, pp. 738–744.

GAO (1999) Airline deregulation: Changes in airfares, service quality, and barriers to entry. GAO/RCED-99-92.

Gruyer, N. and Lenoir, N. (2003) Auctioning airport slots. *Paper presented at the ATRS conference*, Toulouse, July 2003.

IATA (2005) *Worldwide Scheduling Guidelines.* 12th edn. Available at: www.iata.org/NR/ContentConnector/CS2000/SiteInterface/sites/whatwedo/scheduling/file/fdc/WSG-12thEd.pdf (accessed May 2008).

IATA (2008) Economic Briefing, *The Impact of the Recession on Air Traffic Volumes*, December.

Kleit, A.N. and Kobayashi, B.H. (1996) Market failure or market efficiency? Evidence on airport slot usage. *Research in Transportation Economics*, vol. 4, 1–32.

Levine, M.E. (2009) Airport congestion. When theory meets reality. *Yale Journal on Regulation*, vol. 26, pp. 37–88.

Matthews, B. and Menaz, B. (2003) *Airport Capacity: The Problem of Slot Allocation.* Leeds: Institute for Transport Studies, University of Leeds.

Morrison, S.A. and Winston, C. (2007) Another look at airport congestion pricing. *American Economic Review*, vol. 97, no. 5, pp. 1970–1977.

Mott MacDonald (2006) *Study on the Impact of the Introduction of Secondary Trading at Community Airports.* Volume 1. Commissioned by the European Commission.

NERA (2004) Study to assess the effects of different slot allocation schemes. A final report for the European Commission, DG Tren.

Petroccione, L. (2007) *Delta's Operation Clockwork. Transforming the Fundamentals of an Airline.* Available at: www.airneth.nl/serve_file.php?dType=dDocument&id=308 (accessed May 2008).

Sickmann, J. (2006) Airport slot allocation. Diskussionspapier Nr. 51, Institut für Volkswirtschaftslehre.

Starkie, D. (1998) Allocating airport slots. A role for the market? *Journal of Air Transport Management*, vol. 4, no. 2, pp. 111–116.

Starkie, D. (2007) The dilemma of slot concentration at network hubs. In: Czerny, A., Forsyth, P., Gillen, D. and Nieneier, H.-M. (eds.) *How to Make Slots Work.* Aldershot: Ashgate.

Werson, M. and Burghouwt, G. (2007) Airport planning in free market regimes. *Journal of Airport Management*, vol. 1, no. 4, pp. 38–55.

15 Assessing the impact of Open Skies agreements

David E. Pitfield

1 Introduction

At the most recent meetings of the Air Transport Research Society, held in Abu Dhabi in June 2009, a paper by Eichinger, Drotleff and Fongern (2009) explored the schedule changes seen to result from the EU–US Open Skies Agreement[1] and described it as muted. Another paper at the same meeting raised the issue of the counterfactual. As Pitfield (2009a) noted, the observed scheduled changes may not all be attributable to the Agreement. These issues in causality suggest a methodology needs to be adopted that can deal with this difficulty.

Earlier work on alliances by Iatrou and Alamdari (2005) suggested that airlines benefited from the formation of alliances[2] and, in particular, the advent of code sharing and the gaining of immunity from US Antitrust legislation when countries signed individual open skies agreements with the USA. Iatrou and Alamdari (2005) surveyed and reported on the expectations and perceived impacts of alliances. There is an expectation of a positive impact on traffic on a route as well as on the shares of the alliance members and these impacts will be greater if the participating airlines operate hub and spoke systems based at both the origin and the destination. In addition, these impacts are thought to reach fruition 'between 1 and 2 years of the inception of the partnerships' (Iatrou and Alamdari, 2005, p. 129) and will be greater from the inception of antitrust immunity. These findings were based on surveys of managers' opinions. These open skies agreements are shown in Table 15.1 for Europe (Pitfield, 2009b).

In Pitfield (2007b) a methodology was used to see if these opinions were empirically founded in evidence of changes in market share or total passengers on the routes. No such evidence was found but the methodology used may well be appropriate to deal with the issue of the counterfactual in passenger numbers in the assessment of the EU–US Agreement. If the first application of the model can produce good fit for the period before any interventions, then the significance of those interventions when added to the model will demonstrate their contribution. It was suggested that this methodology could address the significance of the change in passenger numbers attributable to the EU–US Open Skies Agreement. The conclusion of the assessment of alliances was that,

Table 15.1 The European Open Skies bilaterals[1]

Country	Date
Netherlands	14/10/92
Belgium[2]	1/3/95
Finland	24/3/95
Denmark	26/4/95
Norway	26/4/95
Sweden	26/4/95
Luxembourg	6/6/95
Austria	14/6/95
Czech Republic	8/12/95
Germany[3]	29/2/96
Italy[4]	11/11/98
Portugal	22/12/99
Malta	12/10/00
Poland	31/5/01
France	19/10/01

Source: Button (2008) repeated in Button (2009).

Notes
1   The full list for the US is at US Department of State (2009).
2,3 Provisional.
4   Comity and Reciprocity.

It is hard to see how these results can be viewed as compatible with the views of the Brattle Group (2002) that the spread of open skies agreements will increase transatlantic traffic. Open skies agreements do not seem to result in either a significant growth in traffic or in increased competition. Indeed, the strength of the alliances could act as a barrier to entry, contrary to the rhetoric that surrounds open skies policies.

(Pitfield, 2007b: 201)

2 The need to assess Open Skies agreements

Several industry-oriented meetings have been set up to discuss the EU–US Open Skies Agreement and the impending advent of the policy led to some considerable research effort by consultancies for the EU by Brattle (2002) and Booz Allen Hamilton (2007). These works, along with the more emotive views of the industry, including those of airlines and regulators, are summarised in Pitfield (2009a, 2009b) and a special issue of the *Journal of Air Transport Management* contains some of the key papers from the AirNeth conferences held in anticipation of the Agreement in Belgium in 2008, for example, Button (2009) and Humphreys and Morrell (2009).

Brattle and Booz Allen Hamilton were both anticipating an open aviation area but the actual Agreement was implemented, subject to a suspension clause, short of the items that motivated that clause, that is, the absence of full ownership and full cabotage rights.

Indeed, the main provisions summarised in Pitfield (2009a, 2009b) are:

- Removal of restrictions on route rights – any EU airline is allowed to fly from any EU city to any US city. Conversely, any US airline can fly into any EU airport and from there onto third destinations. In addition, EU airlines can fly between the US and non-EU countries that are members of ECAA, the European Common Aviation Area, such as Norway and Croatia. The unequal treatment of cabotage is an issue; although US airlines can fly onwards in Europe, EU airlines cannot fly domestically in the US.
- Foreign ownership – the main change here is that US companies can now only own 49 per cent of the voting rights in European Airlines, whereas European Airlines can still hold only 25 per cent in US airlines, although they can own more in non-voting shares. It is the intransigence of the US position here, as well as on cabotage, that has led first to a delay in the implementation of the Agreement and then the EU's right to suspend the Agreement if insufficient progress towards a revised Agreement is made by mid-2010.

Whereas the earlier work on alliances was concerned just with passenger numbers attributable to a change in the regulatory environment, the assessments suggested by these two reports covers not only the resultant passenger numbers, that can be assessed in a similar way as before, but also the changes in airline costs, competition and cooperation. The passenger numbers can be a result of a stimulation of demand following the fall in output restrictions or to a fall in prices due to a fall in costs due to a stimulus to efficiency. Prices may also fall due to increased cooperation, although this lessening of market power may be less easy to see. To the extent that all these things happen, subject to estimates of price elasticity, there is a rise in consumer surplus. Clearly these issues are of some policy significance.

It is obvious that attributing any change in passenger numbers to these causes is difficult. In the first instance, just identifying passenger growth due to the Agreement is important. In addition, to deal with the other issues requires better information on airline costs, on fare variations and their causes as well as to account for the counterfactual. It may well be the case that our ambitions must be limited to the assessment of passenger numbers and this is the subject of the empirical part of this chapter.

3 The approach to assessment

The difficulties with costs and fares data are dealt with in Pitfield (2009a, 2009b). In short, cost data is lacking, except at a periodicity that does not tie in with passenger data and then only for larger airlines. No data is regularly gathered on changes in fares offered on transatlantic flights and to derive elasticities would require linking this to demand. Passenger data for the affected north Atlantic sector is kept by the US Bureau of Transportation statistics and is freely available online from 1990.

It seems that assessment of the impact is largely hampered by the absence of relevant data. The exception is passengers. However, to attribute the change in passengers to the Agreement means that the counterfactual needs to be addressed. What would the traffic have been if the EU–US Agreement had not been signed? If that can be determined, then the difference between this and the actual traffic is that due to the Agreement. A time series model, given the monthly periodicity of the data, is appropriate and the long time history from 1990 is helpful.

The approach is to model the passenger data up to the start of the Agreement and then to allow for an intervention variable to capture the additional effect of the Agreement. This variable can be specified as a short, sharp shock, as it was when the impact of Ryanair start-ups was investigated (Pitfield, 2007a), or as a gradual term when impacts of alliance formation were investigated (Pitfield, 2007b). To avoid confounding influences, despite the fact that the time period covered is nearly 20 years and will contain a variety of economic peaks and troughs, specific allowance will be made for the events of September 2001 as well as the current global downturn. Past experience suggests that the former will again be found to be immediately influential whereas the latter may not for the reasons addressed in this paragraph although its impact at the time of writing is short in the time series data and it may be longer in its actual impact than previous recessions since 1990 that are embodied in the variations in the data since 1990.

4 An overview of ARIMA modelling and goodness-of-fit

Wei (1994) contains an introduction to ARIMA modelling, intervention analysis and the assessment of the fit of the model to the data. Another very useful guide is McDowell et al. (1980). In a variety of publications, including Pitfield (2007a, 2007b, 2008), the author has used these techniques in air transport applications so the following description is bound to owe something to these previous papers.

Acceptable goodness-of-fit statistics will be generated by a model and the residuals will be white noise if the model replicates the main movements in the data. In this case, all the indigenous factors that cause the original data to vary will be covered by the model.

ARIMA models are described by three parameters, (p,d,q). p is the order of a vector of autoregressive parameters $AR(p)$, d is the degree of differencing and q refers to the order of a vector of moving average parameters, $MA(q)$. So an ARIMA(1,0,0) or AR(1) model can be written as

$$Y_t = \varphi_1 Y_{t-1} + a_t \tag{1}$$

and using the backshift operator, $B\ Y_t = Y_{t-1}$

$$(1 - \varphi_1 B)Y_t = a_t \tag{2}$$

where Y_t is the time series data and a_t is the disturbance or random shock at time t. There is a tendency to favour parsimonious models as well as to avoid some mixed models which may suffer from parameter redundancy (McDowell *et al.*, 1980).[3]

It may be necessary to difference the data Y_t to ensure stationarity. If so a (1,1,0) model results and Y_t is replaced by $z_t = Y_t - Y_{t-1}$ and the backshift operator now is in terms of z_t as B $z_t = z_{t-1}$

If the model has a seasonal component, for example, if the data is gathered over a long period of time and is recorded for short intervals within this period as it is for the data used here, then it will be necessary to specify a seasonal ARIMA model. These are also described by three parameters (P,D,Q)S where P is the order of a seasonal autoregressive vector, D is the degree of seasonal differencing and Q refers to the order of a vector of moving average parameters. S is equal to 12 as the data is monthly with an annual periodicity. So a SAR(1) or Seasonal ARIMA(1,0,0)12 model can be written as

$$Y_t = \Phi_{12} Y_{t-12} + a_t \tag{3}$$

and using the backshift operator, B^{12}, which as it is raised to a power involves repeating it,

$$(1 - \Phi_{12} B^{12})\, Y_t = a_t \tag{4}$$

If seasonal differencing is required, then this model is applied to the seasonal differences, $w_t = Y_t - Y_{t-12}$.

Combining the two model components multiplicatively, gives an ARIMA(p,d,q)(P,D,Q)S model which can be generally represented as

$$\varphi_P(B^S)\, \Phi_p(B)(1 - B)^d(1 - B^S)^D z_t = \theta_q(B)\, \Theta_Q(B^S) a_t \tag{5}$$

Variations can be derived from (5), for example an ARIMA (1,1,0)(1,1,0)12 is applied to the regularly and seasonally differenced data where

$$w_t = z_t - z_{t-12} = (Y_t - Y_{t-1}) - (Y_{t-12} - Y_{t-13})$$

and is given by

$$w_t = \varphi_1 w_{t-1} + \Phi_{12} w_{t-12} - \varphi_1 \Phi_{12} w_{t-13} + a_t \tag{6}$$

and using the backshift operators, B and B^{12} now applied to w_t

$$(1 - \varphi_1 B)(1 - \Phi_{12} B^{12}) w_t = a_t \tag{7}$$

Inspection of the Autocorrelation Coefficient Function (ACF) and Partial Auto-correlation Coefficient Function (PACF) determine p,d,q and P,D,Q as indicated above, although it is the consensus that this process is as much art as science.

For the monthly traffic data a model is calibrated, including seasonal components, as this is appropriate for this data.

The procedures followed for calibrating the passenger data model is described below. For the monthly data, from 1990, to ensure that the series has a constant variance a logarithmic transformation may be necessary. ACF and PACF plots are examined at 12-month lags to establish whether seasonal differencing is required. The ACF and PACF plots are then used to determine whether an AR or MA model is appropriate along with the number of parameters, with a preference to avoid some mixed models and those with a large number of parameters. ACF and PACF plots are then calculated again for the residuals of this model to see what the non-seasonal form is and whether non-seasonal differencing is required. The residuals from this combined model must have white noise residuals. This will be shown by the Box–Ljung Q statistics and the ACF of the residuals.

The model is determined for the data before the commencement of the Agreement, then the same model form, plus intervention variables, is applied to the whole data series to establish the impact on the total series of the start of the Agreement or the start of BA's *Open Skies* service. This can then be compared to the actual size of the passenger numbers and inferences can be drawn on the impact of the start of service. A picture of a BA *Open Skies* Boeing 757 in this livery is shown landing at New York John F. Kennedy Airport (JFK) in December 2008 in Figure 15.1.

Figure 15.1 BA *Open Skies* Boeing 757.

An abrupt step function is used initially for the intervention term even though it might take a variety of forms, for example, individual pulses or gradual interventions. Other forms are subsequently investigated if intervention effects are hard to estimate. These resulting coefficients are then properly interpreted as representing the impact on the whole time series. It is also necessary to cater for the impact of any other exogenous impacts on the data and this is done for the terrorist attacks of 9/11 where it is obvious that the effects are marked as well as the recent global economic downturn, although the start date for this could be the subject of a debate.

Visual inspection is sufficient to ensure that the model replicates the cycles in the data, given that the residuals are white noise but the assessment of the general applicability of the fit requires a formal assessment and this can be undertaken using the root mean square error. This is

$$\text{RMSE} = \sqrt{1/T \sum_{t=1}^{T} (Y_t^s - Y_t^a)^2} \tag{8}$$

where Y_t^s = forecast value of Y_t

Y_t^a = the actual values and T = time periods

Comparison between model fits is difficult as this statistic is influenced by the absolute scale of the errors. Theil's inequality coefficient, U, is used to counteract this difficulty as the denominator of the coefficient corrects for differences in scale.

$$U = \sqrt{1/T \sum_{t=1}^{T} (Y_t^s - Y_t^a)^2} \Big/ \sqrt{1/T \sum_{t=1}^{T} (Y_t^s)^2} + \sqrt{1/T \sum_{t=1}^{T} (Y_t^a)^2} \tag{9}$$

In addition, it can be broken down into the bias, the variance and the covariance proportions of U where U^M is an indication of systematic error, U^S indicates the ability of the model to replicate the degree of variability in the data and U^C shows the unsystematic error.

$$U^M = (\bar{Y}^s - \bar{Y}^a)^2 \Big/ (1/T) \sum (Y_t^s - Y_t^a)^2 \tag{10}$$

$$U^S = (\sigma_s - \sigma_a)^2 \Big/ (1/T) \sum (Y_t^s - Y_t^a)^2 \tag{11}$$

$$U^C = 2(1-\rho)\sigma_s\sigma_a \Big/ (1/T) \sum (Y_t^s - Y_t^a)^2 \tag{12}$$

U^M, U^S and U^M sum to 1 and ideally, U^M, $U^S = 0$ and $U^c = 1$ (Pindyck and Rubinfeld, 1998).

In addition, Stationary R-Squared and Normalised Bayesian Information Criterion (Normalised BIC) are shown. The former has a range of negative infinity to 1 with positive values showing that the stationary part of the model is superior to a simple mean baseline model.[4] The Normalised BIC is a measure of overall fit that also accounts for model complexity so it is useful for examining different models of a single series.[5]

5 Empirical studies

5.1 Supply side changes

The abrupt changes at London Heathrow (LHR) between 2007 and 2008 were first shown by Cole (2008) and reproduced in Pitfield (2009a, 2009b). The interest of the US carriers in gaining access to such an important, if slot constrained hub, are well known and the changes reflect that. These are illustrated in Table 15.2 taken from Cole (2008). The jockeying for valued LHR slots by alliance partners is interesting and these often represent moves from London Gatwick (LGW) to LHR. In Figures 15.2 and 15.3 illustrations are made of the planned slot allocations in 2009.

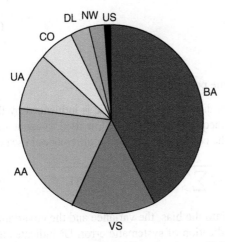

Figure 15.2 LHR–US airline slot shares, 2009.

Table 15.2 Sources of Open Skies slots

Airline	Slots
Air France	Reduced Paris from 12 to 7 per day: 3 to DL, 1 CO, 1 AF to Los Angeles (LAX)
KLM	Dropped 2 to Eindhoven (EIN) and reduced Rotterdam (RTM) by 1: Funded Northwest's (NW) Detroit (DET), Minneapolis (MSP), Seattle (SEA) Service as Skyteam partner
Alitalia	Dropped 3 at Milan Malpensa (MXP) as part of strategic retrenchment: 1 to CO, 1 to US Airways (US) and 1 BA
GB Airways	Sold LHR slots: 2 to CO, 1 to BA, 1 to Qatar Airways (QR)
Iberia	Dropped 1 to Bilbao (BIO): Funded 2nd AA Dallas (DFW) move to LHR from LGW

Source: Cole (2008).

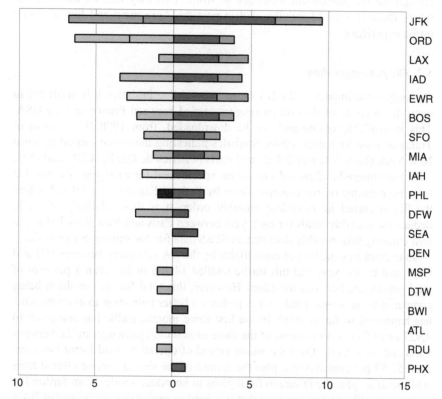

Figure 15.3 LHR–US: US airports served by airline and daily frequency, 2009.

As a result of examining these changes and the frequencies offered the most important candidate routes for assessment by volume are London (Heathrow, Gatwick, Stansted and Luton, respectively LHR, LGW, STN, LTN)–New York (Kennedy and Newark, JFK, EWR), London–Chicago (O'Hare and Midway, ORD, MDW), London–Los Angeles (LAX) and London–Washington Dulles (IAD).[6] In each case the total traffic at origin city and destination city must be addressed to cover cases where flights are switched, say between LHR and LGW or between JFK or EWR.

Further, a similar approach could be taken to investigate the impact of Virgin America (VX) that set up in August 2007 as a result of the ownership changes in the Agreement and operates between western and eastern seaboard cities in the USA. At present the airports served are LAX, San Diego (SAN), San Francisco (SFO), Las Vegas (LAS), JFK, IAD and Seattle (SEA).

In addition the BA initiative of setting up a new subsidiary airline, first in Paris and then in AMS can also be assessed. It is this venture that is the empirical focus of the chapter, and Paris is concentrated on as the AMS service finished in August 2009 so the length of service post the Agreement may not be long enough for the assessment technique to work. This may also be true of Paris where there is only 12 months of data post the Agreement and less of actual traffic experience.

5.2 *The passenger data*

To analyse the impact of the BA *Open Skies* airline initiative it is necessary to avail the analysis of data on passengers carried between France and the USA. This is available online and can be downloaded, from 1990 (US Bureau of Transportation Statistics, 1990). Statistics indicating the traffic carried between New York (both JFK and EWR) and Paris (Charles de Gaulle, CDG and Orly, ORY) are filtered and pasted into a new spreadsheet for each year. Flights that have no passengers, for example those by Federal Express, are deleted before the file is sorted in ascending monthly order. It is then relatively trivial to deduce the monthly totals for each year between Paris and New York before, in turn entering this monthly data into an SPSS data file for subsequent analysis.

June 2008 saw the first of these flights by the BA subsidiary between JFK and ORY and by the year end this traffic totalled 14,406 or less than 1 per cent of total passengers between the cities. However, this total for six months is being compared to an annual total so it is perhaps a better indication to examine what has happened so far in 2009. In the first three months traffic has amounted to 4,927 and this is 1.49 per cent of the three-month total passenger traffic between Paris and New York. Over the whole period of operation, load factor has averaged 51.59 per cent and this, plus the demise of the similar service offered from AMS to JFK, plus the failure to fulfil plans to introduce service from further EU major cities, like Milan, suggests that it is hard to expect that the impact of BA's *Open Skies* has been significant, but a time series analysis with intervention analysis will determine this.

Figure 15.4 shows the monthly passenger traffic from 1990 to the first quarter of 2009 between Paris and New York. It can be seen that traffic has a cyclical pattern over each year peaking in the summer months and declining in winter. Initially this variation was large and it has declined over the period. Peaks have tended to rise from about early 2002 and troughs have been less steep over much of the period.

5.3 *The results of the assessment*

The procedures outlined in section 4 were followed. Preliminary analysis reveals that there are outliers in the series, most notably in late 2001, so the need to explicitly model 9/11 is empirically justified. The interpretation of the ACF and PACF plots suggests alternative models as appropriate to the data up to September 2001 and indeed, it is not clear that a logarithmic transformation is required to ensure a constant variance, so there are a variety of models that are alternatively specified in terms of passengers or the logarithm of passengers. These include (2,0,1) (1,0,0)12, and (1,0,0) (0,1,1)12 on the original data and on the

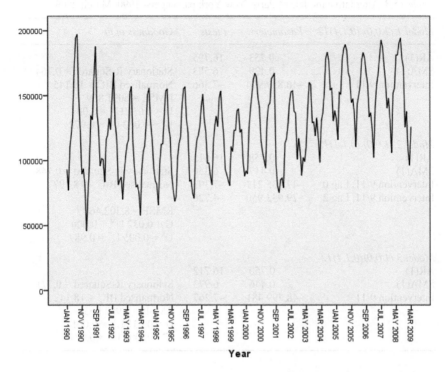

Figure 15.4 Paris–New York passenger traffic by month, January 1990–March 2009.

logarithmic transformations. The goodness-of-fit statistics and the relative parsimony along with the ACF of the residuals suggest the latter form is the preferred model applied to the original data with no constant term.

Applying the intervention variables yields no significant impacts for the Open Skies Agreement, BA's start-up of *Open Skies* in Paris or of the current economic downturn.[7] This is true whether these interventions are specified as steps, exponential increases, or pulses.[8]

The impact of the terrorist attacks in 2001 is significant and alternative specifications indicate marginally different impacts. The coefficient of $-46,859.97$ ($t = -7.366$) indicates an abrupt drop in passengers when a continuous step change is specified. Compared to September the year before, this is a 31 per cent fall. If this intervention is allowed to have lagged impacts specified, then at lag 0 there is a decline of $47,135.21$ ($t = -7.393$) and at lag 2, in November 2001, there is a further impact of $-29,933.95$ ($t = -4.726$). Although the goodness-of-fit of this model is slightly inferior, Table 15.3 shows the results for both of these models (Model 1 and Model 2). It also shows the best results from specifying the 2001 intervention as a simple pulse that gives the best overall goodness-of-fit statistics (Model 3). The intervention is then $-48,799.48$ with a slightly reduced $t = -7.267$.

Table 15.3 Alternative models of Paris–New York passengers, 1990–March 2009

Model 1 (1,0,0) (0,1,1)12	Parameters	t tests	Goodness of fit
AR(1)	0.753	16.795	
SMA(1)	0.429	6.583	Stationary R-Squared = 0.764
Intervention 9/11	−46,859.974	−7.366	Normalised BIC = 18.145
			RMSE = 8091.859
			U = 0.031 U^M = 0.004
			U^S = 0.002 U^C = 0.972
Model 2 (1,0,0) (0,1,1)12			
AR(1)	0.758	16.615	
SMA(1)	0.417	6.350	Stationary R-Squared = 0.748
Intervention 9/11, Lag 0	−47,135.211	−7.393	Normalised BIC = 18.197
Intervention 9/11, Lag 2	−29,933.950	−4.726	
			RMSE = 8,302.462
			U = 0.032 U^M = 0.000
			U^S = 0.005 U^C = 0.987
Model 3 (1,0,0)(0,1,1)12			
AR(1)	0.750	16.712	
SMA(1)	0.446	6.973	Stationary R-Squared = 0.771
Intervention 9/11	−48,799.481	−7.267	Normalised BIC = 18.142
			RMSE = 7,982.063
			U = 0.031 U^M = 0.001
			U^S = 0.001 U^C = 0.971

Figure 15.5 shows the ACF plot of the residuals from Model 3, Table 15.3. It can be seen that these are white noise as they are within the confidence levels for all lags shown. Figure 15.6 demonstrates that this model also replicates the turning movements of the original series while its goodness-of-fit is demonstrated by the statistics given in Table 15.3.

The model fit could be improved if another intervention variable were allowed to account for the level shift outlier identified in November 2003. Investigating this month in some detail shows New York–Paris traffic at 62,668 of which Air France carried 28,476 and the US carriers, Delta, Continental and American carried 23,477. The difference is the passengers carried by Air India. Paris–New York totals 56,391 of which Air France has 26,591, the US airlines, 22,197 with the balance due to Air India. It may be that the shift is due to Air India's operation. However, this started in December 2002 and so it may be, but this seems unlikely that comparing the two Novembers gives rise to the outlier and, if this is the case, an intervention term should be specified for December 2002, not November 2003. Traffic between the two Novembers differed by 18,230.

6 Conclusions

The intervention analysis here failed to find a significant effect of the start of service of BA's *Open Skies* airline from Orly, but given the scale of the

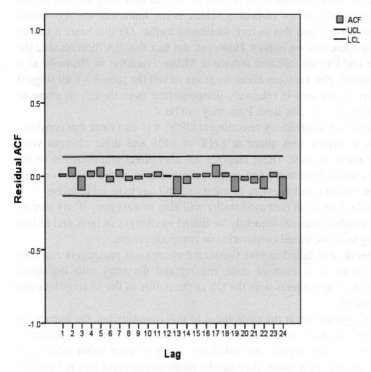

Figure 15.5 Residual ACF from Model 3, Table 2.

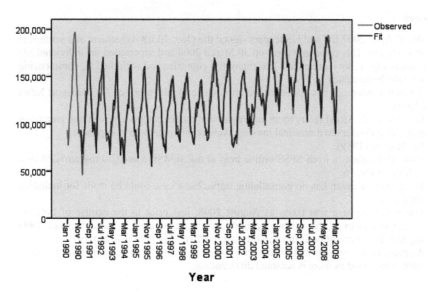

Figure 15.6 Paris–New York passenger traffic by month, January 1990–March 2009.

Paris–New York traffic and its relative size, as well as how long the service has been in operation, this is not surprising. There is no doubt that the Agreement facilitated this service and this in turn facilitated traffic. On this basis it cannot be argued that there was no impact. However, the fact that BA discontinued the AMS service and has not initiated service at Milan, Frankfurt or Brussels, as it originally planned, plus rumours about its desire to sell the subsidiary all suggest that the degree of success is relatively disappointing even though its share of high-yielding business traffic from Paris may not be.

In addition to BA's subsidiary operating at ORY, it is also clear that considerable changes in supply took place at LHR in 2008 and these changes were largely maintained in 2009. These changes are also directly attributable to the EU–US Open Skies Agreement and empirical estimation of the impact on passenger numbers from London to key destinations still has to be undertaken.

Considerable changes in data availability will also be necessary if any change in passenger numbers can subsequently be linked to changes in fares and airline costs resulting from increased cooperation or competitiveness.

Previous work also failed to find significant changes in passengers and alliance market share as a result of code sharing and the entry into individual country open-skies agreements with the US so the nature of the findings here are consistent with this.

Although they were never the main focus of this investigation, the impacts of September 2001 can be seen to vary depending on the model and variable specification. However, the impacts are relatively close to each other whichever model is chosen and, as a result, they can be taken to represent a robust indication of the impact, which is considerable.

Notes

1 On 30 April 2007 EU and US leaders signed the Open Skies Agreement at a summit in Washington. This came into force on 30 March 2008 and superseded the individual EU country Open Sky Agreements that many EU countries had with the US, commencing with the Netherlands in 1992.
2 A recent conference has discussed the importance of alliances, see Air Transport News (2009).
3 In Table 15.3, AR(1) refers to an autoregressive model component with one parameter and SMA(1) refers to a seasonal moving average one-parameter component.
4 See Harvey (1989).
5 This information is from SPSS online help at mk:@MSITStore:C:\Program%20Files\ SPSSInc\SPSS16.
6 Washington Reagan has no transatlantic traffic but a case could be made for including Baltimore.
7 The start date here was taken as August 2008, just prior to the demise of Lehman Brothers. However, the various economic cycles contained in the data since 1990 suggest this intervention is unnecessary irrespective of its start date or form.
8 As there is no non-seasonal differencing, steps and pulses can be examined. The constant is excluded as there is seasonal differencing.

References

Air Transport News (2009) *The Importance of Airline Alliances Conference*, Beijing, China, September 2009 at www.airtransportnews.aero/print_analysis.pl?id=779.

Brattle Group (2002) *The Economic Impact of an EU–US Open Aviation Area*, Washington, DC: Brattle Group.

Booz Allen Hamilton (2007) *The Economic Impacts of an Open Aviation Area between the EU and the US*, Brussels: European Commission, TREN/05/MD/S07.5260.

Button, K.J. (2008) The Impact of EU–US 'Open Skies' Agreement on Airline Market Structures and Airline Networks. Paper presented to Airneth workshop on the implications of the EU–US Open Sky Agreement, 6 March 2008, The Hague.

Button, K.J. (2009) The impact of EU–US 'Open Skies' Agreement on Airline Market Structures and Airline Networks, *Journal of Air Transport Management*, 15, 59–71.

Cole, J. (2008) Implementing EU–US Open Skies at Heathrow. Paper presented at the Airneth second annual conference 'EU–US Open Skies: Competition and change in the worldwide aviation market', 17 April 2008, The Hague.

Eichinger, A., Drotleff, W. and Fongern, T.A. (2009) Muted Reactions – Assessing the Impact of the EU/US Open Skies Agreement. Paper presented at the 13th ATRS World Conference, Abu Dhabi, UAE, 27–30 June 2009.

Harvey, A.C. (1989) *Forecasting, Structural Time Series Models and the Kalman Filter*, Cambridge: Cambridge University Press.

Humphreys, B. and Morrell, P. (2009) The Potential Impacts of the EU/US Open Skies Agreement: What will happen at Heathrow after spring 2008, *Journal of Air Transport Management*, 15, 72–77.

Iatrou, K. and Alamdari, F. (2005) The Empirical Analysis of the Impact of Alliances on Airline Operations, *Journal of Air Transport Management*, 11, 127–134.

McDowall, D., McCleary, R., Meidinger, E.E. and Hay, R.A. (1980) *Interrupted Time Series Analysis*, Beverley Hills: Sage Publications.

Pindyck, R.S. and Rubinfeld, D.L. (1998) *Econometric Models and Economic Forecasts*, London: McGraw Hill.

Pitfield, D.E. (2007a) Ryanair's Impact on Airline Market Share from the London Area Airports: A time series analysis, *Journal of Transport Economics and Policy*, 41, 75–92.

Pitfield, D.E. (2007b) The impact on traffic, market shares and concentration of airline alliances on selected European–US routes, *Journal of Air Transport Management*, 13, 192–202.

Pitfield, D.E. (2008) The Southwest Effect: A time series analysis on passengers carried by selected routes and a market share comparison, *Journal of Air Transport Management*, 14, 113–122.

Pitfield, D.E. (2009a) The EU–US Open Skies Agreement: How can its impact be assessed? Paper presented at the 13th ATRS World Conference, Abu Dhabi, UAE, 27–30 June 2009.

Pitfield, D.E. (2009b) The Assessment of the EU–US Open Skies Agreement: The counterfactual and other difficulties, *Journal of Air Transport Management*, 15, 308–314.

US Bureau of Transportation Statistics (all dates from 1990), Air Carriers:T100 – International Segment (All Carriers) at www.transtats.bts.gov/Fields.asp?Table_ID=261.

US Department of State (2009) at www.state.gov/e/eeb/rls/othr/ata/114805.htm.

Wei, W.S. (1994) *Time Series Analysis: Univariate and Multivariate Methods*, Redwood, CA: Addison-Wesley.

16 The impact of North Atlantic passenger services on airports

Anne Graham

1 Introduction

It is the aim of this chapter to assess the impact that recent aviation developments on the North Atlantic route have had on airports. Only passenger services
are being considered. The North Atlantic is the largest inter-regional route in the
world, accounting for around a quarter of all inter-regional traffic. According to
the International Air Transport Association (IATA) in 2008 435 billion revenue
passenger kilometres (RPKs) were flown on this route which was 13 per cent of
all global domestic and international traffic (IATA, 2009a). Eurostat (2009)
reported that there were about 60 million transatlantic passengers in 2007, with
over 50 million on US routes. Twenty-two million passengers, representing one-
third of the total transatlantic traffic, flew on routes to and from the UK.

There have been a number of important events related to the North Atlantic
route in recent years. The terrorist attacks of 9/11 and subsequent developments
such as the Iraq War in 2003 and the outbreak of SARS in the Far East meant
that the first years of the twenty-first century were very uncertain ones for North
Atlantic services. Demand hardly grew and many airlines focused on cost reduction and cutting capacity. It was not until 2004 that the industry entered into a
period of recovery and that an overall growth trend returned. It is from this time
until the current date that is the focus here.

In the next section an overview of North Atlantic traffic characteristics is provided. This is followed by an assessment of how this traffic is dispersed, particularly between major hubs such as London Heathrow, Paris, Frankfurt and
Amsterdam and other smaller secondary cities and regional airports. Special
attention is given to the UK and Germany which are the two most important
transatlantic markets. Next, consideration is given to the influence on airports of
more specialist airline operations. First, premium traffic services are explored,
which have become particularly relevant since Concorde ceased operating from
the UK and France to the US in 2003. Second, developments associated with
low-fare leisure traffic, provided both by charters and low-cost carriers (LCCs),
are investigated. This is followed by an assessment of the most significant regulatory change of recent years, namely the EU–US 'open skies' agreement which
came into force in March 2008. Conclusions are then drawn with consideration

of prospects for the future, both with regard to the major short-term problems associated with the effects of the credit crunch and the severe economic recession which the industry now faces, and also the more long term.

2 Traffic overview

Figure 16.1 shows annual RPKs on the North Atlantic route since 2000. The impact of 9/11 in 2001 and SARS and the Iraq War in 2003 can clearly be observed with the growth not returning until 2004. Up until mid-2008, there was a steady increase in traffic but then traffic began to fall and evidence from the Association of European Airlines (AEA) (albeit that this just covers European carriers) showed a decline of 6.9 per cent for the first eight months of 2009 compared to the previous year (AEA, 2009). Premium traffic on the North Atlantic, which globally accounts for a fifth of this type of demand and close to a third of all revenues, was particularly depressed during this period and showed a decline of 15 per cent (IATA, 2009b).

Figure 16.2 shows that traffic to and from the UK accounts for around a third of the total US traffic, followed by Germany with a market of about half this size. No other European country has a market share of greater than around 10 per cent. At most European airports transatlantic passengers make up less than 10 per cent of the total passenger traffic (Table 16.1). The exceptions are the major airports of London Heathrow, Paris Charles de Gaulle, Frankfurt and Amsterdam. This is partly as a result of the three major European carriers (BA, Air France-KLM, Lufthansa) consolidating their services at their major hubs whilst the other European carriers tend to concentrate more on serving niche city-pairs. An unusual airport is Shannon airport in Ireland where North Atlantic

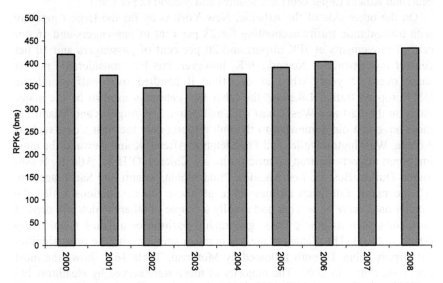

Figure 16.1 Passenger traffic on the North Atlantic 2000–2008 (source: Boeing (2009)).

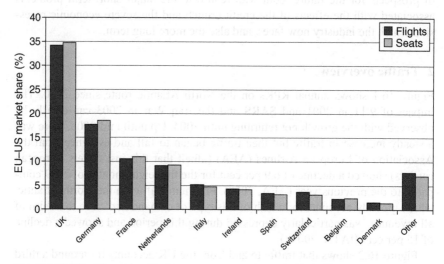

Figure 16.2 EU–US services by country – summer season 2008 (source: OAG/anna.aero).

traffic has traditionally accounted for a significant share of the total traffic because regulatory requirements up until 2008 made it obligatory for carriers to make a stopover at this airport. Since the average aircraft size for transatlantic services tends to be larger than that used for the higher volume of short-haul flights (albeit that the average size of aircraft across the Atlantic has been decreasing) these flights account for a smaller proportion of total aircraft movements, for example Frankfurt (8 per cent), Amsterdam (6 per cent), Zurich (5 per cent) and Athens (3 per cent) and Munich and Madrid (2 per cent).

On the other side of the Atlantic, New York is by far the largest gateway with transatlantic traffic accounting for 28 per cent of passengers and 16 per cent of movements at JFK airport and 20 per cent of passengers and 10 per cent of movements at Newark. JFK, however, has lost considerable market share over the years when at one time it handled over half of all the US–European traffic. Likewise the other key gateways used to be the major cities on the East and West Coast such as Boston, Los Angeles and Miami but these have lost out somewhat to the hub airports near the East Coast such as Atlanta, Washington Dulles and Philadelphia. After JFK and Newark, the most important airports for transatlantic traffic are Chicago O'Hare, Atlanta, Washington Dulles, Boston, Los Angeles, Philadelphia, Miami and San Francisco. All the major European airlines serve all these ten destinations whilst the smaller ones serve New York and usually a couple of others which will depend on factors such as ethnic links, geographic position or alliance membership (Dennis, 2007). The Canadian market is much smaller with the most significant airport being Toronto followed by Montreal. Table 16.2 shows the most important routes in 2007. The majority of these were served by Heathrow but there were also two routes from Paris.

At the major EU airports, there is a high proportion of connecting passengers. For example at the UK airports of Heathrow, Gatwick and Manchester, only 49 per cent of all transatlantic passengers in 2005 were on point-to-point services. A further 27 per cent had connections at the UK airports, 17 per cent at the North American airports and 7 per cent at both ends (CAA, 2007a). On certain routes the proportion of international transfers may approach or even exceed 50 per cent. For example in 2006 the Detroit route had 64 per cent international

Table 16.1 Transatlantic passenger traffic by major European airports 2008

Airport	Transatlantic passengers (000s)	Total passengers (000s)	Transatlantic market share (%)
London LHR	15,132	67,055	22.6
Paris CDG	8,621	60,875	14.2
Frankfurt	8,076	53,192	15.2
Amsterdam	5,885	47,430	12.4
London LGW	3,378	34,206	9.9
Munich	2,094	34,421	6.1
Manchester	1,896	21,219	8.9
Dublin	1,748	23,467	7.4
Madrid	1,707	50,526	3.4
Zurich	1,628	22,044	7.4
Rome FCO (*)	1,307	32,947	4.0
Brussels	1,220	18,480	6.6
Copenhagen	787	21,530	3.7
Dusseldorf	774	18,103	4.3
Barcelona	635	30,250	2.1
Milan MXP	590	19,014	3.1
Shannon	575	3,170	18.1
Athens	558	16,376	3.4
Stockholm	512	19,992	2.6
Glasgow	412	8,179	5.0

Sources: Airport websites and annual reports.

Note
(*) 2007.

Table 16.2 Major transatlantic passenger routes 2007

		Passengers (000s)	Flights (000s)
London Heathrow	New York JFK	2,839	13.5
Paris Charles de Gaulle	New York JFK	1,729	9.6
London Heathrow	Chicago	1,605	8.5
London Heathrow	Los Angeles	1,406	6.1
Paris Charles de Gaulle	Montreal	1,057	3.9
London Heathrow	Washington Dulles	1,055	5.4
London Heathrow	San Francisco	1,032	3.6
London Heathrow	Toronto	1,024	4.9
London Heathrow	Boston	889	4.3

Source: Eurostat (2009).

transfers, Montreal 51 per cent, Phoenix 49 per cent, Toronto 47 per cent and Vancouver 46 per cent (CAA, 2008). These transfer passengers may be going to another European country or somewhere much further such as India which is a popular ultimate origin/destination for such transfer traffic.

Clearly this transfer traffic has cost implications for airports. On the one hand certain passenger costs may be reduced because transfer passengers tend not to use landside areas. On the other hand they need specialist facilities, such as transfer baggage systems, which will push costs up. In terms of revenue generation, transfer passengers may often pay reduced passenger charges. At Amsterdam it is about 40 per cent of the normal passenger charge, at Frankfurt around 50 per cent, at Paris around 60 per cent, whilst at Heathrow airport there is no discount. Moreover, transfer passengers will not pay out money on commercial facilities such as car parking and car hire but they may be good spenders on the airside area if they have some time to wait for their connection. Another important factor as regards non-aeronautical revenue is that North American travellers tend to be rather low spenders overall on commercial facilities. This was well illustrated after 9/11 when average commercial spend per passenger at Heathrow airport actually went up due to the smaller proportion of North American travellers.

3 New route development

Whilst a considerable share of transatlantic traffic goes through the major European hubs, there has been a growth in new routes in recent years from smaller capital city airports and regional airports. One key development here has been the use of smaller and often narrowbody aircraft such as the Boeing 757 with around 170–200 seats which has been used to serve these thinner routes by some US carriers. Most notably Continental has developed a number of new routes using this aircraft into its Newark hub, for example from Barcelona, Oslo, Stockholm and a selection of UK and German regional points. Delta has also added services from UK and German airports and other destinations such as Nice and Venice into its Atlanta hub – this time by primarily shifting its 767s from domestic to international operations. All these services have been highly significant for the smaller airports and the surrounding area as they have given them a direct link into a US hub with many connecting possibilities. This is important as if such services do not feed into a hub or the major gateway of New York they are difficult to sustain unless there is some past migration patterns which will generate significant VFR traffic, as with the Canadian routes of Belfast to Toronto or Lyons to Montreal, or if they serve a major tourist destination such as Orlando.

Specifically in the UK between 2003 and 2006 the share of narrowbody aircraft from UK regional airports and the US increased from 12 per cent in 2003 to 44 per cent in 2006 (CAA, 2007). In 2003 there were 11 services which were daily or more from five UK airports but by 2007 this peaked at 20 services from 11 UK airports (Table 16.3). Continental's services to Edinburgh and Belfast International were considered important enough to justify assistance from the Route Development Fund which was financed by regional development agencies

Table 16.3 UK–US services at UK airports 2003–2009

	UK airports with US scheduled services	Airports served	Total US routes (with at least a daily service) at regional airports
2003	5	Heathrow, Gatwick, Manchester, Birmingham, Glasgow	11
2004	6	Heathrow, Gatwick, Manchester, Birmingham, Glasgow, Edinburgh	14
2005	9	Heathrow, Gatwick, Stansted, Manchester, Birmingham, Glasgow, Edinburgh, Belfast Int, Bristol	16
2006	9	Heathrow, Gatwick, Stansted, Manchester, Birmingham, Glasgow, Edinburgh, Belfast Int, Bristol	18
2007	11	Heathrow, Gatwick, Stansted, Luton, Manchester, Birmingham, Glasgow, Edinburgh, Belfast Int, Bristol, Liverpool	20
2008	10	Heathrow, Gatwick, Manchester, Stansted, Luton, Birmingham, Glasgow, Edinburgh, Belfast Int, Bristol	16
2009	10	Heathrow, Gatwick, Manchester, Stansted, Luton, Birmingham, Glasgow, Edinburgh, Belfast Int, Bristol	15

Sources: CAA (2007b), OAG.

with the aim of supporting services which helped promote business links or inbound tourism (Graham and Dennis, 2007). Overall the market share from the regional airports increased from 11 per cent in 2003 to 16 per cent in 2007 although this dropped back a little in 2008 because the 'open skies' agreement caused an increase in services from Heathrow and a few operations such as American's Boston–Manchester route were terminated. In the second biggest market, Germany, the regional airports have also increased their passenger market share from 17 per cent in 2003 to 30 per cent in 2008 (Table 16.4). This was the result of a number of new services such as Continental's 757 operations from Berlin and Hamburg in 2005 and Cologne/Bonn in 2006 (although discontinued in 2009). At Dusseldorf other additions included a new Delta Atlanta service in 2006 and a Northwest Detroit service in 2007 (although discontinued in 2009).

4 The impact of specialist airline services

4.1 Premium traffic

Since 1976 the key routes from JFK to Heathrow and Paris had been served by BA and Air France's Concorde operations. However, in 2000 the aircraft experienced its only major crash and this event combined with the traffic downturn in subsequent years, and steeply rising maintenance costs, meant that Concorde

Table 16.4 UK and German airport passenger market share 2003–2008 (per cent)

	2003	2004	2005	2006	2007	2008
UK						
Belfast Int	0	0	1	1	1	1
Birmingham	1	1	1	1	1	1
Edinburgh	0	0	1	1	1	1
Gatwick	22	21	21	21	21	16
Glasgow	2	2	2	3	2	2
Heathrow	67	65	64	64	63	70
Manchester	8	9	9	9	9	9
Other	0	0	1	1	2	1
Total	100	100	100	100	100	100
Germany						
Berlin Tegel	0	0	1	2	2	2
Cologne Bonn	0	0	0	1	1	1
Dusseldorf	2	2	3	4	5	7
Frankfurt	83	80	77	74	72	70
Hamburg	0	0	1	1	2	1
Munich	13	16	17	17	18	18
Stuttgart	2	2	1	1	1	1
Total	100	100	100	100	100	100

Sources: UK CAA and Destatis.

Note
Totals may not add up due to rounding.

was withdrawn from service in 2003 by both airlines. The retirement of these services created a fresh opportunity to look at premium traffic transatlantic services. Already in 2002 Lufthansa had contracted the Swiss-based airline Privatair to provide a six days a week premium service using the Boeing business jet on its behalf on the Dusseldorf–Newark route. Following the success of this it introduced similar services on the Munich–Newark and Dusseldorf–Chicago routes in 2003 and by 2009 Lufthansa only used Privatair on a few Middle Eastern and Indian destinations. However, Privatair also operated a premium service for Lufthansa's partner Swiss on the Zurich–Newark route and for Air France-KLM on the Amsterdam–Houston route.

Since these services are operated on behalf of the main carrier they face limited competition and can take advantage of all the marketing and alliance opportunities that these major airlines offer. They operate out of airports that already have transatlantic services and since the passenger volume is relatively low they only have marginal impacts on the airport. However, in the last few years there have been a number of other proposals for new premium services flying from alternative airports which could have had a more significant effect. For example, there were proposals for Blue Fox to fly from Stansted and Fly First from Luton. Also the airline City Star, which already linked Aberdeen with Norwegian oil-related destinations, proposed a business class flight from Aberdeen to Houston in 2008 but went out of business before this started.

There have been a few premium class airlines that have entered into service (Aviation Strategy, 2007). First to operate was EoS in October 2005 with a service from Stansted to JFK. It was joined at Stansted in November 2005 by MaxJet which also flew to JFK. MaxJet subsequently went on to serve Washington, Las Vegas and Los Angeles. Meanwhile at Luton airport, another premium class airline SilverJet started operations in January 2007 to Newark. Although the type of product and price varied for these three airlines, they all offered comfort and luxury away from the more crowded and congested terminals of Heathrow and Gatwick. However, they did not last, with MaxJet ceasing operations in December 2007 followed by EoS in April 2008 and SilverJet in May 2008. The weakness of the model was that frequencies were low, there were generally poor connections available and very few opportunities for back-up aircraft when problems arose. It was difficult for them to compete with the frequent flyer points and corporate travel policy discounts that the major airlines offered. Moreover, rising fuel prices, extra capacity due to the 'open skies' agreement, lack of available funding due to the credit crunch and a sharp decline in demand (particularly related to the large premium transatlantic market associated with the banking sector) brought additional problems to these carriers.

Figure 16.3 shows the passenger numbers carried on these services. At the peak in Autumn 2007 close to 30,000 monthly passengers were flying through Stansted and Luton although this was clearly rather minimal compared to the much higher monthly volumes of over one million passengers at Heathrow and over 300,000 passengers at Gatwick at the same time. Since these passengers had a much shorter check-in time than for normal long-haul passengers, this reduced the opportunity for generating commercial revenue from them at the shops and catering facilities. At Luton airport a dedicated terminal service was provided. This terminal, which was leased to Silverjet, was 10,000 square feet and could handle up to 200 passengers at any one time. It had its own dedicated security which allowed for 20-minute check-in without bags and a 45-minute check-in with bags. Check-in was undertaken at the passenger's own seat using a laptop. This terminal is currently empty.

Whilst the passenger numbers were small, the development of these specialist carriers undoubtedly had some influence on American Airlines' decision to return to Stansted after a number of years in October 2008 with a service to New York. This was short lived though as they pulled out in July 2009 blaming rocketing fuel prices and softening demand. Also competitive pressures from these new airlines are likely to have played some role in encouraging BA to announce in 2008 that it was to launch in 2009 a London City airport premium service to New York (which was actually a London airport which EoS was also considering for services) – particularly as it had lost its business market competitive edge somewhat since it retired Concorde. The service began in September 2009 and was the first time that London City had had a transatlantic service. BA has re-introduced Concorde's 001 and 002 flight numbers. BA is using an A318 and due to runway restrictions at London City the westbound flight is required to make a fuel stop at Shannon airport where passengers at the same time clear US immigration and customs. More generally the EU–US 'open skies' agreement has provided the possibility for carriers, such as BA and Virgin, to set up premium services from countries that they have previously not served. This is discussed later.

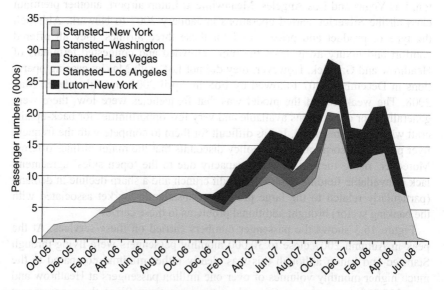

Figure 16.3 Monthly passenger traffic on Stansted and Luton routes to US, November 2005 to August 2008 (source: CAA).

4.2 Low-fare services

At the other end of the market are passengers who are travelling primarily for holiday or VFR reasons and are seeking a relatively low price service. Traditionally some of the holiday traffic was carried on charter traffic (although never as much as on European routes) but primarily because of regulatory reasons, both in Europe and Canada, most of these services have now become, or have been reclassified as, scheduled services. As a result, for example, on UK transatlantic routes charter traffic has fluctuated around just 3–5 per cent of total traffic since 2003. Nevertheless, most operations serving the leisure market still remain similar to charter services in a number of ways as they tend to be fairly low frequency, focused on point-to-point traffic and linked closely to tour operating activities. They are operated from both the major airports and the regions by airlines such as Air Canada and Air Transat in Canada, and Thomson/TUI, Thomas Cook, LTU and Eurofly in Europe.

There has also been the development of some new routes to serve this market which has given certain airports access to this traffic for the first time. Flyglobespan, a British airline which had previously served European leisure routes, began its first long-haul service from Glasgow to Orlando Sanford in 2006. Then in 2007 it added services from Glasgow to Boston and Liverpool to New York (the airport's first US route) but this route was discontinued after just six months. It operated services from a number of UK airports (Gatwick, Manchester, Edinburgh, Glasgow, Belfast) and Dublin to Canada and Orlando but failed in 2009. In 2005 Zoom Airlines Inc (a Canadian airline) began offering services for the leisure market between Canada and the UK and France and in 2007 a sister airline, Zoom Airlines Ltd, was set up in the UK and commenced flights from Gatwick to New York. In the summer of 2008 it expanded its services from Gatwick to San Diego and Fort Lauderdale but then in August of the same year the Zoom companies went out of business.

However, none of these services can be considered to be pure low-cost services as have been developed in Europe, for example with carriers such as easyJet and Ryanair. To date there are very few examples of long-haul low-cost services, with the notable examples of Jetstar, Air Asia X and the failed Oasis, and there has been considerable debate as to the feasibility of transferring the low-cost model to long-haul operations (Wensveen and Leick, 2009; Francis *et al.*, 2007). However, Ryanair did announce that it planned to offer services from Stansted and Dublin to destinations such as New York, Florida, Los Angeles, San Francisco and Boston with fares beginning at around $10 before taxes but as yet it has not introduced such services (BBC, 2008). The services would have been kept independent of Ryanair's short-haul services similar to AirAsia and AirAsia X operations. Ryanair also planned a premium cabin where the prices would be considerably higher. A distinct advantage that Ryanair would have over other airlines that have started services from Stansted or Luton where connecting services have not been possible, is that it may be able to pick up a considerable volume of self-connecting passengers flying into Stansted from other points in Ryanair's network.

5 The EU–US Open Skies Agreement

Whilst the mid-2000s saw some interesting developments as regards new routes and services, by far the most significant event was the signing in April 2007 of the 'open skies' agreement between the 27 EU member states and the US, following 11 rounds and over four years of extensive talks, which came into effect on 30 March 2008. All EU airlines are now able to operate direct flights to the US from anywhere in Europe and not just from their home country. All restrictions on routes, prices, or the number of weekly flights were removed. The ultimate objective of the European Commission is to have a transatlantic Open Aviation Area where there is a single air transport market between the EU and the US with free flows of investment and no restrictions on access to both domestic and international air services. Hence this 2007 agreement was just the first stage of wider negotiations which have already begun again (Ezard, 2008).

In the past, a number of regulatory changes have had major impacts on airports, most notably US domestic deregulation which led to increased domestic hub development and more recently European liberalisation which provided many regional airports with more opportunities to compete for direct European services. However, in this case the impact of EU–US open skies on airports seems likely to be less significant as the majority of European countries, with a few exceptions such as UK, Spain and Hungary, already had open skies bilateral agreements with the US. Moreover, in the UK, regional airports had been covered by virtual open skies conditions with the US for some time. Hence in reality the main effect of the new agreement was the opening up of Heathrow to additional carriers and services. Previously the 'Bermuda II' limitations (named after the Bermuda II UK–US bilateral agreement) meant that only two carriers from each country, namely BA and Virgin from the UK and American and United from the US, could operate transatlantic services from the airport. There were also some restrictions on the individual routes that could be flown. The new situation means that there are no longer any limits on the number of carriers or services offered.

Heathrow is generally considered to be a more attractive airport for transatlantic services than other London airports for a number of reasons. It has a larger catchment area, particularly for business traffic, there are greater connection opportunities and it is often perceived as being closer to Central London. However, much of its attraction comes from its ability to generate higher yields for the airlines rather than to just give access to additional passengers (Humphreys and Morrell, 2009). This is very much related to the higher share of business travellers using Heathrow. For example in 2008 37 per cent of passengers at Heathrow were flying for business purposes as opposed to only 16 per cent at Gatwick (CAA, 2009).

Table 16.5 shows the new routes that were launched at Heathrow when open skies came into effect at the end of March 2008. For the first time the four US carriers Continental, Delta, Northwest and US Airways had access to Heathrow and as a consequence a number of their Gatwick services were terminated or

Table 16.5 New US routes at Heathrow starting 30 March 2008

Carrier	US destination	Weekly frequency	Comment
American	Raleigh-Durham	7	Moved from Gatwick
American	Dallas-Fort Worth	14	Moved from Gatwick
British Airways	Houston	14	Moved from Gatwick
British Airways	Dallas-FW	7	Moved from Gatwick
Continental	Houston	14	Dropped 2nd daily flight from Gatwick
Continental	Newark	14	Dropped 3rd daily flight from Gatwick
Delta	Atlanta	7	
Delta	JFK	14	Dropped 2nd daily flight from Gatwick
Northwest	Minneapolis	7	Moved from Gatwick
Northwest	Detroit	7	
Northwest	Seattle	7	
United	Denver	7	
US Airways	Philadelphia	7	

Source: OAG.

reduced in frequency. BA and American also shifted some services from Gatwick. Overall in May 2008 25,500 daily seats were offered on flights from Heathrow to the US representing a 19 per cent increase from 21,500 in the previous year. The US airports to benefit the most from increased transatlantic capacity at Heathrow were Denver (115 per cent increase), Seattle (38 per cent), Atlanta (29 per cent), Philadelphia (29 per cent) and Newark (21 per cent). By contrast the seats offered at Gatwick fell by 33 per cent from 6,900 to 4,700 (Halstead, 2008). Hence Gatwick's position as a major transatlantic gateway, which had been protected by the previous Bermuda II bilateral agreement, was lost and now it is left with a smaller number of predominantly leisure-focused routes.

Table 16.6 shows the monthly traffic trends at Heathrow and Gatwick. The significant increase from April 2008 at Heathrow from both new services and from traffic which has been shifted from Gatwick can clearly be seen. Traffic at Heathrow continued to grow all year in 2008 although the substantial decreases in the later months at Gatwick, primarily due to the economic recession starting to bite, meant that overall a loss in traffic from London was recorded.

Although open skies provided for a sizeable increase in theoretical airline capacity at Heathrow, the major practical problem was slot constraints. After the signing of the agreement in April 2007 there was a considerable amount of slot buying and swapping to enable new services to come into operation for the summer 2008 season. This meant that slot prices soared and, for example, it was reported that Continental paid $209 million for its four daily slots pairs to Newark and Houston (Button, 2009). Airlines such as GB Airways and Alitalia traded some slots. In addition the US carriers acquired or leased slots from their respective alliance partners. For example Northwest acquired its six new slot pairs for its Detroit, Minneapolis and Seattle services by leasing them from KLM who reduced its frequencies to Rotterdam and shifted its Eindhoven flights to

Table16.6 UK–US passenger numbers (000s) at Heathrow and Gatwick Airport 2007–2008

	Heathrow			Gatwick		
	2007	2008	Change	2007	2008	Change
January	803.3	795.7	−7.6	271.3	261.8	−9.5
February	678.1	706.2	28.1	235.6	235.7	0.1
March	916.2	933.2	17.0	328.5	320.2	−8.3
April	977.9	1,061.0	83.1	347.7	258.3	−89.4
May	990.5	1,135.3	144.8	352.2	241.6	−110.6
June	1,081.5	1,249.7	168.2	393.1	252.0	−141.1
July	1,076.2	1,279.5	203.3	409.9	263.4	−146.5
August	1,085.1	1,303.0	217.9	415.1	276.8	−138.3
September	992.5	1,117.8	125.3	363.2	197.0	−166.2
October	992.6	1,088.1	95.5	351.4	205.0	−146.4
November	889.0	909.6	20.6	307.2	175.0	−132.2
December	939.5	1,021.9	82.4	325.1	167.1	−158.0

Source: UK CAA.

London City Airport. Likewise Delta leased three slots pairs from Air France to support its flights to Atlanta and JFK. This was achieved by Air France reducing the frequency of its flights on the Paris route (Buyck, 2008).

Whilst US carrier activity increased significantly at Heathrow with open skies, the only non-UK European carrier to start a new US service from Heathrow was Air France-KLM. It launched a daily service to Los Angeles, which had a code share with Delta. This route already had a significant amount of capacity with services offered by BA, Virgin, United, American and Air New Zealand and so the Air France-KLM services accounted for only around 10 per cent of flights. Moreover, connecting possibilities were limited since neither Air France nor Delta had hubs at Los Angeles or Heathrow and so it was not at all unexpected when the carrier abandoned this route after only six months of operation. Meanwhile the UK-based carrier BMI decided not to introduce transatlantic services from Heathrow although it had long campaigned for the right to do so. In fact in November 2008 it decided to terminate its Manchester services to Chicago and Las Vegas as well, which it had been operating from the years 2001 and 2004 respectively. This news came just after BA had abandoned its JFK service from the same airport.

It can be argued that as Heathrow has now been fully opened up to transatlantic services, carriers will divert their attention here and call a halt to the growth of regional services, since this may have simply been driven by their inability to serve Heathrow. However, it has been observed that the London and regional routes serve different types of passengers, for example on Continental's operations where UK residents accounted for less than a quarter of London passengers but over 60 per cent of regional passengers (CAA, 2007b). Hence in this case open skies should not necessarily mean that it makes sense to abandon the regional routes.

At other airports, the impact of open skies has been fairly limited except in the notable case of Shannon airport in Ireland. In the traditional bilateral agreement between Ireland and the US until the 1990s all airlines had been required to make a stopover at Shannon if they were serving Dublin. This was undertaken to boost passenger numbers at Shannon airport (which has been experiencing a steady decline in traffic) and to help support tourism and industry in the west of Ireland region. However, it delayed journeys for passengers and placed extra costs on the airlines (Barrett, 2009). An amendment to the bilateral in 1993 meant that only 50 per cent of flights had to make the stopover and then in 2005 new changes to the bilateral meant that the stopover was to be phased out (and three new US destinations could be added). This was then incorporated into the EU–US open skies agreement which meant that by March 2008 there was no longer any requirement for a compulsory stop at Shannon. The reduction in traffic at Shannon and subsequent increase at Dublin can clearly be seen from Figure 16.4. Shannon has reacted by developing an incentive scheme for transatlantic services that offers a discount on airport charges of up to 50 per cent. Moreover, since 1986 the airport has offered a US immigration pre-clearance facility to enable passengers to clear immigration in Ireland rather than in the US but it also added customs services to this in summer 2009 which it hopes will prove attractive to airlines and corporate jets, like the BA premium service from London City airport.

Outside of the UK and Ireland, the only other significant development has been BA's 'Open Skies' airline. This premium class airline (originally called L'Avion) started flying between Paris Orly to Newark in 2007. BA took over the airline in 2008 and began 757 operations in June between Paris-Orly and JFK and subsequently added Amsterdam as well (but withdrew this service in August

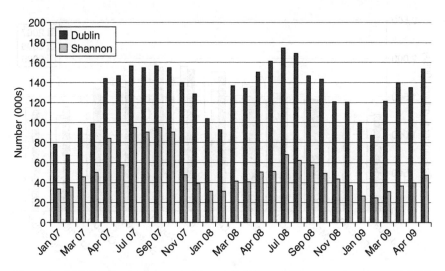

Figure 16.4 Irish–US passenger numbers at Dublin and Shannon airports 2007–2009 (source: Irish CSO).

2009 because of poor performance of this route). It also originally had plans to offer transatlantic services from Dublin, Frankfurt, Madrid, Brussels and Rome but these have currently been abandoned. By positioning itself at other European airports there is less of a risk of cannibalisation of its premium traffic at Heathrow (although this could have some effect on its premium connecting traffic) but the overall airport impact, given the limited traffic volumes, is likely to be fairly marginal. In 2007 Virgin also announced that it was going to set up an all-premium service based at other European airports but it has subsequently put these plans on hold, arguing that it was a too risky venture given that the first stage of open skies could be reversed if no agreement on the second stage negotiations is reached by 2010.

6 Conclusions and future prospects

At the time of writing, the world was in the midst of a very severe economic recession which had caused traffic numbers to contract in most regions of the world. Specifically on the North Atlantic the latest available figures for transatlantic traffic from UK and Germany (from the major airports of Heathrow, Gatwick, Frankfurt and Munich) showed a decline in 2008 compared to 2007 from autumn onwards (Figure 16.5). Traffic was also depressed in the early months of 2009 and overall IATA was forecasting that global passenger demand for this year will be down by 4 per cent (IATA, 2009c).

After five years of consecutive summers of major capacity gains on the route, the summer of 2009 saw a decrease in flights offered of around 8 per cent compared with 2008 (Ranson *et al.*, 2009). US carriers eliminated 169 daily flights but added 106, giving a net change of –63. Non-US carriers eliminated more

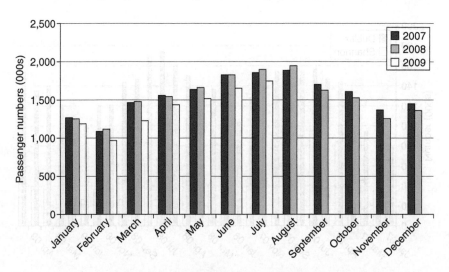

Figure 16.5 North Atlantic passenger numbers at UK and German airports 2007–2009. (a) Heathrow and Gatwick (source: UK CAA).

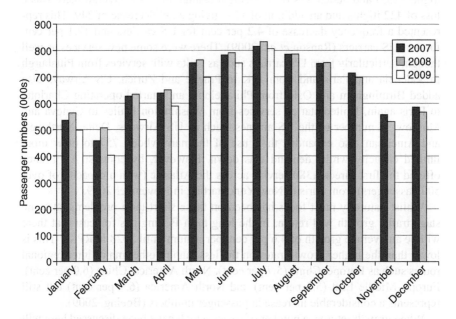

Figure 16.5 Continued.
(b) Frankfurt (source: Destatis).

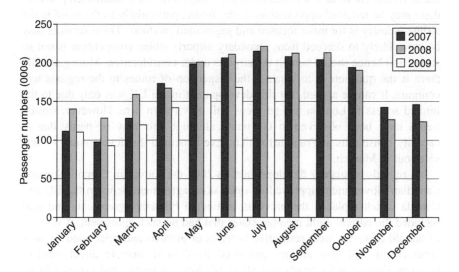

Figure 16.5 Continued.
(c) Munich (source: Destatis).

flights (253) and added less (67), giving a change of –249. Overall there was a loss of 422 flights and an addition of 173, giving a net decrease of 249. This represented a frequency decrease of 4.2 per cent for US carriers and 12.1 per cent for non-US carriers (Ranson *et al.*, 2009). There were some new services as well though, particularly from US carriers such as Delta with services from Pittsburgh to Valencia and Paris and from JFK to Prague and Zurich. US Airways also added Birmingham and Oslo from Philadelphia and started operating Charlotte to Paris again. United started services from Washington Dulles to Geneva and Moscow. A number of the US airlines, such as US Airways, Delta, Northwest and American also expanded their use of the narrowbody 757 to offer more limited capacity whilst demand was down. However, by contrast Air France offered the first direct A380 service across the Atlantic (with a capacity of over 500 passengers) from Paris to New York starting in November 2009.

Whilst naturally most focus has been on these short-term problems, at some stage traffic growth will return. In the long term Boeing has forecast that there will be an average growth of 4.6 per cent per annum until 2028 in RPKs. This is lower than the higher growth rates on the less mature other major inter-regional routes such as Europe–China (5.7 per cent), North America–China (6.0 per cent), Europe–Middle East (5.5 per cent) and North America (6.9 per cent) but still represents a considerable increase in passenger numbers (Boeing, 2009).

When growth returns, a number of issues which have been discussed here will need to be revisited. First, the extent to which there is scope for specialist services, both premium or LCC. Whilst the economic downturn does not encourage the development of new services (except perhaps with well-established players), there may be renewed opportunities in the future, particularly as the trend in the airline industry is for more focused and segmented products. These services may be more likely to succeed from secondary airports where competition is not so strong and hence should benefit the airports under consideration. More generally there is the question as to whether the dispersion of routes to the regions will continue. It can be argued that this development in the UK was only due to the limited access in London and so focus will now return here. However, similar trends have been observed in Germany, although this may be partly due to capacity constraints at Frankfurt which have benefited the development of services out of Munich.

As regards regulatory developments, in 2008 the European Commission and Canadian Government approved an open skies agreement between the EU and Canada which replaced the previous individual bilateral agreements and also included the current eight member states that had no such agreement. A number of the old bilaterals were restrictive in terms of markets and prices and the new arrangement will give airlines unlimited freedom to operate direct services between Europe and Canada and all restrictions on routes and prices will be removed. Moreover, there will be a gradual liberalisation of the foreign ownership rules and other traffic rights as the two regions move to an Open Aviation Area. However, the potential impact of such developments cannot be expected to be as significant as with the US given the smaller market size.

With the exception of the BA Open Skies project and the short-lived daily Heathrow–Los Angeles flight offered by Air France, the US agreement has in reality seen carriers staying put at their own hubs and those of their alliance partners, and hence has had only limited effects on airports. Clearly the most noteworthy impact has been on Heathrow but now that all the carriers have secured a presence at the airport, any future developments are likely to be more limited and with upward pressure on slot prices if the airlines choose to add incremental slots to their networks. One major uncertainty was associated with the second stage of this agreement which could have led to a possibility of reverting back to the bilateral structure if no deal was signed. However, this was achieved in June 2010 which provided for reciprocal liberalisation on airline ownership and control (although the US legislative changes have yet to be approved) and greater access for EU airlines to the 'Fly America' programme. It also agreed greater cooperation in areas such as security, employee rights and security.

References

AEA (2009) 'European airline traffic in the last two months "Disappointing" says AEA', press release 9 October. Online. Available: www.aea.be/press/releases/index.html (accessed 18 October 2009).

Aviation Strategy (2007) 'Premium transatlantic airlines: how important are they?' *Aviation Strategy*, July/August, 13–21.

Barrett, S. (2009) 'EU/US Open Skies – Competition and change in the world aviation market: The implications for the Irish aviation market', *Journal of Air Transport Management* 15(2), 78–82.

BBC (2008) 'Ryanair set for £8 flights to US, news report 2 November'. Online. Available: http://news.bbc.co.uk/1/hi/business/7705169.stm (accessed 15 November 2008).

Boeing (2009) *Current market outlook 2009–2028*. Online. Available: www.boeing.com/commercial/cmo/pdf/Boeing_Current_Market_Outlook_2009_to_2028.pdf (accessed 10 October 2009).

Button, K. (2009) 'The impact of US–EU Open Skies agreement on airline market structures and airline networks', *Journal of Air Transport Management*, 15(2), 59–71.

Buyck, C. (2008) 'A slow opening', *Air Transport World*, March, 25–30.

CAA (2007a) *Connecting the continents – Long haul passenger operations from the UK*, CAP 771. Online. Available: www.caa.co.uk/docs/33/CAP771.pdf (accessed 5 April 2008).

CAA (2007b) *Air services at UK regional airports*, CAP 775. Online. Available: www.caa.co.uk/cap775 (accessed 5 April 2008).

CAA (2008) *Civil Aviation Authority response to HM Treasury consultation on aviation duty*, 24 April. Online. Available: www.caa.co.uk/default.aspx?catid=697&pagetype=90&pageid=9597 (accessed 15 November 2008).

CAA (2009) *CAA passenger survey report 2008*. Online. Available: http://www.caa.co.uk/surveys (accessed 20 October 2009).

Dennis, N. (2007) 'Competition and change in the long-haul markets from Europe', *Journal of Air Transportation*, 12(2), 4–26.

Eurostat (2009) 'Air passenger transport in Europe in 2007', *Eurostat Statistics in focus 1/2009*. Online. Available: epp.eurostat.ec.europa.eu/cache/ITY_OFFPUB/KS-SF-09-001/EN/KS-SF-09-001-EN.PDF (accessed 20 February 2009).

Ezard, K. (2008) 'Back in the ring', *Airline Business*, May, 66–68.

Francis, G., Dennis, N., Ison, S. and Humphreys, I. (2007) 'The transferability of the low-cost model to long-haul airline operations', *Tourism Management*, 28(2), 391–398.

Graham, A. and Dennis, N. (2007) 'Airport traffic and financial performance: A UK and Ireland case study', *Journal of Transport Geography*, 15(3), 161–171.

Halstead, J. (2008) 'British Airways grows in strength – despite the LHR fiasco', *Aviation Strategy*, May, 4–9.

Humphreys, B. and Morrell, P. (2009) 'The potential impacts of the EU/US Open Sky Agreement: What will happen at Heathrow after spring 2008', *Journal of Air Transport Management*, 15(2), 72–77.

IATA (2009a) *World air transport statistics*, 53rd edn, Geneva: IATA.

IATA (2009b) *Premium traffic monitor*, August. Online. Available: www.iata.org/whatwedo/economics (accessed 20 October 2009).

IATA (2009c) 'Deeper losses forecast – falling yields, rising fuel costs', press release 15 September. Online. Available: www.iata.org/pressroom/pr/2009-09-15-01.htm) (accessed 20 October 2009).

Ranson, I., Sobie, B. and Kirby, M. (2009) 'Cutting to fit', *Airline Business*, June, 34–42.

Wensveen, J.G. and Leick, R. (2009) 'The long-haul low-cost carrier: A unique business model', *Journal of Air Transport Management*, 15 (3).

17 Effects of emission trading schemes

Yulai Wan and Anming Zhang

1 Introduction

Climate change has aroused much public concern around the world in recent years. The rapid growth in air traffic over the last few decades has led to a significant increase in greenhouse gas (GHG) emissions from the aviation sector, and these emissions are expected to continue to grow rapidly in the future. According to OECD (2008), air transport's share of total transportation carbon dioxide (CO_2) emissions could, based on a "business as usual scenario," grow from 14.8 percent in 2010 to 23.0 percent in 2050. (The transport sector emitted approximately 23 percent of total world CO_2 emissions in 2006.) This is due partly to more readily available environmentally friendly energy in the future for ground-based transportation compared to air transportation, and partly to faster growth of air transport than other modes.

Significant public pressure has been mounted on both the aviation industry and its regulators to better control GHG emissions. European Commission (2005) discussed an array of policy instruments considered by the Commission of European Communities before their recommendation of implementing an emission trading scheme (ETS). Earlier, Carlsson (1999) classified various emission reduction policies into incentive-based (e.g., tax, emission charges and tradable permits) and command-and-control (e.g., standards, emission limits and restrictions on flight movements) regulations, and compared the effectiveness of these two policy types. A comprehensive list of aviation climate change mitigation measures available for policy makers is given in Forsyth (2008). Table 17.1 summarizes various emission reduction regulations based on these (and other) studies.

Table 17.1 also lists possible responses by airlines and airports to various emission reduction policies, reflecting the fact that the aviation industry will likely respond to the challenges from environmental regulations. Alamdari and Brewer (1994), for instance, surveyed about 20 airlines to explore possible reactions that might be preferred by carriers faced with tightening environmental policies. Forsyth (2008) provided a list of emission reduction options available for industry practitioners faced with GHG emission reduction pressures imposed by regulators.

Table 17.1 Emission reduction policies and possible responses by airlines and airports

	Government policy	Possible airline response	Possible airport response
Technological	Emission standard	Aircraft development (engines/winglets and fuel efficiency) Fleet renewal (fuel-efficient aircraft, larger and lighter aircraft) Alternative fuels	Alternative fuels Ground facility energy efficient system and design
Operational	Air traffic control (ATC) improvement Flight movement restrictions Emission limits	Cruise altitude/speed optimization Ascending/descending procedures optimization Interior weight reduction Network (route) optimization Adjustments in load factor, seat density and frequency	Airport reforms (less taxi time, less airport congestion) Airport operational savings Supporting airport access by public transit Restriction on access of high-emission aircraft
Strategic	Airport development control Promote rail transport	Voluntary carbon offsets Green airline branding Rail (multimodal) feeder development	Voluntary carbon offsets
Economic incentive (market-based)	Tax incentives Fuel tax Emission (carbon) tax Emission trading scheme (ETS) Airfare tax Emission charges	Fare increase	Airport emission charges Congestion pricing Inducing airlines to adopt GHG-reducing ground practice

Sources: Summarized from Forsyth (2008), Vlek and Vogels (2000), Sgouridis (2009), Alamdari and Brewer (1994), Bresson (2009), Reimer and Putnam (2007) and European Commission (2005).

Consideration of possible industrial responses turns out to be important when we classify the effects of ETS into the direct impacts and indirect impacts. Note that the policy objective of reducing emissions can be achieved either directly through increasing the cost of air travel and thereby suppressing the demand, or indirectly through inducing further emission reduction measures initialized by the aviation sector (carriers, airports, aircraft manufacturers, etc.) trying to lower costs and restore demand by improving fuel and other operating efficiencies. When estimating the effects of certain emission reduction policy, therefore, we need to investigate both the direct and indirect impacts induced by the reactions of various players in the aviation industry. Figure 17.1 shows the paths through which the climate change policies affect the economy and environment at the aggregate level. For a particular air travel market, usually a route, other subtle issues, such as the strategic interactions among airports and airlines and airline competition, will also influence the effectiveness of climate change mitigation policies, which are not depicted in Figure 17.1.

As can be seen from the figure, the path of the direct impacts is straight-forward and it is relatively easy to quantify and analyze these effects based on the status quo of the airline industry prior to the implementation of any emission policy, since no potential reactions from airlines and airports are taken into consideration. A number of studies, both journal articles and research reports, have investigated and estimated the direct impacts. These studies, mostly empirical, assume that factors such as airline flight frequency, aircraft fuel efficiency, network structure and competitive environment remain unchanged. As a result,

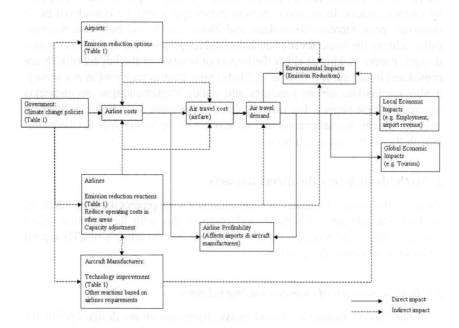

Figure 17.1 Impacts of climate change policies.

emission control policies simply impose an extra cost on airlines, which then pass the additional cost onto the passengers by raising fares. Owing to the inherent heterogeneity of each carrier's strategy (e.g., business model), operation (e.g., route and hub airport selection, fleet mix) and performance (e.g., emission efficiency), the amounts of fare increase differ among the carriers. This will in turn induce a new distribution of passengers and lead to changes in competitive positioning among airlines and airports. Note that even though the airline/airport reactions are not considered, the demand loss on a certain route for a particular airline may be attributed not only to its own price elasticity, but also to the substitution effects of other transport modes, alternative destinations and routes, as well as competing airlines. Finally, unlike the direct impacts, the indirect impacts are much more subtle and difficult to analyze. This is due either to the lack of data as GHG emission policies were not mandatorily applied in the aviation industry until recently, or to the complexity of the issue itself as emission policies can trigger strategic behavior and interaction among the actors (airlines, airports, etc.) at various linkages as depicted in Figure 17.1. As a result, studies on the indirect impacts are relatively rare.

We organize our literature review along the lines of the direct and indirect impacts. Furthermore, given the global character of climate change, unilateral implementation of GHG emission policies may lead to airline competition, tourist distribution, transport modal shift and other issues. These issues, together with the effectiveness of unilateral policies in terms of emission reduction, will also be examined in our review. Finally, emission trading and emission taxation are two major climate-change policies that are widely implemented or proposed by various sectors. In aviation, as both policy types may be considered as de facto fuel price increase (Brueckner and Zhang, 2009) and both can, theoretically, achieve the same level of emission reduction provided appropriate policy designs, papers looking at either the impact of taxation or the impact of ETS are considered in this survey.[1] Table 17.2 lists major studies reviewed in our survey; it also summarizes airline reactions and policy implementation environments covered in these papers. The possible (direct) reactions to emission policies by airports, aircraft manufacturers and air navigation operators will not be examined further in this survey, however.

2 Methods to assess the direct impacts

To assess the potential impacts of ETS, various studies project the future demand for emission without any scheme and compare this with the situation where certain designs of ETS were adopted. It turns out that the impacts of ETS depend on how the scheme is designed.

2.1 Design elements of emission trading schemes

Wit *et al.* (2005) provide a comprehensive discussion on the design options for elements in ETS. Below, we list the most important elements.

Cap: As in a cap-and-trade system, the cap is the total number of permits allocated to the aviation sector, reflecting the total amount of emissions allowed. Theoretically, if the cap is set at the level where marginal benefit equals marginal abatement cost, social optimum is achieved. In practice, sometimes the cap is determined as a proportion of historical emissions. The proposed EU-ETS sets the cap for 2012 – the first year of imposition of ETS on EU markets – at 97 percent of the average of 2004–2006 emissions by aircraft operators included in the scheme.

Allowance allocation methods: The baseline method sets a historical emission baseline for each trading entity, and each entity is then required to purchase allowances from the market for emissions above its baseline. Both the *grandfathering approach* and the *benchmarking approach* grant a certain proportion of allowances to the trading entities for free and the rest by auction. The grandfathering approach distributes the free allowances based on each trading entity's share of historical emissions, while the benchmarking approach distributes the free allowances based on historical shares of output levels such as revenue tonne-kilometers (RTK) and revenue passenger-kilometers (RPK). Alternatively, all the allowances may be auctioned. If free allocation is allowed, the decision on the base (monitoring) year to calculate the share of emission or output will be an issue. EU-ETS will adopt the benchmarking method to grant 85 percent of the allowances freely, taking 2010 as the monitoring year. Section 2.2 discusses the impacts of applying different allowance allocation rules.

Trading entity: Various players in the aviation sector, such as airports, airlines, aircraft manufacturers and jet fuel suppliers, can be potential trading entities. The proposed Australian, New Zealand and US ETS require fuel suppliers to surrender allowances, while EU-ETS considers airlines as the trading entities. Following the principle of "polluters pay," airlines are preferred trading entities. Compared with other players in the aviation sector, airlines usually have direct control over a large range of emission abatement measures (Wit *et al.*, 2005).

Geographic scope: Theoretically, it is socially optimal to implement a global scheme in which all the flights and all the other emitting sectors are covered, so that potential distortions in competition and leakage of emissions can be avoided. However, owing to various political and practical concerns, this cannot be achieved by any of the proposed schemes right now. For example, EU-ETS includes emissions from all the domestic flights, intra-EU flights and flights to/from the EU, but does not cover automobiles. It is, therefore, important to analyze potential distortions associated with the "unilateral" actions. The effects of unilateral ETS will be discussed in later sections.

2.2 Impacts of various allowance allocation methods

While it is commonly regarded that 100 percent auction provides the most incentives for emission reduction and the least possibility of distortion, considering the burdens the trading entities will have to bear and the difficulties they may

Table 17.2 List of major papers reviewed in this survey

	Airline responses						Policy implementation environment						Impacts		
	Impact path	Rerouting path	New tech/ efficiency improvement	Aircraft size/seat capacity	Frequency	Load factor	Imperfect competition	Mode substitution	Business models	Short-/ long-haul	Business/ leisure passenger	Unilateral adoption/ Asymmetric development	Fare/ cost increase	Demand	Emission
Alamdari and Brewer (1994)	Indirect		X											X	X
Albers et al. (2009)	Direct												X	X	X
Boon et al. (2007)	Direct			X	X								X	X	X
Brueckner and Zhang (2009)	Both						X						X	X	X
Carlsson (2002)	Indirect						X						X	X	X
Ernst & Young (2007)	Direct						X	X	X				X	X	X
FitzGerald and Tol (2007)	Direct											X		X	X
Forsyth (2008)	Direct							X					X	X	X
Frontier Economics (2006)	Direct												X	X	X
Hofer et al. (2009)	Direct						X	X			X		X	X	X
Jamin et al. (2004)	Indirect						X	X						X	X
Lu (2009)	Direct							X			X		X	X	X
Mayor and Tol (2009)	Direct			X										X	X
Miyoshi and Mason (2009a)	Indirect									X		X	X	X	X

	Airline responses					Policy implementation environment							Impacts		
	Impact path	Rerouting	New tech/efficiency improvement	Aircraft size/seat capacity	Frequency	Load factor	Imperfect competition	Mode substitution models	Business models	Short-/long-haul	Business/leisure passenger	Unilateral adoption/Asymmetric development	Fare/cost increase	Demand	Emission
Miyoshi and Mason (2009b)	Indirect					x			x	x				x	x^a
Morrell (2007)	Direct			x					x						x
Morrell (2009)	Indirect								x						
Morrell and Lu (2007)	Indirect		x												
Scheelhaase and Grimme (2007)	Direct								x		x				x
Scheelhaase et al. (2009a)	Direct								x						
Scheelhaase et al. (2009b)	Direct							x			x				x
Tol (2007)	Direct														x
Vivid Economics (2007)	Direct						x				x	x		x	x	x
Vivid Economics (2008)	Direct		x				x				x	x		x	x	x
Wit et al. (2002)	Both			x											x	x
Wit et al. (2005)	Both		x												x	x
Yuen and Zhang (2009)	Direct														x	x

Note

a Study the impacts on emission efficiency.

face in funding emission reduction projects, an ETS may allocate part of the allowances to the trading entities for free. The initial purpose of free allocation is to provide financial compensation for the sectors included in the scheme so as to partially offset possible losses relative to the pre-scheme situation (Boon et al., 2007). As the granted allowances can be sold at market price, the issue of windfall profits can arise. For example, under perfect competition or Bertrand oligopoly with free allowance allocation, airlines may purchase all the allowances needed from the market, pass all the allowance acquisition costs into ticket prices, and sell free allowances to the market. In this case, these airlines will be able to earn positive windfall profits which are exactly equal to the values of allowances granted (Forsyth, 2008). Note that prior to emission trading, these airlines can only earn zero economic profit.

Positive windfall profits are more likely realized with one-off permit allocation. In the case of a repeated scheme in which the number of allowances granted will be updated periodically based on the airlines' realized outputs, the possibility of gaining windfall profits is relatively low (Boon et al., 2007). Under a repeated scheme, airlines have an incentive to continue staying in the market, or keeping high output levels even if doing so is not efficient economically, in order to obtain more free allowances in the future. This effect intensifies airline competition and restricts the ability to pass all the cost to passengers. Since the gain from selling free allowances needs to offset the loss from overproduction, the net gain becomes smaller.

With regard to providing the incentive to reduce emissions through technical and operational measures, repeated benchmarking is more effective than one-off benchmarking or grandfathering. Since grandfathering allocates free allowances based on the share of emissions, it favors less environmentally efficient airlines (Morrell, 2007). On the other hand, with repeated benchmarking, if an airline is able to reduce emissions while increasing output at the same time, it will have more free allowances to sell in the next period.

As mentioned previously, when free allocation is allowed, choice of the base year also plays an important role. For instance, in the proposed EU-ETS, the free allowance allocation is benchmarked on the 2010 output levels and therefore airlines may have incentives to drastically increase their RTK or RPK in 2010, which may be neither economically efficient nor environmentally friendly (Scheelhaase et al., 2009a). This situation will not happen if the benchmark is based on the year in which the output levels have already been realized. Morrell (2007) pointed out that a later base year favors fast-growing airlines relative to an earlier base year.

It is also noted that the freely allocated allowances may serve as an entry barrier. Since the free allowances are de facto lump-sum subsidies, the incumbents may cross-subsidize marginally unprofitable routes; consequently, the potential entrants' incentive to enter those routes will be reduced (Forsyth, 2008). More detailed analysis on the pros and cons of various allocation methods can be found in Wit et al. (2005), Boon et al. (2007), Frontier Economics (2006) and Morrell (2007).

2.3 Steps in assessing the direct impacts

Various models have been employed to assess the direct impacts of ETS. For example, FitzGerald and Tol (2007) use the Hamburg Tourism Model (HTM), whereas Wit *et al.* (2005) apply the AERO model.[2] Based on the works reviewed in this survey, we generalize the approaches to predicting the direct impacts into the following eight steps:

1   Forecast business-as-usual traffic demand and emission demand. Some studies establish their own forecasting approaches, while others choose to directly apply the published traffic growth rates from other studies. Sometimes the projected emissions are adjusted by automatic emission efficiency growth (e.g., a 1 percent annual efficiency improvement) or a pre-set fleet renewal rate.

2   Calculate free allowances allocated based on allowance allocation rules specified by the scheme.

3   Make assumptions about allowance prices and derive the allowance acquisition cost. Two approaches are available to calculate the allowance acquisition cost: the first one considers the allowances purchased and excludes those freely allocated. The total acquisition cost is then the permit price multiplied by the difference between the allowances needed (from step 1) and the allowances freely granted (from step 2). In this approach, the free allowance allocation method matters. The second approach counts the costs of all the allowances freely allocated, auctioned and purchased, as surrendering free allowances incurs opportunity cost. The total acquisition cost is then the permit price multiplied by the total number of allowances needed. The cost increase per unit is lower in the first approach and hence the first approach will likely induce lower airfare increase and cause smaller impacts than the second approach.

4   Calculate the cost increase per RPK, per RTK, or per passenger. This is simply to divide the allowance acquisition cost by the projected traffic demand.

5   Make assumptions about the cost pass-through rate. Airlines, as the trading entities, may suffer cost increase when participating in ETS. To restore profitability, airlines will try to pass some or all of the cost increase to passengers by raising fares. Most existing works trying to quantify the impact of ETS assume that the allowance acquisition cost will be fully passed onto final consumers (i.e., passengers), since some reports have claimed that the aviation industry is competitive and hence is likely to fully pass the extra cost (e.g., Boon *et al.*, 2007). However, this assumption has been challenged by a number of studies. Table 17.3 shows that, theoretically, the cost pass-through rates depend on various assumptions regarding air travel demands, market structures, etc. PWC (2005) conducts a regression analysis based on fuel price increase and indicates that the cost pass-through for full service carriers is about 105 percent, while that

Table 17.3 Summary of studies on cost pass-through rates

	Influencing factor	Economic model/reasoning	Conclusion/Remarks
Frontier Economics (2006)	Marginal cost	Even under perfect competition, if the marginal cost curve is increasing, increase in equilibrium price is lower than the upward shift of marginal cost.	Full pass-through may not be achieved even in perfectly competitive market.
Ernst & Young (2007)	Competition	Cournot competition under linear demand. The resulting rate is $n/(n+1)$.	100% pass-through is unlikely in most of the cases.
	Congested airport	When the airport capacity is constrained, the airlines have slot rents. The equilibrium airfare is decided by the demand curve and is not affected by a small shift of marginal cost.	Zero cost pass-through for flights from congested airports.
Boon et al. (2007)	Type of competition	In Bertrand competition, even oligopoly market can achieve perfect competition results and hence full cost pass-through.	In aviation markets, Bertrand competition is more likely than Cournot competition and cost is likely to be fully passed through.
	Periodic benchmark updating	When the free allowance allocation method is repeated benchmarking based on the volume of the base year, airlines may have incentive to lower price and boost traffic for the years the benchmark is based.	Under repeated benchmarking, the ability to pass through all the extra allowance cost is limited.
Vivid Economics (2007)	Demand curve	In Cournot competition, the pass-through rate depends on the curvature of the demand curve and the number of firms.	The cost pass-through rate may exceed 100% under non-linear demand.
	Airline strategy	In Cournot model, the pass-through rate also depends on the objective of the firms: maximize profit, sales or market share.	The cost pass-through rate is closest to 100% under sales-maximization, and is furthest from 100% under profit-maximization.

Forsyth (2008)	Congested airports	In competitive market, flights from uncongested airports increases price. This shifts the demand for congested airports outward and hence increases the price of flights from congested airports.
	Capacity constrained routes	As in the case of congested airports with no demand shift, the airlines will have to absorb all the cost increase and generate less profit.	Capacity of some international routes may be regulated by aviation service agreements. To restore profitability, the regulators may further restrict capacity and raise price.
	Asymmetric coverage of ETS in slot constrained airports	The initial price is p1 for all flights from this airport. Only flight A is covered by the scheme with extra marginal cost t. Then, the demand for flight A will shift downward by t, while the total demand by less than t. The new price which clears the market drops to p2.	Then, flight A incurs charges p2+t> p1 and part of the cost is passed through instead of full cost.
	Free allocation of allowance	If the airline's objective is cost recovery instead of profit maximization, it may set a lower price at the average cost (excluding opportunity cost) level, rather than at the marginal cost level (including opportunity cost).	The price increase is to cover the expenditure of purchased allowances and hence is lower than the opportunity cost of allowances.
	Long run effect	If free entry is allowed in Cournot competition, price will be kept low to just cover the cost of the marginal firm. After imposition of ETS, cost raises and the marginal firms incur loss and exit the market, and price increases until the original profitability is restored.	At the new equilibrium, the extra permit cost should be fully passed through to passengers.

of low-cost carriers is lower, at 90 percent. Vivid Economics (2007) estimates the pass-through rate for a sample of flights departing from the UK,
assuming Cournot competition with iso-elasticity demands or linear
demands. The report predicts a wide range of cost pass-through rates, but
suggests that 100 percent or even higher pass-through rates may be highly
possible.

6   Calculate fare increase. The increase in airfare is the cost increase per passenger multiplied by the cost pass-through rate.

7   Obtain percentage changes in demand relative to the business-as-usual
demand. Once the price increase is determined, it is straightforward to
quantify the changes in demand if the price elasticity of demand is known.
Most of the empirical papers included in this survey assumed constant
price elasticity. Further, instead of estimating the price elasticity, these
papers tried to pick up reasonable values from published works (based on
the authors' own judgment). Some papers surveyed here (e.g., Frontier
Economics, 2006; Lu, 2009; Vivid Economics, 2007) have reviewed the
published results of price elasticity estimation. One special case is the
HTM employed by FitzGerald and Tol (2007) where the price elasticity for
each country of origin is estimated from a modified version of Bigano *et al.*
(2006)'s holiday destination choice model. Another interesting case is
given in Jamin *et al.* (2004) where the authors fit a city-pair gravity model,
resulting in a price elasticity dependent on both air travel costs and automobile travel costs.

8   Calculate emission reduction in the aviation sector due to the drop in
demand.

3 Direct impacts on airfare, demand and emission

Even if an ETS treats all the players equally, airlines' relative positions may
change post-ETS, owing to differential business models and operational strategies. In this section, we focus our discussion on the direct impacts of ETS and
thus, the emission reduction in the aviation sector corresponds to the demand
reduction from the airfare increase. While it is obvious that fare increase will in
general reduce aviation demand, the magnitude of such impacts may differ
among business models and discriminate treatments between leisure and business passengers. The comparisons will be given below.

3.1 Compare business models: LCCs vs. FSCs

In comparison between full service carriers (FSCs) and low-cost carriers (LCCs),
we find that various studies have reached a consistent conclusion that ETS
impacts more negatively on LCCs than on FSCs, provided that no supply-side
responses are exerted. More specifically, LCCs are expected to encounter a
larger decline in profit margin, a higher percentage fare increase, and a more
severe demand reduction than FSCs. This is because LCCs usually have a higher

growth rate and serve a larger share of price-sensitive passengers. Even though LCCs may have a lower (absolute) fare increase, the percentage reduction in demand is far greater than that of FSCs. In terms of absolute profit change, however, the adverse impact on FSCs is greater. Morrell (2007) indicates that since the low-cost market only started its rapid growth after 2000 LCCs would be better off if the free allowances were allocated based on airlines' performance in later years. He further suggests that grandfathering favors generally less fuel efficient network carriers, while benchmarking narrows down the difference of price changes between FSCs and LCCs and would make relatively fuel efficient LCCs better off. This latter observation was confirmed by Scheelhaase and Grimme (2007) who found that, because of its relatively higher fuel efficiency, Ryanair may be granted more free allowances than needed by the benchmarking approach. The results on the ETS impacts for different business models are summarized in Table 17.4.

Regarding charter or holiday airlines, Morrell (2007) finds that the charter airline studied, namely Britannia, would benefit from benchmarking and outperform both the FSC (British Airways) and LCC (easyJet), because of its longer average stage length and higher load factor. In Scheelhaase and Grimme (2007), the holiday airline, namely Condor, would perform much better, in the sense of obtaining more allowances than needed, under the benchmarking approach. Under the grandfathering approach, however, Condor's position would be worsened dramatically relative to the FSC (Lufthansa), because Condor has a much higher predicted growth rate than Lufthansa.[3] Since the grandfathering approach relies on the historical share of emissions, the number of free allowances allocated to Condor is so low that the holiday airline has to purchase a large proportion of allowances from the market and hence suffers from a much higher allowance acquisition cost. In addition to this, Condor is more fuel efficient, leading to a much better situation under benchmarking.

Unlike the other papers in Table 17.4 that quantify the economic impacts of ETS on airlines, Lu (2009) considers an environmental charge which aims to reduce the social cost of noise and engine emission. When estimating the social cost of engine emission, emissions at both the "landing and take-off" (LTO) cycle and the cruise stage are included and costs of both climate change and air pollution are estimated. (The detailed estimation method is presented in Lu and Morrell, 2001.) This environmental charge is therefore different from conventional airport environmental charges which only consider noise and local air pollution around the airport. Table 17.4 presents her results concerning business passengers for British Airways and Air France-KLM and leisure passengers for easyJet. Although Lu (2009) does not directly study the impacts of ETS and, because of the inclusion of more externalities than GHG emissions, the environmental charges are supposed to be higher than ETS cost on the per passenger basis, the qualitative difference between the two FSCs and the LCC studied should be similar to the rest of empirical studies on ETS. The LCC has lower social cost per passenger, but more adversely affected by the policy than the FSCs.

Table 17.4 ETS impacts for different business models

Study (Allowance price, per tCO₂)	Business model	Price elasticity	Impacts
Ernst & Young (2007)[ab] €6, 30, 60	FSC	-1.5 ~ -0.8	Profit-margin drop (%): 0.3, 1.6, 3.1 — Profit drop (€ billions): 5.2, 23.8, 47.0
	LCC	-1.5	Profit-margin drop (%): 0.9, 3.9, 8.7 — Profit drop (€ billions): 1.3, 5.1, 10.8
	Cargo	-1.6 ~ -0.8	Profit-margin drop (%): 0.9, 3.8, 8.8 — Profit drop (€ billions): 3.0, 11.6, 26.6
Frontier Economics (2006)[b] €27 ~ 40	FSC	-0.8	Demand drop (%): 2 ~ 3 — Revenue change (%): 0.5 ~ 0.8 — Fare increase (%): 2.5 ~ 4
	LCC	-1.5	Demand drop (%): 7.5 ~ 12 — Revenue change (%): -2.5 ~ -4.0 — Fare increase (%): 5 ~ 8
Morrell (2007)[cd] US$40	FSC	NA	Fare increase (US$) — Grandfather: 0.41, Benchmark: 1.76, Auction: 4.18
	LCC		Fare increase (US$) — Grandfather: 2.17, Benchmark: 3.49, Auction: 5.87
	Charter		Fare increase (US$) — Grandfather: 0.63, Benchmark: -0.53, Auction: 3.00
Lu (2009)[de]	FSC	-0.7	Fare increase (€): 4.69 ~ 7.58 — Demand drop (%): 0.9 ~ 1.3 — Social cost
	LCC	-1.52	Fare increase (€): 3.38 ~ 3.53 — Demand drop (%): 7.1 ~ 7.8 — Social cost

				Fare increase (€)	Demand drop (%)	Acquisition cost (% of revenue)
Scheelhaase and Grimme (2007)[df]	€15 ~ 30	FSC	Business: −0.9 ~ −0.5	0.04 ~ 1.74	0.02 ~ 1.51	0.03 ~ 0.84
		LCC	Leisure: −1.5 ~ −1.1	0.34 ~ 1.33	0.78 ~ 5.56	0.77 ~ 3.02
		Holiday		0.37 ~ 2.97	0.24 ~ 2.44	0.41 ~ 1.98
		Regional		0.26 ~ 1.01	0.28 ~ 2.03	0.10 ~ 0.52

Notes

Unless specified in the notes below, the following hold: (1) the pass-through rate is assumed to be 100%; (2) if free allowances are granted, the acquisition cost only counts the expenditure on additional allowances needed for operation; and (3) the prediction is on an aggregate level.

FSC: Full service carriers; LCC: Low cost carriers; Cargo: Cargo carriers; Holiday: Holiday airlines; Regional: Regional airlines.

a Pass-through rate: FSC = 29%, LCC = 30%, Cargo = 29%.

b The acquisition cost includes the opportunity cost. This is equivalent to 100% auction.

c Assume ETS only covers domestic and intra-EU flights.

d The estimation is based on a few selected airlines and routes, rather than on an aggregate level.

e The policy studied in this paper is environmental charge.

f The paper considers three ETS options for different allowance price levels: Option 1 applies a grandfathering approach and covers only Intra-EU flights, with an allowance price of €15; option 2 applies a benchmarking approach and covers only Intra-EU flights, with an allowance price of €20; and option 3 uses grandfathering for all flights using EU airports, with an allowance price of €30.

3.2 Compare business and leisure passengers

Airlines usually price-discriminate between business passengers and leisure passengers to extract more consumer surplus as business passengers are less price sensitive than leisure passengers. Airlines' ability to pass-through cost increase to leisure passengers is relatively restricted as compared to a mix of business and leisure passengers on board (Vivid Economics, 2007). Lu (2009) demonstrates, using a sample of intra-EU flights, that even if the airfares of both passenger types increase by the same amount, the demand reduction is about 4.5–7.8 percent in the leisure market and about 0.9–1.9 percent in the business market. Two underlying causes are attributed to this result: (1) the original price in the business market is much higher and thus the percentage price increase is much lower; and (2) the business market has a lower price elasticity of demand.

Following the above argument, the impacts of ETS may vary among carriers who have different business–leisure passenger splits. Vivid Economics (2008) argues that leisure passengers are more likely to have a flat linear demand whereas, on the other hand, business passengers or a mixture of business and leisure passengers are more likely to have a constant elasticity demand.[4] In a Cournot oligopoly, if the demand curves have constant price elasticity, airlines with smaller market shares pre-ETS may, post-ETS, gain market shares from larger airlines if the cost–pass-through rate is greater than 100 percent. In contrast, under a linear demand, small firms lose market share to large firms post-ETS, suggesting that if LCCs or charter carriers compete in a Cournot fashion, ETS tends to strengthen the position of dominant airlines. Vivid Economics (2008) calibrated the post-ETS profit reduction in terms of the percentage of pre-ETS emission cost for a sample of routes to and from the UK.[5] In that study, the impact on profit reduction ranges from 15 to 40 percent under constant elasticity demands, whereas the reduction range is 40–70 percent under linear demands.

Airlines may as well treat these two groups of passengers separately when trying to pass the emission cost to passengers. Scheelhaase and Grimme (2007) show that by shifting the allowance cost only to business passengers instead of all passengers, Ryanair would be able to cut the demand reduction by almost 80 percent, from 5.56 percent to 1.2 percent, under grandfathering with allowance price of €30/tCO$_2$. However, the same method would only cut Lufthansa's demand reduction by about 70 percent, from 1.51 percent to 0.44 percent. This distinction is due partly to the fact that Ryanair has a smaller share of business passengers than Lufthansa, and by passing cost only onto business passengers, its leisure passengers would be retained. This example suggests that there might be some incentive for different airline business models to change their leisure–business passenger split.

3.3 Emission reduction in the aviation sector

Table 17.5 reports the effect of EU-ETS on emission reduction within the aviation sector.[6] A number of observations emerge from the table: first, the amount of emission reduction is positively correlated with the cost–pass-through rate. Second, since the supply effect is not included and the demand effect is the same over the years, the amount of emission reduction within the aviation sector barely increases over the years. Wit *et al.* (2005) claim that supply-side responses, in the long run, may contribute about half of the reductions within the aviation sector. Third, the aviation sector is only able to achieve a marginally small fraction of the emission reduction target, and the remaining tranche of the target is met by purchasing allowances from other sectors that are capable of reducing emission in a much cheaper way.

In accordance with the above analysis, several studies about levying tax on CO_2 emitted, carbon or fuel in international aviation show that the impact of taxation on travel demand and hence emission reduction is limited. The three studies listed in Table 17.6 applied three completely different models, but reached the same conclusion: that taxation is not effective in achieving emission reduction within the aviation sector. Olsthoorn (2001) claims that in order to keep the 2050 emission at the 2000 level, a fuel tax of US$1,500 per tonne is needed and this emission target could only be achieved under the most environmentally friendly scenario in which the projected 2050 emission is reduced by about 70 percent. Such a tax would raise the share of fuel costs to 90 percent of the total airline costs.

4 Effects on airline competition

Owing to various political and practical reasons, most aviation incentive-based emission control policies are implemented unilaterally within one country or one

Table 17.5 Effects of EU-ETS on emission reduction within the aviation sector (million tonne CO_2)

Prediction year	Cost–pass-through rate		Allowance price			
			€10	*€15*	*€30*	*€45*
2020	100%[a]			6.4		17.7
	47.3%			3.5		10.2
	75%					14.3
	50%					10.8
2012	100%[a]			6.0		16.5
	47.3%			3.0		8.1
	100%[b]	Aviation sector	2.0		5.6	
		Other sectors	20.7		17.1	

Sources: Wit *et al.* (2005) and Boon *et al.* (2007).

Notes

Wit *et al.* and Boon *et al.* use the same simulation model (AERO), but examine different scheme designs.

a All flights, domestic, intra-EU and to/from EU are covered by the scheme, 100% auction.

b All flight segments within the EU airspace are covered by the scheme, 100% auction.

Table 17.6 Effect of taxation on emission reduction within the aviation sector

	Tax type	Tax level	Policy coverage	Emission reduction rate (% of business-as-usual emission)
Wit et al. (2002)	CO_2 emission tax	€10/tCO_2 €30/tCO_2 €50/tCO_2	All flights via EU airspace	1.0 3.1 4.9
Tol (2007)[a]	Carbon tax	US$1,000/tC	Global international aviation	Substitution to domestic flights not allowed: 0.81 ~ 1.67 Substitution to domestic flights allowed: 7.59
Olsthoorn (2001)[b]	Jet fuel tax	US$1,000/t fuel US$1,250/t fuel US$1,500/t fuel	Global international aviation	21 ~ 45 28 ~ 59 33 ~ 70

Notes

a About 3.67 tonne of CO_2 contains 1 tonne of carbon and thus US$1,000/tC is equivalent to US$272/t$CO_2$, or US$80 per tonne fuel.

b The emission reduction rate is calculated based on Olsthoorn (2001)'s results. US$1,000/t fuel = US$34,060/tCO_2. The left numbers of the emission reduction rates are the percentage of reduction under the most emission intensive global economy scenario, and the right numbers are under the least emission intensive global economy scenario.

region. Perhaps the most prominent example of unilateral action is the proposed inclusion of aviation sector into the EU-ETS: as proposed in Directive 2008/101/ EC, starting from 2012, EU-ETS will cover all the flights – domestic, intra-EU and to/from EU – as long as they land at/take off from airports in the EU. This is so far the largest emission trading scheme for aircraft CO_2 emission. Compared with other proposed schemes, EU-ETS attempts to include as wide a scope of flights as possible, but it does not include motor vehicles, thereby creating a potential carbon leakage between transport modes.[7] Another example may be the Kyoto Protocol: as of May 2008, over 180 countries have ratified the Protocol. However, the Kyoto Protocol only covers domestic aviation emissions and some large polluting countries, such as the US and China, either have not ratified the Protocol or have no responsibility for limiting carbon emissions to a predetermined level. As a consequence, this scheme may also be considered as a unilateral regulation.

If an ETS is not implemented globally – either throughout geographical areas or across transportation modes – undesired consequences might occur. In particular, failure to include all the commercial aviation routes in the world in the scheme can distort the competition between carriers who set their base in and outside, respectively, the geographical region covered by the scheme. It can also cause changes in destination choices of tourists and harm the tourism industry of certain countries. Similarly, imposition of ETS can affect passengers' choices of transport modes if surface transportation is not properly covered by similar emission reduction policies.

This section will discuss the effect on airline competition, whereas the next section will discuss the other two effects. To illustrate the effect on airline competition, we consider the proposed EU-ETS. Although both the EU carriers and non-EU carriers are covered in this scheme, the EU carriers may face more disadvantages than their foreign rivals. Below, we list a number of situations where the EU carriers may encounter disadvantages relative to non-EU carriers.

1   Increased airfare induced by the EU-ETS may slow down the growth of the European aviation market. The shrink in the size of EU carriers' home market (relative to that of the non-EU competitors) may raise costs of EU network carriers via the effect of economies of traffic density, resulting in a detriment to the competitive position of European airlines. Wit *et al.* (2005) argue that since the fare increase is small, the change in market size should be marginal and the aforementioned effects on EU carriers should be minimal.
2   Since a large number of routes operated by non-EU network carriers are not covered by the scheme, those carriers are able to deploy the cleanest aircraft on routes inside the scheme while at the same time distributing less fuel efficient aircraft to other routes. If a benchmarking allocation rule is applied, the non-EU carriers may benefit from beating the benchmark and thus being awarded more allowances than needed while saving the cost and effort of adopting the state-of-the-art cleaner technology.

3   The EU-ETS covers almost all the flights of EU-based carriers, both short-haul and long-haul, while it only covers the long-haul intercontinental flights of non-EU carriers. As long-haul flights are more fuel efficient than short-haul flights, non-EU carriers are able to achieve a higher average emission efficiency and obtain more free allowances under benchmarking. This has been quantitatively demonstrated by Scheelhaase *et al.* (2009b) who attempt to forecast the costs of acquiring additional allowances under the proposed EU-ETS following Directive 2008/101/EC for different groups of airlines in 2012. In their study, non-EU network carriers obtain the highest share (73.6 percent) of the allowances needed for their 2012 operation, while the EU-based network carrier group is granted freely the lowest share (65.6 percent) of the allowances needed.

4   Non-EU carriers may try to cross-subsidize their international routes to and from Europe with the profit of domestic operations outside of the scheme. European Commission (2005) argues that this kind of cross-subsidization is unlikely, provided that the pre-ETS operation is optimal. Since the profit of non-EU carriers on routes outside of the scheme will not be affected, no extra profit will be available post-ETS to subsidize the European routes inside the scheme. Thus, if cross-subsidization were profitable, non-EU carriers would have already done so regardless of imposition of the scheme.

Analytically, Yuen and Zhang (2009) study the impact of unilaterally implementing a GHG control measure by levying a tax on flights using airports within the Country H (home). In their model, two competitors, one home airline and one foreign airline, serve the same pair of cities with connecting flights, one in Country H and the other in Country F (foreign). Each carrier uses its hub airport in its own country for flight connection (see Figure 17.2). The home government first decides the level of tax at home airports, which is then followed by airline competition in Cournot form. Yuen and Zhang show that if the home government does not take too much account of its airline's profit and is able to set individual taxes on the hub-and-spoke airports respectively, both airlines will increase fares, the total output will decrease, and the output of the home airline will definitely decrease. However, since the foreign carrier's fare increases less than the home carrier's fare, the foreign carrier's output may either decrease or increase. In the case of rising foreign output (and hence foreign market share), the unilateral tax makes the foreign airline better off relative to the home airline. Moreover, total world GHG emission might increase if the emission efficiency of the foreign airline is below some threshold. Thus, the unilateral action may, while reducing carbon emissions in that region, actually raise total carbon emissions – an effect that is similar to the "pollution haven hypothesis" discussed in the environmental economics literature (e.g., Copeland and Taylor, 1994).

Yuen and Zhang (2009) further investigate the impact of implementing the Kyoto Protocol. Assume that Country H (e.g., Germany) has ratified while Country F (e.g., the US) has not, the government of Country H will maximize its social welfare by choosing an optimal domestic flight emission charge, while

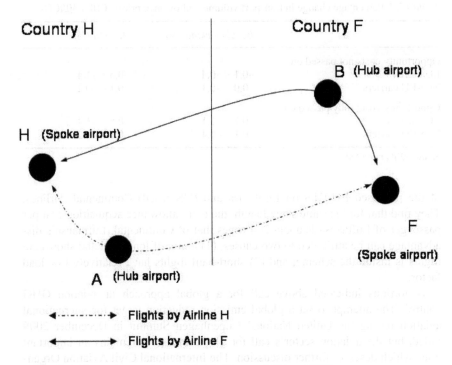

Figure 17.2 Network structure modeled in Yuen and Zhang (2009).

taking both home airline's profit and emissions from the domestic AH leg into consideration. Since the foreign airline does not operate flights within Country H, only the home airline is subject to the emission charge. The foreign airline will obtain a competitive advantage, as the home airline will have to increase fares, losing market share of this city-pair market to its foreign competitor. Consequently, emissions from the home domestic leg (AH) decrease. The total output of the HF market decreases and hence emissions from the international legs (HB and FA) also decrease. However, this does not guarantee a reduction in total GHG emissions, since the emissions from the foreign domestic market will likely increase. Thus, if the foreign airline is highly inefficient, the net effect will be an increase in global emissions. For instance, there is some empirical evidence suggesting that domestic flights in Europe emit, on average, less CO_2 per passenger-km than those in the US (Yuen and Zhang, 2009).

Empirically, using the AERO model Wit *et al.* (2005) predict the impacts on transport-volume changes for both the EU and non-EU carriers. As presented in Table 17.7, non-EU carriers have a better position than EU carriers, as the latter suffer a higher percentage decline in demand than the former by a factor of 4 to 7. Considering that a significantly larger amount of traffic of EU carriers is inside the scheme than that of non-EU carriers, the absolute demand reduction of EU carriers is substantial. Scheelhaase *et al.* (2009a) investigate the impacts

Table 17.7 Percentage change in transport volume – allowance prices: €10 ~ 30/tCO$_2$

	Benchmarking (%)	Auction (%)
Opportunity costs not passed on		
EU carriers	−0.1 ~ −0.4	−0.5 ~ −1.4
Non-EU carriers	0.0 ~ −0.1	−0.1 ~ −0.2
Opportunity costs fully passed on		
EU carriers	−0.7 ~ −2.1	−0.5 ~ −1.4
Non-EU carriers	−0.1 ~ −0.4	−0.1 ~ −0.2

Source: Wit *et al.* (2005).

of the proposed EU-ETS on Lufthansa and (US-based) Continental Airlines. They find that for the same stage length, the extra allowance acquisition cost per passenger of Lufthansa is about 2–4 times that of Continental. Lufthansa's disadvantage can be attributed to two causes: (1) a mix of long-haul and short-haul flights is inside the scheme; and (2) short-haul flights have relatively low load factor.

Distortions indicated above call for a global approach in aviation GHG control. The attempt to set a global emission reduction target for international aviation during the United Nations' Copenhagen Summit in December 2009 failed, but the aviation sector's call for global measures remains an important issue which deserves further discussion. The International Civil Aviation Organization (ICAO) is also trying to design a global mechanism although the progress has been slow and a general agreement among the member states has not yet been reached.

5 Effects on tourist destinations and transport modes

5.1 Tourist destination choices

We locate three papers in which emission trading or carbon taxation in Europe has been examined for their impacts on international tourist distributions and emissions. Tol (2007) studies the effects of a (hypothetical) global carbon tax and a European carbon tax, while FitzGerald and Tol (2007) investigate the effects of EU-ETS (Table 17.8). The global carbon tax on international tourists would achieve 0.81 percent emission reduction, while this reduction falls to 0.19 percent if only tourists to/from EU countries are taxed. If international tourists are able to substitute an overseas holiday with a domestic holiday, the emission reduction from international tourism aviation improves further to 7.59 percent under a global tax.[8] Under EU-ETS with allowance price at €240/tC, the HTM model predicts that the global emission reduction would be less than 0.14 percent. Overall, the total emission reduction from the aviation sector is small even with a very high tax rate or allowance price regardless of the policy imposed.

Table 17.8 Predicated impact of emission policies on tourist distribution and welfare in 2010

Regions	Change in distribution of international tourists				Welfare change (million €)	
	Global carbon tax (US$1000/tC)[a]	EU carbon tax (US$1000/tC)[a]	Difference (global − EU)[a]	EU-ETS (€240/tC)[b]	EU-ETS (€23/tCO₂)[c]	
					Consumer surplus	Producer surplus
Central/Eastern Europe	+	−	−		All EU excl. UK:	All EU excl. UK:
Western Europe	−	+	−		−2,758	−448
EU island nations (e.g., Cyprus, Ireland)	−	−	−			
UK	−	−	+		−349	−145
China	−	−	+	+	All non-EU:	All non-EU:
India	+	+	+	(in general)	−6,998	779
China/India's neighbors	+		+			
Hong Kong	++	−	+	++		
South Korea	+	+	−	++		
Japan	+		+	(in general)		
Middle East	+	−	+			
North America	−	−	+			
South America	−	+				
Africa	−	+	+			
Australasia	−	+	+			
World	na	na	na	na	−10,106	185

Notes

− Assume full opportunity cost pass on and grandfathering in emission trading.

a Summarized from Tol (2007).

b Summarized from FitzGerald and Tol (2007).

c Summarized from Mayor and Tol (2009).

++: very high increase; +: increase; −: decrease; −−: very high decrease.

In general, the regulated region loses market share to non-regulated regions. When an emission tax is imposed, destinations closer to the origin are facing a relatively high price increase because the LTO cycle is the most inefficient stage of a flight. Under a global scheme, tourists tend to shift from long-distance trips to medium ones, from medium-haul air travel to short-haul ground transport, and from short-haul flights to medium-haul flights. Therefore, regions which usually need to be reached by a long flight from major origins of international tourists suffer (e.g., the Americas, Australasia, Africa) and regions that cannot be reached by ground transport lose both short-haul and long-haul tourists (e.g., UK and European island nations). Countries neighboring China and India are expected to gain, because they can be reached from the two most populated countries with medium-haul flights. In a European scheme, European island countries which cannot be reached by ground transportation would lose the most, followed by other European countries on the mainland, but the total number of tourists destined for Europe would fall by less than 0.6 percent (FitzGerald and Tol, 2007). Compared to existing airfare levels and other holiday expenditures, the fare increase from emission trading is relatively marginal and hence the European countries would not encounter a substantial fall in the number of tourists (Wit *et al.*, 2005). European tourists would travel less, and non-EU tourists would turn away from Europe, to other parts of the world. Mayor and Tol (2009) further estimate world welfare changes contributed directly by the aviation sector if EU-ETS were imposed. They find that huge consumer-surplus loss would occur everywhere in the world. Furthermore, non-EU airlines would be able to obtain positive changes in producer surplus, which offset the negative changes in producer surplus suffered by EU airlines.

One interesting observation by Mayor and Tol (2009) is that if the UK air passenger duty (APD) and the Netherlands' boarding tax are considered along with EU-ETS, the combined effect is almost equal to the sum of the effects of each policy implemented alone. This may stem from the model settings where the price elasticity of individual countries is constant.

5.2 Transport mode choices

Airfare rise driven by emission trading may provide incentives for short-haul travelers to divert to ground transportations such as automobile or high-speed rail. Automobiles consume fuel and generate GHG emission as well, while high-speed railways consume electricity which may be supplied by power plants that are major GHG emitters. In this sense, the impact of fare rise on the changes in emissions also depends largely on the share of passengers diverting from aircraft to automobile or train. Jamin *et al.* (2004) estimate a city-pair gravity model based on domestic US passenger air traffic data. In their model, two transportation modes, air and road, compete for passengers in each city-pair market, and the share of traffic by air is determined by a logit model based on passengers' utilities of traveling by air and by car respectively. The regression results show that when all factors (i.e., the total costs of time, transport and lodging) are equal, automobile is slightly preferred to air travel. If the average cost of air travel increases by 10 percent, the air travel market will lose 8 percent of the demand to auto.

Hofer *et al.* (2009) apply the "cross elasticity" estimated by the US Bureau of Transportation Statistics on US domestic markets, suggesting that a 1 percent air traffic demand drop will induce traffic increase in auto mode by 0.041 percent. Based on other assumptions made in their paper, this means that a 10 percent airfare increase is translated to a 2.4 percent traffic loss from air to auto. This ratio is much lower than the estimation by Jamin *et al.* (2004), but note that Jamin *et al.* assume the total number of trips is not affected by the travel costs.

With regard to a shift from aviation to high-speed rail, Jamin *et al.* (2004) show that if ten planned high-speed railway corridors were constructed and were able to capture one-third of the demand in affected air transport markets, the environmental improvement would be modest in the sense that CO_2 emission would drop by 0.7 percent (and NO_x by 1 percent). According to the authors, city-pairs affected by the high-speed rail constitute only 7 percent of the US domestic air travel market and hence high-speed rail has a relatively small impact on nationwide emissions. In the case of a substitution between air and automobile, Hofer *et al.* (2009) find that a 2 percent airfare tax on US domestic markets would eventually increase automobile traffic by 0.094 percent which generates 1.65 billion lbs of CO_2 emissions. Nonetheless, this substitution effect would be offset by the drop in aviation demand and the nationwide net effect is a reduction in emission of 3.44 billion lbs. However, they also demonstrate in a sensitivity analysis that the net emission would rise if the cross-elasticity is higher than 0.13 percent.[9] Besides, since short-haul air trips are more likely to be replaced by auto trips, the adverse impact on the environment is more likely to occur in these markets.

In summary, the above two empirical studies suggest that, in the case of US domestic air transport, the diversion to high-speed rail would only have a small positive effect, while the diversion to automobile would not have a negative effect unless the diversion rate between air and automobile were very high.

6 Indirect impacts

We have so far discussed the direct impacts of ETS through cost and fare increases. With regard to the indirect impacts, a complete treatment of the full indirect linkages shown in Figure 17.1 is non-existent at the moment. Empirical analysis of the indirect impacts is challenging, since interactions among all the players in the aviation sector and various second-order effects need to be captured and theoretical work on these effects is still limited. Nevertheless, some empirical and analytical attempts to study part of the linkages have emerged. One stream tries to construct the relationship between emission efficiency and various service quality and aircraft design decisions, such as aircraft size, flight frequency and load factor. Another tries to study the effects of ETS on airline network structure. There are also papers that examine the incentives for technology improvement. These studies are discussed below.

6.1 Aircraft size, frequency, load factor and flight distance

Scheelhaase *et al.* (2009a) point out a trade-off between two strategies: large aircraft with lower frequency to reduce emission, vs. small aircraft with higher frequency to compete for passengers. The question is then what responses of airlines to the emission control policies, such as ETS, will elicit. Carlsson (2002) limits his study on airline responses in terms of flight frequency. In his (inverse) demand function, airfare is decreasing in the number of passengers and increasing in frequency (i.e., service quality). The government charges each flight a flat environmental tax and maximizes social welfare. For a monopoly airline, Carlsson shows that both the number of passengers and flight frequency would decrease because of the per-flight tax. With two competing airlines, environmental charges would reduce total passengers, but the changes in flight frequency are undetermined for both individual airlines and the market as a whole.

Brueckner and Zhang (2009) consider more dimensions of airline responses than the above studies; they allow airlines to make decisions on fare, frequency, load factor, aircraft fuel efficiency and seat capacity in the context of a de facto fuel price increase caused by emission charges or ETS. Their analytical model considers two airlines competing in a city-pair market. Airline *i*'s total cost of serving the market is denoted as follows:

$$f_i \cdot [r_i e_i s_i + g(e_i, s_i)] k i = 1, 2 \tag{1}$$

where f is frequency (the number of flights), r is per unit fuel price, e denotes fuel consumption per seat per flight hour (i.e., the inverse of fuel efficiency), s is the seat capacity of each flight and k is flight hours. Further, $g(e, s)$ denotes the aircraft capital cost per hour flown, which is decreasing in e and increasing in s, meaning that more fuel efficient/larger aircraft are more expensive. In addition, $g(e, s)/s$ is decreasing in s to reflect economies of aircraft size.

On the demand side, the number of passengers choosing airline *i* is:

$$q_i = \frac{1}{2} - \frac{1}{\alpha} \left(p_i - p_j + \frac{\gamma}{f_i} + \lambda l_i - \frac{\gamma}{f_j} - \lambda l_j \right) i = 1, 2 \quad j = 1, 2 \quad i \neq j \tag{2}$$

where p is ticket price and l is load factor. Assume that passengers with different preferred departure times are uniformly distributed throughout a day and the time intervals between two flights are equal. Then, γ/f is a passenger's cost of not able to depart at his/her preferred time (the so-called frequency delay) with γ being the (positive) cost parameter. Another type of delay cost, the stochastic delay, is incurred when a passenger is denied of boarding on an oversold flight with more passengers showing than the number of available seats. This cost is given by λl, with λ being the cost parameter. Furthermore, the choice of airlines is affected by passengers' brand loyalty which is uniformly distributed on $[-\alpha/2, \alpha/2]$. Finally, the demand specification is derived under the assumption of inelastic demand at the market level.

Given the demand and cost specifications, the profit function can be written for each airline. Each airline will choose p, l, f, e and s to maximize its profit. After examining the resulting Nash equilibrium, Brueckner and Zhang (2009) conclude that a de facto fuel price increase owing to emission trading will induce the airlines to raise fares, reduce flight frequency, increase load factor and choose more fuel efficient aircraft, while keeping their seat capacities unchanged. In particular, the fare increase is decomposed into four channels: (1) a positive direct effect from fuel price increase; (2) a negative second-order effect from less fuel consumption through airlines' improving fuel efficiency; (3) a positive second-order effect from higher capital cost via airlines' buying/leasing more efficient aircraft; and (4) a negative indirect effect from lower per passenger cost through airlines choosing higher load factors. As can be seen, (2), (3) and (4) can be considered as the indirect impacts of ETS in our classification.[10]

As indicated earlier, EU-ETS will apply the benchmarking approach to emission allowance allocations. This implies that airlines achieving lower than average emissions per RTK (or per RPK) would be rewarded. As a consequence, airlines might have an incentive to improve fuel efficiency by changing aircraft size, load factor, route distance, flight frequency, etc. This and related issues have attracted several recent empirical investigations. For instance, Morrell (2009) examines various types of aircraft and finds a strong negative correlation between fuel consumption per available seat and seat capacity for short-/medium-haul aircraft. For long-haul aircraft, this relationship is much weaker and is not statistically significant if double-deckers (e.g., A380) are included in the sample. Miyoshi and Mason (2009a) observe that in general large aircraft operating long-haul flights have higher fuel efficiency than small short-haul aircraft, but that the efficiency of large aircraft decreases with stage length, since more fuel has to be carried. Miyoshi and Mason (2009b) apply a log-linear model to a sample of UK carriers and find that seat capacity, load factor and stage length are all negatively correlated with carbon emission per passenger-km. Furthermore, flights operated on routes with high market concentration and by carriers with small market share tend to be less fuel efficient, and LCCs are more efficient than network carriers. Another interesting finding in Miyoshi and Mason (2009b) is that carbon emission per passenger-km has a negative correlation with frequency. Their explanation is that offering more flights will attract more passengers and the increase in passenger-km then outweighs the increase in emission.

6.2 Network structure

To illustrate the impact of emission regulations on airline networks, we first consider an origin-destination (OD) market with one city in the regulated home area and the other in the unregulated foreign area. Albers *et al.* (2009) investigate three routing possibilities given in this case under the proposed EU-ETS: (1) one-stop flight with the stop within the EU; (2) direct flight; and (3) one-stop flight with the stop outside of the EU. Table 17.9 shows the additional costs per

Table 17.9 Additional costs per origin-destination passenger under the proposed EU-ETS

Routing type	Origin	Stopover	Destination	Additional costs per passenger (€)
1	Newark	Frankfurt	Cologne	16.08
2	Newark	–	Cologne	9.27
3	Newark	Zurich	Cologne	1.74
1	Newark	Frankfurt	Dusseldorf	12.33
2	New York (JFK)	–	Dusseldorf	13.84
3	Newark	Zurich	Dusseldorf	3.18
2	Singapore	–	Frankfurt	19.77
3	Singapore	Zurich	Frankfurt	1.48
3	Singapore	Istanbul	Frankfurt	4.69
3	Singapore	Dubai	Frankfurt	13.04

Source: Albers *et al.* (2009).

Notes
Routing type: 1 = one-stop flight with the stop within EU; 2 = direct flight; 3 = one-stop flight with the stop outside of EU.
Assume a 50–50 leisure-business passenger split and €20/tCO2 allowance price.

passenger for OD pairs selected from the study. Note that while the direct routing generally performs better than the routing of having a stop within the EU-ETS area, this is not always the case (e.g., New York–Dusseldorf). Further, having a stop outside of the scheme area always generates a much lower cost than transiting at an airport inside the scheme area. The cost difference between the EU stop flight and the direct flight is relatively small as compared with the cost difference between the two one-stop alternatives. It seems that airlines that have already had a hub operation at airports just outside the scheme area would have an advantage after the implementation of an ETS.

In comparison between the direct flight and the non-EU stop flight, Scheelhaase *et al.* (2009b) present an example of a round trip between Frankfurt and Singapore. If the allowance price is €40 and the allowance costs are fully passed through to passengers, the trip price would increase by €85 for direct flights operated by Lufthansa or Singapore Airlines. On the other hand, for the flights operated by Emirates with a stop-over at Dubai, the price increase would be less than €35. Nevertheless, compared with the price of a direct flight for such a long-haul trip, the €50 difference is a small saving and would hardly be a good reason for passengers putting up with the trouble of having one more stop. Wit *et al.* (2005) argue that rerouting from the direct flight to the non-EU stop flight is very unlikely, because the change incurs costs of additional airport charges and fuel consumption which are likely to outweigh the cost savings from surrendering fewer allowances.

Next, consider an OD trip with all the feasible routes fully covered by ETS. This case is fundamentally different from the above case, in the sense that geographical restriction of the scheme does not play a role. As a result, whether a direct flight or an indirect flight is preferred depends on fuel efficiency as well as various operational decisions made by airlines. Morrell and Lu (2007) evaluate the increase in social environmental costs caused by accommodating an extra of 150 passengers traveling between origin and destination, either indirectly with a stop or directly.[11] Their major finding is that accommodating the additional passengers with direct flights will induce less environmental cost than using indirect flights. The difference becomes smaller if the two routings are closer in their great circle distances. Jamin *et al.* (2004) explore the impacts on GHG emission if all indirect flights in the US domestic market were replaced by direct flights. The authors find that in such an extreme case, CO_2 emission would decline by 10 percent, of which 4 percent is due to the reduction in average total trip length and 6 percent is due to the reduction in the number of take-offs. Scheelhaase *et al.* (2009a) argue that because of the difference in fuel efficiency between short-haul connecting flights and long-haul direct flights, ETS would provide an incentive for airlines to offer more direct long-haul flights instead of hubbing. However, such cost savings from switching to direct flights barely offset the benefit of hubbing, as the ETS-related cost constitutes only a small share of total cost.

Scheelhaase *et al.* (2009a) further point out that the fuel efficiency of a hub-and-spoke system may be improved with larger aircraft and lower flight frequencies. However, an effective and marketable hub-and-spoke system usually requires high frequencies facilitated with small aircraft. To some extent, this "dilemma" is addressed in Brueckner and Zhang (2009) with a simple model of three equally distant cities. They show that under a hub-and-spoke network, airlines tend to use more fuel efficient and larger aircraft while providing more flights, than under a point-to-point network.[12] Moreover, Brueckner and Zhang investigate whether imposition of airline emission charges will tend to alter current network structures, perhaps causing a shift away from the dominant hub-and-spoke structure. They find that a hub-and-spoke system is favored only if the economy of aircraft size is large enough; otherwise, a shift away from the hub-and-spoke to point-to-point systems might be expected.

6.3 *Technology improvement*

Brueckner and Zhang (2009) model the capital cost as a function of aircraft fuel efficiency and show that emission charges would induce airlines to choose more efficient aircraft. In the short run, however, the ability to improve aircraft fuel efficiency may be limited. Wit *et al.* (2002) consider retrofitting wings with winglets or wingtip devices and retrofitting of riblets as possible short-term technical measures. The authors find that these measures provide more emission reduction and DOC ("direct operating cost") reduction on long-haul flights than short-haul flights.[13] However, emission charges tend to elicit short-haul small aircraft to adopt these measures.

In the medium-to-long run, accelerating fleet renewal with currently available technology is a viable option. Wit *et al.* (2002) conclude that imposition of an emission charge at €30/tCO_2 will, on average, lower the "lowest cost aircraft age" – the age at which DOC per RTK is the lowest – by one year. This result suggests that a moderate emission charge may be able to induce earlier phase-out of older and less fuel efficient aircraft. In the longer run airlines may, as predicted by Brueckner and Zhang (2009), invest in new technology for cleaner aircraft and more efficient engines. This is perhaps the most desirable airline response from the environment perspective and is in accord with the long-run benefits of emission trading. However, since investment in cleaner technology can be risky and the recovery cycle is long, airlines must take future environmental policy into consideration. As suggested by Carlsson (1999), in the long run the incentives to invest in new technology depend on the predicted future regulations rather than the present regulations.

7 Concluding remarks

Our review of the research on the effect of emission trading schemes (ETS) in air transport has revealed an important and active strand of literature. The research has improved our understanding on the issue. At the aggregate level, studies have reached fairly consistent conclusions on the impacts of ETS within the aviation sector. For example, LCCs would be more adversely affected by ETS than FSCs although LCCs are generally more fuel efficient. The differential impacts arise because following the imposition of ETS, LCCs tend to have a higher percentage price increase and, owing to serving more price sensitive passengers, suffer a greater percentage decline in demand than FSCs. Charter airlines may, because of their high fuel efficiency owing to high load factors and long flight distance, benefit from ETS, if the benchmarking allocation method is applied. In the short run and without adequate supply-side responses, the amount of emission reduction within the aviation sector induced by the direct impacts is found to be relatively small.

Existing empirical and analytical studies have also indicated that unilateral adoption of ETS may distort airline competition with airlines based inside the ETS region facing competitive disadvantages at least in the short run. However, it is not clear to what an extent such a distortion would occur, and how in the longer run airlines will respond with their choices of network structure, aircraft size and fuel efficiency. In terms of the tourism industry, countries not implementing an ETS may benefit in that they may gain international tourists from the ETS region. Several studies have also examined the important issue of "carbon leakage," and have provided conditions under which failure to implement a global ETS – both geographically and across transport modes – actually raises total world carbon emissions. One of the conditions is those routes or modes that gain more passengers post-ETS are highly inefficient in fuel consumption. It is noted that current empirical studies on mode substitutions suggest that shifting air passengers to high-speed rails would have a small positive effect on emission reduction, while shifting air passengers to automobiles would not have adverse impacts on total emissions unless the diversion rate between air and automobile trips is very high.

With regard to the indirect impacts, imposition of ETS may result in airlines' raising fares, improving aircraft fuel efficiency, increasing load factor and reducing flight frequency. However, no determinate results have emerged regarding the ETS impact on airline routing and network structures. A point-to-point system does not necessarily outperform a hub-and-spoke system even if all the routes are covered by the ETS. Having a hub just outside the ETS region might be beneficial to an airline if the costs of switching hub airports or adding stops are offset by the benefit of paying less for emission allowances.

We end this review with the observation that to improve our understanding of the effects of emission trading schemes and further provide helpful policy guidance, both the direct and indirect impacts need to be thoroughly investigated. The existing literature appears to focus on the direct, short-run impacts. It is also observed that the papers are primarily empirical and institutional studies. Theoretical work is still relatively rare but is nevertheless important in guiding empirical investigation as well as in the policy discussions. We expect that more analytical work and work combining both the direct and indirect channels of ETS impact will be developed in the literature. Hence, future reviews of the effects of emission trading schemes will have much to say on the important interactions among the policies, aviation and environmental impacts, as well as overall social welfare.

Notes

1 For example, Carlsson and Hammar (2002) assert that ETS with fully auctioned permits has almost the same characteristics of an emission charge and that, while emission reduction under ETS is known, emission charge may be preferred under uncertainty. Nevertheless, ETS has some special features, including the emission allowance allocation rules, base year selection, decision on open or close trading, which are not at issue in taxation.

2 Descriptions of the HTM and AERO model are available in Tol (2007) and Vlek and Vogels (2000), respectively.

3 In this sense, Condor, while a traditional charter airline, shares some characteristics of a low-cost carrier.

4 The rationale offered in Vivid Economics is that among business passengers or the mixed passengers, some of them have very high willingness to pay and the rest have increasing numbers of passengers less willing to pay and hence the demand curve is close to an iso-elasticity demand curve. In contrast, the proportion of leisure passengers who are prepared to pay a very high price is much smaller and the willingness to pay may tend to be uniformly distributed among leisure passengers for a range of lower prices, resulting in a nearly linear demand.

5 The pre-ETS emission cost is the production of post-ETS allowance price and pre-ETS emission level.

6 Note that with a cap-and-trade system, assuming no emission leakage, the total amount of emission reduction of the specific GHG regulated is predetermined. If radiative forcing is considered, one tonne of CO_2 emitted by aircraft flying in the sky is estimated to have around two to four times of the impact of the same amount of CO_2 emitted on the ground (IPCC, 2001). Another estimate by Henderson and Wickrama (1999) is around 2.5 times. Thus, change in the amount of radiative forcing is unknown under the cap-and-trade system on CO_2 if the aviation sector is allowed to

trade allowances with other sectors, although the amount of CO_2 emission reduction is fixed. The issue of global emission reduction with possible leakage will be discussed in Sections 4 and 5.

7 Emissions from the vehicle fuel production and automobile manufacturing activities are included in EU-ETS, but emissions from using automobiles, the largest tranche of GHG emissions in the transportation sector, have yet to be included. The European Council started to consider including road transportation in 2007. No agreement has been reached yet. In EU-ETS, the rail sector is indirectly affected by the electricity production process, since emissions from electricity producers are covered.

8 Carbon emissions from taking domestic holidays were not counted in Tol (2007), since the author was only interested in the effects on international tourism.

9 This is equivalent to the situation in which a 10 percent increase in fares causes 7.5 percent of air traffic to divert to automobiles. This figure is closer to the estimation of Jamin *et al.* (2004).

10 Sgouridis (2009) discussed in detail a range of emission reduction alternatives for airlines and potential competitive advantages if any of the alternatives is adopted. The study is mostly descriptive, with some illustrative simulations.

11 In Morrell and Lu (2007)'s setting, prior to the addition of 150 passengers, there are flights on the two spoke segments, but no direct flights. If all the 150 new passengers are accommodated by the original indirect flights, the airline will switch to larger aircraft. Further, their social environment costs include noise, local air pollution around the airports, and CO_2 emissions during both the LTO cycle and the cruise stage.

12 This is in contrast to the "common" result, discussed above, that direct flights are more fuel efficient. The difference might be explained by different definitions of "fuel efficiency": the "generally defined" fuel efficiency is the amount of fuel burned per RPK affected by various operational measures. In Brueckner and Zhang (2009), on the other hand, fuel efficiency is a property attached to aircraft and so it is not affected by load factor, seat capacity and flight distance.

13 DOC includes the direct flying cost (crew and fuel), maintenance cost, aircraft depreciation cost, landing fees, insurance and finance cost.

References

Alamdari, F.E. and Brewer, D. (1994) "Taxation policy for aircraft emissions," *Transport Policy*, 1(3): 149–159.

Albers, S., Buhne, J. and Peters, H. (2009) "Will the EU-ETS instigate airline network reconfigurations?" *Journal of Air Transport Management*, 15: 1–6.

Bigano, A., Hamilton, J.M. and Tol, R.S.J. (2006) "The impact of climate on holiday destination choice," *Climatic Change*, 76: 389–406.

Boon, B., Davidson, M., Faber, J. and van Velzen, A. (2007) "Allocation of allowances for aviation in the EU ETS: the impact on the profitability of the aviation sector under high levels of auctioning," CE Delft.

Bresson, J. (2009) "Impact of NOx emissions regulation – cost benefit analysis," paper presented at the 13th ATRS World Conference, Abu Dhabi, June 2009.

Brueckner, J.K. and Zhang, A. (2009) "Airline emission charges: effects on airfares, service quality, and aircraft design," paper presented at the 4th Kuhmo Nectar Summer School and Conference, Copenhagen, July 2009.

Carlsson, F. (1999) "Incentive-based environmental regulation of domestic civil aviation in Sweden," *Transport Policy*, 6: 75–82.

Carlsson, F. (2002) "Environmental charges in airline markets," *Transportation Research Part D*, 7: 137–153.

Carlsson, F. and Hammar, H. (2002) "Incentive-based regulation of CO2 emissions from international aviation," *Journal of Air Transport Management*, 8: 365–372.

Copeland, B.R. and Taylor, M.S. (1994) "North–south trade and the environment," *Quarterly Journal of Economics*, 109, 755–787.

European Commission (2005) "Annex to the communication from the Commission: reducing the climate change impact of aviation – impact assessment COM (2005) 459 final," *Commission Staff Working Document*, Brussels.

Ernst & Young (2007) "Analysis of the EC proposal to include aviation activities in the emissions trading scheme," York Aviation, June 1, 2007.

FitzGerald, J. and Tol, R.S.J. (2007) "Airline emissions of carbon dioxide in the European trading system," *CESIfo Forum*, January 2007.

Forsyth, P. (2008) "The impact of climate change policy on competition in the air transport industry," discussion paper, OECD/ITF, Paris.

Frontier Economics (2006) "Economic consideration of extending the EU ETS to include aviation," paper prepared for the European Low Fares Airlines Association (ELFAA), March 2006.

Henderson, S.C. and Wickrama, U.K. (1999) "Aircraft emissions: current inventories and future scenarios," in J.E. Penner, D.H. Lister, D.J. Griggs, D.J. Dokken and M. McFarland (eds.) *Aviation and the Global Atmosphere: A Special Report of IPCC Working Groups I and III*, Cambridge: Cambridge University Press.

Hofer, C., Dresner, M. and Windle, R. (2009) "The environmental effects of airline carbon emissions taxation in the U.S.," *Transportation Research Part D*, 15 (1): 37–45.

IPCC (Intergovernmental Panel on Climate Change) (2001) *Climate Change 2001: The Scientific Basis. Contribution of Working Group I to the Third Assessment Report of the IPCC*, eds. J.T. Houghton, Y. Ding, D.J. Griggs, M. Noguer, P.J. van der Linden, X. Dai, K. Maskell and C.A. Johnson, Cambridge: Cambridge University Press.

Jamin, S., Shafer, A., Ben-Akiva, M.E. and Waitz, I.A. (2004) "Aviation emissions and abatement policies in the United States: a city-pair analysis," *Transportation Research Part D*, 9: 295–317.

Lu, C. (2009) "The implications of environmental costs on air passenger demand for different airline business models," *Journal of Air Transport Management*, 15: 158–165.

Lu, C. and Morrell, P. (2001) "Evaluation and implications of environmental charges on commercial flights," *Transport Reviews*, 21(3): 377–395.

Mayor, K. and Tol, R.S.J. (2009) "The impact of European climate change regulations on international tourist markets," *Transportation Research Part D*, 15 (1): 26–36.

Miyoshi, C. and Mason, K.J. (2009a) "The carbon emissions of selected airlines and aircraft types in three geographic markets," *Journal of Air Transport Management*, 15: 138–147.

Miyoshi, C. and Mason, K.J. (2009b) "Airline business models: evolution and their impact on the carbon efficiency of air transport in the intra-EU market," paper presented at the 13th ATRS World Conference, Abu Dhabi, June 2009.

Morrell, P. (2007) "An evaluation of possible EU air transport emissions trading scheme allocation methods," *Energy Policy*, 35: 5562–5570.

Morrell, P. (2009) "The potential for European aviation CO2 emissions reduction through the use of larger jet aircraft," *Journal of Air Transport Management*, 15: 151–157.

Morrell, P. and Lu, C. (2007) "The environmental cost implication of hub–hub versus hub by-pass flight networks," *Transportation Research Part D*, 12: 143–157.

OECD (2008) "Transport outlook 2008: focusing on CO2 emissions from road vehicles," Organization of Economic Cooperation and Development (OECD) Discussion Paper No. 2008–13, May.

Olsthoorn, X. (2001) "Carbon dioxide emissions from international aviation: 1950–2050," *Journal of Air Transport Management*, 7: 87–93.

PWC (2005) "Aviation emissions and policy instruments," London: Price Waterhouse Coopers.

Reimer, D.S. and Putnam, J.E. (2007) "The law of aviation-related climate change: the airport proprietor's role in reducing greenhouse gas emissions," *Airport Management*, 2(1): 82–95.

Scheelhaase, J.D. and Grimme, W.G. (2007) "Emissions trading for international aviation – an estimation of the economic impact on selected European airlines," *Journal of Air Transport Management*, 13: 253–263.

Scheelhaase, J.D., Grimme, W.G. and Schaefer, M. (2009a) "The inclusion of aviation into the EU emission trading scheme – impacts on competition between European and non-European network airlines," *Transportation Research Part D*, 15 (1): 14–25.

Scheelhaase, J.D., Schaefer, M., Grimme, W.G. and Maertens, S. (2009b) "EU-legislation tackling aviation's CO2 emissions: model-based empirical estimation of the economic and ecologic impact of the EU-emissions trading scheme on the international aviation sector," paper presented at the 13th ATRS World Conference, Abu Dhabi, June 2009.

Sgouridis, S. (2009) "Successful airline strategies in a carbon-constrained future: scenario analysis for investigating the options," paper presented at the 13th ATRS World Conference, Abu Dhabi, June 2009.

Tol, R.S.J. (2007) "The impact of a carbon tax on international tourism," *Transportation Research Part D*, 12: 129–142.

Vivid Economics (2007) "A study to estimate ticket price changes for aviation in the EU ETS," a report for the Department for Environment, Food and Rural Affairs (Defra) and the Department for Transport (DfT), UK, November 2007.

Vivid Economics (2008) "A study to estimate the impacts of emissions trading on profits in aviation," a report for the Department for Environment, Food and Rural Affairs (Defra) and the Department for Transport (DfT), UK, January 2008.

Vlek, S. and Vogels, M. (2000) "AERO – Aviation emissions and evaluation of reduction options," *Air and Space Europe*, 2(3): 41–44.

Wit, R.C.N., Dings, J.M.W., Mendes de Leon, P., Thwaites, L., Peeters, P., Greenwood, D. and Doganis, R. (2002) "Economic incentives to mitigate greenhouse gas emissions from air transport in Europe," CE Delft, July 2002.

Wit, R.C.N., Boon, B.H., van Velzen, A., Cames, M., Deuber, O. and Lee, D.S. (2005) "Giving wings to emission trading-Inclusion of aviation under the European emission trading system (ETS): design and impacts," CE Delft, July 2005.

Yuen, A.C.L. and Zhang, A. (2009) "Unilateral GHG control measure and aviation industry: a theoretical analysis," paper presented at the 4th Kuhmo Nectar Summer School and Conference, Copenhagen, July 2009.

18 Competition between airlines and high-speed rail

Werner Rothengatter

1 Introduction

The development of transport demand after opening of high-speed railway (HSR) lines between big agglomerations shows that fierce competition between air transport and HSR may occur on distances up to 1,000 km. In most cases a modal competition between air and rail occurs on travel distances between 400 and 800 km. Below 400 km road transport is the main competitor of the railways. Beyond 800 km air transport has such big advantages that the modal share of the railways is fading away. There are only a few cases for long-distance HSR such as the corridor between Seville and Barcelona with an overall length of 1,102 km and a total travel time of 5 hrs 42 min.

In this chapter the European development of air traffic and high-speed rail on major relationships is compiled and discussed in the first two parts. The third part presents empirical findings on the competition between short-distance air transport, in particular operated by low-cost carriers (LCC), and HSR. In some cases the competitive performance of HSR appears encouraging, but there are also a number of cases for which the huge investment in HSR has not proven financially viable (see Adler and Nash, 2008). If the occupancy rates are low then the environmental advantages of HSR compared with LCC are shrinking such that the question arises whether the expansion plans for HSR should be streamlined or the competitive power of HSR could be improved by state policies towards competing modes in the future.

In the fourth part the possibilities for increasing the competitive power of HSR are analysed. First of all the barriers to fair competition are analysed, as they can be found in the fields of taxation, subsidisation and regulation. It will be shown that the state support given for constructing the infrastructure is widely compensated by discriminatory state policy on the operation side. This will be demonstrated in particular using the example of CO_2-emission trading in the EU. Second, the management capacity of European railway companies will be discussed critically. European legislation has provided the necessary conditions for a re-organisation of the railway companies to increase competitiveness. The present economic crisis, however, has strengthened the political wings, which are in favour of an increasing state influence on the network economies, again.

This might lead to more intense state interventions in the rail market which inter-rupt the process of railway reform towards a more commercial orientation of the railway companies.

The fifth part will summarise the main conclusions on the potential of HSR on the one hand and on the barriers to HSR development on the other hand. HSR extension is not possible without the significant financial assistance of the state. There is high probability that the budget problems of the European states will increase after the economic crisis. Therefore there are some doubts about the financial feasibility of the very optimistic expansion plans of some European countries.

2 Air transport dynamics

2.1 Growth and market share

Air transport has grown most dynamically in the past decades. Air traffic per-formance (pkm) in the EU27 has increased by 70.4 per cent between 1995 and 2007 (Figure 18.1). Modal split developed from 6.3 per cent (1995) to 8.8 per cent (2007). During this period the share of railways dropped from 6.6 per cent to 6.1 per cent.

2.2 The success of low-cost carriers (LCC)

The rapid growth of air transport has been driven to a wide extent by the upturn of LCC. While the business model of LCC has been known since 1971 (US carrier South West; Laker's Skytrain) and started in Europe with Ryanair as early as 1991 the powerful push came in the late 1990s after the completion of

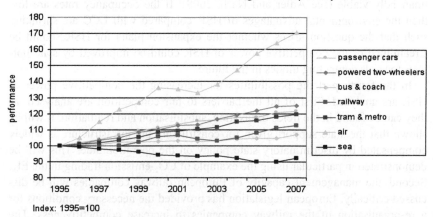

Figure 18.1 Development of air traffic in EU27 (source: Energy and Transport. Facts and Figures (2009)).

the liberalisation of the EU air transport market. Presently 31 LCC are regis-tered on the EU market with about 40,000 starts per day, a seat capacity of 6.2 million and a market share of about one-third (see DLR and ADV, 2009). While some carriers are specialised on low-cost flights only (Ryanair and easyJet are number 1 and 2) others apply mixed business concepts, like Air Berlin (number 3 on LCC market). Figure 18.2 exhibits the rapid market expansion of LCC since 2002.

While the growth of LCC exploded between 1998 and 2003 it had slowed down by 2008 (see Figure 18.3). In the year 2009 LCC stagnated; however, their market share keeps growing because the LCC low price strategies diverted traffic from network and charter carriers to LCC during the economic crisis (see Figure 18.2).

The main reason for this success story of LCC is the low tariffs which become possible through a related low-cost business strategy, consisting of the following components:

- single passenger class;
- single type of aircraft;
- minimum optional equipment, minimum unpaid extra service;
- simple tariff scheme, direct sales, no agent service;
- using cheap secondary airports, simple boarding equipment;
- fast turnaround processes;
- direct flights, simple round tours, no hubbing;

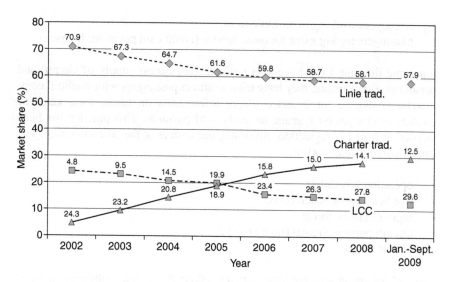

Figure 18.2 Development of market shares of LCC in Germany in percentages (source: DLR and ADV (2009)).

Notes
Linie trad.: Network carriers; Charter trad: Charter carriers; LCC: Low-Cost Carriers.

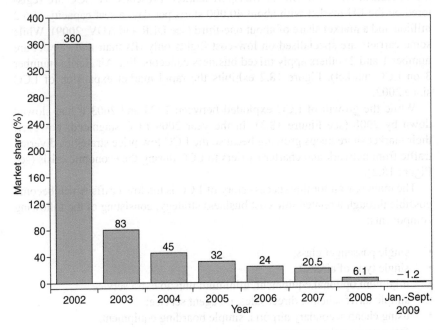

Figure 18.3 Development of growth rates of LCC in Germany in percentages (source: DLR and ADV (2009)).

- employees working in multiple roles;
- passengers paying extra for basic service (credit card payment, luggage).

For some time the LCC have also profited from excess supply of aircraft and personnel. Furthermore, they have tried to attract passengers with doubtful commercial strategies, for instance hiding information on taxes, fees, kerosene charges or charges on luggage or credit card payment. This practice has been stopped now by EU regulation. Analysing the sources of the cost advantages one can classify five categories:

- operation schedules;
- overhead services and costs;
- input of labour force;
- aircraft purchase/rental (high orders);
- airport choice.

Some of the advantages are temporary and others due to state subsidies. Some of the options mentioned above have been squeezed out or are also used now by network carriers. Therefore, the expansion phase of LCC seems to be turning into a phase of consolidation. Nevertheless LCC will play a major role on short and medium distances and will be the main competitors on corridors served by HSR.

3 European experience with high-speed rail

3.1 HSR network and planned extensions

If high speed is defined as including all railway links which allow for a maximum speed of 200 km/h and more, then the European HSR network is already advanced, as can be seen in Figure 18.4. However, trains operating on links with a maximum speed of 200 km/h can only be competitive on smaller distances or in combination with links allowing for much higher speeds. Therefore, the information on those parts of the European rail network, which allow for speeds of 250 km/h or more, is more relevant.

Table 18.1 shows that the length of the European HSR_{250} network is about 5,800 km. France, which has been the European pioneer of HSR since 1981, has the largest HSR network with about 1,900 km, followed by Spain (1,600 km) and Germany (1,300 km).

While the HSR networks in France and Spain have been constructed in the past on the base of clear corridor concepts (Italy is also on the way to complete a coherent North–South corridor) the German HSR network is rather fragmented. HSR sections are combined with conventional rail sections to construct complete lines with mixed speeds. Therefore the competitiveness of HSR on connections between large cities is still modest. The travel times between Munich and Berlin (503 km[1]) is about 6 hrs, Cologne–Berlin (475 km) about 4 hrs 15 min and Frankfurt–Berlin (423 km) about 4 hrs. On city pairs which are connected by coherent high-speed links (Cologne–Frankfurt (152 km), Hanover–Berlin (245 km), Hamburg–Berlin (255 km) the air service has been abolished after introducing HSR.

Figure 18.4 European high-speed rail network 2007 (source: UIC).

Table 18.1 Length of railway links allowing for speeds of 250 km/h or higher

	BE	DE	ES	FR	IT	UK	EU
1990		90		699	224		1,013
2000	58	636	471	1,278	248		2,691
2008	120	1,300	1,594	1,893	744	113	5,764

Source: EU Energy and Transport Facts and Figures, 2009.

3.2 Planned HSR network in Europe

The concept of Transeuropean Networks for Transport (TEN-T), which has been developed by the EU Commission since 1990, leading to the guidelines of 1996 and their revision in 2004, favours the development of HSR in Europe, which is regarded a backbone of interurban passenger transport. Fourteen out of 30 corridors in the 2004 guidelines are related to HSR. The international (border crossing) parts of the TEN-T are widely in line with the national infrastructure development plans, because a co-finance by the EU Commission (in general: up to 50 per cent of the planning costs and up to 10 per cent of the construction costs) is possible. Figure 18.5 shows the expansion plans for links >250 km/h speed until the year 2020. It can be seen that France and Italy are following corridor-based expansion strategies. Also border-crossing links (France–Spain; Italy–Austria; Portugal–Spain) are in the focus. The Spanish concept is turning from corridor to a network orientation and plans to use HSR also to provide equal rail service to all regions. The planned network density for HSR is unusually high and might call for further action – either streamlining of the concept or strategies towards competing modes.

In France the plans exhibited by Figure 18.5 have meanwhile been extended by the Grenelle programme, which foresees building 2,000 km of HSR until 2020 – which would mean a doubling of the network compared with 2008. Table 18.2 gives some details on the new links planned in a medium term.

3.3 Performance of HSR in Europe

Rail transport showed a modest development in the phase 2001–2004 when economic growth was low in countries with higher modal shares of the railways. Since 2004 the railways have significantly gained market share again (see Figure 18.1). This is due in particular to HSR service, which could be improved considerably after the opening of some important links (sections of Madrid–Barcelona until completion 2008, Cologne–Frankfurt 2002, Paris–Beaudrecourt 2007, London–Folkestone 2007).

Figure 18.6 gives an example of the effect of adding a missing link to an important HSR corridor. The accomplishment of the section London–Folkestone (Channel Tunnel), of the corridors London–Paris and London–Brussels was planned for the late 1990s, but for a number of reasons it came ten years late in 2007. Again, one realises the kink in the development of passenger demand

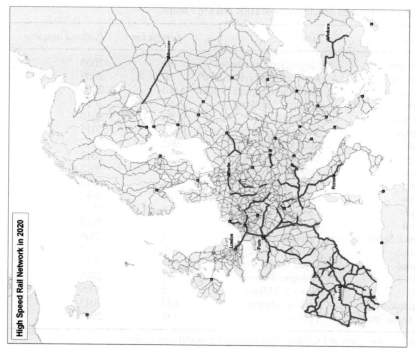

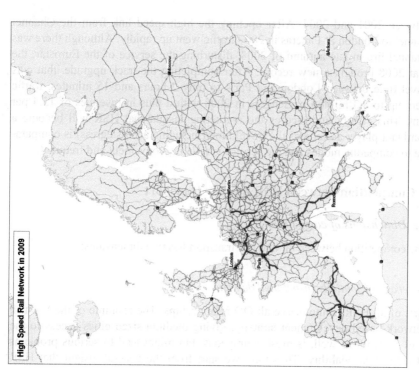

Figure 18.5 Planned development of the European HSR network (source: Rothengatter and Szimba, compiled from different sources).

Table 18.2 Planned development of HSR links in Europe

Country	Link	Length km	Planned opening
Belgium	Liège–German Border	36	2009
Belgium	Antwerp–Dutch Border	36	2009
Netherlands	Schiphol–Belgium Border	120	2009
Germany	Munich–Augsburg	62	2010
Germany	Gröhers–Erfurt	98	2010
Germany	Nuremberg–Erfurt	218	2015
Spain	Madrid–Murcia	902	2017
Spain	Vitoria–San Sebastian	175	2012
Spain	Bobadilla–Granada	50	2012
Spain	Variante de Pajares	88	2012
Spain	Ourense–Santiago	109	2012
Spain	La Coruna–Vigo	158	2012
Spain	Barcelona–Figueras	132	2012
France/Spain	Perpignan–Figueras	44	2009
France	Nimes–Montpellier	70	2012
France	Dijon–Mulhouse	140	2012
Italy	Bologna–Firenze	77	2009
Italy	Novara–Milano	55	2009
Portugal/Spain	Lisboa–Madrid	644	2013
Portugal/Spain	Porto–Vigo	145	2018

Source: Rothengatter and Szimba, 2009; compiled from different sources.

between 2001 and 2004. After opening the high-speed link from the Channel Tunnel to London St Pancras in 2007 traffic went up rapidly. Although there was a tunnel fire in late autumn of 2008, disturbing the service of the Eurostar, the year 2008 brought a new record. After completing the track upgrade, that cuts travel time between London and Paris to only 2 hours and 15 minutes, traffic went up to 8.3 million passengers in 2008 with a plus in revenues of 15.4 per cent. This clearly underscores the marketing insight that HSR will become a dominant player as soon as the travel time (including access/egress) is comparable to competing modes and the service is reliable, convenient and frequent.

4 Competition between HSR and air transport

4.1 Dimensions of competition

The competition between air and rail transport has two dimensions:

Coverage of spatially distributed demand

First of all HSR cannot serve all OD relationships. The example of the Spanish network-based development strategy, giving medium-sized cities access to the HSR network as well, is most courageous, but might lead to serious problems with financial viability. Therefore, we start from the general insight that HSR

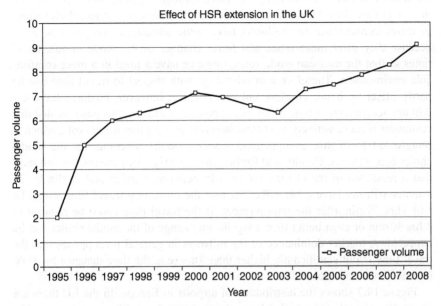

Figure 18.6 Growth of Eurostar patronage 1995–2008 (source: Eurotunnel).

can only be provided successfully on busy corridors. As soon as patronage is low then the advantage of railways in terms of low unit costs of transport and low external effects will vanish. This means first that HSR has to be combined with efficient regional transport such that regions in the neighbourhood of HSR stations can also profit from the better railway service. But second, this will not be sufficient to give all regions equal access to HSR. The distribution of rail demand potential in Europe is not comparable to Japan where the major part of the population is concentrated alongside a narrow band on the main island Honshu and the major cities are lined up like pearls on a string.

Therefore there will remain territorial spatial "natural" monopolies for air transport. The development of regional airports in the past two decades has partly created and partly strengthened this monopoly position. Airports are distributed over the European space after two decades of dynamic development in a way that most of the regions have good access to an airport and are served with attractive flight patterns (see Figure 4.1). Furthermore, the possibility of the railways providing a service comparable to the airlines is becoming difficult at OD distances beyond 800 km and almost hopeless beyond 1,000 km.

Quality of service in densely populated corridors

In densely populated corridors there is in principle a high demand potential for railway service. To explore this potential the railway service quality should come close to that of the airlines, expressed through the generalised cost including travel time, travel costs, convenience and frequency of service. With respect to travel convenience the railways have some advantage compared with air because they offer more space and fewer changes of the mode or idle travel times so that the user can work, relax, move or have a meal in a more comfortable environment. Therefore a disadvantage with respect to travel time can be partly offset by better comfort and convenience; however, business travellers will not accept a large time difference. Travel demand analysis has revealed that customers react sensitively in critical intervals of the generalised costs, which is represented by highly asymmetrical reaction (logit) functions for the modal choice (see Mandel, Gaudry and Rothengatter, 1997).[2] This means, for instance, that a reduction of travel time for the trip between Munich and Berlin by 30 minutes will not have a big effect because the remaining travel time would be still 5 hrs 30 min after the improvement. If the travel time could be reduced to 4 hrs 30 min or even better then a significant change of the modal choice can be expected. A market dominance of the railways in general presupposes that the travel time is not significantly higher than 3 hrs (e.g. the time distance by TGV between Paris and Marseille).

Figure 18.7 shows the distribution of airports in Europe. In the EU there are about 400 airports, of which 31 count more than ten million passengers, 101 between 1.5 and ten million, 143 between 150,000 and 1.5 million and 111 between 15,000 and 150,000. The airports served altogether 790 million passengers in 2007 of which 520 million were within the EU (figures from Energy and Transport, Facts and Figures, 2009). Comparing the density of airport distribution with the existing and planned HSR network in Europe one can conclude:

- On every major HSR corridor there is competition with air transport.
- Air transport is able to offer many direct OD flight connections, which cannot be contested by HSR.
- Air transport has little sunk cost and can be adjusted very flexibly to demand by frequency of service and size of aircraft.
- Air transport has several airport options in agglomerations and can choose the least cost alternatives.

4.2 The impacts of low-cost carriers

The market share of HSR is in the first instance a function of travel time (Figure 18.8). If travel time is between 3 and 4 hrs then a market share of about 50 per cent can be expected, as a rule of thumb.

The market entry of low-cost air carriers (LCA) had big impacts on the market share of the railways. Figure 18.9 shows that the losses of rail were in places substantial (Cologne–Munich, Cologne–Berlin). The main reasons are reduced travel time and lower fares for early booking.

Steer Davies Gleave (2006) have carried out a scenario study for the EU Commission to derive the probable impacts of HSR extensions on demand and modal split (see Figure 18.10). In several scenarios they show the importance of taxes, internalisation of externalities and the effects of lower tariffs following a cost reduction for HSR.

It is most important for the competitiveness of the railways to operate HSR with a high occupancy of seats. Figure 18.11 compares the competitive situations per seat and per passenger. It reveals that competitiveness in many cases is a matter of occupancy rates. This is also a potential barrier for the further development of HSR in Europe. If planned HSR links combine regions with lower density it will be difficult to achieve a positive financial return in the future.

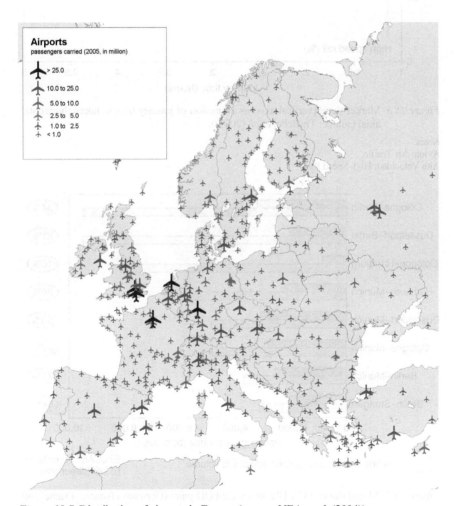

Figure 18.7 Distribution of airports in Europe (source: NEA *et al.* (2004)).

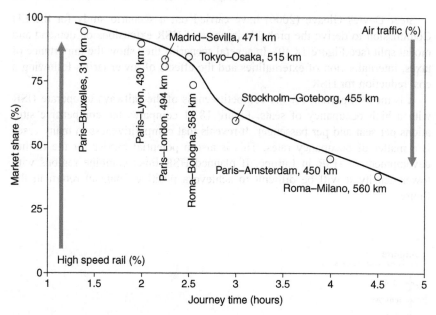

Figure 18.8 Market share (vertical axis) as a function of journey time in hours (horizontal axis) (source: Tractebel *et al.* (2009)).

Notes
Avion: Air Traffic.
Alta Velocidad: High Speed Rail.

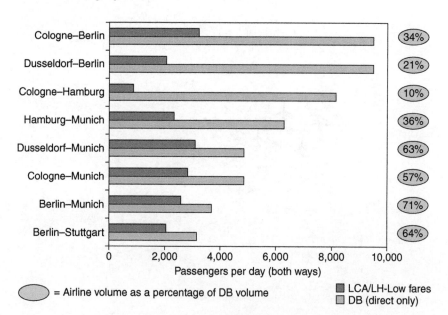

Figure 18.9 Modal shares LCA/DB on selected OD pairs (Germany) (source: Friebel and Niffka (2005)).

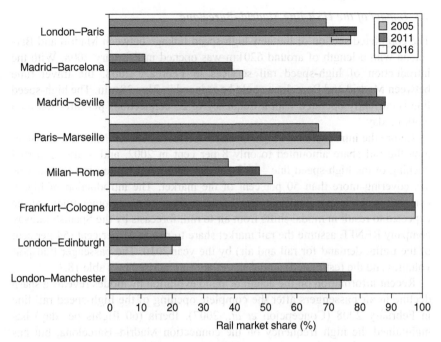

Figure 18.10 Projected modal shares for HSR in an environmental taxation scenario (source: Steer Davis Gleave (2006)).

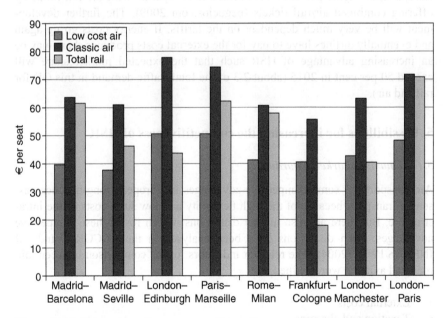

Figure 18.11 Comparison of average operating costs per seat (source: Steer Davis Gleave (2006)).

4.3 Impact of the HSR line Madrid–Barcelona

The completed section of the new high-speed linkage between Madrid and Barcelona with a length of around 620 km was opened in February 2008. With the introduction of high-speed rail services in February 2008, the travel time between Madrid and Barcelona could be reduced to 2 hrs 38 min. The high-speed line is currently operated with a frequency of 25 connections per direction on a working day.

Before the introduction of high-speed rail services between Madrid and Barcelona the rail share amounted to only 8 per cent in 2002, and – after a partial opening of the high-speed line – to 9 per cent in 2006. The dominant mode was air, covering more than 50 per cent of the market. The introduction of highly competitive high-speed rail services between these two agglomerations can be expected to result in modal shifts from air to rail: forecasts by the Spanish railway company RENFE assume the rail market share to rise to 41 per cent (54 per cent of the traffic demand for rail and air) by the year 2010. The passenger transport volumes and the (estimated) modal shares are summarised by Table 18.3.

Recent information on the actual demand evolution by modes reveals a sharp decline in air passengers after the complete opening of the high-speed rail line in February 2008 (Concepcion et al., 2007): Iberia (60 flights per day) has maintained the high frequency on the connection Madrid–Barcelona, but has reduced the number of seats offered by 20 per cent through operating smaller aircraft. Also Spanair (11 flights per day) has decided to reduce capacity. Air Europa (four flights per day) has decided to co-operate with the rail mode by offering combined air/rail tickets (negocios.com 2009). The further development will be very much dependent on the tariffs. If energy costs go up again and eventually airlines have to pay for the external costs produced there may be an increasing advantage of HSR such that the expected market share will exceed 50 per cent in 2015 (about 2/3 of the total traffic demand in this OD for rail and air).

5 Possibilities for increasing the competitiveness of HSR

5.1 Removing market distortions

Air transport has some competitive advantages in European long-distance passenger transport, because of the high flexibility and low sunk costs of the infrastructure. But there are also market distortions, which foster these competitive advantages. Such distortions have been analysed in the FACORA study of INFRAS/IWW (2004). The relevant indicators for the comparison between rail, road and aviation were defined as:[3]

- External costs
- Taxation and charging
- Infrastructure investments and public sector contributions.

External costs

The main sources of external costs of transport are air pollution, noise, accidents and climate change. INFRAS/IWW have calculated that rail passenger transport is three to four times more efficient with respect to external costs than aviation. The main reason is the high contribution of aviation to climate change. As these comparisons are based on unit cost figures the loading of transport vehicles is a key factor for the result. Loading of aircraft on short distance flights is between 65 and 80 per cent, with low-cost carriers at the top of the list. The loading factor for TGV trains is also in this range as the operation schedules of TGV are adjusted to the demand profile over the day. Deutsche Bahn applies a different operation schedule and offers fixed schedules over the day, not adjusting to the peaks and lows of demand. Furthermore, the number of seats in an ICE3 is greater than in a TGV (450 versus 370 seats). Therefore the ICE loading factor is slightly below 50 per cent on average.

The relatively high occupancy rate of HSR is one reason – besides modern technology with energy recycling – for the fact that the specific energy consumption per passenger km is lower than for conventional intercity trains, on average. The latter have an occupancy rate in Germany between 30 and 40 per cent. This reflects in the following average consumption of energy for different rail modes:

Rail is much more energy efficient than air transport on short flight distances (relationship 1:6). This advantage diminishes with increasing distance and reduces to 1:2 on distances over 1,000 km. These average figures vary with the occupancy rates and the relative importance of upstream effects of infrastructure provision.

Table 18.3 Development of passenger demand and modal split on the relation Madrid–Barcelona

	2002[1]	2006[2]	2008[3]	2010[3]
Modal share (in percent)				
Passenger car	24	33	28	22
Coach	5	5	4	2
Rail	8	9	31	41
Air	64	53	37	35
Passenger volume (in mill. passenger p.a.)				
Total	6.3	7.5	8.5	9.5

Sources: 1 Lopéz-Pita and Robusté (2005); 2 RENFE (2008); 3 forecast by RENFE (2008).

Table 18.4 Energy consumption of passenger rail transport in Wh/km

	Conventional rail	*Highspeed rail*
Energy consumption/seat	35	39
Energy consumption/pass.	76	70

Source: Tractebel *et al.*, 2009.

Taxation and charging

Comparing the taxation/charging regimes one can summarise:

1   International air transport in Europe is free of value added tax.
2   Air transport is free of fuel and energy taxation.
3   Air transport is presently not included in the European Emission Trading System and will be only partly included after 2013.

The Chicago Convention of 1944 has put international aviation outside the national taxation rules. The tax regulation for railways is different in Europe. In the case of VAT it varies from zero to the general tax rate. In Germany the railways have to pay the full VAT (19 per cent), which leads to the consequence that the tariffs of low-cost carriers may be lower than the VAT, which the railway company has to pay. Fuel taxes are more relevant for freight trains with diesel traction while HSR is driven by electrical propulsion. In some countries energy taxes have to be paid by the railway companies.

All producers of electrical energy (also railway companies) are included in the European Emission Trading System, which was introduced in 2005 as a follow-up of the Kyoto Protocol. In the past the major part of CO_2 emission allowances has been allocated free of charge according to grandfather rules. Beginning with the year 2013 all allowances will be auctioned off. According to the new Directive 2008/101/EC the aviation sector will be included in the ETS beginning with the year 2013. The most important regulations are:

• All flights are included which arrive/depart at EU aerodromes, beginning on 1 January 2012.
• In the year 2012 the number of allowances equal 97 per cent of historical CO_2 emissions. From 1 January 2013 the number of allowances will be reduced to 95 per cent of historical emissions. Further reductions will be decided for each subsequent period.
• From 1 January 2013, 15 per cent of allowances will be auctioned. This percentage may be increased as part of the general review of this Directive.
• In each period a special reserve of 3 per cent of total allowances is given for operators entering into business and operators in the start-up phase, showing growth rates of 18 per cent and more. This is limited to one million allowances.[4]
• At least 15 months before the start of each period the Commission shall calculate and adopt a decision setting out the conditions (e.g. the number of allowances).
• Third country measures to reduce the climate change impact of aviation can lead to compensation agreements (to avoid double charging).

Directive 2008/101/EC is a big step forward to include the aviation sector in the EU climate policy. Although the impacts on the cost side of aviation will be very low in the initial phase the new system can create incentives for the airline carriers to use fuel-efficient aircraft and operate them with high occupancy rates. However, looking at the details of the Directive one discovers severe discriminations against the railways. They will have to buy 100 per cent of CO_2 emission allowances beginning with the year 2013 while aviation will have to buy only 15 per cent in the initial phase. The medium- and long-term development is still open. This leads to the paradoxical situation that the environmental regulations for taxation and charging are disadvantaging the environmentally much more friendly railway industry. Figure 18.12 shows the estimated results of the discriminatory emission trading rules for the case of Deutsche Bahn AG.

If the EU Directive is implemented without further adjustments this would yield a clear market loss by the railways compared with road and air (light columns). If, alternatively, all modes would have to pay the same unit charge for emitting a ton of CO_2 this would lead to a harmonised treatment and would result in the effects exhibited by the dark columns, indicating a clear advantage of the railways compared with the competitors in a harmonised trading system.

Infrastructure investments and public sector contributions

Infrastructure investments in HSR are associated with high sunk costs. Because of the duration and the complexity of the legal processes involved with land acquisition and social requirements uncertainty on the cost side is very high. On the demand side the expected passenger volume often will not be achieved in the first years after opening; rather it can take more than a decade and may need the

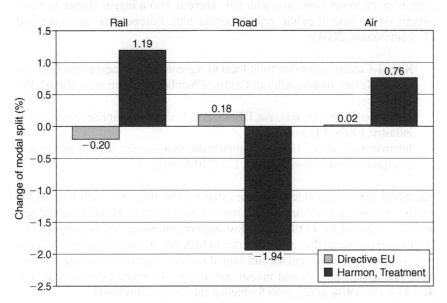

Figure 18.12 Impacts of the EU Directive 2008/101/EC on modal split in percentages (source: ZEW (2009)).

accomplishment of complementary investments before the full performance of an HSR link is reached. Therefore – flanked by the state ownership of incumbent railway companies – the provision of HSR infrastructure is in general planned and financed by the state.

Big HSR projects belong to the category of state-procured mega-projects, which has been subject to several critical scientific analyses (see Flyvbjerg *et al.*, 2003; TRT *et al.*, 2008). In a number of cases such mega-projects are characterised by massive cost overruns and overestimations of demand. The main reasons for planning failures are (1) the intrinsic incentives of main stakeholders to manipulate planning figures to promote a project and help to pass the major barriers in the political procurement process, (2) the length of the process and changes of the economic environment during planning and construction period. In some cases complementary investments have been assumed to be realised which did not come true. Usually a mix of wrong incentives and unexpected changes of the environment are causing planning failures and contribute to the negative image of mega HSR projects. Despite these difficulties two major HSR projects were procured as PPP projects, naturally with strong support of the states, the EU Commission and the EIB:

- Perpignan–Figueras, BOT Model, Rail Concession France/Spain;
- Channel Tunnel Rail Link, DBFO Model, from Folkestone to London St Pancras.

In the case of aviation the fixed investment in the infrastructure causing sunk costs is much lower compared with rail. There is also a bigger chance to build airports on the base of public–private partnerships. European examples are (see EU Commission, 2004):

- Kassel–Calden, extension from local to regional airport, agreement between city of Kassel, municipality of Calden, Chamber of Commerce, Kassel, EU assistance;
- International airport, Warsaw, DBFO, Polish airport enterprise, construction industry, banks, EU assistance;
- International airport, Hamburg, agreement between city, city-owned airport enterprise, construction industry, EU (EIB loans).

Successful airports are able to finance extensions by their own cash flow, as for instance Fraport in Frankfurt (fourth runway, terminals) or Munich (second terminal co-financed by Lufthansa). Most airport companies for big airports are breaking even financially, in general due to high non-aviation revenues. It is not easy to check to what extent the full capital costs are recovered because in many cases public start-up aids and investment support for major extensions are not paid back (see IWW *et al.*, 2006 for hidden subsidies of this kind).

In the past 20 years many regional airports have been established, partly due to the changed political situation, which made it possible to change former military to civil airports. Many of these regional airports are heavily subsidised by the local public authorities and offer low starting/landing fees to the airlines. The political hope is that these airports turn into job machines, in particular in regions lagging behind economically. Low-cost airlines are making use of these favourable supply conditions, which combine the advantages of low costs for runways and ground service with stable conditions for starting/landing operations. In several cases the arrangements with low-cost carriers were in conflict with European law (Directives for subsidisation and competition). Examples are the airports of Charleroi and Strasbourg. Furthermore, there are numerous examples for massive subsidisation within the legal rules. Figure 18.13 demonstrates such a case of huge subsidisation. The airport Hahn, located in a remote area of Rhineland-Palatinate, was developed from a former military airport after 1990. When Fraport, the former 65 per cent owner of Hahn, tried to improve on the financial situation by increasing starting/landing fees after ten years of losses, Ryanair responded with the announcement to leave Hahn. The state of Rhineland-Palatinate then took over the shares of Fraport and announced that it would keep the fees stable, to avoid a loss of 6,000–8,000 jobs in an area with high unemployment. Looking at Figure 18.13 one should remember that the passenger volume has increased considerably in the decade presented, finally reaching about 4 million passengers per year. However, the increase of passenger turnover had little influence on the financial returns because of the special arrangements with the air carriers.

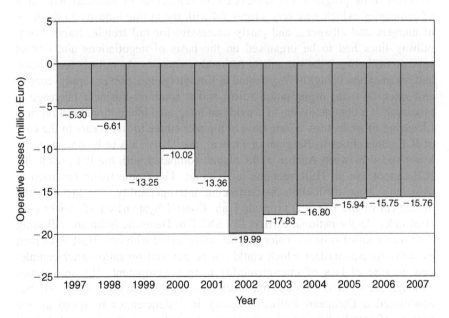

Figure 18.13 Development of operating deficits of Hahn Airport (source: Hahn Airport Company).

The Hahn example can be regarded as a prototype for the situation of many regional airports. Note that the investment grants given by the federal state and the state of Rhineland-Palatinate have not been considered in the upper graph. The authorities find themselves in a most complex negotiation situation and can be extorted easily by low-cost airlines. This seems to be a clear competitive advantage compared with HSR because the airline industry is able to start the operation on an airport without major barriers to entry and sunk costs.

5.2 Improving on competitiveness of the railway organisations

5.2.1 Liberalisation process

The aviation industry has been deregulated in Europe through four liberalisation packages in the 1990s, ending with free cabotage in Europe. Railway liberalisation has been lagging behind for at least one decade, if one considers that the liberalisation Directives were decided in 2001, the relevant conditions for their introduction ("railway packages") date from 2004, and free access to the market for international passenger service will come in 2010. The reason is that neither the states nor their incumbent rail companies are interested in fast progress; only the European Commission is pushing the liberalisation process actively.

The railway reform in Europe was successful in some countries with respect to the efficiency and financial viability of national and regional rail transport. However, little progress was achieved with respect to the internationalisation of companies, which was very successful with the airline industry in the form of mergers and alliances, and partly successful for rail freight. International railway lines had to be organised on the basis of negotiations and mutual agreements between the incumbent national companies. As railway technology and organisation is highly fragmented in Europe (gauge, power supply, control and safety system, organisation rules) and a common business language is missing it is a complex issue to provide an integrated international rail service. Licensing of trains took a long time in the past (three to four years in the case of ICE connections to Belgium or France), the Thalys has to be operated at a lower speed between Aachen and Cologne compared with the ICE, while the ICE cannot use all HSR sections in Belgium. The Commission has tried to overcome these difficulties by enforcing interoperability, for instance the instalment of the ETCS (European Train Control System) on all newly built HSR links. As the national carriers like SNCF or Deutsche Bahn are still using their own control systems major difficulties occurred with new HSR links such as Antwerp–Amsterdam which could not be put into operation after completion because of lack of interoperability in train equipment. This means that although the Commission has put much emphasis on interoperability and has established a European Railway Agency in Valenciennes to speed up the process of standardisation of technology, the railway sector is much behind aviation with this respect.

5.2.2 New forms of organisation

The formation of new organisations can be expected with respect to three directions:

- multilateral agreements,
- mergers, alliances of national rail companies,
- co-operations, alliances with airlines,
- new international HSR companies.

The pressure stemming from opening up access to the international rail passenger transport market will lead to a reorganisation of international passenger transport service. According to the second railway package published in 2002 it will be possible to extend national HSR service to neighbouring countries. However, as services and facilities of the neighbours' incumbents have to be used one cannot expect that such an extension of services will be achieved without some type of cooperation. More probably multi-lateral agreements will be prepared to serve particular corridors with interoperable technology and harmonised service systems for the clients. Mergers and alliances will be a further step forward in this direction. Some incumbent companies might establish common daughter companies, which operate on particular corridors. Examples are Thalys (SNCF, SCNB, DB; since 1996), Eurostar (SNCF, SNCB, British Rail; since 1994), Artesia (SNCF, Trenitalia; since 2000) or Alleo (SNCF, DB; since 2007). In principle, new companies (e.g. low-cost rail lines) could enter the market, but this is not highly probable because of the complex railway technology and the network effects, which favour the incumbents.

Cooperation between airlines and rail companies has emerged in some cases. Deutsche Lufthansa and Deutsche Bahn cooperate under the flag "Airail" on the corridor Cologne–Frankfurt–Stuttgart such that air passengers booked on an international flight from Frankfurt can check in at Cologne or Stuttgart and access Frankfurt by rail in reserved compartments. The LH flight connections Frankfurt–Cologne or Frankfurt–Stuttgart have been abolished. The same holds for SNCF feeder services from Brussels or Lille to Charles de Gaulle airport.

Within the framework of the Third Railway Package, the EU has paved the way for opening up access to the railway infrastructure by the year 2010 for those operators wishing to provide international services, including the possibility of cabotage (EU 2007).[5] The opening-up of international rail markets has resulted in ambitious plans for new service operators, which may significantly change the European high-speed rail market in the future. Two examples are briefly presented in the following.

In September 2008, Air France founded a joint subsidiary with Veolia, a French private company that is a major public transport service provider in several countries, in order to provide international high-speed rail services, for instance on routes like Paris–Amsterdam and Paris–London. The services are scheduled to start in the second half of 2010. The motivation for the airline to offer its own high-speed rail services is threefold: first, after the completion of several new high-speed rail lines in Europe, the air mode has lost significant market shares against rail; second, providing services on relatively short distances tends to be a less lucrative market segment for airlines, by simultaneously spending scarce airport capacities that otherwise could be available for more lucrative medium- and long-distance flights; and third, the sharp rise in the oil price in 2008 has supported the airline's strategy of entering the less oil price-sensitive rail market.

In 2006, the Italian railway company Nuovo Trasporto Viaggiatori (NTV) was founded by a consortium of Italian industrialists, with the aim of providing high-speed rail services in Italy. The French railway company SNCF holds 20 per cent of NTV's shares. Starting from 2011, NTV plans to operate 25 new high-speed trains on the high-speed railway network, connecting the cities Bari, Bologna, Florence, Milan, Naples, Rome, Salerno, Turin and Venice, by offering more than 54 journeys per day and providing 13.5 million train-km. per year (NTV 2009).[6] NTV expects to carry around ten million passengers per year, as soon as the planned operation capacity is reached.

With this ambitious plan, NTV benefits from the decision of the Italian government to open up the domestic long-distance rail market as soon as 2010, well ahead of the deadline stipulated by the European Union (2015). NTV will contribute to enhancing the level of service provided by the rail mode and can be expected to become a potent competitor not only for airlines that operate domestic connections, but also for the state railway company FS.

6 Conclusions

The competitive situation is characterised as follows:

1   Air transport has comparatively low sunk costs and can adjust more flexibly to demand development. Because of the high density of airport locations in Europe it can cover the area in a targeted way.
2   Regional airports, which are often used by low-cost carriers, are usually subsidised and far from breaking even.
3   The judgements of courts allow for an extensive interpretation of the subsidisation regulation stated in the EC treaty.
4   Air transport causes external costs, in particular CO_2 emissions, which are not internalised. International aviation is free of taxation on value added and fuel.
5   HSR is bound to corridors connecting agglomerations, needs very high fixed investments and is less flexible.
6   HSR needs a high occupancy rate to become as cost efficient as air transport.
7   HSR as an environmentally friendly transportation mode has to pay considerable fuel and eco taxes, and in some countries VAT as well.
8   In many cases the provision of HSR links is subsidised by the state through grants for infrastructure construction. This is motivated strongly by the

presumed environmental friendliness of rail travel. But as aviation is heavily subsidised as well by various sources it can offer lower tariffs. In such cases modal share of HSR, occupancy rates and positive environmental impacts may be low.

9 The economic crisis has stopped the process of commercialisation and privatisation of incumbent railway companies. For instance, the planned sale of 24.9 per cent of DB AG shares had to be cancelled. It follows from such observations that the state influence may increase in the medium term. This will not foster the management efficiency of the state-owned incumbents, in general.

10 In France, Italy and Spain there are plans to increase the HSR network substantially. This will improve the competitive power of the railways, if new private consortia emerge to foster competition with the incumbent state railways.

The private initiatives to enter the market of HSR are most promising and appear sustainable. HSR and air transport are commercial services, which in the long run can be financed completely by market revenues. Therefore the role of the state should be limited to an internalisation of external costs, a facilitation of risk-taking through state guarantees and the legal planning processes associated with infrastructure provision. Investment grants without repayment are only temporarily justified as long as there is no full internalisation of externalities.

This means for the railways that a consequent continuation of the path of railway reform towards fully commercialised railway companies provides the best option, operating internationally on an interoperable network, competing or cooperating with the airline industry depending on business opportunities. Subsidisation of air traffic should be stopped completely, in particular if it leads to counterproductive traffic diversion from rail to air. A full integration of air transport into the ETS and an ambitious internalisation strategy for externalities will lead to fair competition among the traffic modes and limit the growth of environmentally undesired traffic activity.

Notes

1 All distances given in this paragraph are flight distances. Railway distances or centre-to-centre distances are up to 20 per cent higher.
2 A logit function can well represent the discrete choice of the transport mode of a traveller. The theory has been established by Nobel Prize Laureate D. McFadden and has induced manifold extensions and empirical applications (e.g.: BenAkiva and Lerman, 1985).
3 INFRAS/IWW also discuss the influence of safety and social regulations but this refers to the competition road/rail and is not relevant for the competition air/rail.
4 One allowance corresponds to 1 ton of CO_2 or 0.27 tons of carbon.
5 European Union (2007): Further integration of the European rail system: third railway package. http://europa.eu/legislation_summaries/transport/rail_transport/l24457_en.htm.
6 www.ntvspa.it/en/nuovo-trasporto-viaggiatori/39/3/high-speed-railways-italy-city-time-frequency-travel.

342   *W. Rothengatter*

References

Adler, N., C. Nash and E. Pels (2008) High-speed rail and air transport competition: game engineering as tool for cost–benefit analysis. ITS Working Paper. Leeds. Mimeo.

Ben Akiva, M. and S. Lerman (1985) *Discrete choice analysis*. Cambridge Mass.

Concepción, R., R. Espinho and J.C. Martín (2007) Competition of high-speed train with air transport: The case of Madrid–Barcelona, *Journal of Air Transport Management*, 13: 277–284.

DLR and ADV (2009) *Low cost monitor 2/2009*. Cologne.

European Commission (2009) *Energy and transport in figures*. Brussels.

European Commission (2004) *Resource book on PPP studies*. Brussels.

European Commission (2001) "Time to decide". White Paper on Common Transport Policy. Brussels.

Flyvbjerg, B., N. Bruzelius and W. Rothengatter (2003) *Megaprojects and risk. An anatomy of ambition*. Cheltenham.

Friebel, G. and M. Niffka (2005) Functioning of inter-modal competition in the transportation market. Evidence from the entry of low-cost airlines in Germany. Working Paper. University of Toulouse.

Ifeu und Öko-Institut (2009) *CO2-Emissionen in Gramm je Personenkilometer; Studie im Auftrag der DB AG. Datenbasis 2008*. Heidelberg.

INFRAS/IWW (2004) *FACORA. Facts on competition in the European transport market. Study for the UIC*. Paris. Authors: M. Maibach and W. Rothengatter (lead), C. Schreyer, N. Schmid, C. Doll, A. Ott.

INFRAS (2009) *Energiepolitische Rahmenbedingungen. Wettbewerbssituation zwischen den europäischen Bahnen. Studie im Auftrag der DB AG*. Zürich.

IWW, MKmetric and FhG ISI (2006) *Wegekosten und Wegekostendeckung des Luftverkehrs im intermodalen Vergleich. (Infrastructure Costs and their Recovery of Air Transport in an Intermodal Comparison)*. Study for Lufthansa. Karlsruhe.

López-Pita, A. and F. Robusté (2005) Impact of high-speed lines in relation to very high frequency air services, *Journal of Public Transportation*, 8 (2): 15–35.

Mandel, B., M. Gaudry and W. Rothengatter (1997) A disaggregate box-cox logit mode choice model of intercity passenger travel in Germany and its implications for high-speed rail demand forecasts, *The Annals of Regional Science*, 31 (2): 99–120.

NEA, COWI, IWW and NESTEAR (2004) *TEN-STAC*. Study for the European Commission. Rijswijk.

RENFE (2008) *El AVE reinará en la ruta BCN-Madrid pero no hundirá ni al avión ni al bus*. Madrid.

Rothengatter, W. and E. Szimba (2009) Transport demand, transport and climate policy in Europe – status quo and developments. Background Paper on Europe. Contribution to the JR Central Study on Intercity Transport. (Lead by ITPS). Tokyo.

Steer Davies Gleave (2006) *Air and rail competition and complementarity*. Report to the European Commission. London.

Tractebel Engineering and MVV Consulting (2009) *Étude sur l'État de Développement et les Perspectives d'Avenir du Réseau Transeuropéen de Chemin de Fer à Grande Vitesse*. Study for the European Commission, DG TREN, Brussels.

TRT (lead) CSIL, EPFL, FhG ISI, IIP, ITPS, IWW, NESTEAR (2008) *EVA-TREN*. Project for the European Commission. Milan.

ZEW (2009) *Wettbewerb und Umweltregulierung im Verkehr. Eine Analyse zur unterschiedlichen Einbindung der Verkehrsarten in den Emissionshandel. Studie im Auftrag der DB AG*. Mannheim.

19 Consolidation in the air transport industry and antitrust enforcement in Europe

Marco Benacchio

1 Introduction

This contribution addresses the role and the tools of competition policy in the evaluation of the consolidation phase which is re-shaping the air transport industry, after the implementation of the EU deregulation packages.

Competition is crucial to any liberalization process, where regulatory authorities should retreat and economic agents take over. Only free and open markets, in fact, force companies to compete on their merits. If competition, by its nature, implies rivalry and foreclosure, the issue is to keep the competitive strategies within the space of compliance with competition law, which now probably represents the main current form of public intervention in the sector (Gillen-Morrison, 2005).

In this contest, the role for antitrust rules enforcers should not be to influence the market outcomes, but – as a referee – to preserve the contestability of the air transport markets in the light of the current regulation. No preference towards any specific institutional design or airline size should be given by the regulator. It is for the market to find the optimal structure, whereas the goal of competition policy is to make sure that liberalized markets remain accessible for competitors and that consumers can fully take advantage of liberalization benefits.

Public action, in fact, needs to be non-distorting and clearly different from the past governmental policy action in the aviation business in Europe which, due to the radical involvement of national interests, heavily influenced the industry equilibrium till the beginning of the third millennium.[1]

At the same time, no dogmatic approach on the "neutrality" of the antitrust intervention should be emphasized. The market itself is a "social institution" (implying the interaction of private and public economic agents, including regulators) and the public intervention (in terms of rules and market control) is a necessary element in consideration of the many deviations experienced from the perfect competition model (Caffè, 1986). Competition policy therefore needs to be clearly market-oriented in the application of its leading principles to a concept of workable competition promoting efficient market outcomes and incentives to maximize social welfare.

2 The institutional framework of civil aviation in EU and emerging market forces

2.1 Internal market

Civil aviation in EU makes a very important contribution to the European economy.[2] The actual significant scale, notwithstanding the economic downturn, is mainly a consequence of the liberalization of air transport in the 1990s and the creation of an internal open market. The increase in the number of airlines is clearly a sign of the dynamic nature of the sector especially in consideration of the several carriers that have been taken over or ceased trading in the meantime.[3]

Consumers have been the principal beneficiaries of the EU liberalization of the airline industry as this policy has led to more routes, greater choice and an increased overall quality of service.

As to market equilibrium, the almost full liberalization of the aviation sector and airports and the free market access regime for intra-Community routes has made it possible for newcomers to join the market, making life difficult for the monopoly power of the national flag carriers. Some of these carriers were suffering badly from the "distressed state airlines syndrome" (Doganis, 2001), since their corporate culture, focused on rent exploitation in un-contestable markets, could not adjust to the mechanism of the free market system and related competitive environment (Autorità Garante, 2005).

2.2 Slot allocation

A deregulated market tends to increase the number of market players, creating additional pressure on airport infrastructure. There is a general consensus upon the fact that the actual slot allocation rule – mainly based on grandfather's right[4] – represents a barrier to entry, although alternative market solutions are not a panacea for all the likely distortions. They may in fact incur failures or worse competition outcomes. It is not by chance that alternative slot allocation schemes have been accurately analysed by the EU Commission since 2001, but a full implementation seems to be quite far off (Mott McDonald, 2006).

The recent Communication adopted by the Commission in April 2008 on the application of Regulation (EEC) No 95/93 on common rules for the allocation of slots at Community airports, may open up a radically new framework of allocation and exchange.[5]

In the opposite sense, in May 2009, the European Parliament – as an urgent measure to prevent airline companies from suffering the consequences of the economic slowdown – adopted a legislative report that relaxed rules on the allocation of slots, allowing airlines not to lose unused ones: air carriers will be entitled to the same series of slots during the summer 2010 scheduling season as were allocated to them during the summer 2009 season, even if they use them less than 80 per cent of the time this year.

2.3 Reduced public intervention

Along with the liberalization process, the public intervention in the airline sector, which was quite significant till the 1990s, is partially decreasing, but not completely fading out, although representing a less relevant element of interaction for competition policy than in the recent past.[6]

Apart from the issue of state aid control by the Commission, the policy of protecting the weak "state-controlled" carrier from real competition corresponded to a significant distortion of the competitive process. Paradoxically, in many cases such a policy was shown to be short-sighted in the long run, implying a faster road to weakness for the protected player. In fact, by allowing extra profits and/or extra costs, the incentive for the incumbent to increase efficiency and effectiveness as a way of competing was reduced (leading to overstaffing, cost and X-inefficiencies, short-sighted rent-seeking policies).[7]

Recently, several privatization processes took place in the airline industry, as a step towards complete privatization processes. Privatization processes, in any case, may be non-neutral schemes, as they could be evaluated as a state aid in case of no public and transparent procedure or prior airline's debts cancellation by a public body. Besides state ownership, capital mobility is still imperfect since, with reference to the EU, to maintain the status of Community carrier (and the relative traffic rights) at least a percentage of the share of an airline has to be in the hands of EU investors. Even more radical measures of this kind occur in the US (Carney and Dostaler, 2006). Governments that have otherwise adopted liberal commercial aviation policies continue to require that domestic owners hold upwards of 50 per cent of an airline's voting equity.

2.4 Emergent market forces and reaction strategies

At least at the beginning of the liberalization stage, the strengthening of competition between airlines as a result of new players entering the market, and a general wider contestability on EU routes, speeded up the erosion of the previously "captive" markets, although not at the same magnitude for different flag carriers (Macchiati-Piacentino, 2006).

In parallel, deeper forms of cooperation, mainly at intercontinental level, have been exploited by full service carriers in order to perform better in terms of efficiency and network coverage (Pels, 2001). Strategic alliances among major world-wide carriers re-shaped the supply of international air transport by developing a few intensive interconnected hub-and-spoke networks. Where the commercial strategies of partners are coordinated (e.g. frequent flyer programmes), alliances resemble an oligopolistic outcome. The vast literature on strategic alliances in the air transport sector highlighted private/social costs and benefits deriving from cooperation agreements (e.g. Brueckner, 2003; Brueckner and Pels, 2005).

Moreover, the liberalization process has allowed the emergence and fast development of a new type of airline in Europe, a radically new player – the so-called "low-cost carrier" – offering a no-frills point-to-point new product which, in return for a simpler service and/or the use of secondary airports, provides very competitive prices. The main role of low-cost carriers has been to develop additional air transport for price-sensitive passengers. But as the new product gained in popularity, route coverage and frequencies, it also implied changes induced in the demand side, promoting a growing competition with full service carriers for the needs of tourists and some less time-sensitive business travellers.

The reaction by full service carriers to new players, including low-cost carriers, had been focusing on different kinds of strategies (Brueckner and Pels, 2005):

- cooperation strategies with other traditional carriers at international level, with the aim of reducing the competition among partners on Member States' domestic routes while exploiting cost economies and competitive advantages on international connections where competition takes place between big alliances;
- Exclusionary practices (such as predation and anticompetitive use of over-capacity) put in practice by a still dominant player (i.e. the former monopolist) against new entrants, mainly on national routes, in order to reduce their ability to survive as real competitors. Such a strategy usually occurs in the first stage of the liberalization, when the competitive pressure is weak and the market power of the incumbent still relevant.
- consolidation strategies (from code sharing to mergers) on domestic markets with competitors, in order to recoup a quasi-monopolistic market position after the reduction of the market share of the main player (Dennis, 2005). The strategy usually refers to a mature phase of liberalization.

3 Consolidation in the air transport sector and the intervention by competition authorities at EU level

Enforcing full compliance with EU and national competition rules ensures that the benefits of liberalization are not cancelled out by anti-competitive mergers, agreements or abusive practices.

With regard to scheduled air passenger services, the focus is currently on mergers and alliances, which represent the most up-to-date issue in the light of the emerging trend of the industry since the beginning of the new century, after almost ten years of progressive liberalization of market access conditions. Efforts at liberalization, in fact, go hand-in-hand with the industry's need for cooperation and consolidation, to create synergies to survive and compete in a global economy (Nordic Competition Authorities, 2002).

Nevertheless, behind the goals of efficiency-seeking and supply rationalization, consolidation strategies pose serious issues from the point of view of competition policy. In fact, the increasing number of independent players which characterized the first years of the liberalization process tends to reduce or stabilize (also as an effect of the financial difficulties for airlines occurring after the

9/11 incident, and, more recently, due to the economic downturn), with the likely consequences on the reduction of consumer welfare.

Looking at the consolidated jurisprudence at EU and national levels in the field of evaluation of mergers and alliances, it appears that there is a generally positive attitude in the antitrust assessment to highly complementary airline alliances and mergers that can bring important benefits to passengers by connecting networks, offering new services and generating efficiencies across the aviation value chain. In any case, it is crucial that the economic benefits of airline alliances or mergers are passed on to passengers in terms of price, quantity, quality. And the degree of competition left is the best assurance for the pass-on to the consumers (European Competition Authorities, 2006).

Moreover, a generally positive approach cannot ignore the negative effects that airline consolidation has on individual markets (for overlapping routes connecting the hub airports of the parties or congested airports).

4 Merger control in the airline industry: (a) the definition of the relevant market

A key element in identifying whether a merger or alliance will give rise to competition concerns is the definition of the relevant market. This is a crucial step in any antitrust evaluation; guidelines may help in encoding the definition process that, in any case, should be performed on a case-by-case basis.

4.1 The product

Scheduled air traffic services between a point of origin and a point of destination (O&D) is the basic product. However, airlines form heterogeneous groups which significantly differ among themselves, mainly in relation to (1) the operating model and (2) the level of service offered to passengers. As to the first distinction, network carriers operate complex "hub-and-spoke" systems, while "point-to-point" carriers in principle operate each single route independently of the others. Although the latter are not hub carriers, they normally converge their traffic at certain airports (base airports), where they base a certain number of aircraft and concentrate some of their connections. With reference to the qualitative features carriers compete on, some airlines offer ancillary services to the basic transport service (full service carriers), while others focus the commercial offer on the mere transport service, by reducing the level of complementary services (no-frills carriers) and operating from/to secondary airports.

4.2 The origin and destination approach and the issue of airport substitutability

In line with the Commission's findings, the markets for passenger air transport can be defined on the basis of individual routes or bundles of routes between a point of origin and a point of destination, to the extent that there is substitutability between them for passengers. According to the O&D approach, every combination of a point of origin and a point of destination is therefore to be considered a separate market from the consumer's point of view (demand-based approach). In the case of adjacent airports with overlapping catchment areas, some of the passengers for whom the overlapping catchment area represents the origin or the destination of the travel, may consider those airports as substitutes. The assessment of substitution relies on a number of factors, including the number of potential passengers attracted by the overlapping catchment areas, the frequency and schedules of the service at different airports, the difference in the total duration of the journey – including transfer time to terminals – and the difference in the total travel costs.

The emergence of low-cost carriers, focused on point-to-point connections mainly to/from regional airports, postulates a more accurate analysis of airport substitutability for different patterns of passengers, in relation to the possible ways to segment the demand.[8]

4.3 Segmentation of the demand

The demand-based approach to market definition postulates a distinction between different groups of passengers, since different services may be substitutable for different kinds of customers. Reflecting the established practice, the distinctions between time-sensitive and non-time-sensitive passengers, as well as between point-to-point passengers and connecting ones, are usually assessed. Generally, time-sensitive passengers, who are not flexible in terms of departure/arrival time, expect faster connections, more frequencies, a higher level of punctuality than non-time-sensitive ones, and the possibility of changing their reservation at short notice. Non-time-sensitive passengers, on the contrary, are interested in obtaining the lowest fares and are willing to accept longer travel time and less flexibility (Dresner, 2006).

The issue of the most appropriate proxies to be used to identify the two subgroups is debated, since data on whether passengers are time-sensitive or not are unavailable, and non-time-sensitive passengers are decreasingly represented by the distinction between business and leisure travellers, since cost-sensitiveness is growing even in some categories of business travellers. The assessment of the passengers holding restricted or unrestricted tickets could be a guiding principle, although it needs a case by case implementation.[9]

The degree of substitutability between low-cost flights and "traditional" services increases the difficulty in market segmentation. The quality of on-board services, the availability of fidelity programmes, the range of destination served, the airports and the aircrafts used and the type of tickets and pricing policies (restrictions vs. flexibility) influence the likely substitutability for different kinds of consumers (Gillen and Morrison, 2003).

The issue of airport substitutability has been affected too in a number of cases by the distinction between time-sensitive and non-time-sensitive passengers. Data analysis and the results of market tests show that airports were less dependent on their main catchment areas for non-time-sensitive travellers compared to time-sensitive ones.

Finally, as to the distinction between O&D and connecting passengers, the two categories are normally considered to belong to different markets.

4.4 Substitutability with indirect flights and alternative transport modes

Indirect flights imply more stops and take longer than non-stop flights. This is why they are generally considered more inconvenient and less attractive to consumers, at least on short-haul flights.

Another aspect which is growing in importance, according to recent technological and commercial developments, is the question whether certain alternative modes of transport belong to the same product market as air services. Already in several EU cases high-speed rail connections have been considered as a possible intermodal alternative to air travel also when time-sensitive passengers are concerned. Despite the dis-homogeneity of rail connections within Europe, the issue will surely become even more relevant as the quality of rail transport grows in terms of speed and frequency available in connecting major cities, in comparison with the longer times spent in the airport due to increasing security controls.[10]

4.5 Market definition and supply-side effects

Antitrust market definition firmly relies on a demand-side approach on a route by route basis. In fact, following a small but significant and non-transitory price increase on a given route, the customers would not choose another destination to fly to.

Nevertheless, for some cases, the mere O&D approach seems to support a fragmented market definition which does not capture all the relevant competition issues involved. The issue relates to the role of the supply-side substitutability (or network effects), that can be taken into account when competitive constraints from the supply side affect the range of choice for consumers. This refers to the possibility of competitors reacting to a price increase on a given route by entering into competition on that route.

The argument is quite a fascinating one but the outlined competitive constraints have to be sufficiently immediate and effective. If a number of barriers to entry related to investments, strategies and time prevent carriers from reacting to competition by opening new routes, the effect of supply-side substitution cannot therefore be regarded as equivalent to demand substitution effects for their effectiveness and immediacy.

Thus, network effects should be considered along with the route by route analysis when assessing the competitive effects of the consolidation – recognizing that the single O&D markets are not entirely independent from each other.[11]

5 Merger control in the airline industry: (b) the competitive assessment

The welfare effects of airline mergers and alliances are twofold. Efficiency gains in terms of cost reductions and quality improvements need to be compared with the risk of elimination or restriction of competition on the affected routes. The network effects of the industry increase the complexity in the assessment (Nordic Competition Authorities, 2002).

For the purpose of this section we will consider the market dominance test (i.e. the creation or strengthening of a dominant position due to the consolidation process) as the basis for establishing whether a merger leads to a significant restriction or elimination of competition. The general presumption is that both mergers and alliances will result in the total elimination of actual and potential competition between the involved parties on the routes affected.

The fact that the antitrust authorities have the duty to ensure that competition on all markets (routes) is maintained explains why the assessment of overlapping effects (which affect actual competition) is usually more severe than the assessment of the complementary effects (addressing potential competition issues).

5.1 Market shares as the basic criteria

From a legal and economic point of view the key question to be answered is how much competition remains in the market after the consolidation process. A number of criteria should be taken into account in assessing market power, differing in terms of relevance in each case (a checklist cannot automatically be applied).

The combined market share of the parties in the relevant markets is, of course, the primary indicator, providing information on the positioning of the parties and their competitors. Different proxies are used when calculating market shares. Besides the actual number of O&D passengers carried, the number of frequencies (i.e. the number of slots operated on single routes) sometimes gives a better perspective of the competition conditions on the route, for the strategic value of slot allocation. On the basis of these proxies, market power is more likely to exist if a carrier has a persistently high market share (in terms of absolute thresholds and/or relative to other competitors).

5.2 Barriers to entry

The signalling value of market shares needs further refinements in order to assess the real effects of the merger on competition. As an example, a 60 percent market share on several O&D markets may lead to different concerns according to different market entry conditions. They are usually sorted according to (1) structural, (2) regulatory and (3) behavioural factors; each one partially explains network effects (Nordic Competition Authorities, 2002; Commission Decision case M4439 Ryanair/Aer Lingus, 2007).

- Structural factors mainly relate to slot shortages in congested airports, the number and quality of frequencies (peak hours), the range of destinations offered and the access to airport services. In general, structural barriers to entry will be particularly high on markets where the merged entities operate a hub (or base) airport on both ends of the route, since the ability to attract connecting traffic to the concerned airport is a critical factor which can make entry particularly unattractive in consideration of the fixed costs necessary for the establishment of a base (Commission Decision case M4439 Ryanair/Aer Lingus, 2007). The reputation of the incumbent airline may also act as a significant barrier to entry since new entrants will face higher sunk costs associated with promotion and brand advertising than the established airline which holds a recognizable brand.
- Regulatory factors today mainly refer to administrative slot allocation systems, since other administrative barriers (such as the framework of computer reservation system (CRS) and tariff conferences) lost importance due to the liberalization process of the industry and the emergence of internet-based distribution systems).
- Strategic behaviour (i.e. the reputation of the incumbent as an aggressive player) affects the potential for predatory conduct and retaliation such as strategic pricing, frequency increase, fidelity programmes, corporate discount deals, loyalty schemes applied to travel agents.

In the light of this checklist, competition authorities establish, on a route by route basis, which of the outlined conditions of market entry exist and whether market power resulting from these factors is likely to reduce or eliminate competition. As a consequence, mergers and alliances can be accepted even when the parties have high market shares on overlapping routes, provided that there are no barriers to entry and the remaining actual, and potential, competition is sufficient to influence and constrain the competitive behaviour of the merged entities.[12] On the other side, lower market shares, in the presence of relevant entry barriers, may lead to an assessment of market power which requires a prohibition or an authorization subject to remedies.

5.3 The role for "hub" or "base" airport economies and the minimum efficient scale

Carriers benefit from economies of scale and scope when they operate a hub or have a base in the airport. Sales and marketing costs, customer service facilities and costs associated with flight cancellations would in fact decrease if they are recovered over a larger fleet and a wider portfolio of routes. Moreover, the flexibility (reduction of opportunity costs) in switching slots and other assets (such as crew staff) from one route to another, in managing connections adjusting the supply to anticipated fluctuation in demand, increases with the size of the base. Large-scale carriers may also benefit from a stronger negotiation power in purchasing services from airports, reflecting their greater volumes.

The outlined airport advantages can increase with the size of the hub/base, so that competition effects of the merger will depend also on the scale of the operation carried out by other carriers at that airport. In particular, in the case Ryanair/Aer Lingus, a significant effort has been devoted by the Commission to measure the base's cost economies (De La Mano, 2008).

5.4 Existing competition

When a merger leads to very high market shares on a large number of overlapping routes, the magnitude of the removal of existing competition between carriers depends also on how much the merged entities were close competitors on the affected routes. The closeness of competition depends on size and market position, on the degree of similarity of the business model and of the operating costs structure which reflects on price setting. Moreover, time series analysis can show how much the merging entities were reacting to each other's commercial strategies in terms of price, frequency and capacity deployment on different routes.

The real possibility of expanding the supply on those routes is the main competition constraint exerted by remaining competitors. The credibility of the competition constraint should be assessed in consideration of the existing barriers as well as of the economic incentives to increase the competitive pressure against the merged entity. In general, non-base competitors are considered as more vulnerable and less likely to exert a competitive constraint than carriers with a base at the same airport.

5.5 Potential competition

The issue of potential entrants as a competition constraint able to discipline the conduct of the merged entities probably refers to the most difficult and slippery part of the *ex ante* competitive assessment. How likely is the entry by other airlines? Will it be effective in exerting a potentially competitive constraint taking into account the size and the features of the market? Again, the focus is on the existing barriers to entry; a stronger emphasis should be given to the economic evaluation of the incentive to enter new routes where a big competitor is already established and benefiting from advantages in terms of reputation and cost economies.

Summing up, to consider actual or potential entry as a sufficient competitive constraint on the merging parties, it must be shown to be likely, timely and sufficient to deter any potential anti-competitive effects of the merger.

5.6 The role for efficiencies

Efficiencies, usually of a technical nature, represent positive welfare effects resulting from the merger or alliance. It is possible, in theory, that efficiencies brought about by a merger counteract the effect on competition, and, in particular, the potential harm to consumers that it might otherwise cause.

In order to be evaluated by competition authorities, claimed efficiency has to be verified and quantified. The net welfare effect will be positive if passengers benefit to a reasonable extent from the expected efficiency gains. As an example, efficiencies claimed on the basis of an increasing load factor post-merger need to be proved to be transferred to passengers. The competitive pressure exerted from the remaining competitors operating on each route, or from a likely potential new entrant, is an immediate indicator of the sustainability of a pass-on to consumers. In addition, efficiencies should be considered only when a causal connection between the consolidation and the possible benefits is likely (merger specificity).

In general it is highly unlikely that a merger leading to a market position approaching that of a monopoly, or leading to a similar level of market power, can be declared compatible with the common market, on the ground that efficiency gains would be sufficient to counteract its potential anticompetitive effects. This can partially explain why the Commission, within the numerous assessments of competition effects induced by mergers and alliances in the air transport sector, has never considered efficiency gains as sufficient to offset anticompetitive outcomes of the consolidation.

6 Merger control in the airline industry: (c) decisions with remedies

It is likely that a merger or alliance will raise particular competition concerns in relation to one or more specific routes, but, in most cases, will not raise significant concerns in relation to the majority of routes affected. In such cases the competition authority faces a trade-off between the overall positive welfare effect the merger or alliance is expected to have and the risk that effective competition will not be maintained on every affected route. In this case the appropriate approach is to impose adequate remedies to deal with the competition concerns identified. Of the many decisions that have been taken in the last ten years for cooperative agreements and mergers in air transport by the EU Commission,[13] just one merger has been prohibited.[14]

As a rule, when designing remedies the principle of proportionality has to be taken into account.[15]

With respect to the air traffic sector, the design of remedies which have to be effective in preventing the anticompetitive effects of a merger or alliance is a relatively complex task. In order to calibrate the remedy, it has to be considered whether or not the markets affected are characterized by significant entry barriers. In the majority of cases, in fact, remedies are directed at reducing existing entry barriers and enabling new airlines to enter the market.

As far as mergers are concerned, structural remedies are considered more straightforward than behavioural remedies since they are generally more clearly defined and easier to enforce, in comparison to behavioural remedies (which, in any case, have been imposed as well to tackle competition concerns).

The question of which remedies are appropriate in order to maintain effective competition in a particular case cannot be answered in general terms, since they depend on the competition analysis in each single case. The following types of remedies have been applied in a number of cases:

- obligations regarding the surrender of slots at congested airports,
- obligations regarding interlining and code sharing agreements,
- obligations to enter into intermodal agreements,
- obligations to open up frequent flyer programmes to new entrants,
- obligations to freeze or reduce frequencies,
- obligations related to price reduction mechanism.

For the purpose of this chapter, only structural remedies will be addressed.

6.1 Surrender of slots

Such obligations have been considered to be essential in situations where potential entrants would not have been able to obtain slots at the airport at one or both ends of a route in question through the normal slot allocation procedure, due to congestion. The competition assessment in the air transport cases showed that an open and equal access to airport slots remains the key factor in ensuring competition in the aviation market.

As previously outlined, the lack of adequate take-off and landing slots is generally the main barrier for potential entrants. The number of slots surrendered needs to be high enough to enable competitors to operate a sufficient number of frequencies on the routes where the anticompetitive effects have been assessed to exercise a significant competitive constraint on the parties. The availability of slots, in fact, defines the contestability of the market, even in the case of high market shares.

The current system by which incumbent airlines have "grandfather rights" to slots at congested airports makes it very difficult for new entrant airlines to obtain access to hub airports. It is a case of regulation affecting competition conditions, especially when there is significant excess demand for slots at a number of EU airports. For this reason, slot surrender remains an essential remedy in order to secure effective access to the market for newcomers, notwithstanding difficulties of technical implementation and monitoring and the circumstance for which – being rights not in the ownership of carriers – slots are released for free. Only the recent Commission Communication on the application of Regulation (EEC) No. 95/93 on common rules for the allocation of slots at Community airports finally opens up to one-to-one exchange of slots "for monetary and other consideration". The likely effects of the new opportunities will be experienced in the near future.

In the Air France/KLM merger decision (2004) the European Commission updated the "slot surrender" remedy scheme. First, the duration of the obligation to surrender slots is unlimited. Slots may be claimed by competitors at any point in the future, although the parties may be released from the obligation under a review clause. In case of utilization below the 80 percent threshold, slots are given back to the coordinator and not to the dominant carrier. Second, in order to make entry more attractive, under certain conditions new entrants may be able to obtain grandfather rights for the slots released so that, once a new entrant has operated this route for a minimum of a number of IATA seasons, it may thereafter use the slots released at its discretion for any other city pair. This standard, up to now, still represents a guideline.

7 Considerations on the likely need to update the antitrust toolbox

A new season for merger control activity is expected by competition authorities as a result of the effects of the economic downturn. This should lead to a crucial question in terms of competition policy: do the ongoing major changes in the aviation sector also require changes in the antitrust toolbox in order to properly intervene to preserve a sufficient and effective degree of competition? And how should an up-to-date competitive assessment be approached which remains formally consistent with the consolidated jurisprudence of recent case law?

The topic is quite relevant for the eventual impact on future proceedings. In the following some preliminary considerations are developed.

7.1 Definition of the relevant markets

This preliminary step is crucial since it identifies the boundaries of the space where market power can be effectively exerted. The O&D approach is revealed to be the most appropriate and solid way to define the relevant market from the demand side since the supply-side effects can be better caught during the competition assessment. But within the O&D markets, more efforts should be dedicated to evaluate the degree of competition between different air transport services. This leads directly to the issue of the segmentation of the demand. Does the difference between time-sensitive and non-time-sensitive passengers hold when fare structures are getting simpler (not only for low costs but to some extent also for traditional carriers)? Moreover, is that distinction still appropriate? In recent years, in fact, price-sensitivity of business customers has increased over time due to new possibilities to book cheaper flights with low-cost carriers that, in the meantime, have increased the frequencies on routes between important city pairs to a relatively high number. The fact that the supply of a new product – such as the no-frills point-to-point air services – has changed the pattern of the demand and its willingness to pay, is something that still has not been taken fully into account when defining the relevant market.

Finally, with reference to intermodal competition, deeper analysis is needed on the competition constraints exerted by high-speed trains as substitute for air transport services (especially on connection between major city pairs).

7.2 Competition assessment

The degree of competition left after the merger/alliance, and to what extent it acts as a competition constraint on the incumbent, are at the core of the antitrust analysis. The computation of market shares on the basis of slot availability (frequencies) contributes to a better representation of the competitive scenario than the mere number of the passengers carried, by taking into account supply-side effects. Slots, in fact – due also to a conservative regulation – are the most critical assets to successfully compete, especially in congested airports.

Furthermore, a realistic competitive threat – actual or potential – is based on the possibility of operating at a minimally efficient scale on a given route and at a given airport. This has to do with the concept of operation with a base airport with considerable cost savings and increased flexibility. In recognizing the importance of the operational scale in assessing the effectiveness of the competition constraint, the competitive assessment – and the eventual remedies imposed – should therefore be focused more on the credibility of the competitors' threat than on the number of competitors (i.e. "pluralism" is not always a synonym for competition, especially in network industries). This has the consequence that market analysis has to explore also the potential of single O&D markets, not only in terms of the existing barriers to entry, but also of the likely sustainable demand.

With reference to the assessment of strategic barriers to entry, it is doubtful whether the role of reputation effects should be emphasized or not (as in the Ryanair/Aer Lingus case; Spector and Chapsal, 2008). On one side it surely relates to the incumbent's advantages which are not easily replicated by competitors, but, on the other, it is closely linked to the concept of "competition on the merits" which should be preserved with appropriate incentives.

A final word on vertical effects. The increasing importance of airports in the operation of the airline business is creating a strong incentive for carriers to integrate with airport services. Requests for dedicated terminals, acquisition of shares in main hub airports or strategic destination bases represent an emerging trend that competition enforcers have to evaluate by facing the trade-off between efficiency gains and the risk of increasing barriers to entry.

7.3 Remedies design

According to an economic analysis based on the assessment of the effectiveness of the competition left after the merger/alliance, slot release is by far the most far-sighted remedy, especially in the light of the current regulation on slot allocation.[16]

Nevertheless, different implementations of the slot release remedy can lead to different results in terms of market outcomes. A preliminary consideration concerns the scope of the remedies: if they aim at maximizing the number of players on single routes, they could be inefficient in terms of competition constraints exerted by new entrants. The minimum scale required to compete within a network industry suggests, on the contrary, giving priority in accessing the released slot to already operating competitors, in order to strengthen their counterbalance power.

Other considerations may be raised when competitive concerns are not strictly "route-specific", but, for instance, related to the profitability of entry in the bundle of routes originating from the base airport by actual and potential competitors. Up to now, in fact, consistently with the O&D market definition and the competition assessment based on single markets (i.e. routes), remedies have always been market-targeted; they modify competition conditions in each market where the market power of the merging entities cannot be countervailed by competitors. The market-related scheme prevents the risk of a decreasing supply in a given market after the intervention by the competition authority, which would damage consumers in the short run. But in specific cases, especially when the airport cannot increase its capacity, the remedy could be ineffective in promoting real competition.

Appropriate remedies should in fact incentivize at least one competitor to operate from the base airport where limitations occur, according to a scale that allows the exploitation of base economies comparable to those of the merging entities. This leads to the radical conclusion that, when the "incentive" is not sufficient, the remedy will not be sufficient to restore competition. And this holds even if it allows the operation of a number of slots and market share on single markets decreases significantly. That is to say that competitive concerns may go beyond specific market concerns. The risk of such a radical analysis is to evaluate as un-remediable (to be prohibited) a number of mergers due to market considerations other than the technical slot availability; this seems to go far beyond the established procedure of slot release in order to allow competitors (actual and potential) the possibility of entering single routes.

A second question concerns the route-specificity of the remedies. Route-specific remedies might in fact reduce the likelihood of new entries and, hence, might make the discipline of potential competition much weaker and less effective. On the other hand, if in order to be effective remedies have to be not strictly route-related, they may become inconsistent with the demand-based market definition, by ignoring the routes affected by the merger.

Some of the answers which can be given to these questions might undermine the market definition approach traditionally privileged in antitrust analysis in the airline industry. For instance, if one believes that slot release can be more effective without restricting its use to specific routes (i.e. the overlap routes) it means that market power is wrongly assessed by the traditional market definition. However, an assessment fully based on the availability of slots at the airport level which does not take into consideration the degree of substitutability between different routes from the demand side, should cope with some distributive issues which are not typical of antitrust analysis.

In conclusion, the challenge of designing effective remedies not in contrast with the market definition (or the other way round) in the air transport industry is surely one of the main nodes of modern antitrust enforcement, also taking into consideration the potentially static effects in terms of quantity on specific routes. May, otherwise, a splendid inconsistency between market definition and remedies be sustainable?

Notes

1 In the period 2000–2001 can be located the last significant interventions by EU Member states in order to subsidize and re-capitalize flag carriers. The first bankruptcies of publicly owned carriers (Sabena and Swiss) occurred in 2001. In the current scenario of economic crisis, the recapitalization schemes of nationally owned carriers are starting to emerge again (e.g. Alitalia, Austrian Airlines), even if in a privatization perspective.

2 Updated data on traffic volumes and economic output are available on the Air Transport Portal of the European Commission, see http://ec.europa.eu/transport/air/internal_market/internal_market_en.htm – (accessed October 2009).

3 The number of scheduled airlines established in the European Economic Area has increased steadily from 1992, reaching a maximum in the years 2002–2003, while now it is almost stable (the EU enlargement offsets the ceased activities).

4 Council Regulation (EEC) 95/93 on common rules for the allocation of slots at Community airports partially amended by EC Regulation 793/2004, was the first step to lay down a number of transparent, non-discriminatory rules.

5 Communication from the Commission "On the application of Regulation (EEC) No 95/93 on common rules for the allocation of slots at Community airports, as amended".

6 Several re-capitalizations of former flag carriers occurred in the EU and were authorized according to State Aid legislation: Sabena (1991, 1995), Iberia (1992, 1995), Aer Lingus (1993), Tap (1994), Olympic Airways (1994), Air France (1994, 1998), Alitalia (1997, 2001).

7 The several situations of dramatic financial distresses led to technical "bankruptcy" only in the case of Sabena and Swiss Air, both in 2001.

8 A side-effect of the growing low-cost market share of air traffic within the EU might be the likely identification of another category of the demand, the so-called "destination insensitive customers", which can consider flying to different destinations on the basis of the price, without having an *ex ante* preference.

9 As an example, in the case of the merger between Ryanair and Aer Lingus (case M4439), the Commission did not segment the markets in consideration of the similar service offered by the two carriers which operated more than 80 percent of the routes from/to Dublin.

10 Cf. "Air and rail competition and complementarity" Final Report (August 2006) prepared for the European Commission DG TREN by Steer Davies Gleave, available at http://ec.europa.eu/transport/air_portal/internal_market/studies/index_en.htm (accessed October 2009).

11 More radically, it can be said that merger-related network effects in terms of market power could be demonstrated more effectively in relation to a market defined as the whole relevant network, than with regard to single O&D pairs. In the Sky Team investigation, for instance, for the first time the Commission is examining the competition effects of a global alliance in its quasi-totality. The peculiarity of the case can suggest a different approach to market definition. A decision is expected in 2010.

12 In the case of KLM/Northwest (in OJ 2002 C 264/11), the European Commission accepted a combined market share of up to 90 percent on the direct overlap routes (without imposing remedies) since no significant entry barriers were identified.

13 The most recent cases are: (i) for mergers, M.5440 Lufthansa/Austrian Airlines (2009), M.3940 Lufthansa/Eurowings (2005), M.3770 Lufthansa/Swiss (2005),

M.3280 Air France/KLM (2004); (ii) for alliances COMP/37.984 Skyteam (under investigation), COMP/37.749 Austrian Airlines/SAS (2005), COMP/38.479 British Airways/Iberia/GBAirways (2003), COMP/38.284 Air France/Alitalia (2004), COMP/37.730 Deutsche Lufthansa/Austrian Airlines (2002), COMP/38.477 British Airways/SN Brussels Airlines (2003).

14 The Ryanair/Aer Lingus (M4439) case represents the first antitrust evaluation of a merger between low-cost carriers, both operating from the airport of Dublin. It has been probably the first case where the competitive concerns have been analysed according to the "base competition" paradigm.

Ryanair offered various remedies to solve the competition issues identified. However, the Commission decided that the scope of these remedies was insufficient to ensure that customers would not be harmed by the transaction. In particular, the limited number of "slots" offered was unlikely to stimulate market entry of a size necessary to replace the competitive pressure currently exercised by Aer Lingus.

15 See Notice on remedies acceptable under the Council Regulation (EEC) 4064/89 and under the Commission Regulation (EC) 447/98, OJ 2001/C 68/03.

16 A market-oriented regulation for slot allocation – where slots become marketable assets for airlines – could also remove the drawback of a structural measure (the slot release) which has no economic compensation.

References

Autorità Garante della Concorrenza e del Mercato (2005) Dinamiche tariffarie del trasporto aereo passeggeri. Indagine conoscitiva IC24. Available at: www.agcm.it (accessed October 2009).

Brueckner, J.K. (2003) The benefit of codesharing and antitrust immunity for international passengers, with an application to the Star Alliance. *Journal of Air Transport Management*, vol. 3, pp. 323–342.

Brueckner, J.K. and Pels, E. (2005) European arline mergers, alliance consolidation and consumer welfare. *Journal of Air Transport Management*, vol. 11, pp. 27–41.

Caffè, F. (1986) *In difesa del welfare state*. Turin: Rosenberg & Sellier.

Carney, M. and Dostaler, I. (2006) Airline ownership and control: A corporate governance perspective. *Journal of Air Transport Management*, vol. 12, pp. 63–75.

De La Mano, M. (2008) Analyse quantitative de l'affaire Ryanair–Aer Lingus. *Revue Lamy de la Concurrence*, no. 14, pp. 9–11.

Dennis, N. (2005) Industry consolidation and future airline network structures in Europe. *Journal of Air Transport Management*, vol. 11, pp. 175–183.

Doganis, R. (2001) *The airline business in the 21st Century*. London: Routledge. London.

Dresner, M. (2006) Leisure versus business passengers: Similarities, differences and implications. *Journal of Air Transport Management*, vol. 12, pp. 28–32.

European Competition Authorities (2004) Mergers and Alliances in civil aviation. Available at www.oft.gov.uk/shared_oft/mergers_ea02/ecareportcivilaviation.pdf (accessed October 2009).

European Competition Authorities (2006) Code-Sharing agreements in scheduled passenger air transport. *European Competition Journal*, vol. 2, no. 2, 263–284.

Gillen, D. and Morrison, W.G. (2003) Bundling, integration and the delivered price of the air travel: are low-cost carriers full-service competitors? *Journal of Air Transport Management*, vol. 9, pp. 15–23.

Gillen, D. and Morrison, W.G. (2005) Regulation, competition and network evolution in aviation. *Journal of Air Transport Management*, vol. 11, pp. 161–174.

Macchiati, A. and Piacentino, D. (2006) *Mercato e politiche pubbliche nell'industria del trasporto aereo.* Bologna: Il Mulino.

McDonald, M. (2006) Study on the impact of the introduction of secondary trading at community airports. Report commissioned by the European Commission.

Nordic Competition Authorities (2002) Competitive Airlines – Towards a more vigorous competition policy in relation to the air travel market. Available at: www.kkv.se/t/ IFramePage____1687.aspx (accessed October 2009).

Pels, E. (2001) Economic analysis of airline alliances. *Journal of Air Transport Management,* vol. 7, pp. 3–7.

Spector, D. and Chapsal, A. (2008) La décision Ryanair/Aer Lingus: un nouveau standard de qualité. *Revue Lamy de la Concurrence,* no. 14, pp. 12–13.

European antitrust cases:

Mergers (http://ec.europa.eu/comm/competition/mergers/cases)

Case M5440 Lufthansa/Austrian Airlines
Case M4439 – Ryanair/Aer Lingus
Case M3940 – Lufthansa/Eurowings
Case M3770 – Lufthansa/Swiss
Case M3280 – Air France/KLM

Alliances (http://ec.europa.eu/comm/competition/antitrust/cases/index.html)

Case COMP/37.984 – Skyteam
Case COMP/38.284 – Air France/Alitalia
Case COMP/37.749 – Austrian Airlines/SAS
Case COMP/38.479 – British Airways/Iberia/GB Airways
Case COMP/37.730 – Lufthansa/Austrian Airlines
Case COMP/38.477 – British Airways/SN Brussels Airlines

20 Regulatory constraints in Europe or "how free are you?"

Mia Wouters

1 Governmental intervention: a forced choice?

The chapters written in this book concern "critical issues in air transport economics and business". At first glance, the writings of a lawyer would not fit this bill, but in today's air transport industry the line between law and economics is really thin and in the current deregulated environment, these will affect each other more than ever. The combination of law and economics invariably leads to "a policy". But what actually is "the policy of air transport", or the role of the government/policy maker?

Air transport is the most regulated sector in our society, even after deregulation.[1] One could ask: why? What makes air transport different from maritime or road transport and how can we legitimize the intervention of the Government in all aspects of air transport?

Taking into account the overall economic and financial situation of today's airlines, where prosperity is seen as a rare bird, the question should be asked whether the aviation industry can ever be ready for total independence from government intervention. Government intervention is almost as old as aviation itself and certainly as old as commercial aviation. But unlike in other industries, it never ceased intervening.

The earliest instances of governmental control of the movements in airspace are most probably the Paris Police Ordinances of 1784 and 1819 putting a restraint on the use of the Montgolfier balloons.[2] Hot air balloons remained cumbersome especially at the end of the nineteenth century, following Germany's launch of hot air balloons over French territory to spy on the troops. Protests were made in 1908 and the French Government decided at the end of that year to invite European Powers to participate in a conference on the regulation of air navigation. Thus, on 10 May 1910 representatives of 19 European countries assembled for the first time in Paris to decide on the legal nature of airspace and on the establishment of a framework for international aviation. The French and German delegations were in favour of freedom of the air, based on the model of Hugo Grotius' *Mare Liberum*.[3] The British insisted on complete state sovereignty and control over the airspace. The conference adjourned on 29 June 1910 with no convention having been signed; thus, technically, the diplomatic convention should have been seen as a failure.

However, in the absence of an agreement, in 1911 the British declared de facto their sovereignty over the airspace above their country. Other European countries quickly followed suit. After the First World War, the Peace Conference of 1919 tried to complete the work begun in 1910.[4] Although the resulting Paris Convention did not define the term "airspace", it declared in Article 1 that a subjacent State had complete and exclusive sovereignty in the airspace above it. In the end the US and Russia failed to ratify the Paris Convention. With two world powers missing, the impact of the Convention was rather limited.

Following the end of the Second World War,[5] at a time when aviation was turning itself into a commercial activity, governments decided to rethink the "Paris principle" in Chicago. Although President Roosevelt called for an open sky that could be exploited for the good of mankind,[6] the British (rightly?) feared that the American aviation structure and fleet, and its large manufacturing capacity which had remained undamaged during the war, would end up dominating Europe which was left behind in a ravaged state.[7] Despite American efforts to make airspace free, the governments present at Chicago[8] decided to take the "Paris principle" up again: the airspace above the soil belongs to and will be controlled by the country owning the soil.

The final acceptance of the principle that the territory is three-dimensional and that the airspace above national lands and waters is part of the territory of the subjacent State, entailed the application of all the absolute and exclusive powers that historically had been attributed to Sovereign States with regard to the use of their national land. This can be seen as a first major step to legitimizing governmental intervention, a step which was never undone. But this means that commercial aviation now became a very cumbersome exercise with traffic rights forming part of the natural resources of governments and those governments wanting, of course, their own nationals to benefit from the commercialization of these resources.[9]

Thus when an airline decides to enter the international market, a strange sequence of diplomatic manoeuvres will ensue.[10] Unlike other businesses, before an international airline can enter new markets, lengthy government-to-government discussions are required.

In brief, worldwide, governments determine the "freedom" of the players on the air transport market.

2 Developments in Europe – the legal framework

On 1 January 1958, the Treaty of Rome came into effect, establishing the EEC. The aim was to create a true common market in which goods, services, labour and capital could freely move. Article 3(f) of the Treaty of Rome specifically provides for the adoption of a common policy in the sphere of transport. In Articles 74–84 of Title IV, the principles of the Treaty of Rome are applied to the transport sector, but Article 75 stresses the distinctive features of transport, which are for instance its dependency on infrastructure, the lack of elasticity of supply and demand, the public service aspect and the particular sensitivity to conjuncture and infrastructure costs. Articles 74–84 exempt air transport from the workings of the general rules on the common market. They will not be directly applicable to air transport; the Council (Member States) still needs to decide how air transport is affected by them.

This different approach affecting air transport was enhanced when, in November 1962, transport was explicitly withdrawn from the scope of Regulation 17/62 which contained the provisions for the implementation of the old Articles 85 and 86 on competition law. Thus for almost 30 years, civil aviation remained outside the main process of European integration. The development of a European air transport policy had to take into account an exceptional political sensitivity of the Member States. This was the result of a high degree of public funding that had led to a severe level of national regulation,[11] which in turn resulted in protectionism of the national air transport sector. Although by Treaty placed under the obligation to act, neither the Council nor the Member States were inclined to take decisions furthering a common European regime concerning air transport. National governments did not want to lose their grip on aviation. The process of liberalization therefore became a political struggle in which, in the end, the European Court of Justice had to arbitrate.

Countering the resistance of the Member States and the European Council to the introduction of competition in the air transport sector, both the European Commission and the Court, supported by the European Parliament, expressed their willingness to subject air transport step-by-step to the workings of the competition rules. It was indeed clear that liberalization in Europe should gradually be introduced.[12] Given the scope of the changes that would be brought about, the progressive nature of the process of liberalization was considered as a prerequisite.

The goal of the Commission's First Memorandum of 1979 was to start a debate on the contents of an integrated European air policy in which national governments would necessarily lose their prerogatives. The ongoing deregulation process in the US influenced the debate on the pursuit of the regulatory process in Europe. The basic idea brought forward in the following Second Memorandum, in 1984, was the belief that the existing system did not sufficiently enhance competition between airlines and thus the productivity of the airlines was not optimum and that services could be provided at a lower cost. But the Commission also made it clear that it would use all means to try to avoid the US model of deregulation which, in its opinion, would lead to harmful competition.[13]

The Second Memorandum did retain the bilateral system, whereby Member States allow access to their airspace to air carriers from another Member State within the framework of bilateral service agreements. Where the First and the Second Memoranda were only opinions expressed by the Commission, the First Package was adopted three years later by the Council in 1987.This followed the implementation of the Single European Act in 1986, whereby decisions of the Council were no longer subject to the unanimity rule. Unanimity of all of the European Member States was no longer necessary to change the existing concept. The First Package was a first significant step towards a common European air transport policy. It represented the implicit conviction that the completion of a common market was as relevant to air transport as to any other sector. This was a first attempt towards a situation in which Member States would, little by little, lose full control.

Contrary to new proposals from the European Commission, the Council, however, maintained in its Second Package in 1990, the principles of the First Package and opted not to affect the existing relations between the airlines and their governments. The Council made it clear that nothing in the Second Package would prejudice a government's control over its own airlines. We had to wait for the Third Package in 1992 for a full liberalization in Europe. The Third Package was intended to be the finishing touch to the liberalization of air transport in a single market and no longer required "national" ownership of the carrier.

Thus a "common European Aviation Area" was created in which all European airlines are free to fly with a "European Nationality".[14] The only requirement for EU carriers to operate within Europe was/is that they were/are majority owned and controlled by EU citizens and that their principal place of business was/is within the EU. Further topics regulated by the three Regulations that constituted the Third Package were the freedom of establishment and freedom to provide services, free traffic rights between airports in the EU, no capacity restraints, free pricing and as of 1997 full cabotage. This opened up a lot of possibilities.

3 Safeguarding the common aviation market

In 2006, after more than ten years of its entry into force, the Commission assessed the Third Package and found it had largely played its role, allowing for unprecedented expansion of air transport in Europe, sweeping away old monopolies and intensifying competition to the benefit of the consumer. Europe had gradually moved from protected and fragmented national markets towards a single and liberalized internal market. It was felt that the liberalization of the internal aviation market had favoured the transformation of air transport services into a more efficient and affordable service.

But ten years later, the Third Package was up for revision because, despite all its success, the Commission found that most of the Community airlines still suffered from overcapacity and excessive fragmentation of the market. The inconsistent application of the Third Package across the Member States and the lingering restrictions on intra-Community air services were to blame for this. According to the Commission, airlines do not yet benefit from a level playing field. In practice they found varying levels of application within the different Member States with regards to the requirements of the operating licence; discrimination between EU carriers on the basis of nationality and discriminatory treatment concerning routes to third countries. The Commission also ascertained that the rules governing the leasing contracts on aircraft with a crew from third countries were inconsistently applied and held that passengers were not reaping the full benefits of the internal market because of the lack of price transparency and due to practices which discriminate on the basis of the place of their residence.

The revision of the Third Package was not intended to radically change the legal framework but merely to make a series of adjustments in order to address the above-mentioned problems. The new Regulation *on the common rules for the operation of air services in the Community*, consolidates the different Regulations of the Third Package and will safeguard the common aviation market in the coming years. It will ensure an efficient and homogeneous application of Community legislation via stricter and more precise application criteria for operating licences, leasing of aircraft, public service obligations and traffic distribution rules. It reinforces the internal market by lifting still existing restrictions on the provision of air services and it enhances consumer rights by promoting price transparency and non-discrimination.[15] The Third Package was intended to create a European framework, independent from national restrictions. As long as you stay within the set framework, you are free to operate. But how free is this, or where are the boundaries of the framework?

4 Regulation no. 1008/2008 of the European Parliament and of the Council of 24 September 2008 on the common rules for the operation of air services in the community[16]

4.1 Operating licence

In order to operate, all airlines need to be in possession of an Operating Licence. According to the non-discrimination principle of the Regulation, every company that meets a number of criteria in respect of economic and technical fitness, is entitled to be granted an Operating Licence. This non-discrimination requirement is important, because without it Member States would have the total freedom to decide in a discretionary manner whether they "need" a new carrier or not. A Member State shall issue an Operating Licence (OL) to a requesting airline if the applicant:

- has its principal place of business in a European Member State;
- is mainly involved in air transport and is more than 50 per cent owned and controlled by nationals of a European Member State;
- has a valid AOC (Aircraft Operating Licence which guarantees technical fitness) issued by the same Member State as the one it is seeking the OL from;
- has at least one aircraft at its disposal by means of ownership or dry leasing. This requirement was inserted to avoid the creation of a virtual air carrier;
- proves its financial health, meaning that the-airline-to-be needs to submit a valid business plan for at least three years of operation. This business plan shall give details regarding any financial links the applicant has with other commercial activities in which it is directly or indirectly engaged. The

business plan has to demonstrate that the airline will realistically be able to meet its obligations for the next two years and that it can pay for its fixed operational costs for at least three months without further income. Exceptions to these requirements are granted for the operation of small aircraft. An air carrier must at all times be able to demonstrate to the Member State that issued the licence, that it continuously meets the financial requirements. Financial fitness of air carriers is deemed to be of the greatest importance. Normal commercial conditions are not possible if air carriers, when exposed to market risks, are not able to take commercial decisions that are market-based. It was decided that airlines, like any other business, should face the risk of going bankrupt;

• has insured itself to cover its liability with respect to mail and abides by Regulation 785/2004 which sets out quite detailed insurance requirements with regards to passengers, luggage and cargo;

• is of good repute as well as the persons managing the airline's operations. They should under no circumstances have been declared bankrupt.

The Member State to whom the application for an operating licence is made shall take a decision on the application within three months after the necessary information has been provided. A possible refusal must indicate the reasons therefor. When a Member State has issued an Operational Licence, it only stays valid as long as the airline complies with the above-mentioned requirements. The licensing Member State has to monitor the airline to this end. This requires Member States to reinforce supervision of the operating licences and to suspend or revoke them when the requirements of the Regulation are no longer met.

Leasing of aircraft

The Regulation strengthens the requirements for the leasing of aircraft. It was deemed that the wet-leasing of aircraft from third countries provides for important flexibility. This practice, however, has some disadvantages and possibly could entail severe safety risks. Therefore, the Regulation introduces stricter requirements with regard to the leasing of aircraft, to minimize the risk of adverse consequences and to enhance safety. Community air carriers that abide by the Community safety requirements may freely operate wet-leased aircraft, provided these aircraft are registered within the Community.

For dry-leased aircraft and other wet-lease agreements, prior approval is needed. When a Community carrier wants to wet-lease an aircraft from a third country, such will only be accepted if Community safety requirements are met and the leasing is temporarily necessary to satisfy an exceptional or an excessive seasonal capacity need. Aircraft may also be leased from third countries to overcome operational difficulties provided, however, it is not possible to lease the required capacity on the European market under reasonable terms.

4.2 Access to routes

The Articles of the Regulation concerning "access to routes" are to ensure open access for any Community air carrier to all of the air routes situated within the EU. Market access is thus completely open and a Community carrier basically can start operations between any two airports within the EU. A Member State may not, except for environmental or public service reasons, refuse a Community carrier access to an airport which lies in its territory. The Regulation does, however, include safeguard clauses when dealing with situations where the open market does not provide satisfactory service.

4.2.1 Public service obligation

Competition may not in all instances provide air services where they are needed. To deal with such situations the possibility of Public Service Obligations (PSO) has been introduced. If a route which falls within the ambit of the Regulation and its operation can be qualified as a Public Service Obligation, it can receive beneficial treatment. PSOs basically amount to an obligation to operate routes at a certain quality level of service. If this would lead to a situation which is not commercially interesting to operate, Member States are allowed to give compensation.

Air services that are eligible to be endowed with the status of a PSO can include services between any Community airport and a Community airport serving a peripheral or development region or can be air services on a thin route to a regional airport, provided such a service is vital for the economic and social development of the region which the airport serves. Airlines bidding for a PSO must ensure minimum provisions of scheduled air services on that route and must satisfy fixed standards of continuity, regularity, pricing or minimum capacity. A PSO can only be given provided no airline would be willing to give these kinds of undertakings and operate under these conditions, in case they were only considering their commercial interest.

Member States are allowed, to a certain degree, to protect carriers operating a PSO. If there were no carriers willing to operate the route under consideration for endowment with PSO, the Member State is allowed to reserve the operation of that route for a period of three years to only one carrier. Carriers operating a PSO shall be elected through the process of public tendering. The text of such tender is published in the Official Journal. Member States are only allowed to compensate for PSOs in a cost-related manner and this shall be based on the costs and the revenue generated by the PSO.

Further safeguards in the Regulation concerning free market operations, are: (a) provisions on the distribution of traffic between airports that serve the same city or conurbation; (b) limitations of traffic for environmental measures; and (c) the refusal, limitation or imposition of conditions on the exercise of traffic rights in case of unforeseeable and unavoidable circumstances in the short run. Such actions shall be proportional, transparent and based on objective and non-discriminatory criteria.

4.3 *Provisions on pricing*

Together with the European Directive 2005/29 concerning unfair business-to-consumer commercial practices and Regulation 80/2009 on a Code of Conduct for Computer Reservation Systems; the Regulation under discussion puts an obligation on the air carriers operating from a Community airport to indicate the final price of the flight ticket, at the outset of the booking process. The price first advertised on a website or other types of media should thus be the final amount the consumer will have to pay. In addition, the Regulation requests that the consumer should be given a detailed breakdown of all the price elements. If taxes, fees and charges are to be added to the basic air fare, they need to be specified.

Thus the price of a ticket clearly and individually has to show:

a   the basic air fare or air rate;
b   the taxes;
c   the airport charges – both (b) and (c) are imposed on a per passenger basis and directly traceable to third parties such as airports and governments, and
d   the other charges which are levied by the airlines themselves. This last category includes fuel charges; booking fee/service, fee/ticket issuing charges; insurance charges; security charges (these are the airlines' own security fees and are in addition to the security charges imposed by airports under (c)); possible VAT on domestic flights; air traffic control charges (charged by airport authorities, air navigation service providers and Eurocontrol for air navigation services) and any other charge which can include, for instance, a war premium, environmental taxes, landing charges, over-flight charges and charges for the use of the airport outside usual service hours.

Optional price supplements (such as luggage and cancellation insurance) must be communicated in a clear, transparent and unambiguous way and at the start of the booking process and their acceptance by the customer should be made on an "opt-in" basis!

A current in-depth study made by the European Commission, Directorate for Consumer Affairs, found that airlines frequently include parts of their basic operational costs (mentioned under "(d) other charges") into what appear to be the obligatory "taxes and charges" (mentioned under (b) and (c)). It is perceived that this misleads consumers and falsely attracts consumers into buying seemingly cheaper tickets. The study also exposed that the current terminology used by airlines to describe the different taxes, fees and charges is often hazy and/or abundant, which makes it extremely difficult for consumers to compare the different offers.

5 How free are you?

Stuck within a worldwide framework which the governments created in 1944, along the lines of the Chicago Convention and by which governments are prominently present in all aspects of public air transport, nothing basically changed over the last 65 years. Although at the regional level national interests had to make way for a European interest, on a worldwide level, the bilateral system still prevails. Within IACO, different countries have gone through the theoretical exercise of what it would mean to the world to abandon the sovereignty of airspace, but the question remains hypothetical. Open Skies Agreements[17] are punching holes in the wall of governmental dominance but as long as the ownership and effective control of airlines can be traced back to the nationality of its stakeholders, the wall will not give way.

Your freedom to carry out and structure your business is subordinated by the model the authorities have decided on.

Notes

1 Pilarski, A.M. (2007) *Why Can't We Make Money in Aviation,* Cornwall: Ashgate, pp. 180–189.
2 Cooper, J.C. (1967) *Backgrounds of International Public Air Law, Yearbook of Air and Space Law 1965,* Montreal: McGill University Press, pp. 3–21.
3 Mateesco Matte, N. (1981) *Treatise on air-aeronautical law.* Montreal: McGill University Press.
4 Dempsey, P.S. (1987) *Law and Foreign Policy in International Aviation,* New York: Transnational Publishers, pp. 7–21.
5 Weber, L. (2007) *International Civil Aviation Organization. An introduction,* Alphen aan den Rijn: Kluwer Law International.
6 Guldiman, W. (1989) The market regulation of international air transport, in Nicolas Matte Mateesco, *Liber Amicorum,* Paris: Editions A. Pedonne, pp. 121–129.
7 Rhoades, D. (2003) *Evolution of International Aviation; Phoenix Rising,* Cornwall: Ashgate Publishing Limited, pp. 13–29.
8 The Convention on International Civil Aviation (Chicago Convention) was signed in Chicago on 7 December 1944 by 52 signatory states and established the International Civil Aviation Organization (ICAO), a specialized agency of the United Nations charged with the coordination and regulation of international air transport. It received the requisite 26th ratification on 5 March 1947 and went into effect on 4 April 1947. In October of the same year, the ICAO became a specialized agency of the United Nations Economic and Social Council (ECOSOC).
9 van Fenema, H. (1992) Substantial ownership and effective control as airpolitical criteria, in *Air and Space Law: de Lege Ferenda, Essays in honour of Henri Wassenberg,* Dordrecht: Martinus Nijhoff Publishers, pp. 27–41.
10 Mendes de Leon, P.M.J. (1992) De lege ferenda: explanation and application to public international air law, in *Air and Space Law: de Lege Frerenda, Essays in honour of Henri Wassenberg,* Dordrecht: Martinus Nijhoff Publishers, pp. 53–61.
11 Dempsey, P.S. (2004) *European Aviation Law,* The Hague: Kluwer Law International, p. 3.
12 Doganis, R. (2001) *The Airline Business in the 21st Century,* London: Routledge, p. 38.
13 On destructive competition in the US, see Dempsey, P.S. and Gesell, L.E (1997) *Airline Management Strategies for the 21st Century,* Chandler: Coast Aire Publications, pp. 455–463.
14 Bartlik, M. (2007) *The Impact of EU Law on the Regulation of International Air Transportation,* Cornwall: Ashgate Publishing Limited, p. 15.
15 Proposal for a Regulation of the European Parliament and of the Council on common rules for the operation of air transport services in the Community, presented by the Commission, COM(2006) 396 final.
16 Official Journal L. 293 from 31/10/2008; pp. 0003–0020.
17 Liberal Air Service Agreements.

21 Essential airline marketing strategies

Joel Zhengyi Shon

The concept of marketing can be quite confusing to those who are unfamiliar with business, management, and economics. They might wonder: what is the difference between marketing and sales? Is there anything else that marketing can do other than advertise? Why and in what way is marketing related to economics? Marketing researchers have analyzed these important issues in great detail over the past 50 years. Even though they have come up with quite a number of well-formulated and well-founded theories, these theories are sometimes rather difficult to read and understand for most of us. To put it in the simplest terms: marketing is an intermediary, helping supply to meet demand on the market. Without marketing processes and activities, transaction costs may become too high, leaving all parties involved in the transaction process without ever reaching an agreement. Obviously, marketing has other effects as well, though this is perhaps the most critical one. In short, marketing creates both a virtual and a physical marketplace, and then has demand meet supply in these marketplaces, which is the basic principle of business operations and of economic theory. In this chapter, we discuss essential airline marketing strategies. Researchers may find interesting and most up-to-date topics in each of the sections, which might have value for further studies.

1 Airline marketing strategies – what you really need to know

Most people have already read plenty of marketing ideas and have learned basic marketing concepts from newspaper columns and business magazines, but what is the entire picture of marketing? In this section, the most important and basic elements of marketing are introduced. Readers will understand the role that marketing plays, and will then be ready for advanced marketing knowledge.

Airline marketing is just like regular marketing, but marketers are marketing airline services. The first thing everyone needs to know is that professionals usually divide marketing strategies into four categories: Product, Price, Place, and Promotion. Combined, these are usually called "the marketing mix," or "the 4Ps." Some scholars and professionals have added additional Ps to the original four, thus creating 5Ps, 6Ps, even 7Ps, but these extended definitions are not as popular as the original one. The 4Ps still form the bedrock of most marketing plans that marketers draw up, meaning that when people talk about marketing strategies, they base many of their decisions on these four categories. Any marketer should know what the 4Ps mean in his or her specific field. To the airline marketer, *product* means the delivery of services to airlines' customers, *price* means the fare that airlines charge their customers for the service. Sometimes price also refers to total costs, which includes searching, handling, and delivery costs. This definition leads airlines to another decision factor: Place.

Though there are minor differences in the various definitions of *place*, it usually refers to the channels that airlines use to sell their products and services. The more channels airlines apply, the easier it gets for their customers to reach the airlines' products and services. A broader channel strategy will result in lower total costs paid by customers, and in more business opportunities. However, airlines' marketing costs will also increase with the number of the channels applied. A favorable trade-off between price and place is often a key success factor (KSF) of a lot of businesses.

The last of the four Ps is *promotion*, which is a variety of tools that will make customers know the product, love the product, and hopefully buy the product. However, it's hard to find an effective tool that is capable of doing all these things at the same time. That is to say, different promotion strategies are usually needed in order for customers to know, to love, or to buy the product.

In addition to the 4Ps, many other important marketing topics and/or concepts are discussed in marketing journals and in business magazines, such as consumer behavior, customer satisfaction, price discrimination, market segmentation, and the product life cycle. Basically, all these concepts are derived from the 4Ps. As long as the concept of the 4Ps is understood, the other marketing concepts won't be too hard to understand either.

2 Market segmentation and product differentiation

Why do airlines need different classes such as first class and business class? Why do airline images differ? Does it matter if airlines do not segment? What if the target market is shared with competitors? In this chapter, the art of market segmentation and product differentiation is introduced. Airlines constantly use these skills, which form the core elements of their product strategy.

The answer to all of the questions above involves product strategies. Different types of customers exist: some are rich, some are not. Some passengers' travel costs are reimbursed by taxpayers and/or their bosses, while other passengers pay for their own tickets. Some passengers travel for business, while others travel for leisure only. Wealthy customers might be willing to pay more to get a larger and more private seat during their flight for added comfort and privacy: these passengers are what the airlines call business travelers, but not all business travelers fly business class.

Generally speaking, most business class fares are 1.5 times higher than economy class fares, while first class fares are twice as high. The physical space on the aircraft as well as the luggage allowances airlines reserve for business and first class travelers are also approximately 1.5 times and two times more than those of economy class travelers (www.smarttravelasia.com, 2009). Some airlines, such as ANA, EVA, and Air France, have introduced a product strategy of "luxury economy" or "premium economy" class, which offers its passengers 20 percent more space at a fare that is also 20 percent higher. These airlines attempt to persuade the more well-off customers to upgrade from the basic economy class fare to an economy class fare that, while still affordable, provides more comfort.

Some airlines focus on the higher-end markets: business and first class travelers. The cabin interior of the legendary supersonic Concorde is an excellent example thereof. This famous and luxury aircraft was equipped with first and business class only. Normally, in order to attract business and first class passengers, airlines need to offer dedicated check-in counters, as well as finely-decorated lounge facilities, complete with food, beverages, and newspapers. However, if the market size of these well-off passengers is not big enough, it may prove too costly to run these facilities. When BA and Air France still operated Concorde (before the plane officially retired from regular service in 2003), Concorde passengers were treated to caviar and champagne in business and first class lounges right after they checked in at their dedicated counter. Not surprisingly, first and business class cabins are usually crowded on city pairs that link commercial centers, such as New York–London, New York–Hong Kong, and London–Singapore. For many business travelers, travel costs are covered by their employers, so they don't need to worry too much about fare levels.

Nevertheless, not everyone can afford the high fares of first or business class. Although they are sometimes able to, well-off customers may still not be willing to spend that much money on airline tickets. Some companies are already asking

Figure 21.1 First class cabin layout of Singapore Airlines A380.

their managers and other high-level executives to travel economy class in order to save costs. In microeconomic theory, the differences between "needs," "wants," and "desires" are the basis for structuring utility, preferences, and demand functions. Only a few of the desires can eventually turn into real demand. Business and first class travel is a very good example in interpreting this theory.

In general, the number of mid-income travelers is much higher than the number of high-income ones. As a result, airlines need to offer a different product to this market. Low-cost carriers, also known as LCCs or budget airlines, are typical for a business model of product differentiation. Using cheap and efficient aircraft equipped with a single class (economy class), LCCs are usually able to carry a lot more passengers than legacy carriers can. In several specific markets with a large number of commuters, legacy carriers also opt for a single economy-class cabin layout to meet the huge demand in the market. Japan Airlines used to operate Boeing 747-400s with a single economy class to carry more than 500 passengers per aircraft from Tokyo to Osaka.

Not all airlines succeed with their products, however. Technology usually sets limits to product design. A number of carriers have attempted to offer "long-haul" low-cost services, but the aircraft capable of long-distance flights are usually very expensive. And reducing costs on long-haul low-cost operations seems to be almost like mission impossible. Moreover, the range of the maximum payload of most aircraft models has made a single-class cabin design practically impossible for cross-Pacific or cross-Atlantic flights. In order to offer such long-distance flights, business and first class are essentially required in order to reduce the total number of passengers and luggage on board. If not, the aircraft would otherwise not be able to cross the ocean before its fuel burnt out.

We have now learned that there are different types of customers and that each of these types request different products and services to meet their specific needs. However, market segmentation has its limitations. Some segments are not easy to reach, some are too costly to promote, and some are too small to be profitable. Moreover, certain laws and regulations also restrict the possibility of certain types of segmentation. After all, all international flights have become non-smoking flights now, rendering air travel a nightmare to cigarette lovers. Airlines know that this particular segment exists, and they know that if flights allowed onboard smoking they would attract a lot of business, but airlines are legally prohibited to cater to this segment. Other segmentation techniques could result in discrimination disputes, either racial or sexual.

Product design problems that airlines face are almost identical to what other companies face. So what is so special about airline marketing then? In order to be able to answer this question, we need to further examine the airlines' core product, which is service. Compared to physical products, service has different attributes. First of all, it's intangible. Passengers do not really own anything after they have bought a ticket. Passengers do not pay and get the airplane, nor do they get the decorations on the airplane, not even the beautiful flight attendants. Passengers pay the airline to take them from point A to point B. So it's quite difficult for airlines to compete with the core product of basic transportation service, because all of the carriers take their passengers to their destinations (barring any accidents). Hence, airlines can only compete with one another on the extended product, for example, having nicer cabin interior designs, softer seats, or more exquisite meals. Although these extended services may help, most passengers prefer aspects such as punctuality and safety, as well as a greater frequency and less travel time. Other service attributes are much less important.

Figure 21.2 All economy class layout of Budget Airline.

The reason passengers ask for greater frequencies comes from the three attributes of services: perishability, simultaneous production and consumption, and variability. No inventory can be stored for service goods. Unlike physical products that can be stored in case supply temporarily exceeds demand, service production and consumption always take place at the same time. So passengers need greater service frequency to meet their variable demand, which is exactly the third attribute of services. Services, and transport services in particular, always have peak and off-peak demand cycles. Airlines need to accommodate capacity to meet peak demand. That is why fleet sizes are usually bigger than average demand levels. Nevertheless, surplus supply is a huge waste during off-peak flights. In the long run, the interest paid on the over-investment that is needed to create the over-size fleet is one of the major factors of airlines' financial deficits.

Last but not least, services are also inseparable. Passengers cannot ask airlines to drop them off halfway down the flight and then have them pick them up again a few days later to continue their flight. Some may argue that airlines provide stopover services – however, that is a completely different product design. Stopovers are not simply transfers; passengers check out from the airline's service and then check in again later. Stopovers may create utilities to those travelers who would like to visit more places for either leisure or business purposes. In such circumstances, airlines usually sell stopover tickets at higher fares, or at least charge an additional airport tax. If stopovers are allowed, airlines have the responsibility to take the passengers to both the stopover point and the final destination, which is different from city-pair services. If there is no particular reason not to do so, passengers traveling between city pairs usually prefer direct flights in order to reduce travel time as well as reducing the risk of delays and accidents at transfer airports.

However, there is one exception: the island hopper flight of Continental Airlines. The island hopper flight travels from Guam to Hawaii and stops at five other islands in between. Many aviation enthusiasts take the island hopper flight instead of many other, direct flights sold at a much cheaper fare. They do so because they want to enjoy the frequent take-offs and landings as well as the beautiful scenery overlooking the Micronesian islands.

3 Service quality vs. air fare

The business model of budget airlines, also known as low-cost carriers (LCC), is not a particularly profitable business model, but it is one that definitely affects markets tremendously because budget airlines usually sell tickets at prices lower than average costs of most legacy carriers. Why is this model so competitive? It is not just because of the low fares that these budget airlines offer. From the PZB model introduced by Parasuraman *et al.* (1985), the success of LCCs can be explained by the concepts of customer satisfaction.

The Low-Cost Carrier model is currently a popular business model in the airline industry. Using a single-cabin design in the same aircraft model has reduced not only aircraft procurement costs, but operational costs as well. This is one of the very few examples of economies of scale we can find in the airline industry. For further cost reductions, the LCCs scrap normally free-of-charge cabin amenities, such as meals, beverages, newspapers, and inflight entertainment. In other words, all the services that passengers want during a flight now carry their own price tags: passengers need to pay for them. By doing so, the LCC is able to offer a much lower fare in the market.

Since there is only economy class in a typical LCC cabin, LCC passengers have few choices. The seats provided by the LCCs are always small. By removing the services that passengers used to have, LCC service quality may be seen as far from satisfactory. However, such a straightforward way of thinking is not necessarily a correct one. Customer satisfaction is measured by the gap between expectation and reality. This was a famous theory of satisfaction introduced by Parasuraman *et al.* known as the PZB model in the 1980s (Parasuraman *et al.*, 1985). Passengers on board LCCs would usually not expect a high quality of service, based on their previous experiences. They also believe that the service they should expect is what they have paid for. Research held in the Chinese market revealed that most of the passengers onboard LCCs were satisfied with the service they provided.

So why is it that these LCC passengers are satisfied? Using the PZB model, Shon, Chen, and Chiou (2007) tried to analyze the gap between expected and perceived service quality. Trip characteristics and personal characteristics, which may have certain effects on service quality, were also included in order to have a better constructed research model, which is shown in Figure 21.3. Finally, a clear definition of airline service quality is needed. IATA (International Air Transportation Association) has categorized and defined airline service quality from an industrial perspective. According to IATA, airline services can be divided into nine different major categories: seat reservation, ground service,

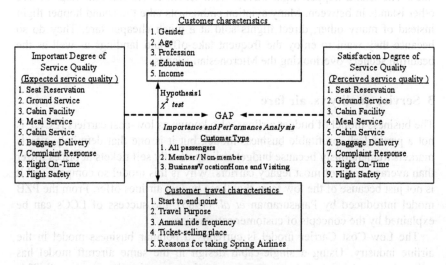

Figure 21.3 Research framework of airline service quality.

cabin facility, meal service, cabin service, baggage delivery, complaint response, flight on-time, and flight safety. To find the customer's perception of the airline service quality, these nine factors are all measured on a five-degree Likert scale. The higher the score given by passengers, the better the service quality, and vice versa. The analytical tool applied in the research is called the IPA (Importance-Performance Analysis) model developed by Martilla and James (1977). The IPA model simultaneously identifies the X axis value of relative importance as expected service quality, and the Y axis value of performance of service or product attributes as perceived service quality. The Origin is exactly the average score given by the passengers of both relative importance and performance of attributes.

The results are plotted graphically on a two-dimensional grid. Attribute importance is listed on the vertical axis while satisfaction level is displayed on the horizontal axis, as depicted in Figure 21.4, resulting in four quadrants. Factors located in Quadrant I are perceived as high expectation and high per-formance, while factors in Quadrant IV are perceived as low expectation and low performance.

From the data collected in the Chinese LCC market, only flight on-time and complaint responses fall into Quadrant I, indicating that their performances are lower than their expectations. The factors of meal service and cabin facility, which legacy carriers usually focus on, are not part of LCC passengers' expecta-tions. As a whole, overall service quality of LCCs can be very high because the airlines have already satisfied the passengers' basic needs and wants, and have successfully educated their passengers to realize what they should not expect. In the original IPA model, the suggested strategies for factors that fall in the four Quadrants are "Keep Up the Good Work" (Quadrant I), "Concentrate Here" (Quadrant II), "Low Priority" (Quadrant III), and "Possible Overkill" (Quadrant

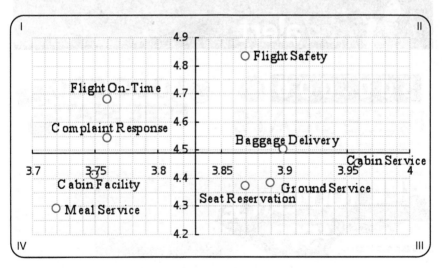

Figure 21.4 IPA model of LCC service quality.

IV). Does this mean that the LCC in this study should concentrate on flight on-time and complaint responses? Interestingly, however, based on statistical data from the government, the airline in question already ranked first on the 2006 punctuality list, which was announced prior to the service quality survey in 2007. The airline in question has probably done too much to raise the expectations of its passengers.

In addition to removing unnecessary services, one key success factor within the LCC business model is to maximize utilization of aircraft and employees, reducing the average cost of each available seat-kilometer. Turnover time of LCCs can be as low as 30 minutes, and even less in China. The daily average operation hours of any LCC aircraft can be 1.5 times higher than those of legacy carrier aircraft. LCCs usually do not set up hub-and-spoke networks to reduce the risk of schedule delays at the hub airports. Direct flights also increase the utility of travelers between city pairs. As a result, LCCs can be more cost-effective, and more punctual as well.

Cost-effectiveness can be found in the pricing strategy of LCCs. Starting from 2008, Air Asia, the biggest LCC in Asia, has offered half to one million of its seats for free twice a year. Passengers only need to pay the necessary fees and taxes. US-based JetBlue airways, another famous LCC, launched a new product called AYCJ (All-You-Can-Jet) in 2009, offering passengers unlimited flights in a 30-day period at a fixed rate. They obviously still needed to pay taxes and fees. Such pricing strategies are not new to the transport industry, and are similar to monthly passes of Mass Rapid Transit (MRT) or railway services, and free-of-charge bus or shuttle services. But to the airline industry, these pricing techniques can be considered revolutionary.

Figure 21.5 Famous pricing strategy of low-cost carriers.

In fact, legacy carriers had low-fare products long before LCCs entered the market. They are familiar with quoting different prices for the same economy class seat. This is quite similar to price discrimination in microeconomic theory. Airlines said that this pricing strategy is for yield management and profit maximization, but it also looks like the airlines have increased producer surplus by decreasing consumer surplus. Though total social welfare may not decrease, some economists still believe this is a kind of exploitation (Samuelson and Marks, 2003). However, if the airlines are making money through unfair competition or information asymmetry, why don't we see any surplus profits in the industry?

It is because of the ideology of airline product design. One of the basic principles in price discrimination is that products carrying different prices must be homogeneous. One could argue that services in economy class are all the same, but they are actually quite different because of their booking classes, which have different fare rules, or different ticket restrictions. The less passengers pay for a ticket, the more restrictions apply to their airline tickets. Some restrictions are easy to recognize, including early booking, ticket validation duration, outbound/inbound validation dates, minimum stay duration, maximum stay duration, weekend flights restrictions, over-weekend requirement, block-out dates, penalties on rebooking, refunding, and cancellations. However, there are other restrictions as well that are not that common to see in the market. For instance, there is a "standby" ticket, which does not allow passengers to confirm their booking before the final call of the flight. That is to say, passengers can only wait at the standby counter for the first available flight. Once there is a seat available, the first passenger can then check in and board. In extreme cases, the first available seat may come up after several days of standing by. On the other hand, the standby ticket fare is obviously extremely low, usually less than 30 percent of the regular fare. Another example is the hand-luggage-only fare. Passengers on low-cost airlines are used to carrying their luggage onboard and paying for the check-in luggage. Nowadays, even some legacy carriers, US Airways and American Airlines for example, have removed the free check-in luggage allowance, and this policy has been gaining popularity in the industry.

Since ticket flexibility is different, the costs in each booking class are different as well. Hence, economists do not really think that airline yield management is price discrimination. However, all businesses want to sell their product at a higher price to generate more revenues. Not surprisingly, the number of discount-fare tickets is usually limited on each flight. Airlines always want passengers to pay more, even if passengers do not really need the flexibility offered with the higher-fare tickets. Sometimes the lower-fare product is very hard to come by, and is then defined as a promotional strategy rather than a pricing strategy.

4 Effective promotion

Marketing costs can sometimes be quite high, but their effect is often hard to evaluate. How can we save some money, and spend it in the most efficient way? This section introduces several effective promotional strategies, including fare promotion, spokespersons, and customer loyalty programs. However, limitations to promotion still exist. Hence, marketers should spend their resources in the most effective, but not necessarily the most popular way.

Promotion is the strategy to attract customers' attention, or to change customers' mindsets. Using promotional activities, airlines wish to be acknowledged or be chosen by customers. It is more or less a psychological game between airlines and passengers.

It is widely believed that the most common and useful promotional strategy is *fare promotion*. However, fare promotion can be very dangerous, since passengers are able to find a psychological bottom of the fare level, and then get used to this fare level. Passengers might be led to believe by the fare-promotion strategy that airlines are always able to offer this kind of service at such a low fare level. When they need the same service again, they will search for similar fares on the market. In other words, if airlines overemphasize their fare-promotion strategy, passengers will easily switch to any other airline that is able to provide the same low fare or even lower fares. In addition, fare promotion can have very negative effects on the airline's long-term financial performance. As a result, airlines always have limited seats on promotion fares, which are usually defined as short-term promotions. That is why tickets on promotion fares are always hard to come by.

In fact, airlines love loyal customers much more than the low-yield and fast-switching passengers. The most popular way for airlines to create customer loyalty is by setting up a *Frequent Flyer Program (FFP)*. This program is a predecessor of CRM, Customer Relationship Management. Airlines record the flight history of registered members, rewarding them in some way when they reach a certain number of flights or have traveled a certain distance threshold. Traditionally, free upgrades and free tickets have been the most popular rewards for members who have earned enough miles – nowadays, passengers can also use their miles to buy free accommodation, food, entertainment, or even donations to charities. Dozens of studies and market responses have shown that FFP is an effective marketing tool, but it is also quite expensive. Since miles owners are the airlines' loyal customers, the number of free seats for the FFP cannot be too limited. That is to say, a certain number of total seats available are not for sale, but for marketing purposes only. This will effectively lower the short-term sales revenues on the income statement, but marketers believe that, in the long run, this promotion strategy can be very helpful to the bottom line. That is why most of the airlines choose to set up FFPs. One simple way to solve the problem of revenue losses is to designate holiday demand peaks as block-out dates for free miles tickets. On these special dates, passengers are not allowed to travel with free reward tickets. However, setting more restrictions on the FFP benefits will result in reduced attractiveness of the program.

In addition to FFPs, airlines will also try to differentiate by offering different services and products in order to cater to consumers' preferences and to foster loyalties. However, it is usually expensive to do so. Airlines want to do a lot of promotions, but they always want to pay less. Strategic alliances with other industries are one popular solution for airlines to cut down promotion costs. It's easier and cheaper to cooperate with credit card companies, hotel groups, or even shops and restaurants to do promotions for airlines. In addition to their own loyalty programs, each individual business offers their loyalty members benefits from allied business partners' programs as well. It is not surprising then that passengers are now offered discounts at hotels, restaurants, and department stores as long as they carry the airline FFP membership. They can even trade many of the above-mentioned services for free. There are also strategic alliances within the airline industry. If two or more airlines are not competing in the same market, they can even share the benefits of FFP mileage for their passengers to create more utilities and loyalties. That is why we see the global alliances Star Alliance, One World, and SkyTeam grow at such a fast pace. However, not all airlines believe these global alliances are worth investing in. Some airlines might find joining these global alliances too expensive and therefore choose not to join them.

Among all of these strategies that airlines can use, the concept of *spokespersons* is one good way to attract the attention of passengers. Using spokespersons has long been a strategy applied in marketing management. In the early days, spokespersons were seen as an endorsement or testimonial. In the nineteenth century, this marketing strategy was commonly applied by pharmaceutical companies that wanted to introduce new drugs. In those days, even influential figures such as Pope Leo XIII and Queen Victoria endorsed a number of drugs and other products. Around the globe, consumers went wild for the products or manufacturers that the British monarch approved. Nowadays, spokespersons are still popular in marketing activities. Whether they would be famous athletes or music artistes, spokespersons can be found in almost any industry.

Spokespersons are not just a popular topic in marketing management, they are popular in marketing research as well. In 1958, Fritz Heider proposed the so-called Balance Theory, which led psychologists to analyze the fundamental theoretical structure of endorsements. The Balance Theory is a motivational theory of attitude change, which conceptualizes the consistency motive as a drive toward psychological balance. Heider proposed that "sentiment" or "liking relationships" are balanced if the affect valence in a system multiplies out to a positive result. On the basis of this theory, psychologists were then able to find the fundamental theoretical structure of endorsements, which is also believed to be the most important attributes of spokespersons. Mowen and Brown (1980) introduced the Balance Theory into marketing fields by substituting P, O, X (Person, Other person, and Object) with P, C, S (Product, Customer, and Spokesperson). The theory proposed that, if a person liked a celebrity and believed (due to the endorsement) that the celebrity in question liked a certain product, that person would tend to like the product more, in order to achieve psychological balance.

In some Asian nations, spokespersons are quite easily found in the airline industry. In 2005, one of these airlines started to use spokespersons. Eva Airways paid royalties to Japanese company Sanrio in exchange for the right to use its famous fictional character Hello Kitty. And in 2007, China Airlines

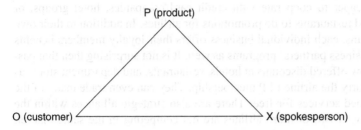

Figure 21.6 The application of balance theory in testimonial advertisement (source: Mowen and Brown (1980)).

contracted a supermodel as its spokesperson. Both of these airlines asked their respective spokespersons to participate in numerous additional marketing activities, next to television ads and printed ads. For example, the latter airline took a series of photos of its supermodel and used these in give-away calendars. The former airline painted its aircraft with the fictional character. All of the duty-free merchandise, souvenirs, and catering tools on board the painted aircraft also featured the character. These two spokespersons are widely believed to have been quite successful in attracting their customers' attention. For example, prices of the above-mentioned give-away calendar were soaring on various auction sites, due to the limited number of those calendars, while the other airline had to deal with passengers stealing cabin decorations with the fictional character on them. The airlines found the spokespersons to be a very effective way to attract the media. The airlines did not have a hard time to get covered in every newspaper or on the evening news – not to mention on websites and radio stations. It was almost like free advertising.

In fact, the two spokespersons were quite different in the market they penetrated. The Hello Kitty character was first introduced by Eva Airways. It mostly attracted young female travelers, and families traveling with children. As a counter-strategy, the most logical market segment China Airline could go for was the business segment. Using the supermodel, China Airlines focused on males, aged 25–45, who were frequent flyers in the business market. Most passengers in this segment would certainly be attracted by the supermodel.

To analyze the effectiveness of airline spokespersons, a marketing research based on these two airlines (in the same country in order to reduce cultural differences) was conducted in 2009 (Chen, Shon, and Chen, 2009a). The research not only examined the responses from the market, but also the impact of spokespersons on passengers' behavior in choosing an airline. Research showed that spokespersons have some, but not a huge impact on the airline selection process of passengers. Given these findings, spokespersons in the airline industry are not as important as they are in other industries, such as pharmaceuticals or sports equipments, nor can they be the key success factors of an airline. In practice, using spokespersons has its limitations. Though it can be a very effective promotion strategy for media exposure, as well as a very effective competitive

Figure 21.7 Hello Kitty as a spokesperson in EVA AIR.*

2009

Enjoy the Moment!
中華航空 Cindy

Figure 21.8 Supermodel as a spokesperson in China Airlines.

advantage within the airline industry, it will never be able to increase total demand. Promotion strategy usually focuses on the competition within the airline industry only, or between airlines and other transport modes, especially High Speed Rail. After all, total demand heavily relies on the local and global economy. If the macroeconomic environment deteriorates, the market can hardly be saved by spokespersons. Despite the fact that rising oil prices and the global financial crisis have created the worst recession in 80 years during the research period, the research findings still reveal several important observations. First of all, any marketing strategy can be easily duplicated, which can thus decrease its effect. Second, to counter the first problem, even spokespersons should be segmented to meet different types of customers. Finally, total travel demand in the market is much more important than marketing strategy, especially in a small market.

It has been observed that the number of golf fans increased considerably when Tiger Woods spoke for Nike Golf products. Nonetheless, spokespersons of the airlines can only speak on behalf of their airlines instead on behalf of the entire travel market. One way to increase total travel demand between city pairs is by using strategic alliances with local governments. Promoting tourist attractions and business activities together with local governments and traditional tourism businesses as well as business of MICE industry (Meeting, Incentive Travel, Conference, and Exhibition) will increase the total demand for air transportation in regions that are accessible by air in an effective way. Las Vegas CES, Hannover CeBIT, and Guangzhou CantonFair are all good examples of this promotion strategy. But what if the spokespersons were able to speak on behalf of the travel market? Would they be able to increase total travel demand? One interesting case we found in Korea and Taiwan was that both governments have hired popular movie stars as spokespersons for the tourism industry for several years now. As fans living outside of these countries wanted to participate in the activities hosted by these movie stars, air travel increased. Though it is a different story for airline spokespersons, we are still confident about the possibilities and the potential that using spokespersons offers (Chen *et al.*, 2009b).

5 Future marketing issues

Digital marketing, Corporate Social Responsibility (CSR), individual marketing are the most important issues in marketing in the next ten years. It may be a nightmare to airlines if these arising issues are not well managed. In this chapter, we introduce the essential knowledge of all future marketing issues. Readers should at least be conscious of these important issues, and be prepared to face the challenges ahead.

Marketing management theories have been developed for almost 50 years. Long before any hypotheses were verified, people already had marketing skills for more than a thousand years. The above-mentioned concepts are not new, though some may not sound familiar. Nevertheless, since the introduction of the internet in the early 1990s, things have started to become different. For the first time ever, marketers were able to focus on different target markets, segmented by websites, communities, and other online social networks. Information technology nowadays is able to keep track of all transactions of each and every customer. These records can then be analyzed by professionals trying to identify consumers' preferences, purchase behavior, and shopping locations. Customer Relationship Management (CRM) is no longer just textbook theory. Customer X's anniversary, his kid's birthday, even his wife's favorite restaurant: it has become information that is completely traceable. Marketers are now able to deliver more precise marketing plans, incorporating their customers' personal characteristics as well as their purchase history. Consumers' experiences are the best references for marketers to make decisions on.

On the other hand, surplus profits because of information asymmetry have become a thing of the past, as consumers are now able to get virtually all the information about their products in order for them to make their purchasing decisions. Comparing prices of the product they want in both virtual and physical stores is just one click away. Consumers are finally able to just buy it online, and have it delivered to their homes.

Airlines are facing the same marketing environment as other service industries. *E-Commerce* has been a big topic for airlines since the early 2000s. Airlines used to sell tickets through travel agents, but nowadays they need to have a website, have online booking facilities, complete with ticketing transaction capabilities, and airlines now have to interact with their customers directly instead of through travel agents. Although issuing paperless tickets may save airlines big money, its downside is that customers are able to compare prices and schedules by themselves. In the late 1990s, before the internet became as ubiquitous as it is now, only travel agents could afford very expensive *computer reservation systems (CRSs)*, which could only be developed by just a few, big airlines. These megacarriers were feeding the CRSs with biased flight information in order to increase the odds of selling more tickets. These competitive advantages soon disappeared after internet-based search engines were developed. Websites with fare-comparison services can be found everywhere nowadays. For each itinerary the consumer enters as a search query, these search engines compare all the different fares of airlines and travel websites. No airline is therefore able to hide.

Last but not least, this chapter deals with *corporate social responsibility (CSR)*. Global warming has taught both consumers and marketers to be conscious of CSR. Some passengers and airlines care a great deal about *environmental protection*. However, environmental protection is not the only issue in CSR, as global warming is not the only issue in environmental protection. Long before Greenhouse Gases (GHGs) became a household name, aircraft noise had always been the focus of environmental organizations concerned about aviation activities and their impact on the environment. In the 1980s, concerns about SOx emitted from aircraft engines were widespread as this gas led to acid rain, which is harmful to plants and to human health. Since 2000, greenhouse gases and carbon dioxide appear to have become the main focus instead. Some airlines are moving fast, and have started to buy offsets or have started to fund *CDM (Clean Development Mechanism)* projects to neutralize the GHGs they emit. Introducing such green initiatives creates a positive corporate image of these airlines, even though most of the carbon offset funds come from voluntary contributions of passengers.

As mentioned earlier, eco-friendly is not the only CSR issue in the aviation industry. Being user-friendly, *labor-friendly*, community-friendly, and even being competitor-friendly are all aspects of CSR. Among all these "friendly" issues, the relationship between airlines and their employees is the most critical one. Airlines and airports are very labor-intensive operations. They need a skilled and well-trained workforce, which can be quite expensive, in order to ensure smooth and safe operations every day. Lay-offs and salary cuts are usually the first remedies when airlines and airports start losing money. To minimize labor costs, it is still quite common in the air transport industry to have your staff work overtime. As a result, it is not that surprising to see employees of both airlines and airports strike in such cases. Not only do labor protests such as these hurt the airline's corporate image, they also generate real financial losses because of cancelled flights and because of compensations to customers. Moreover, strikes can lead to accidents and disasters, for example, in China in March 2008, 18 flights of China Eastern Airlines returned to their home base without landing at their original destination airports. The pilots went on strike, but they did so in a very dangerous way. Shortly after this incident, the government Bureau of Aviation in China revoked China Eastern Airlines' operating license in several profitable markets. The airline suffered a total loss of 0.45 billion RMB, approximately 66 million US dollars, because of this penalty. China Eastern Airlines' stock price was plummeting for 20 consecutive days following the incident. The president and CEO were forced to resign, and the stock price never recovered in the 18 months that followed. No wonder that more and more business consultancies are now focusing on CSR performances as well as on financial performances.

The relationship between management and employees not only affects the stability of the airline, it also deeply affects the second CSR issue – *customer relationship*. In the previous example of China Eastern Airlines, several passengers sued the airline because they believed that such behavior was criminal as it put public safety at risk, while others sued and demanded compensation for incurred losses because of the incident. Another lesson learnt is that employees are an organization's internal customers, who need to be treated just as nicely as external customers are treated. Earlier research has shown that internal-customer satisfaction is likely to have positive effects on external-customer satisfaction (Berry, 1981; Cahill, 1995; Gummesson, 1987; Heskett *et al.*, 1994). One study (Chen and Chang, 2005) also indicated that job satisfaction levels affected airline employees' willingness to serve, as well as affecting their service attitude. Willingness and attitude are major components of service quality, which is the key to customer satisfaction. It is therefore not too far-fetched to assume that internal-customer satisfaction also has positive effects on external-customer satisfaction in the airline industry.

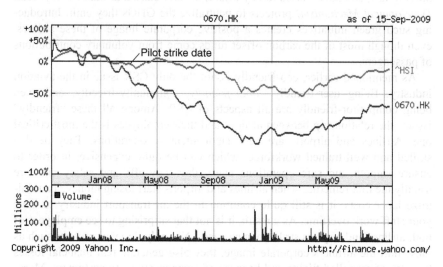

Figure 21.9 Stock price of China Eastern Airlines before and after pilot strike.

So why are customer relationships that important? For most airlines, customer relationships mean business opportunities. If certain airlines are unwilling to invest in maintaining good relationships with their customers, competitors will be more than happy to do just that in their place instead. That is why CRM is now so popular in marketing management. In addition to taking into account business considerations, it is also important to see your customers as your stakeholders. That is the social responsibility of an organization. For a long time, consumers were the weakest link in the supply chain, because consumers did not have any rights with regard to their interaction with either the products they purchased or with their suppliers. Consumers had little ground on which to defend themselves against faulty or defective products, or against misleading or deceptive advertising methods. Although consumerism has steadily risen over the last 50 years, there are several regions where consumers are still treated unfairly. Bad experiences where passengers complain about airlines' service failures exist even in developed countries. Most service failures are the result of schedule delays, luggage lost/damaged, or of employees' attitude problems. If airlines do not immediately correct these problems, customers' perception of the airline can be seriously damaged. Bad experiences such as these often turn into complaints filed with the responsible government agency. US FAA receives over 5,000 passenger complaints a year.

Passengers are more worried about the inconvenience caused by schedule delays than the airline's possible financial losses. It makes no difference whether the reason behind the delay was a technical problem or weather conditions: passengers are always affected the most. The problem can be even worse when luggage is lost or damaged. Lost or damaged luggage is often caused by airport workers at the airport of departure or transfer, but it is usually the airline employees at the destination airport that have to face the annoyed customers. However, many airline employees fight against their customers rather than fight for the rights of their customers. Some airlines still do not understand the importance of being considerate and supportive of their customers. As mentioned earlier, information asymmetry is fading away fast. In some cases, consumers already have the power of interpretation when service failures happen. If airlines do not deal with customers' complaints correctly, customers are now able to fight back online. They will not choose the expensive yet inefficient legal system the airlines are familiar with. Instead, the internet is a much better platform they can use to protect their rights.

In the summer of 2009, United Airlines broke a guitar of a passenger who happened to be a musician. The airline refused to fix the broken guitar after several negotiations and as a consequence the annoyed musician then wrote a song, made a music video, and posted it on YouTube. Within two months, over 5.5 million people watched the video "United Breaks Guitars," 22,000 among them left messages expressing their bad experiences with United Airlines. These responses from all over the world put a lot of pressure and also had a lot of negative effects on the airline. If airlines need to be educated by their passengers, lessons can become very expensive. Eventually, United Airlines tried to repair the damaged relationships with its customers, but it did so too late. Loss of the brand image's value and possibly of business as well, or even the fall of its stock price is hundreds, even thousands of times higher than the cost of a single new guitar. This is what customers are able to do nowadays.

If customer relationships, employee satisfaction, and environmental protection are the critical issues in CSR, then connecting with the *community* is just as important. In the aviation industry, airlines do not appear to be well-known for getting along well with the community, at least less than airports are. However, since airlines are the airports' primary clients, airlines should be aware of this particular issue and catch up with airports. Most of the community problems come from conflicts between regional economic developments on the one hand and environmental protection on the other hand. Business activities of airlines and airports can be damaging to the local region, while at the same time these activities create jobs and stimulate regional development. As mentioned earlier, noise was the first form of pollution found to affect communities. As a result, some airports, mostly in Europe and Asia, started to charge all aircraft landing and taking off at them so-called noise fees. These noise fees are paid by airlines and are used to reduce noise pollution around the airport by applying housing insulation, and noise abatement techniques. In some specific areas, noise fees may be used to purchase land and houses that are heavily polluted. In addition to these noise fees, some airports and airlines also finance the creation of public facilities such as libraries, gyms, or education centers in the region around the airport. All these activities are not-for-profit, which is why CSR initiatives are sometimes called "social marketing," because these activities do not focus on any products or services. Airlines just wish to improve their brand image or corporate image, as well as hoping to increase their recognition and customer satisfaction.

After GHG has become the hottest item in CSR, some airlines have introduced voluntary carbon-offset programs, where passengers buy back the carbon they emitted during their flight. Airlines collect the offsets to purchase equivalent certificates or to fund CDM projects. With their customers' help, they try to make their flights carbon-neutral. The carbon-offset program has become popular throughout the world; it effectively separates "greener" airlines from "less green" ones. For the environmentally conscious, there is only one choice. For business travelers whose companies need to comply with "green production" codes and regulations, flying with airlines that have carbon-offset programs has become a necessity. Again, economic incentives seem to have successfully linked social responsibility with sales and revenues.

One last stakeholder in CRS is the *shareholders*. Airline managers and executives should try to seek the best return on investment to maximize production of all available production factors. If they fail to do so, airlines waste Earth's scarce resources. In short, airlines should make investors happy. This is a big problem. Even airlines that do not invest in these social marketing initiatives have a hard time to be profitable. The airline industry has attracted a lot of money, has created numerous jobs, but it has never been a high-return investment, and it is too deeply affected by macroeconomics, both on a regional and global level. During the financial tsunami in 2008 and 2009, from the Far East to the West, we hardly found any profitable airline with positive ROE. As a result, it is almost impossible to make airline investors happy about their investment. A lot of carriers went bankrupt or reorganized during these recessions. And that has definitely been disastrous to several regional economies because they were subsequently not served by any airline. In remote areas, both the locally produced goods as well as the people living there were unable to rely on air transportation anymore. Mass lay-offs will create even more problems. It may sound familiar, though not pleasant, but financial sustainability, or simply breaking even should still be the most important social responsibility of any airline in the world.

6 Concluding remarks: there is always something new with marketing

Airline business is a typical service business. Service marketing therefore plays a critical role in this industry. As described in previous paragraphs of this chapter, marketing is not a new concept in itself, but there have always been new marketing ideas and strategies, which successfully attract customers to airlines. In the Chinese market recently, we observed that Shenzhen Airline had a significantly higher load factor in some regions than other airlines. Shenzhen Airline managed to raise its load factor in a very simple way, which was by introducing a home-made and delicious spicy sauce used in its catering service. On request, flight attendants add two spoons of this spicy sauce to passengers' meals. Passengers who love spicy food will choose Shenzhen Airline because it is the only carrier providing any spicy sauce. Interestingly, most people living in the northeastern and southwestern provinces of China love spicy food. Some say that this

Figure 21.10 The spicy sauce rewarded by mileage of Shenzhen Airline only, not for sale in the market.

spicy sauce is the main reason why Shenzhen Airline has a bigger share in these markets and has a higher yield than competitors on some selected city pairs. Moreover, the airline has prohibited any sales regarding the secret spicy sauce. Spice lovers can only buy the sauce using the airline's privilege miles. As a result, spice lovers flock to Shenzhen Airline in order to accumulate more miles and then spend them on a bottle of its spicy sauce. Since there are 1.3 billion Chinese, the pool of spice lovers is big enough to create a niche market. And at least Shenzhen Airline reaped the benefits of entering this niche market.

Airline service is intangible; it is hard to distinguish between the services of different airlines. Marketing strategies aimed at differentiating service products try to make the intangible tangible. Shenzhen Airline found the key, while others are still searching for better strategies for future competitiveness. In marketing management, there is always something new and creative to be expected. Of course marketing is only one element in the airlines business, but it is definitely the critical one that needs a lot more attention paid to it.

References

Berry, L. L. (1981) "The Employee as Customer." *Journal of Retail Banking*, vol. 3, pp. 25–28.

Cahill, D. J. (1995) "The Managerial Implications of the Learning Organization: A New Tool for Internal Marketing." *Journal of Marketing*, vol. 9(4), pp. 43–51.

Chen, F. Y. and Chang, Y. H. (2005) "Examining airline service quality from a process perspective." *Journal of Air Transport Management*, vol. 11(2), pp. 79–87.

Chen, Y. H., Shon, Z.Y., and Chen, D. J. (2009a). "Who is a better spokesperson of an airline? A super model or a cartoon character?" The 2009 world conference of Air Transportation Research Society, Abu Dhabi, UAE, June, 2009.

Chen, Y. H., Shon, Z.Y., and Chen, D. J. (2009b) "Airline Marketing Strategy with Spokespersons?" *Aerline Magazines*, November, Amsterdam.

Chiou, Y. C., Chen, Y. H., and Shon, Z. Y. (2008) "Examining Low Cost Carrier Service Quality in China Market," the 2008 world conference of Air Transportation Research Society, Athens, Greece, July.

Gummesson, E. (1987) "The New Marketing-Developing Long-Term Interactive Relationship." *Long Range Planning*, vol. 20(4), pp. 10–20.

Heider, F. (1958) *The psychology of interpersonal relations*. New York: John Wiley & Sons.

Heskett, J., John, T. O., Loveman, G. W., Sasser, W. E., and Schlesinger, L. A. (1994) "Putting the Service-Profit Chain to Work." *Harvard Business Review*, March–April, pp. 164–172.

Martilla, J. A. and James, J. C. (1977) "Importance–Performance Analysis." *Journal of Marketing*, January, pp. 77–79.

Mowen, J. C. and Brown, S. W. (1980) "On Explaining and Predicting the Effectiveness of Celebrity Endorser." *Advertising in Consumer Research*, Vol. 8, 99, 437–441.

Parasuraman, A., Zeuthaml, V. A., and Berry, L L. (1985) "A Conceptual Model of Service Quality and Its Implications for Future Research." *Journal of Marketing* (Fall 1985), pp. 41–50.

Samuelson, W. and Marks, S. (2003) *Managerial Economics*, 4th edn, Oxford: John Wiley.

Shon, Z. Y. (2005) "The Impacts of Internal Customer Satisfaction on the Service Attitudes and Willingness to Serve of Airline Employees," the 2005 world conference of Air Transportation Research Society, Rio de Janeiro, Brazil, July. www.smarttravelasia.com.

22 Major challenges for the future of the air transport sector

Rosário Macário and Eddy Van de Voorde

Recent evolutions in the global air transport market, with the emergence of low fare products, have reconfirmed how economic accessibility can generate greater demand for mobility and, concurrently, increased willingness to pay for air travel. Moreover, it is well established that, as people get wealthier, not only are they able to afford to travel further and more often, they also become more pre-pared to pay for goods and services supplied from further afield. In the airline business, these effects have been amplified by evolutions at the supply side, where the emergence of low-fare operators has brought air transport services within financial reach of the lower economic classes. In other words, there is not only a greater willingness to pay, but also an enhanced ability to pay. Air trans-port has thus become much more accessible and socially more inclusive, similar to evolutions witnessed previously in other transport modes. In fact, this is argu-ably the most notable achievement in the sector over the past decade or so.

With globalization, the world economy is also becoming increasingly depend-ent on air transport services. There is, for example, undeniable evidence that a growing share of freight is being conveyed by air: there has been remarkable growth in the all-cargo segment, and the cargo transported by combination airlines now plays a valuable role in ensuring the economic viability of certain routes and in allowing more competitive passenger fares in those flights. At the same time, tourism and business travel have stimulated growth in airport capacity around the world. In two extremes of this evolution, we have seen the emergence of, on the one hand, budget terminals and, on the other, sophisticated terminals with city-like structures, with office space, street infrastructure, restaurants, shops, public services, motorised and pedestrian movements, rush hours, etc. Both types of terminal support millions of jobs in both developed and developing countries. It is beyond doubt that the development of international air transport links is today a driver for the success of economies in this increasingly globalized world.

In addition, the rapid and strong economic development of many Asian coun-tries over the past few decades has presented further opportunities and chal-lenges. Economic progress and rising incomes have likewise translated into greater transport demand, not only for cargo and business travel, but also for leisure. Furthermore, many Asian countries have become increasingly popular as tourist destinations.

Yet, despite these positive factors, IATA insists that these are extremely challenging times for airlines, and not without reason. It refers not only to the sharp economic downturn and the absence of signs of an early recovery, but also to rising oil prices and to the impact of the recent influenza A (H1N1) pandemic. Cash flows are affected by weaker demand, and, after years of fare discounting and cost cutting, there is little scope for further action in these areas. All of the above has created a tension that would appear to be moving the industry closer to a paradigmatic change of its business models.

Despite the undeniable negative impact of cyclical economic events, globalization has indeed opened windows of opportunity that continue to ensure long-term growth in the air transport industry. However, the downstream market of air travel and upstream market of airport and air traffic capacity seem to have lost their understanding of the underlying systemic condition, and the different speed at which they are evolving is threatening to generate a mismatch and to jeopardize the sector's healthy development.

And these are not the only tough challenges that lie ahead. In most developed countries, there is also growing concern with sustainability and the environment. However, interdisciplinary research on environmental attitudes and pro-environmental behaviour has studied people's value orientations and found that they differ in their deeper sentiments towards the environment (Garling, in Hensher and Button, 2003, p. 728). This, in conjunction with an awareness that transport is essential to society's well-being, is today resulting in ambivalent perceptions of and attitudes towards transportation in general. Moreover, while the societal context of transportation, and aviation in particular, is undoubtedly changing, attitudes towards air transport are possibly not as critical as they are towards other modes, especially surface transport.

Nonetheless, an awareness and acknowledgement of the fact that the current technological paradigm in transportation is, by its very nature, unsustainable has formed the basis for research into innovative solutions. In many ways, air transport has long been a leader in technological advances and materials engineering, which has contributed to a historically low-impact footprint for the industry today. What is more, the industry and scientific community continue to strive for more efficient engines, enhanced aerodynamics and cleaner fuels, further highlighting the present concern with achieving a clean and sustainable air transport.

Indeed, the recognition of the complex issues involved in the current technological debate, not only in air transport but in transport in general, has triggered even broader R&D efforts in relation to new engine technologies and cleaner fuels. This evolution, too, is characteristic of the kind of essential tension underlying paradigm shifts, and it has come about in response to a growing awareness of the "anomalies" that cause the unsustainability patterns observed in transport systems today. This has prompted efforts to either advance the conceptualization of new engines and cleaner fuels or to disprove the ability of the current paradigm to properly address the anomalies in respect of sustainability.

In recent years, we have also seen the emergence of a new attitude in the aviation sector, with companies increasingly adopting more environmentally responsible policies. Many airlines are going green, as it were, supporting environmentally friendly projects (such as reforestation to counter CO_2 emissions) and implementing energy reduction measures at three levels: at the strategic level by the use of state-of-the-art equipment; at the tactical level by developing new processes; and at the operational level by implementing new and optimizing existing processes and by changing daily habits (such as increasing air-conditioning temperatures, reducing cabin lighting in long-distance flights, etc.). Transport in general is coming under increasing societal and political pressures to innovate, creating a new policy context that is defined by a striving for climate change mitigation and a reduction in GHG emissions.

The foregoing chapters have painted a clear picture of the consequences of this fundamentally changing context. The conclusions reached by the various authors may be summarized in just a few points, which we shall recap in the next sections: (1) the air transport market is a highly competitive playing field; (2) the industry's business models have undergone profound changes in recent decades; (3) production systems are reaching their limits of improvement, and collaborative solutions are emerging; and (4) the new era is increasingly characterized by collaboration with other transport modes. All these elements are symptomatic of a paradigm shift that requires a strong research agenda for the coming years, as we shall argue in the final section of this chapter.

1 A highly competitive playing field

There is consensus that there is no such thing as a single homogeneous air transport market, as *Hilde Meersman, Eddy Van de Voorde* and *Thierry Vanelslander* highlight in their contribution. However, their evidence for the existence of a configuration of various submarkets that are interconnected and therefore interact adds a further degree of complexity to the analysis of the air transport sector. The trends point towards even fiercer competition within the industry, marked by further specialization, renewed alliances and easy market access, as well as a more prominent role for private investors.

An obvious consequence of the changes in the modus operandi of air transport operators is found in the predictive methods used to understand future developments. In this respect, *Sveinn Vidar Gudmundsson* opens up an extremely important line of research by demonstrating that air transport has characteristics that allow one to approach it through international prediction models that capture the inherent dynamics of the industry. The necessary switch to such prediction models is a direct consequence of the effects of increased competition in the sector.

Moreover, there is evidence that these effects have manifested themselves in both passenger and freight markets. *Franziska Kupfer, Hilde Meersman, Evy Onghena* and *Eddy Van de Voorde* underline how the air freight business model has changed, as freight is no longer approached as a by-product of passenger transport. The analysis provides strong evidence of the volatility of the air cargo market. A similar observation is made in the chapter by *Evy Onghena*, who calls for a more diversified approach to the air cargo market that takes due account of different market behaviours and highlights what is arguably one of the most critical factors in air cargo, namely imbalances on trade routes that lead to imbalances between incoming and outgoing cargo flows, with severe economic consequences. This is a clear example of how business models have to be revised in order that the industry can cope adequately with new contingencies.

2 Uncertainties with transformed business models

Evolutions over the past decades have disrupted the existing air transport business models and, in some instances, have imposed the adoption of such models where none was assumed before. This is clearly the case in the airport sector, as is highlighted by *Rosário Macário* in a contribution that demonstrates how long-term business stability in the airport industry is achievable through a business model that encompasses a clear mission, a well-considered strategy, effective marketing, and efficient and accountable management. Further evidence of this is found in the cases presented by *Douglas Baker* and *Robert Freestone*, who define airports as nodes of high accessibility, both in the context of aviation networks and within the metropolitan space, and that consequently are shaped by global as well as local forces.

This point is further underlined by *Juan Carlos Martín* and *Concepción Román*, who recognize that the competitive pressure created by the emergence of low-fare services has necessitated a re-evaluation of the business model of former legacy carriers, making them more efficient and more market effective. This trend has extended beyond the airlines and also affects other players in the air transport supply chain, resulting in major competitive effects through synergies in systemic markets, despite the fact that EU deregulation has been only partially successful. In a similar line of thought, *Rosário Macário* and *Vasco Reis* confirm that the more competitive environment created by the emergence of low-fare airlines has also caused innovations in relationships with airports and regions.

All these changes to the prevailing business models provide evidence that service marketing is now a critical tool for both airlines and airports. The analysis by *Joel Zhengyi Shon* confirms this and draws attention to the challenges of marketing strategies aimed at differentiating service products that try to make the intangible tangible.

3 Limits to the cooperative production systems

A major area of tension in recent decades has been the need for cost reduction in the production and distribution systems.

Jan Veldhuis, in his analysis of the case of Air France and KLM, concludes that, contrary to common belief, network integration is not necessarily in the interest of consumers. He points out that, while this particular instance of integration has obviously resulted in more connections and better access by air, it is also conceivable that, in some markets, increased levels of competition will go hand in hand with upward pressure on air fares.

Martin Dresner and *David Pitfield* look at alliances as an intermediate form of organization and thus as a way of optimizing cost reduction, and they demonstrate that advantages do accrue for passengers. The specific focus of analysis is on virtual code-sharing and on the question of whether there is a limit to this strategy.

The same question has been raised in relation to airports and hub-and-spoke networks. However, in his contribution, *Kenneth Button* concludes that there is no such thing as a hub-and-spoke network for airline services, but rather that there are a variety of different hub-and-spoke structures that have emerged over time to meet changing market and technological conditions. This brings a new level of complexity to network analysis, since hubs are not independent entities and compete with each other in an imperfect gaming environment. An interesting addition is made to the issue of network limitations in relation to hubs as competition between these hub structures may well lead to the emergence of new forms of business models.

However, congestion problems are persistent. As *Paul Roosens* highlights, airports bear greater responsibility in this respect than en-route structures. More specifically, slot allocation plays a distinct role. The analysis by *Jaap de Wit* and *Guillaume Burghouwt* concludes that there may be tradeoffs between market-based approaches such as primary slot auctioning and/or secondary slot trading to allow an efficient use of slots at congested airports. In fact, the two approaches represent different strategic objectives for airports, i.e. efficient use of scarce airport capacity and sufficient competition in the downstream air transport markets.

Further indications of change in the air transport industry are found in the fact that a new competitor has entered the fray: high-speed rail services. *Werner Rothengatter* analyses this development and presents evidence of HSR's potential to compete with air transport or to at least become an elected partner for specific market segments. This again implies a rethink of the business model for both modes and their production systems.

4 The renewed regulatory mission

With so many fundamental changes on the cards, the regulatory function needs to be rethought in a manner that encompasses a more proactive role of inducement of agents' behaviour through more effective incentives. This topic is dealt with by *Anne Graham*, who presents an analysis of regulatory developments in recent years.

A major regulatory intervention in air transport in recent times has been the adoption of emission trading schemes, as discussed in detail by *Yulai Wan* and *Anming Zhang*. Their analysis focuses on different impacts on different types of airlines, and on the risks of distortion of competition in favour of land modes, causing undesirable strategies whereby airlines raise their fares, which clearly was not envisaged in regulation.

Another important aspect of regulation deals with mergers and alliances, which emerge as a natural evolution of the business model. This is the focus of the contribution by *Marco Benacchio*, who demonstrates convincingly how greatly the competence of regulators needs to be enhanced in order for them to be able to deal adequately with these market changes. These findings are underlined by the analysis of *Mia Wouters*, who broadens the discussion to the regional level of decision-making.

5 A research agenda for a changing industry

As we have read repeatedly in the chapters of this book, recent decades have seen a significant increase in both passenger and freight transport by air; the former due mainly to increased purchasing power in the developed and developing worlds, the latter primarily as a result of changes in the global economy and production systems. In the course of the past 20 years, we have moved from a "stock" economy to a "flow" economy. This phenomenon has gone hand in hand with the relocation of industries, particularly labour-intensive ones, to cut production costs in spite of the fact that goods and materials must now be transported over longer distances from production sites to consumers.

With air transport costs now at historically low levels, the global carriage of passengers has become an integral part of unfolding economic processes. Modern globalization, driven by international corporate mergers and business consolidation at a global scale, has resulted in a greater variety of products from different regions being marketed at lower cost. It has become possible to systematically serve a wider range of customer segments, which has in turn encouraged enterprises to operate under more decentralized structures, supported by modern communications systems, logistics networks and a growing capacity to move people around the globe. The removal of commercial barriers and the creation of common currency zones, as with the European internal market and the euro, has also had a significant impact on corporate planning and thus on people's mobility. Enhanced personal mobility in turn translates into greater opportunities in terms of employment, housing, social contacts, education and healthcare.

Indeed, it is difficult today to envisage vigorous economic growth without an efficient air transport system. Even if we have entered the age of the information society and virtual trade, there is little evidence that this has alleviated existing pressures on mobility. Air transport networks are today indispensable for achieving economic growth, which conversely stimulates demand for transport services and changes the nature of the services desired. (WBCSD, 2004).[1]

Modern innovation literature (Fagerberg *et al.*, 2008) identifies innovation as a system process, the outcome of interactions between firms and markets within a regulatory context. As well as providing sector-wide analyses, the literature discusses national and regional systems of innovation, but transportation – and air transport in particular – is by its very nature a multiregional and multinational business.

Therefore, an analysis of air transportation innovation systems is necessary in order to identify combinations of circumstances and effective policies that can initiate momentous change in order that we can face up to the challenges presented by the paradigmatic change that is already in evidence in air transport today.

However, Fagerberg *et al.* (2008) find that, while the effects of innovation are known, the processes involved are not so well understood, as indeed is largely recognized by the research communities in the various relevant fields (social, economic, technological, political, etc.). Also, there is little understanding of how these systems emerge and change over time, and with what impact on the kind of innovation that emerges. Often, this literature is interested mainly in quantitative indicators of innovation (patents, market share, publications, etc.), while it is less concerned with quality of innovation (e.g. carbon emissions, traffic-reduction benefits, new demand management approaches).

Recent economic and financial evolutions suggest that the world faces important structural challenges that are likely to affect major economic sectors. Combined with the variety of cross-sectional elements influencing the international business landscape today, this gives rise to underlying concerns regarding the growing relevance of factors causing structural disruption. These factors are, directly or indirectly, related to unbalanced patterns of consumption and the depletion of natural resources at unsustainable rates. The issues at hand are attracting ever greater attention from experts, economists, politicians and the general public, especially in the context of critical energy dependency and global environmental impacts.

While prior to the ongoing economic crisis[2] the primary concern used to be rising energy and commodity prices and the ensuing inflationary pressures on the economy, we have since experienced a decline in price indexes and in oil consumption in consequence of a worldwide recession. Yet, this has not fundamentally changed the fact that oil dependency and environmental performance constitute major social and economic issues with direct and indirect impacts in the field of transportation. Moving away from this situation requires a new economic, energy-related and technological paradigm. In this context, there is a danger that decision-makers will reach a point where they are constrained to doing too little too late.

This raises pertinent economic as well as societal questions with profound implications for the way that we envisage the future of transportation, including in relation to the so-called "zero-growth paradigm" and efforts to address resource depletion, environmental damage and loss of biodiversity. These circumstances and their multiple consequences suggest that modern societies face a period of structural adaptation to a new economic paradigm in order to overcome the failures in the current context.

In this new setting, air transport emerges as one of the spearhead sectors towards the paradigm shift in technology and business required by a sustainable economic development based on clean and dependable energy sources that is respectful of the environment and of future generations. In order to be able to cope with this role, the systemic and dynamic characteristics of air transport must be duly taken into account in future modelling efforts. Effectiveness of the instruments developed is critical in a period of paradigmatic flux.

In the long term, it would appear to be prudent and even legitimate, given what we observe in the transport world today, that we should adequately address the question of whether we are indeed on the verge of a paradigm shift. Certainly all the indications are there:

- The cost of resources has reached an unsustainable level, given market prices.
- Business cycle strategies involve only a marginal degree of innovation, which is indicative of a kind of exhaustion of the industry.
- Energy and environmental policies are set to become even stricter, closing the reinforcing loop, as politicians try to catch up with the perception delay in relation to the existence of fundamental problems.[3]

In fact, as Kuhn asserts, discovery starts with the awareness of an anomaly. As new and refined methods and instruments become available, resulting in greater precision and understanding of the paradigm, it becomes easier to recognize that something is wrong: "*Frameworks must be lived with and explored before they can be broken*" (Kuhn, 1969, p. 189).

In this context, and in the face of the present economic situation, some critical aspects must be considered when setting the future research agenda for the air transport sector. This agenda is inevitably and intrinsically complex, but it needs to be ambitious as well.

The future may become more uncertain – or at least our predictive confidence may be affected – if we acknowledge the likelihood of paradigmatic change. So which scenarios can we envisage insofar as air transport's position in the mobility chain is concerned? Shall we witness an evolution towards an individualistic air transport sector with its own markets and structures? Or, on the contrary, an air transport sector that is integrated into the transport chain based on an intermodal rationale? Or will air transport perhaps suffer the effects of an overall reduction in mobility and be superseded by alternative technologies (e.g. ICT, ITS...)? Research efforts should, in our view, be focused on two aspects: (1) a close monitoring of the industry and the supposed symptoms of imminent paradigmatic change; (2) the enhancement of instruments and methods for studying uncertain futures in an industry with an inherently systemic character.

Also, our modelling capabilities must be oriented towards supporting evolutions in policy and business in recognition of a likely change of paradigm in transport in general and its inevitable consequences for air transport in particular.

It is clear today that, to effectively reduce congestion, there is a need for improving cohesion and accessibility. However, it must also be acknowledged that much of the new infrastructure is already in place, and that there is little scope (spatially, financially, politically and in the public opinion) for developing it further. Hence, we need to come up with new ways of increasing the effectiveness and efficiency of existing infrastructures. This requires innovative research into both the soft and the hard aspects of infrastructure development and management.

Technology will obviously continue to play a determining role, but rather as a systems management tool. In other words, research efforts in technology must be put at the service of efficiency of management across transport systems, this being the real merit of technological advances.

We see in the literature as well as the real world that a number of "non-modelling" analyses of transport policy instruments have been undertaken in recent years, whereby the emphasis is firmly on the quality (in terms of efficiency and effectiveness) and sustainability of policy-making. These analyses have been rather divergent, ranging from in-depth looks at specific instruments (e.g. slot pricing) to transversal studies of the effective adoption of a given policy measures or regulation. The methods relied on are also diverse, and have included theorizations on particular instruments as well as case studies. There is consensus in research communities today that efforts must be made in the formulation of policy packages, whereby a combination of synergetic, or at least complementary, instruments is relied upon to deal with the systemic nature of the air transport sector. Policy packaging makes it possible to offset the negative impacts of one instrument with the positive affects of another.

Last, but not least, there have already been clear signs that alliances are moving out of the air transport sector. In fact, this evolution has already been unfolding in air cargo for some years. Research must address the consequences of this "out-of-the-box" movement in the relations between actors and also in the regulatory function that has traditionally been ring-fenced by a modal approach. Even the simple decoupling of the air transport supply chain is conducive to the emergence of third and fourth-party agents whose behaviours and interactions with the rest of the system are not yet clearly understood, despite an awareness of their considerable impact on the efficiency and competitiveness of the industry.

Notes

1 www.eu-conference2004.nl/documents/mobility-full.pdf.
2 In February 2010, at the time of writing this chapter.
3 In Systems Dynamics, this is designated as "Time to Perceive Present Condition" (TPPC).

References

Fagerberg, J., Mowery, D. and Verspagen, B. (2008). "Innovation-systems, path-dependency and policy: The co-evolution of science, technology and innovation policy and industrial structure in a small, resource-based economy," TIK Working Paper on Innovation Studies No. 20080624, Centre for technology, innovation and culture, Oslo.

402   *R. Macário and E. Van de Voorde*

Hensher, D. and Button, K. J. (eds.) (2003) *Handbook of Transport and the Environment*, Oxford: Elsevier.

Kuhn, T. S. (1969) *The Structure of Scientific Revolutions*, Chicago: University of Chicago Press.

WBCSD (2004) World Business Council for Sustainable Development, Mobility 2030: Meeting the Challenges to Sustainability, The Sustainable Mobility Project, Full report, 2004 (available www.eu-conference2004.nl/documents/mobility-full.pdf).

Index

Page numbers in *italics* represent tables. Page numbers in **bold** represent figures.

For Product Safety Concerns and Information please contact our
EU representative GPSR@taylorandfrancis.com Taylor & Francis
Verlag GmbH, Kaufingerstraße 24, 80331 München, Germany